THE RISE AND FALL OF

OSAMA

BIN

LADEN

PETER BERGEN

SIMON & SCHUSTER

NEW YORK LONDON TORONTO SYDNEY NEW DELHI

Simon & Schuster
1230 Avenue of the Americas
New York, NY 10020

Copyright © 2021 by Peter Bergen

First Simon & Schuster hardcover edition August 2021

SIMON & SCHUSTER and colophon are registered trademarks of Simon & Schuster, Inc.

For information about special discounts for bulk purchases,
please contact Simon & Schuster Special Sales
at 1-866-506-1949 or business@simonandschuster.com.

The Simon & Schuster Speakers Bureau can bring authors to your live event.
For more information or to book an event, contact the Simon & Schuster Speakers Bureau
at 1-866-248-3049 or visit our website at www.simonspeakers.com.

Interior design by Ruth Lee-Mui

Manufactured in the United States of America

1   3   5   7   9   10   8   6   4   2

Library of Congress Cataloging-in-Publication Data has been applied for.

ISBN 978-1-9821-7052-3
ISBN 978-1-9821-7054-7 (ebook)

For Grace, Pierre, and Tresha

CONTENTS

A NOTE ON TRANSLITERATION

Arabic names have been transliterated in a manner that is standard for Western readers. I have used "Osama bin Laden" and "al-Qaeda" rather than "Usama bin Ladin" and "al-Qa'ida." I have also used the spelling "Binladin" when referring to the family business, as this is how it generally appears in English. In the case of Arabic names that appear in documents written in English, I have retained the original spelling that was used in the document.

BIN LADEN FAMILY TREE

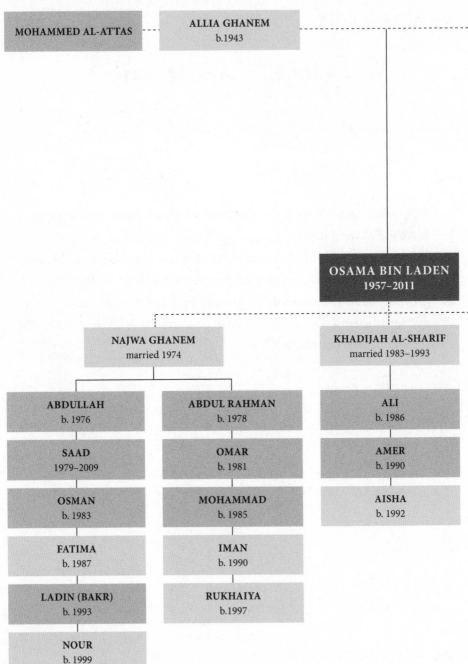

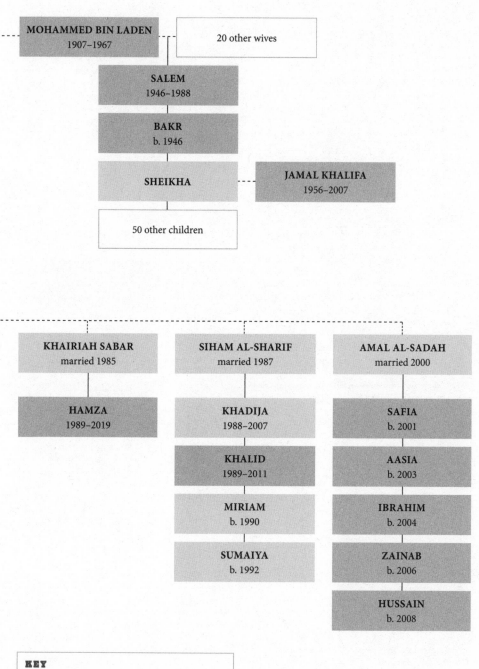

MOHAMMED BIN LADEN 1907–1967		20 other wives
	SALEM 1946–1988	
	BAKR b. 1946	
	SHEIKHA	**JAMAL KHALIFA** 1956–2007
	50 other children	

KHAIRIAH SABAR married 1985	**SIHAM AL-SHARIF** married 1987	**AMAL AL-SADAH** married 2000
HAMZA 1989–2019	**KHADIJA** 1988–2007	**SAFIA** b. 2001
	KHALID 1989–2011	**AASIA** b. 2003
	MIRIAM b. 1990	**IBRAHIM** b. 2004
	SUMAIYA b. 1992	**ZAINAB** b. 2006
		HUSSAIN b. 2008

KEY

Marriage ------   Female

Offspring ———   Male

HOPES AND DREAMS AND FEARS

Targeting the Americans and the Jews by killing them in any corner of the Earth is the greatest of obligations and the most excellent way of gaining nearness to Allah.

—Osama bin Laden

It was Amal's turn with "the Sheikh" as a moonless night settled on Osama bin Laden's compound in Abbottabad, Pakistan, on May 1, 2011. Bin Laden had married Amal, his youngest wife, when she was only sixteen and he was forty-three. Still, their two-and-a-half-decade age difference did not stand in the way of what turned out to be a real love match, much to the fury of bin Laden's three older wives.

In the late 1990s, when bin Laden had first introduced the notion to his older wives of taking a new wife, he had advertised Amal as a "mature" thirty-year-old who knew the Koran by heart. Instead, Amal was a barely educated teenager from rural Yemen who had suddenly arrived in Afghanistan a year before their husband's great victory on 9/11 and she had monopolized much of his time. Bin Laden's older sons were also angered by their father marrying a woman who was even younger than they were. The Yemeni bodyguard who had helped arrange the match between bin Laden and Amal said that because of the family's dim view of this union, bin Laden initially "dragged round his fourth marriage like a ball and chain."

Over time that would change. Amal's firstborn, Safia, came into the world just days after the 9/11 attacks. Bin Laden named her after Safia, the aunt of the Prophet Mohammed who had killed a Jew. Bin Laden explained that he hoped that his daughter Safia would also grow up to kill Jews.

After 9/11, during bin Laden's nine long years on the run, Amal gave birth to another four children in Pakistan. To avoid any troublesome questions about why this Arab woman was choosing to have her babies in provincial cities in Pakistan, the nurses and doctors were told that Amal was deaf and dumb.

Almost a decade after his 9/11 victory, bin Laden, aged fifty-four, had now found what he believed to be the perfect hiding place in Abbottabad. He was living out a comfortable retirement in an obscure Pakistani city in the pleasant foothills of the Himalayas, the kind of urban backwater where few expected him to be hiding. He should have been feeling content.

Yet during the first weeks of 2011, bin Laden was in a state of agitation. History, it seemed, was passing him by. The Arab world was in unprecedented upheaval, and the man who had hoped to bring attention to the frustrations of that world with the deadliest terrorist attack on U.S. territory was being ignored. This is what gnawed at bin Laden more than anything.

Bin Laden was perplexed by how to respond to the momentous events of the Arab Spring uprisings across the Middle East, which had seemed to come out of nowhere at the beginning of the year. In a letter to a top aide bin Laden wrote that these revolutions were the most important developments that the Muslim world had "witnessed for centuries," yet his al-Qaeda terrorist group was playing no role in the wave of protests engulfing the region. He was unsure what to say publicly about the uprisings that in recent months were sweeping away the geriatric, secular dictators who had lorded it over Egypt, Libya, and Tunisia for so many decades. Bin Laden saw these regime changes as an opportunity to try and make himself relevant again.

The challenge posed by the Arab Spring explains why bin Laden was so delighted that he was finally back in touch with Umm Hamza, his third wife, whom he hadn't seen since around the time of the 9/11 attacks. Khairiah Sabar, known by all in the bin Laden family as Umm Hamza—"the mother of Hamza"—was eight years older than bin Laden. He saw her as his intellectual peer, perhaps even as something of a mentor, since her knowledge of the Koran was very deep. He fervently hoped that Umm Hamza, who had a doctorate in child psychology, would help him think through how best to respond publicly to the Arab Spring. He believed she could help him solve a problem: The Arab Spring revolutions were largely instigated by liberals and members of the Muslim Brotherhood—an Islamist movement that al-Qaeda disliked because of its willingness to engage in democratic politics. Could bin Laden nonetheless present himself as the leader of the Arab Spring?

Following 9/11 and the U.S. campaign that months later ousted the Taliban from power in Afghanistan, Umm Hamza had escaped to neighboring Iran with other members of bin Laden's family as well as some of the leaders of al-Qaeda. They lived there under various forms of house arrest for many years. The Iranian regime likely saw these bin Laden family members and leaders of al-Qaeda as potential assets that could be used in negotiations with the United States in the event of a diplomatic agreement with the Americans. But after al-Qaeda kidnapped an Iranian diplomat in Pakistan in 2008, the Iranians and al-Qaeda started quietly negotiating a prisoner swap that involved releasing members of the bin Laden family. In July 2010, Umm Hamza, together with her son, Hamza, set out for the 1,500-mile trip from Tehran to northern Waziristan, an arid, craggy, remote region in Pakistan's tribal belt along its border with Afghanistan where key al-Qaeda members were hiding.

From his Abbottabad hideout bin Laden spent many hours writing letters to them about how they might all reunite. In a letter that he sent to the sixty-two-year-old Umm Hamza in early January 2011 he wrote tenderly, "It comforts me to hear your news, which I have waited for so long in years past. . . . How long have I waited for your departure from Iran."

Bin Laden told Umm Hamza that a member of his team would buy her a computer and some flash drives so she could start providing her "observations and ideas," which bin Laden could then incorporate into his public statements. He explained to his wife that he wanted to "share some of my positions," so together they could formulate what he was going to say publicly on the tenth anniversary of 9/11. He wrote, "We are awaiting the tenth anniversary of the blessed attacks on New York and Washington, which will be in nine months. You are well aware of its importance. . . . So, I sent you all the statements and ideas I have on my computer to contribute to putting together the statements for this important anniversary."

He was excited that he might soon be reunited with Umm Hamza, but he was anxious about his own security and paranoid that the Iranians— who he said were "not to be trusted"—might have inserted electronic tracking devices into the belongings or even the bodies of his family members as they departed Iran in the summer of 2010. He told Umm Hamza that if she had recently visited a dentist in Iran for a filling, she might need to have the filling taken out, as he worried a tracking chip might have been inserted, explaining that "the size of the chip is about the length of a grain of wheat and the width of a fine piece of vermicelli." He went on to tell his wife, "I need to know the date you had the filling, also about any surgery you had, even if it was only minor surgery. If you cannot remember the date, it is fine to give me an approximation."

Knowing that Umm Hamza was stuck in the frigid, mountainous region of Waziristan during the height of winter, he added, "Accompanied with this letter are modest gifts for the cold weather and 25,000 rupees [around $300] for your spending for this period." Al-Qaeda's leader also inquired: "I would like to hear how your health is. Are you comfortable where you are staying? Do you have heating?" Ever cautious about security, bin Laden warned, "Please destroy this letter after reading it."

Bin Laden was specifically worried that the hiding place that he had so carefully constructed in Abbottabad might now be falling apart. After the arrest in Pakistan in 2003 of Khalid Sheikh Mohammed, the operational commander of the 9/11 attacks, bin Laden decided to stop meeting with al-Qaeda members in person, with the exception of his two bodyguards, who were living on the Abbottabad compound with him. The bodyguards were two brothers, Ibrahim and Abrar, who were longtime members of al-Qaeda whose family hailed from northern Pakistan, not far from where bin Laden was hiding in Abbottabad. They did everything for him. The brothers shopped for produce from local markets for the bin Laden family. Crucially, it was one of the brothers who delivered messages to and from al-Qaeda's leader to other senior members of al-Qaeda. Bin Laden was completely dependent on the two brothers both to maintain any semblance of control over al-Qaeda and its far-flung affiliated groups around the globe and also for the basic necessities of life.

By early 2011 the brothers were utterly fed up with all the risks that came with protecting and serving the world's most wanted man. Despite all those risks, the miserly bin Laden was paying them only around $100 a month each. Bin Laden confided to Umm Hamza that the brothers who protected him were "getting exhausted" and were planning to quit. He said relations with the brothers had deteriorated so badly that he could no longer rely on them to escort her across the three hundred miles from Waziristan to Abbottabad so they could at long last be reunited. Bin Laden told her the number of people living at the Abbottabad compound were, according to the brothers, already "large and beyond what they can handle."

Bin Laden was so excited about the possibility of meeting up with his oldest wife he offered that if he wasn't able to "secure your return in the next weeks, I will come to visit you." Traveling to Waziristan to meet with Umm Hamza would have been taking an extraordinary risk for the al-Qaeda leader, who hadn't left his Abbottabad compound during the past five years.

Things got so bad with his two bodyguards that on January 15, 2011, bin Laden took the unusual step of writing the brothers a formal letter, despite the fact that they lived only yards away from him on the compound. In the letter he said the brothers had been so "irritated" in a recent meeting with him that he was resorting to writing them a letter to clarify matters. He asked the brothers to give him adequate time to find substitute protectors.

To accomplish that, he wrote a letter to his top aide, Atiyah Abd al-Rahman, asking if he knew of any Pakistanis who could be trusted with "complete confidence" to replace the two brothers. He was now under pressure because he and the pair had a written agreement to separate by mid-July 2011. The separation meant bin Laden was losing not only the protection of his longtime bodyguards, but also his carefully constructed compound, which, with its walls rising as high as eighteen feet in places, was designed to keep prying eyes out. That's because the Abbottabad compound had been registered in the name of one of the brothers; bin Laden was not its legal owner. He and his family would have to find a new hiding place.

So far, the only candidate to replace bin Laden's bodyguards that Atiyah had proffered was a thirty-five-year-old former shopkeeper with small children who had some experience in the buying and selling of properties, which was an important credential since he would have to help bin Laden relocate. Bin Laden wanted constant updates on the search for his new protector, impatiently urging his top aide, "It would be good if you informed me about the developments about the bodyguard in every message, and there is no problem if you mention that there are no developments."

Over the objections of bin Laden's bodyguards, in mid-February Umm Hamza decided to make the ten-hour trip from Waziristan to Abbottabad, although she left her only child, Hamza, behind.

When Umm Hamza arrived at the Abbottabad compound, the place was packed. There was bin Laden's youngest wife, Amal, and her five children, along with another wife, Siham, with her three children, and four orphaned grandchildren from a daughter of Siham and bin Laden's who had died while giving birth in Pakistan's tribal regions.

By the early spring of 2011 bin Laden's three wives had all settled into the routine they knew well; each of them had signed up for marriage with bin Laden knowing that they were entering a polygamous household, and they all admired him as a great hero of holy war against the infidels. They ranged in age from twenty-eight to sixty-two, and bin Laden was the center of their lives. Bin Laden, for his part, tried to treat all his wives equitably, arranging his compound so each one had her own rudimentary kitchen and living quarters. He also made an effort to please them in the bedroom. He drank Avena, a syrup made from oats that claims to have Viagra-like effects, and he ate copious amounts of olives, which he believed produced similar results. He also regularly applied Just for Men dye to his beard, which had now turned largely white, and also to his graying hair.

Most fugitives try and keep a small footprint while they are on the run and wouldn't dream of bringing a large family with them, but bin Laden reveled in playing the role of a stern, but sometimes indulgent, paterfamilias to those of his kids and grandkids who were living with him. He supervised their playtime, which included cultivating vegetable plots, and he handed out prizes for "best performance" when they recited poems. One of his grandsons, who was around nine years old, recorded a video of a poem about holy war that the family seemed particularly proud of. The boy declaimed, "We have made big strides in Jihad. We fought, and we did not lay down our weapons." Bin Laden watched over his younger sons in the yard shooting a BB gun at birds roosting in trees.

Bin Laden placed great store in holding his family close, even if that put them all in extreme danger. To minimize that danger, he went to great lengths to avoid detection. His two bodyguards installed four separate gas and electricity meters at the compound to ensure that there wasn't ever a suspiciously large gas or electricity bill betraying the presence of the sixteen members of the bin Laden family. They burned all their trash. Bin Laden complained of pain in his heart or kidney, but he never saw a doctor, preferring to treat these ailments with traditional Arab medicine. When he left his three-story residence to tour his spacious compound, he wore a cowboy hat that prevented prying eyes or satellites from recognizing him. He was so careful that in the half decade that he lived at the Abbottabad compound one of the bodyguard's wives never saw him, even though she lived there too. Bin Laden was hidden from even those who lived with him.

To keep shopping trips outside the compound to a minimum, bin

Laden set up what amounted to a small farm that could provide much of the food for his own large family and the eleven members of the body-guards' two families. Dozens of chickens squawked in a pen, cows wandered in a large, muddy yard, apple trees produced considerable fruit, ramshackle greenhouses grew cucumbers and marrows, honey came from a beehive, and grapes grew plentifully on trellises.

At their Abbottabad compound the family lived frugally, not only growing much of their own food, but also avoiding modern comforts such as air-conditioning. Bin Laden enforced his strict Islamic beliefs. In the bin Laden family, girls were completely separated from males at the unusually early age of three. And even when men appeared on TV, the women would leave the room.

There was little in the way of entertainment, although bin Laden devoured news of the Arab Spring on satellite television. If a female news anchor came on, bin Laden used his remote to put up the channel guide on the screen so that it obscured her face.

Bin Laden's bodyguards practiced careful operational security, making phone calls from public phone booths in cities at least an hour's drive from the Abbottabad compound. When one of the bodyguard's young daughters saw video of bin Laden on a television program and recognized him to be the tall Arab man who was living on the Abbottabad compound, the bodyguard banned any further TV watching and any subsequent contact between his family and the bin Laden family, even though they all lived on the same one-acre compound.

Bin Laden could have chosen to cut off all of his communications with anyone in the world outside of his compound, which certainly would have greatly reduced his risk of ever being located, but he wanted to remain relevant as the "emir"—the commander—of al-Qaeda and to maintain control of his organization and its affiliated groups around the Muslim world. Bin Laden's compound was purposefully unconnected to phone lines or the internet because he had a healthy respect for the capabilities of American spy agencies. So he tried to exert control over his jihadist network by writing elaborate memos to his top subordinates that were put on thumb drives and then physically transported by his bodyguard to other trusted members of al-Qaeda. It was not the most efficient way to run a global terror network, like running an international business without the benefit of even nineteenth-century tools like the telegraph or telephone. Sometimes couriers were arrested and often replies were long in coming or they simply got lost, but still bin Laden wanted to micromanage his followers in South Asia, the Middle East, and Africa.

In the missives he wrote in the last months of his life, other than those relating to his own protection, bin Laden was preoccupied with four major issues. He was deeply worried about al-Qaeda's image, which he thought was being tarnished by allied groups who were killing Muslim civilians for no discernible strategic purpose, or who were flirting with using chemical weapons, and he fretted that CIA drone strikes were decimating his group in Pakistan. Bin Laden also wanted to keep al-Qaeda and its affiliates on the offensive, in particular against American targets, especially as the tenth anniversary of 9/11 was approaching and he hadn't been able to repeat a large-scale attack against the United States. Above all, he wanted to intervene in the momentous events of the Arab Spring with a grand public statement that positioned himself as the leader of the revolutions that were rocking the Middle East.

Despite the fact that he ran an organization dedicated to mass murder, bin Laden believed that al-Qaeda needed to maintain a certain image in the Muslim world. In a memo to a top aide, he warned that al-Qaeda's branch in Yemen should be very careful about possibly using "poison" during their operations, suggesting that the use of such chemical weapons might damage their reputation in the media and in "the eyes of the public." In another memo an al-Qaeda official gave a similar warning to members of the group who might use chlorine gas against Kurdish forces in Iraq, saying such a "serious" move required the permission of bin Laden because the gas could be "difficult to control and might harm some people" and that would then "alienate people from us," adding "we have enough problems already." For all the intense concerns of U.S. policymakers after 9/11 that al-Qaeda might deploy weapons of mass destruction, bin Laden himself was quite wary about their use, not on moral grounds, but because he was concerned about how it would play in the media and with ordinary Muslims.

Similarly, bin Laden complained to Atiyah that a recent operation by the Pakistani Taliban had killed Muslim noncombatants. This might seem a strange complaint given that bin Laden had no compunction about killing almost three thousand civilians on 9/11 in the United States, but it fit with bin Laden's general aversion to killing ordinary Muslim civilians living in Islamic countries. He believed it was counterproductive as it alienated the very people whom al-Qaeda was trying to influence.

As the tenth anniversary of his "blessed" 9/11 victory came into view, bin Laden was considering releasing some kind of a mea culpa on behalf of al-Qaeda and its allies. It was not an apology, of course, to the hated Americans, but an attempt to reposition al-Qaeda in the Islamic world as an organization that did not wantonly kill Muslim civilians. He was acutely conscious that al-Qaeda-allied groups like Al-Qaeda in Iraq, al-Shabaab in Somalia, and the Pakistani Taliban in the years since 9/11 had killed many thousands of Muslim civilians, which had undercut al-Qaeda's self-image that it was fighting a true holy war on behalf of all Muslims. He wrote to a top lieutenant during the summer of 2010 saying that he planned to issue a statement in which he would discuss "starting a new phase to correct the mistakes we made . . . and reclaim the trust of a large segment of the population who lost their trust in the jihadis." So badly tarnished had the al-Qaeda brand in bin Laden's mind become that he even considered changing the name of his group. He was seeking a kinder, gentler al-Qaeda.

Bin Laden was also very concerned about the CIA drone campaign in Pakistan's tribal regions on the border with Afghanistan, which was systematically picking off many key leaders of the organization and had also killed his son Saad two years earlier. In a memo that bin Laden wrote to Atiyah, he told him that Pakistan's tribal areas were now becoming too dangerous for his followers. The CIA had launched a record number of strikes into the tribal regions during 2010, a total of 122 strikes that had killed more than seven hundred militants, including key al-Qaeda leaders such as its finance chief and third-in-command, Mustafa Abu al-Yazid.

In a letter to bin Laden an al-Qaeda official provided a vivid description of the death by drone of Yazid on the night of May 22, 2010. The al-Qaeda official wrote that Yazid was staying at the house of a "well-known" supporter of al-Qaeda when a drone started making "distinctive loops that we all know and all the brothers have experienced. They all know that if a plane starts doing these turns, it is going to strike." Yazid and his wife and three daughters and granddaughter were all killed in the strike, according to the official. The official lamented that drones are "still circling our skies every day" and the only relief from them came when there was cloud cover, but "then they come back when the sky is clear." Al-Qaeda had tried to use jamming technology and to hack into the drones "but no result so far," according to the official.

Bin Laden advised his followers not to move around the tribal regions except on overcast days. He complained that "the Americans have great accumulated expertise of photography of the region due to the fact they have been doing it for so many years. They can even distinguish between houses that are frequented by male visitors at a higher rate than is normal." Bin Laden wrote, "I am leaning toward getting most of our brothers out of the area" and he urged his followers to depart for the remote, mountainous Afghan province of Kunar that "due to its rough terrain and many mountains, rivers, and trees, can accommodate hundreds of the brothers without them being spotted by the enemy." (To his own son Hamza, he advised leaving the drone-infested region altogether, and instead to further his religious training in the Persian Gulf kingdom of Qatar.)

Al-Qaeda officials told bin Laden that they were indeed considering moving to Nuristan, a remote, mountainous region of eastern Afghanistan, or to other parts of Pakistan such as Sindh or Balochistan and even to Iran, where a number of al-Qaeda's leaders had lived under house arrest following the fall of the Taliban in late 2001, but had "backed off that idea."

Preoccupied with keeping al-Qaeda and allied groups on the offensive, Bin Laden often went deep in the details with the tactical advice he offered his followers. Far from the prevailing image of the isolated man in a cave, bin Laden tried to be a hands-on manager of al-Qaeda, even a microman-ager. He admonished his Yemeni group that its members should always gas up and eat heartily before they embarked on road trips so that they wouldn't have to stop at gas stations and restaurants monitored by government spies.

In a ten-page letter to the al-Qaeda-aligned group al-Shabaab in So-malia, he ordered that the group not attack Sufi Muslims and also sug-gested a plan to assassinate the president of neighboring Uganda, who had sent his troops to fight al-Shabaab. He went on to give detailed advice about how al-Shabaab could raise its agricultural output by using small dams for irrigation, and he suggested planting palm olive trees imported from Indonesia. He also advised against cutting down too many trees be-cause it was "dangerous for the environment of the region."

Bin Laden had remained in touch with the Taliban leader Mullah Omar, and in the months before he was killed, he sent Mullah Omar a letter intended to be a pep talk about how NATO was tiring of occupying Afghanistan, citing the scheduled pullout of Canadian troops and Presi-dent Barack Obama's announcement in December 2009 that he planned to withdraw all U.S. troops as well.

Bin Laden was also obsessed with finding a way to mark the ap-proaching tenth anniversary of 9/11 and the role he would play in that an-niversary. He was angry that his central goal of attacking the United States again had failed, as had other operations to attack key European targets. In a report on "external operations," an al-Qaeda official explained to bin Laden that a plot to attack the U.S. embassy in Russia had fizzled and that despite sending al-Qaeda members to the U.K. to hit "several tar-gets," these operations had also come to nothing. Al-Qaeda had also sent "three brothers" on a terrorist mission to Denmark, a country that bin Laden loathed because a Danish newspaper had published cartoons of the Prophet Mohammed. But those agents had disappeared.

Bin Laden was eager to memorialize the 9/11 attacks with another spectacular one. He told his deputies that killing President Barack Obama was a high priority, but he also had General David Petraeus, the

then-commander in Afghanistan, in his sights. Bin Laden told his team
not to bother with plots against Vice President Joe Biden, whom he considered "totally unprepared" for the post of president. But he also wanted
to be heard from directly. With that in mind, always acutely conscious
of his own media image, bin Laden batted around ideas about how best
to exploit the fast-approaching tenth anniversary of 9/11 in long memos
to his media advisors, planning for a major public statement to mark the
occasion. Bin Laden told his team that they might think about reaching
out to various journalists who might give him a platform. He suggested
several: Abdel Bari Atwan, a leading Palestinian reporter; and the veteran
Middle East correspondent Robert Fisk of the British *Independent* newspaper; both of them had done interviews with bin Laden during the 1990s
in Afghanistan. He also mused about doing a TV interview with CBS,
which he regarded as the "least biased" of the American TV channels.

In response, an al-Qaeda member—almost certainly Adam Gadahn, an
American who had grown up in California—wrote bin Laden a critique of
the various American news channels, saying, "As for the neutrality of CNN
in English it seems to be in cooperation with the government more than the
others, except Fox News of course. . . . ABC Channel is all right, actually it
could be one of the best channels as far as we're concerned. It's interested
in al-Qaeda issues. . . . The channel is still proud of its interview with the
Sheikh." ABC News had interviewed bin Laden in Afghanistan in 1998.

Above all, bin Laden's major preoccupation was seizing control of the
message emanating from the protest movements that were rocking the
Arab world. A couple of weeks since her joyful arrival at the Abbottabad
compound, Umm Hamza had now settled in, so during the first week of
March 2011 bin Laden started convening almost daily family meetings
with her and with his other older wife, Siham, who had a PhD in Koranic
grammar. A poet and an intellectual, Siham would often edit bin Laden's
writings and along with Umm Hamza played a key, hidden role in formu-
lating his ideas and helping him prepare his public statements.

These meetings to discuss the Arab Spring and other important issues, such as possibly writing a collective biography of bin Laden, were

deemed so important that they were dutifully recorded in detail in a family journal. The journal grew into a 228-page notebook handwritten in Arabic that was titled "The Uprisings: Historic Events and Points of View of Abu Abdullah [bin Laden]." The family meetings would typically start before dinner and then would often resume after dinner in one of the undecorated rooms in the three-story building that was the main house on the bin Laden compound.

On his satellite TV, al-Qaeda's leader watched all the commentary about the uprisings on the BBC and on Arabic channels such as Al Jazeera, commenting on every little detail. During their evening discussions, his wives and adult children "interviewed" him as if he were on television giving his opinions and summarizing the events of the day, while one of his oldest daughters put his words on paper. Bin Laden was trying to recreate something like the excitement that had surrounded the release of his videotaped messages in years past, when tens of millions of people around the world had watched his statements. He could not stand being out of the spotlight at such an important moment in the Arab world, and so he created that spotlight for himself in his own household.

One of the first questions noted in the family journal concerned the striking absence of al-Qaeda's ideas and followers in the Arab Spring uprisings. A family member asked bin Laden: "How come there is no mention of al-Qaeda?" Bin Laden answered concisely and a tad defensively, "Some analysts do mention al-Qaeda." During the family meetings he became excited whenever one of the Arab dictators such as Libya's Muammar Gaddafi invoked the threat of al-Qaeda replacing him if he were overthrown, as it seemed to confirm al-Qaeda's importance. Bin Laden said, "Gaddafi is doing our bidding for us."

It was long bin Laden's goal to instigate regime changes across the Arab world and to replace them with Taliban-style utopias. His strategy to accomplish this was to attack the United States, which was backing the authoritarian regimes in countries such as Egypt and Saudi Arabia, so that the attacks would pressure the Americans to pull out of the Middle East and their client Arab regimes would then subsequently crumble.

That this strategy had spectacularly backfired following the 9/11 attacks didn't seem to occur to bin Laden. As a result of 9/11, the United States had become more involved in the greater Middle East than at any other time in its history, launching wars across the region and establishing large military bases in Afghanistan, Iraq, Kuwait, Qatar, and the United Arab Emirates. Now, in the first months of 2011, bin Laden saw the regime changes that he had long hoped for finally taking place in the Arab world. Those revolutions were driven mostly by young protesters tired of their lives leading nowhere because of the corruption, cruelty, and incompetence of leaders like Egypt's Hosni Mubarak, in power for almost three decades, and Libya's Gaddafi, in power for more than four decades. (During their discussions bin Laden told his family that he had seen the prominent U.S. senator John McCain speaking on an American news channel saying that Gaddafi was crazy. Bin Laden observed, "I agree with him on that.")

During one of the family meetings, bin Laden discussed the possibility of a revolution in Yemen that would depose the dictator, Ali Abdullah Saleh, in power for the past two decades. Bin Laden said that there could be an opportunity for al-Qaeda in Yemen to assassinate Saleh, which certainly would make his organization more relevant.

One of his daughters asked: "Do you think that would succeed?" Bin Laden replied, "If we give detailed instructions for the operation, God willing, it will succeed." But he also complained that "the biggest obstacle is the difficulty of communication between us and the brothers [in al-Qaeda]." So he mused about releasing a "strong poem" entitled "Revolt People of the Arabian Peninsula," which would incite the people of Yemen to rise up. Bin Laden declared grandly, "I welcome my appearance in this stage, especially since it's very well known, our presence as al-Qaeda in Yemen." He seemed to believe that any public statement he made would carry such weight in Yemen that it would guide the protesters in the direction he wanted.

Khalid, the oldest of bin Laden's sons living on the compound, asked his father if, as a result of the Arab revolutions, all the Muslim countries were "united under one caliphate, are we going to attack the West to avenge ourselves for the destruction they have caused, or not?" Bin Laden replied that if there was a caliphate made up of the entire Muslim world he thought the West would make peace with it and that it would also "abandon the Jews." If that happened, it would mean it was a sign of the End of Times and it would signal the arrival of the *Mahdi*, a ruler who would rid the world of all injustice.

Bin Laden, who put great store in dreams, told his family he had just dreamed of Prince Nayef, the powerful Saudi interior minister, who was leading the campaign against al-Qaeda in Saudi Arabia. In the dream bin Laden saw Nayef in a military uniform, which he then took off. To bin Laden the dream meant that the Saudi king would step down peacefully because of the Arab Spring. This, of course, was a total fantasy.

On March 10, 2011, bin Laden asked Umm Hamza and his two oldest daughters, "I would like to know your comments on what you saw on the news that you were watching this afternoon." Bin Laden's kitchen cabinet told their hero that he needed to make a big speech to be released publicly so that he could help guide the Arab Spring. They firmly believed that bin Laden's words could change the course of history.

Two weeks later the family notetaker reported "the news is sweeter than honey." In Yemen, the ancestral home of the bin Laden family, the Yemeni dictator, Saleh, had just started negotiating about stepping down. Bin Laden then remarked that when he traveled in Yemen he felt like he was going back five hundred years and living in the true tribal age of Islam. He observed admiringly, "You don't find a single woman who isn't covered with the *niqab*," referring to the garment that covers the entire face other than the eyes. On April 12, Khalid announced to his family, "I bring you good news. The Yemeni president resigned." The notetaker observed, "Father was right because he had said it will be announced within hours that Saleh will resign." But on that same night Saleh reneged on stepping down.

The next day the family returned to the question of what bin Laden should say publicly about the Arab Spring, noting that a messenger was supposed to arrive in the next few days to pick up letters and messages to and from bin Laden.*

Bin Laden complained that he had been ignored when he released a public statement in January 2004. He said he had urged back then that "we need to hold Arab rulers accountable."

Umm Hamza asked, "Maybe your statement is one of the reasons for the Arab Spring uprisings?"

But of course that was not true. The hundreds of thousands of protesters who risked their lives on the streets of Cairo and Tripoli were not waving any banners of bin Laden, but were simply demanding basic human rights such as free speech and accountable governments. Even bin Laden's family members were dimly aware of this. One of them observed of the Arab Spring's largely peaceful revolutions, "Is it going to have a negative impact that this happened without jihad?" If bin Laden responded to this question his reply wasn't recorded.

On the evening of April 20, the family gathered again to discuss what bin Laden should say publicly about the Arab Spring. The wives and adult children understood that their great hero of jihad was running out of time to stage a comeback. His nineteen-year-old daughter, Sumaiya, urged that with all the fast-moving events around the Middle East, bin Laden "needed to hurry, the statement needs to be issued soon." The big idea that bin Laden kept coming back to was the need to form a *shura*, a consultative council, of the "honest" leaders of the *ummah*, the world community of Muslims. This committee of wise Islamic scholars would direct the revolutions so that they could move in the "right direction," which in bin Laden's mind really meant Taliban-style rule around the Arab world.

Three nights later Sumaiya and her older sister Miriam excitedly discussed that "the statement" by bin Laden was soon going to be recorded.

---

*There was more than one courier servicing bin Laden. The CIA's account of bin Laden's life in Abbottabad focused on only one courier known as "Abu Ahmed al-Kuwaiti"—the father of Ahmed from Kuwait—who was one of the brothers guarding bin Laden at the Abbottabad compound.

Miriam had been making some adjustments to it, which were "very good." Two days later the writer in the family journal observed, "After many consultations which have lasted days, the historical statement about the revolutions have been written, thanks to God, and it will be recorded." On April 30 there were further discussions about the recording of bin Laden's big statement. The notetaker wrote, "The recording needs to take place before the deadline so that we can adjust and make corrections. We should not record late at night because he will look tired, and it will appear in his voice."

Around this time bin Laden made a twelve-minute audio recording celebrating the revolutions in Egypt and Tunisia, saying, "We watch with you this great historic event and we share with you joy and happiness and delight and felicity." As he had discussed during his family meetings, on the tape bin Laden advised that a religious "council" be formed to guide the new governments in Egypt and Tunisia.

The next day, on May 1, 2011, the family notetaker continued to write about bin Laden's statement, observing that he had been silent for so long that there was a danger of creating "a barrier" between him and ordinary Muslims. The notetaker said this meant the next statement from bin Laden needed "to be tight, its meaning important, as it will be the banner for the future we preparing for." The notetaker added that the family would discuss the forthcoming statement again the following day.

Then bin Laden went to bed with his youngest wife, Amal, in his top-floor bedroom together with their three-year-old son, Hussain. Bin Laden and Amal were sleeping when they were startled awake shortly after midnight by a noise that sounded like a strange storm. They heard the unexpected throb of helicopter rotors over their heads and then a loud crash as one of those helicopters landed heavily in a small field inside the walls of bin Laden's large compound.

Amal reached to turn on the light in their bedroom. Bin Laden quickly told her, "No!"

He realized that it was all over.

The Americans had finally found him.

PART I

HOLY WARRIOR

ONE

SPHINX WITHOUT
A RIDDLE?

A sphinx without a riddle.

—Bismarck on Napoleon II

Around the time of the 9/11 attacks, relatively little was known about Osama bin Laden. In the rare television interviews that al-Qaeda's leader had given before then he came across as largely inscrutable, with only an occasional thin, enigmatic smile playing across his lips. He had gone to considerable lengths to keep information about his private life hidden, which wasn't surprising since he had grown up in Saudi Arabia, one of the most closed societies in the world. He also led an organization, al-Qaeda, whose very existence was a well-kept secret for a decade after its founding in the late 1980s. The bin Laden family, one of the richest in the Middle East, had also largely avoided scrutiny. Was the leader of al-Qaeda a sphinx without a riddle?

In recent years a great deal of information has surfaced to illuminate bin Laden and the inner workings of al-Qaeda. First there is the small library of documents found in bin Laden's Abbottabad compound that were released in full only in late 2017, amounting to some 470,000 files. Secondly, many bin Laden associates have finally shown a willingness to talk. The result is that a decade after his death, it is now possible to appraise him in all the many dimensions of his life: as a family man; as a religious zealot; as a battlefield commander; as a terrorist leader; as a fugitive. He was born a young man of contradictions, and he kept adding to them: he adored his wives and children, yet brought ruin to many of them. He was a multimillionaire, but he insisted his family live like paupers. He projected a modest and humble persona that appealed to his followers, but he was also narcissistically obsessed about how his own image played out in the media, and he ignored any advice from the leaders of al-Qaeda that conflicted with his own dogmatic views. He was fanatically religious, yet he was also willing to kill thousands of civilians in the name of Islam, despite the fact that some verses of the Koran emphasize the protections afforded to innocents, even in times of war. He inspired deep loyalty, yet in the end, even his longtime bodyguards turned against him. And while he inflicted the most lethal act of mass murder in United States history, bin Laden failed to achieve any of his strategic goals.

Al-Qaeda's leader is one of the few people of whom it can truly be said changed the course of history. Who could have predicted that in the two decades following the 9/11 attacks he masterminded, the United States would wage various kinds of military operations in seven Muslim countries—in Afghanistan, Iraq, Libya, Pakistan, Somalia, Syria, and Yemen—at the cost of more than $6 trillion and more than seven thousand American lives? In addition, tens of thousands of soldiers from countries allied to the United States died, as did hundreds of thousands of ordinary Afghans, Iraqis, Libyans, Pakistanis, Somalis, Syrians, and Yemenis who were also killed during the "war on terror."

But just as it has taken many years to get a better understanding of the man who launched the 9/11 attacks, it has taken two decades to assess the successes and failures of both al-Qaeda and the United States in the long conflict that followed. This is not to suggest any moral equivalence between the two—but rather to explain where each side miscalculated the other's intentions and actions.

Al-Qaeda did have some tactical successes. Before the 9/11 attacks it deftly exploited its safe haven in Taliban-controlled Afghanistan to train thousands of militants. On 9/11 al-Qaeda carried out the first significant foreign attack against the continental United States since the British burned the White House in 1814. Al-Qaeda used the opportunities presented by the Iraq War to recruit a new generation of militants, planting the seeds for ISIS. And al-Qaeda expanded its affiliated groups from Africa to Asia.

There were also serious American policy failures. They include letting bin Laden escape at the battle of Tora Bora in December 2001, which allowed him to lead his organization for another decade, and the conflation of al-Qaeda with Saddam Hussein, which helped make the case for the Iraq War, a war that ultimately produced the very thing it was supposed to prevent—an alliance between al-Qaeda and Iraqi Baathists.

But bin Laden and al-Qaeda also had many failures of tactics and strategy. For one thing, the United States eventually came up with an increasingly effective tactical playbook against al-Qaeda and other jihadist militant groups—a playbook that largely, if imperfectly, worked, relying on armed drones, a much-expanded intelligence community, and Special Operations Forces raids. It's a playbook that presidents as different as George W. Bush, Barack Obama, and Donald Trump all embraced to varying degrees and that kept the United States largely safe from jihadist terrorism since 9/11.

During the two decades after the 9/11 attacks, al-Qaeda and its affiliates failed to successfully carry out a large-scale lethal terrorist attack in the United States.* Al-Qaeda's failure to strike the United States after 9/11 was neither inevitable nor predictable, especially in the first years after the attacks, when bin Laden and the organization he led continued to plot against Western targets.

The key question about bin Laden is: Why did he build an organization

---

*The only lethal terrorist attack in the United States in the two decades after 9/11 that had any direct connection to al-Qaeda was when its branch in Yemen coordinated with a Saudi air force officer who killed three U.S. sailors at Pensacola Naval Air Station in Florida on December 6, 2019. It wasn't clear whether this attack was directed by al-Qaeda from Yemen, or whether the Saudi officer came up with his own plan and he simply kept al-Qaeda apprised of it as it matured.

dedicated to the mass murders of civilians? It's a question I have been probing since I met bin Laden in 1997 as the producer of his first television interview. There was no single event that turned bin Laden from the shy scion of one of the richest families in the Middle East into the architect of the 9/11 attacks. Rather, bin Laden went through a gradual process of radicalization that first began during his teenage years when he became a religious zealot.

The invasion of Afghanistan by the Soviets in 1979, when bin Laden was twenty-two, turned him into a leading financier of Muslim volunteers from around the globe who were drawn to the Afghan holy war. Eight years later bin Laden led his followers into battle against the Russians. From that battle emerged al-Qaeda, a group dedicated to spreading jihad, holy war, around the world. The introduction of hundreds of thousands of U.S. troops into the holy land of Saudi Arabia in 1990 turned bin Laden's latent anti-Americanism into a passionate hatred of the United States. He started conceiving of the Americans as his main enemy while he was living in exile in Sudan during the first half of the 1990s. His expulsion from Sudan to Afghanistan in 1996 angered him further against the United States, and in the late 1990s the planning for the 9/11 attacks began in earnest.

There was nothing inevitable about bin Laden's transformation over the course of decades from a quiet, humble, religious young man into the leader of a global terrorist network who was intent on killing thousands of civilians. This book is an attempt to explain how that transformation happened.

TWO

ZEALOT

The impression sometimes prevails that the true believer, particularly the religious individual, is a humble person. The truth is that the surrendering and humbling of the self, breeds pride and arrogance. The true believer is apt to see himself as one of the chosen, the salt of the earth, the light of the world, a prince disguised in meekness, who is destined to inherit this earth and the kingdom of heaven too. He who is not of his faith is evil; he who will not listen will perish.

—Eric Hoffer, *The True Believer*

The bin Ladens originally hail from Hadhramaut in Yemen, a region of rocky deserts and boulder-strewn valleys known as wadis bounded to the north by Saudi Arabia's Empty Quarter and the Arabian Sea to the south. *Hadhramaut* means "death is present," an evocatively apt name for a harsh, arid place whose inhabitants have long eked out only the most basic of livings.

One of the larger valleys is Wadi Doan, where the road is not much more than a rocky path shaded by palm trees. The bin Laden ancestral village of al-Rubat lies at the end of Wadi Doan nestling in the shade of honey-colored cliffs that tower above the valley floor by a couple thousand feet. In the village there is a Bin Laden Street, a crumbling, mud-brick bin Laden mansion, and a number of impoverished, distant cousins of the bin Ladens.

Black-robed women flit like wraiths down the alleys of the towns of the wadi, and in the fields women harvest crops while completely swathed in black, shielded from the unremitting sun by distinctive conical hats made of straw. The segregation of the sexes is so rigorously enforced that the women have developed a separate dialect, and the dictates of purdah have shaped the mazelike layout of the tall, mud-brick buildings that are characteristic of Hadhramaut. Small wonder, then, that bin Laden felt so much kinship with Yemen, as he told his wives and children in one of their last family discussions at his compound in Abbottabad.

In the early 1930s the formidable English explorer and writer Freya Stark visited al-Rubat around the time that Osama's father, Mohammed bin Laden, was living there and found "poverty and little commerce." Slavery was still commonplace, and when Stark visited a harem of some dozen women, it was the first time that they had ever met a European woman. Stark observed that most of the men of Hadhramaut had left their native villages to find work in Egypt, or had taken the long sea voyage to Malaysia; staying away for up to twenty years.

Seeking his fortune, which certainly wasn't going to happen in desperately poor al-Rubat, Mohammed bin Laden immigrated to what would soon become the Kingdom of Saudi Arabia, embarking for the seaport city of Jeddah around 1930 together with his brother, Abdullah.

Mohammed had good timing because he arrived in Saudi Arabia as a great gusher of oil wealth was first being tapped that in the decades to come would shower a deluge of petrodollars on the desert kingdom, from which Mohammed would greatly prosper. Mohammed started working as a porter for pilgrims in Jeddah, the port city that had long served as the gateway to the holy city of Mecca, some forty miles away. Later in life Mohammed proudly displayed his porter's bag in one of his palaces. Mohammed, a skilled bricklayer, founded a construction company in 1931. A year later King Abdel Aziz inaugurated the Kingdom of Saudi Arabia, and the following year geologists from Standard Oil of California arrived to begin to prospect for oil fields.

Mohammed bin Laden adeptly ingratiated himself with the source of all the richest contracts in the kingdom, dropping by frequently at King

Abdel Aziz's regular *majlis*, a public meeting where supplicants could lobby the monarch. The king was partially confined to a wheelchair, so Mohammed built him an ingenious ramp on the outside of one of his palaces in Jeddah so that the aging monarch could easily move between the floors of the palace using his car. One thing led to another, and when a British company pulled out of its contract in the early 1950s to build a major road from Jeddah to the holy city of Medina, Mohammed stepped in to save the day and built the highway.

Mohammed, who had only one eye and retained the manners of a laborer with few airs and graces, was now a rich man who had a number of current and former wives. Aged around fifty, Mohammed was visiting the Mediterranean port city of Latakia, Syria, in 1956 when he encountered a beautiful girl in her mid-teens, Allia Ghanem. Allia was from the nearby, desperately poor village of Jabaryoun. The surrounding region of orange groves and olive trees is well known as a home to the Alawites, who are an offshoot of mainstream Shiism. Many Alawite religious practices are secret and they celebrate both Christian and Islamic holidays. As a result, Alawites are considered heretics by orthodox Sunni Muslims such as the bin Ladens. The Ghanems were Alawite, but Mohammed didn't seem to mind. A year after they met in 1957 Allia bore the bin Laden patriarch their first and only child, Osama, who also happened to be Mohammed's eighteenth son. The union between Allia and Mohammed bin Laden was brief; when Osama was two his parents divorced. Allia then married Mohammed al-Attas from a prominent family originally from Hadhramaut who was working as a midlevel manager at the bin Laden construction company. Attas brought Osama up like he was his own son, and he and Allia would also have three sons and a daughter together.

Bin Laden was exceptionally close to his mother. Allia told Osama when he was ten that she was going to take him to visit her family in Syria.

When Osama's biological father, Mohammed, got wind of the trip, he told Osama that if he stayed with him in Saudi Arabia he would buy him a parrot in a cage and a watch.

Osama replied that he wanted to be with his mother.

Mohammed bin Laden told his son that he couldn't be bribed with "earthly things," which was a testament to Osama's true Muslim nature. It was one of the only times that Osama ever had a substantive discussion with his biological father.

Osama often proudly told the story of how Mohammed bin Laden would routinely visit the three holiest Islamic sites during the course of one day, offering his morning prayers in Medina, his afternoon prayers in Mecca, and then his evening prayers in Jerusalem, because he had his own plane. The bin Laden family fortune was deeply intertwined with these holy sites, as Mohammed bin Laden was the sole contractor for their extensive renovations, which brought him not only great riches, but also the considerable prestige of rebuilding the holy places. Bin Laden won the contract to extensively renovate the area in and around the Prophet's Mosque in Medina, expanding the area of the mosque by more than half. He was paid around $19 million during the early 1950s for the renovations. He also built a new airport to service Medina.

Next, Mohammed embarked on a project that was even more ambitious: massively expanding Islam's holiest site, the Ka'ba sanctuary in Mecca, which previously held some fifty thousand pilgrims, so that it could accommodate up to 400,000. The Saudi royal family estimated that this renovation cost $130 million. Mohammed bin Laden was also granted the contract to renovate the third-holiest site in Islam, the Dome of the Rock and al-Aqsa mosque in Jerusalem, the location from which the Prophet Mohammed is supposed to have ascended for his "Night Journey" on a winged horse through the heavens. Mohammed purchased a house in East Jerusalem so he could live close by as the renovation work on the Dome of the Rock and the mosque progressed during the mid-1960s.

The Six-Day War that Israel fought against Egypt, Jordan, and Syria in early June 1967 had a profound effect on the Arab world. The Egyptian government had promised a quick victory against Israel; instead it was a spectacular defeat, and East Jerusalem itself was seized by the Israelis. Mohammed bin Laden was furious. He demanded of the engineers in his construction company, "How many bulldozers do we have?" They told him more than 250. Mohammed asked them, "Can you convert these bulldozers into two hundred and fifty tanks? I want to use these tanks against the Jews, because they have captured our land."

Essam Deraz, an Egyptian army officer who would spend more than a year with bin Laden on the front lines in Afghanistan during the anti-Soviet war in the 1980s, understood that the 1967 defeat was profoundly traumatic to his generation: "It wasn't a military defeat. It became a civilizational defeat. We didn't know that we were so backward, we were so retarded, so behind the rest of the modern civilization. There was an earthquake in the Arab-Islamic personality, not only in Egypt, but in the entire Arab world."

The Palestinian cleric Abdullah Azzam, who in the mid-1980s would become bin Laden's key mentor, took up arms against the Israelis after the Israeli army took his hometown in Palestine during the 1967 war. Azzam, then a twenty-six-year-old high school teacher, moved into neighboring Jordan and joined military training facilities known as "the bases of the sheiks," and he took part in small-scale raids into Israeli territory. These were the beginning of Azzam's forays into what would become effectively his full-time career of fomenting holy war and also writing influential books inciting jihad.

The same year that the hated Israelis seized East Jerusalem, bin Laden, aged ten, suffered a huge personal loss: the death of his father. On September 3, 1967, the small plane that transported Mohammed bin Laden from one construction project to the next crashed while trying to land at a remote landing strip in the far south of Saudi Arabia near the Yemen border, killing both bin Laden and his American pilot. Mohammed was sixty when he died. Despite the fact that bin Laden seldom met his father and seems to have only once had a one-on-one meeting with him, Osama took the death badly. Following his father's death, Osama, always a grave child, became even more subdued, and he increasingly embraced fundamentalist Islam. He later told his own children that the "mental turmoil" caused by the death of his father led him to memorizing the Koran, which he could recite by heart as an adult, a major feat of memory as there are more than six thousand verses in the holy book.

During the next year the future of the bin Laden business hung in the balance; it was the major construction company in Saudi Arabia and many projects were not completed, while the oldest of Mohammed bin Laden's twenty-two sons, Salem, was only twenty-one. Due to Islamic inheritance laws, the sons received just over 2 percent each of the bin Laden company, while his thirty-three daughters received around one percent each, and Mohammed's four current wives received the rest. Salem was responsible for distributing the dividends from the company to his siblings.

King Faisal was so close to Mohammed bin Laden that Osama claimed to a journalist that the king cried for days following his father's untimely death. After the bin Laden family patriarch was killed, King Faisal called in the older bin Laden sons and told them that he would be their "father" and that he was putting the bin Laden company into trusteeship until they were old enough to run it.

A year after his father died, bin Laden, aged eleven, started attending the prestigious Al-Thaghr high school in Jeddah, a school for the elite modeled after British schools, where the boys wore Western-style uniforms of shirts and ties. The curriculum was constantly in a state of development and the school prided itself on its science syllabus. Brian Fyfield-Shayler, an Englishman who had recently graduated from Oxford, taught English at the school to a number of the bin Laden boys, including Osama. Fyfield-Shayler recalled, "Why did I remember Osama? First of all, I would have noticed because of his name, because of the family, and of course, when you walked into a class of anyone of his age, he was literally outstanding because he was taller than his contemporaries." Fyfield-Shayler remembered that bin Laden's English "was not amazing. He was not one of the great brains of that class," but he was extraordinarily courteous, "probably partly because he was a bit shyer than most of the other students."

Four decades later bin Laden gave himself a more generous assessment of his early academic prowess, boasting to his family at his compound in

Abbottabad that both his teachers and his fellow students thought that his parents must have been paying a lot of attention to his schooling. Bin Laden claimed that he was so smart that he would answer his teachers' questions before they had even finished them.

In Abbottabad, a family member had a follow-up question, asking, "Who had the biggest impact on your intellectual growth?" Bin Laden waved the question away, saying he didn't have any key influences, and that since he had been a child he just naturally gravitated to true Islamic thought.

Bin Laden was a member of one of the richest families in Saudi Arabia, yet in many ways he was an outsider: as an only child, and as one of fifty-five children sired by his revered father, whom he had met on only five occasions and who now was dead. Meanwhile, bin Laden's mother was from the Alawite sect, which wasn't considered part of the *ummah*, the community of Muslims, by most Saudis. She had been married to Mohammed only briefly, so she wasn't really treated as a member of the extended bin Laden clan. And despite their fabulous wealth, the bin Ladens originally hailed from rural Yemen, rather than from the Saudi heartlands, so they were not considered to be truly Saudi.

As a young teenager bin Laden seemed discomfited by his status in his family and on rare occasions would tell someone about his feelings, as he did to two young Spanish women he met when he was fourteen while studying at an English-language school in Oxford during the summer of 1971. One of the Spaniards recalled, "I think he needed confidants and for that we became fond of him." Bin Laden told the women that his mother was beautiful, which is what had caught the attention of his father. But he seemed sad when he confided that his brothers all had different mothers and that his own mother was not "a wife of the Koran, but a concubine." A concubine.

At Oxford, bin Laden was accompanied by two seventeen-year-old half-brothers, and the Spanish women thought that all three were Saudi princes. "They invited us to row a boat on the Thames. We were older than them and it amused us that they wanted to pay for the boat rentals."

The Spaniards found bin Laden to be a "very handsome" tall boy who was slow to speak, polite, and quite "deep" for his age. They noticed that, unlike his half-brothers, he did not relish his time in the West. One of Osama's older brothers was always off buying rock and pop albums, while the other brother was a style maven busy updating his wardrobe with the latest accoutrements of the hippie era such as scarves and pointed-toe boots. But Osama had little interest in the "Swinging London" of sex, drugs, and rock 'n' roll, telling the Spanish women that the young foreigners who swarmed around London that summer were a bit crazy.

Four decades later, during one of the family meetings at his Abbottabad compound, bin Laden told his wives and adult children that he had spent a summer as a young teenager studying in Britain, staying for two and a half months, but that when he was asked to repeat the experience the following year, he had refused to go again on the grounds that "a pious Muslim should not go to the lands of the West. I had the impression that they were people of loose morals." He said that while he was impressed when he visited Shakespeare's house in Stratford-upon-Avon, in general the British were "morally degenerate."

While bin Laden was rejecting the West, many of his half-siblings were embracing it. That embrace was led by the oldest brother, Salem, who had attended Millfield, an English boarding school not known for its academics and populated by fabulously wealthy foreigners. Salem quickly adapted to Western ways, playing 1960s hits on his guitar such as "Where Have All the Flowers Gone?" Unlike Osama, most of the bin Ladens were strikingly Westernized and pro-American. After all, they owed much of their vast fortune to the marriage of petro-convenience between the House of Saud and the United States. Eventually, more than a dozen of his siblings would acquire some kind of schooling in the States, and Salem, who was the dominant force in the family after his father's death, went on to buy an estate in Orlando, Florida, that he named "Desert Bear."

Salem was also an indulgent big brother and a Pied Piper of fun who took his siblings on blowout vacations in Europe. He visited Sweden to purchase a fleet of trucks from Volvo for the bin Laden construction company, spending some time in the town of Falun, often with his siblings in tow. The visits were not all business; Salem enjoyed the local discos, and the police in Falun reported that one of the bin Ladens was charged with drunk driving in 1969.

Christina Akerblad owned the Hotel Astoria in Falun where Salem and another brother came to stay in 1970. She recalled, "They had so much money, they didn't know how much money they had." The brothers wore immaculate white shirts from Christian Dior and Yves Saint Laurent, which they used only once and then would throw away. Akerblad asked the bin Laden brothers how they had managed to bring their large Rolls-Royce with them to Sweden. They told her, "We have our own plane."

On a visit to Falun the following year, Salem brought many of his siblings, a visit that was so unusual for the town that a reporter from Falun's newspaper ran a feature about them headlined "Arab Celebrity Visit." The reporter wrote, "Salem bin Laden visited Falun on a combined business and pleasure trip through Europe. He was accompanied by twenty-two members of his family. . . . The young sheikh, who is twenty-six-years old, arrived in his private jet to Borlänge airport, while the rest of the family arrived by car. He has visited the Club Ophelia in Falun. The young sheikh is reportedly a big fan of discos and has visited the discos of Falun at various times in the past."

This vacation was memorialized in a photograph of the twenty-three bin Laden siblings leaning on a pink Cadillac, dressed up in a riot of colors and bell-bottoms, the girls with their long brown hair uncovered. (There is some debate about whether Osama was one of the bin Laden siblings in the photograph. Osama's trip to Oxford for summer school just preceded the bin Laden family trip to Sweden during the first week of September 1971.)

While his many half-brothers were off partying in discos, Osama was charting an altogether different course. At his school in Jeddah, bin Laden, aged fourteen, started attending an after-school Islamic study session led by a Syrian teacher who was in his mid-twenties, physically fit and charismatic. The teacher may or may not have been a member of the Muslim Brotherhood, an organization that seeks to inject Islam into the political sphere. But whatever his formal affiliation, he had a big influence on bin Laden and the other students in the study group. They adopted the style and habits of Islamists, shortening the legs of their trousers in supposed imitation of the Prophet, letting their beards grow, and debating other students about the need for a deeper Islamicization of Muslim societies. Bin Laden later told his family that it was around this time that he first started thinking about jihad.

Bin Laden was three years older than his neighbor Khaled Batarfi when they were growing up in the mid-1970s on Jabal al-Arab Street in Mushrefah. It was a typical middle-class Jeddah neighborhood anchored by both a small mosque where the two friends said their daily prayers, and by a playground where they played soccer after school.

Aged sixteen bin Laden was already displaying a fierce religiosity. When Batarfi was leaving his house to play soccer wearing shorts—which fundamentalist Muslims frown upon—bin Laden just looked at Batarfi's legs and said, "Goodbye." Bin Laden also warned his stepbrothers not to wear short-sleeve shirts or to ogle the maid. And if he passed the maid on the stairs, bin Laden would rearrange his keffiyeh so that he couldn't see her. The kids in his neighborhood avoided using swear words around him because he behaved like a cleric.

Bin Laden fasted every Monday and Thursday just as the Prophet had done, and he also prayed more than the five times a day required by his faith, adding an extra set of prayers in the middle of the night as only the most devout Muslims do. When he invited his friends over to his house they chanted hymns about Palestine. He often said, "Unless we, the new generation, change and become stronger and more educated and more dedicated, we will never reclaim Palestine." He later claimed that he was deeply affected by Israel's invasion of Lebanon in 1982, which he believed was given a green light by the United States, saying, "I cannot forget those unbearable scenes of blood and severed limbs, the corpses of women and children strewn everywhere." As a teenager bin Laden already believed that the Muslim world was "backward" compared with the West and not doing enough to counter Western influence in the Middle East.

Bin Laden certainly had friends, but there was always a reserve about him that suggested he was "kind of a lonely guy," says Batarfi. He was a teenager of few words who did more listening than talking.

He did indulge in some diversions. He and Batarfi enjoyed watching cowboy movies, Bruce Lee karate flicks, and the TV series *Fury*, about a stallion living on an American ranch. The series meshed well with bin Laden's own love of riding. On a desert ranch south of Jeddah, he kept some twenty horses, one of them named Al-Balqa, after a horse ridden by one of the Companions of the Prophet. As many Saudi young men did in a country where gas was almost free and the roads ran smooth and straight across the desert, bin Laden loved driving fast cars, especially a prized white Chrysler tricked out with red leather upholstery.

As sex outside marriage was simply unimaginable for bin Laden, when he turned seventeen he began thinking about a wife. He was very close to his mother, Allia, who frequently visited her family in Syria with Osama in tow. On these trips Osama would often see his younger cousin Najwa, who privately nursed a crush on her tall, monosyllabic, handsome cousin, trembling with excitement when he was in the same room as her. Bin Laden asked his mother if he could marry Najwa, and their families agreed to the match. In 1974 Osama, aged seventeen, and Najwa, aged fifteen, were betrothed. True to bin Laden's fundamentalist beliefs there was no singing or music at their wedding, and laughter and jokes were not encouraged.

Bin Laden and his wife moved in with his mother at her house in Jeddah, where they were given a floor to themselves. Continuing his exceptionally close relationship with his mother, he would kiss her hands and make small talk about her cooking. He was still attending the Al-Thaghr high school, but he was also working on road projects for the Saudi Binladin Group, often operating the heavy equipment himself.

Najwa was soon pregnant and delivered Abdullah, and Osama, as was customary, was now referred to as Abu Abdullah, "the father of Abdullah," his firstborn son. Soon came another son, Abdul Rahman.

When Abdul Rahman was born he had a deformed head, likely caused by hydrocephalus, a buildup of fluid on the brain that causes enlarged heads in infants. Bin Laden decided to go to the United States together with Najwa and their two sons so Abdul Rahman could receive medical attention. It would be his only visit to the country that would become his life's obsession.

During their two-week trip Najwa recalled that she and her husband "did not hate America, yet we did not love it." Najwa's most memorable moment from the trip to the United States was at an airport when a man became so transfixed by her black face veil and all-enveloping abaya that he paced back and forth in front of her gawking in disbelief. Bin Laden told Batarfi that some Americans even took photos of him and his wife in their Arab robes. Bin Laden told another friend, "We were like in a zoo." Najwa and her husband later had a good chuckle about this incident.

After graduating from high school in 1976 bin Laden went to King Abdel Aziz University in Jeddah to study economics and business administration. At the age of nineteen, he soon met Jamal Khalifa, who was a year older and studying science. They became fast friends, drawn to each other by their shared religiosity. Neither of the friends watched movies, listened to music, or took photographs, believing that they were all haram, forbidden by Islam. They did watch the news on TV, and in the days before remote control devices, Khalifa had his son stand by the television so if music came on during a newscast his son could turn it down.

The two friends went riding together out into the desert on bin Laden's beloved Arabian horses, subsisting on dates and water and sleeping on the sand at night. These desert adventures were the beginning of bin Laden's interest in testing himself and toughening himself for a time of privation that he believed would soon be coming.

Both came of age as the Muslim world was experiencing an Islamic resurgence known as "the Awakening." This awakening followed the devastating defeat of the Arab states during the 1967 war with Israel. That defeat had exposed the failings of Egyptian president Gamal Abdel Nasser and his avowedly secular regime, which had promised a swift victory.

The Egyptian writer Sayyid Qutb, a key ideologue for the Muslim

Brotherhood, provided much of the theoretical underpinnings that shaped this Islamic awakening. In his massive multivolume treatise, *In the Shade of the Qur'an*, Qutb argued that Islam was not simply the traditional observation of the five pillars of Islam—the profession of faith, the Hajj pilgrimage to Mecca, the giving of alms to the poor, fasting during Ramadan, and the five daily prayers—it was a whole way of life. Qutb's writings were widely distributed after his execution for purported treason in Cairo in 1966, which made him a martyr for the Muslim Brotherhood movement.

The Awakening had revolutionary features because Qutb's writings contended that most Muslim governmental systems were mired in *Jahiliya*, a state of pre-Islamic ignorance and even barbarism, a charge that was implicitly directed against the authoritarian regimes of the Middle East. In Qutb's polemical book *Milestones*, he provided inspiration for Islamist movements across the Muslim world, explaining that jihad must not only be defensive in nature, but also be waged offensively. Qutb wrote, "The persons who attempt to defend the concept of Islamic jihad by interpreting it in the narrow sense of the current concept of defensive war . . . they lack understanding of the nature of Islam and its primary aim." By implication Qutb was saying that it was a religious duty to take up arms against repressive and corrupt governments in the Muslim world that were not adhering to true Islamic precepts.

In their first years at university Khalifa and bin Laden read Qutb's books, and the two friends also attended lectures at their university given by Sayyid Qutb's brother, Mohammed. Mohammed Qutb was a member of the Muslim Brotherhood in Egypt who had fled persecution and had sought sanctuary in Saudi Arabia. There were a number of Muslim Brothers from Egypt, Iraq, and Syria who were similarly fleeing persecution at home who taught at King Abdel Aziz University when bin Laden and Khalifa were students. These teachers helped shape the Islamist ideology that the two friends were adopting.*

---

*When he became a public figure leading a self-proclaimed jihad, bin Laden never cited Sayyid Qutb's works in support of his actions, probably because Qutb

Khalifa, who probably understood bin Laden as well as anyone, said that he developed a very literal interpretation of Islam that he felt he had to carry out, and he was very much afraid that if did not do so, God would punish him. By the time he was twenty bin Laden was a fully fledged religious zealot, convinced that if he didn't follow his ultra-fundamentalist interpretation of his religion to the letter he would face the wrath of God.

Carmen bin Laden, who married one of bin Laden's half-brothers, remarked that Osama's "fierce piety was intimidating, even to the more religious members of the family." He might have been something of an outsider in the family, but his claims to be a priggish, ultra-observant Muslim were incontestable. And as he became an adult, bin Laden's identity as a person merged with his religious zealotry.

He continued to work for his family construction company, and idolized his father who had built it from nothing and always seemed to be in command while out in the field managing and working on projects. Bin Laden tried to emulate him by driving the bulldozers at the family's building sites himself. Like his father, he ate with the workers and worked from dawn to sundown tirelessly.

Osama decided to skip graduating from university and went to work for the family business full-time. He did so at a moment when his oldest brother, Salem, had taken the reins of the family business. Salem was as adept as his father at ingratiating himself with the Saudi monarchy and generating big contracts from King Fahd, the monarch who had succeeded King Faisal after he was assassinated in 1975. Salem acted as a kind of semiofficial jester in the court of King Fahd, doing things that no one else could get away with like buzzing the king's desert camp in one of the many planes that Salem loved to pilot himself. But Salem was also presiding over a serious business. An authoritative account of Saudi

---

wasn't a cleric with a formal religious education, just like bin Laden himself, who never studied Islam formally. So neither had any real standing to make rulings on Islamic law. Instead, when bin Laden advocated jihad he cited religious authorities such as the medieval Muslim scholar Ibn Taymiyya.

merchant families published in 1979 found that the bin Laden construction business had diversified into a number of areas including engineering, the manufacture of aluminum and concrete, brickmaking, installing air-conditioning systems, and telecommunications.

Bin Laden was twenty-two years old when, seemingly out of nowhere, several hundred Islamist militants seized the Great Mosque in Mecca, the holiest site in the Muslim world, on November 20, 1979. It was the first day of the new century according to the Islamic calendar. The rebels believed that among their ranks was the *Mahdi*, the savior who was prophesied to come at the end of the world to rid it of evil. They were also critical of the corruption of the Saudi monarchy, a critique that bin Laden would echo publicly a decade and a half later.

The bin Laden family knew the Great Mosque well, since they had spent many years expanding and renovating it. Several bin Laden brothers spent weeks at the mosque providing advice to the Saudi security services trying to extirpate the rebels. When the militants fled underground into tunnels beneath the mosque, the bin Ladens brought in equipment to bore holes in the floors so that grenades could be dropped below to kill the rebels. King Fahd conferred with Saudi religious leaders and he ordered the mosque be retaken. The bin Laden family provided blueprints and maps of the Great Mosque to the Saudi Special Forces who stormed it. Some sixty militants were later publicly beheaded.

Bin Laden subsequently reflected on this event, which seems to have precipitated an early skepticism about the Saudi regime. "King Fahd defiled the sanctity of the Great Mosque. He showed stubbornness, acted against the advice of everybody, and sent armored vehicles into the mosque. I still recall the imprint of tracked vehicles on the tiles of the mosque. People still recall that the minarets were covered with black smoke due to their shelling by tanks."

The Saudi royal family saw the rebels' seizure of the Great Mosque as a great threat to their power, just as the Iranian Revolution had been earlier in the year. The Saudi monarchy was determined to ensure that they would not be outflanked on matters of religion by Sunni militants at home or by the Shia militants in Iran. So the Saudi monarchy went back to its roots, and embraced the most austere form of Wahhabi Islam. In the mid-eighteenth century the first Saudi king had allied with Muhammad bin Abdul-Wahhab, a cleric who promoted an extremely harsh interpretation of Sunni Islam. This marriage of convenience had survived for more than two centuries and was the key to the political economy of Saudi Arabia: the Saudi royal family retained absolute authority—so much so that their family name was embedded in the name of the country—while the Wahhabi religious establishment sanctioned that absolute authority.

The Wahhabi religious establishment was now given a free hand: women announcers disappeared on Saudi TV; the religious police could arrest purported malefactors and harass unveiled women; illicit alcohol became much harder to obtain; movie theaters closed, as did music stores; and the Saudis dramatically increased their support to Islamic universities in the country and to charitable organizations that exported hardline Wahhabi ideas around the world.

Carmen bin Laden noticed that the atmosphere in the kingdom changed even in small, subtle ways. Despite the baking heat, bin Laden's wife, Najwa, started routinely wearing gloves outside, as did bin Laden's most observant half-sister, Sheikha.

Three weeks after the end of the Mecca siege there was another momentous event: The "infidel" Soviets invaded Afghanistan. The Soviets were trying to prop up the communist government of Afghanistan, which was facing a growing insurgency. The Soviet occupation of Afghanistan would transform the shy, monosyllabic zealot with a capacious wallet into a leader of men.

THREE

JIHAD

To stand one hour in the battle line in the cause of Allah is better than sixty years of night prayer.

—Abdullah Azzam, a mentor of bin Laden's,
quoting the Prophet Mohammed

In late December 1979 bin Laden was deeply upset when he heard the news that an "infidel" Soviet army had just invaded Afghanistan. The event would turn out to be the most transformative of his life, launching him into a full-time job helping the Afghan resistance and eventually leading to his formation of al-Qaeda.

Bin Laden spent the first two weeks of 1980 gathering donations for the Afghan holy warriors from members of his family and then traveled to Pakistan, where he gave the donations to representatives of the Jamiat-e-Islami, the Islamic Party, which was helping support the jihad against the Soviets.

Abdullah Azzam also was outraged by the Soviet occupation of Afghanistan. He had felt the sting of occupation firsthand during the 1967 war when the Israelis had occupied Jenin in Palestine, where his family lived. Azzam also had guerrilla warfare experience. Following the Israeli occupation he had crossed the border into Jordan where he joined a small group of Palestinian fighters that had launched raids into Israel. Azzam was now emerging both as an important political figure and an authority on matters of Islamic law, as he was a leader of the Muslim Brotherhood in Jordan and had obtained a doctorate in jurisprudence from Al-Azhar University in Cairo, the Vatican of Sunni thought. In 1980 Azzam received an offer to teach at bin Laden's alma mater, King Abdel Aziz University in Jeddah. It was in Jeddah that bin Laden and Azzam fatefully met when bin Laden attended some of Azzam's sermons.

Azzam decided to move to Pakistan in 1981 so he could be closer to the jihad being waged against the Soviets in neighboring Afghanistan and contribute in some way to the holy war. He started promoting the Afghan cause, writing books in Arabic about the war, while collecting donations for the holy cause, and he gave inspirational lectures about the conflict in countries around the world, including in the United States.

Essam al-Ridi, an Egyptian studying to be a pilot at the Ed Boardman Aviation School in Texas, was active in the Muslim American Youth Association, whose convention was held in Fort Worth during the early 1980s. Abdullah Azzam was a star at the convention, where he spoke about the obligation Muslims had to help the Afghan jihad in any way they could. Ridi was so inspired by Azzam's lecture that he moved to Pakistan in 1983 and started working for Azzam, traveling the world to find specialized items needed by the Afghan fighters such as rangefinders, scopes, and night vision equipment.

Similarly, Wael Julaidan, a Saudi from Medina whose family was involved in real estate, was a student in the United States in the mid-1980s studying for a master's degree in range management at the University of Arizona in Tucson. When Azzam spoke in Tucson in 1984, Julaidan was so moved by his lecture that he left for Pakistan to work with Azzam.

Azzam published a book, *Signs of the Most Merciful in the Afghan Holy War*, which recounted stories of the holy warriors in Afghanistan and told of the miracles that were happening to them as a result of God's grace: fighters who were struck by bullets but were not harmed and birds that circled in flocks above the holy warriors to distract Soviet helicopters. This was a leitmotif of Azzam's efforts to recruit Muslims from around the world to aid the Afghan conflict and also to shake loose donations from deep-pocketed Arabs: emphasizing the divine moments taking place in the Afghan jihad. The "martyrs" always died with smiles on their faces and their dead bodies invariably gave off a sweet musk-like odor.

Unlike bin Laden, Azzam was well qualified to pronounce on matters of Islamic jurisprudence, and in 1984 he issued a fatwa, a ruling on Islamic law, that Muslims around the world had an *individual* obligation to fight in the Afghan holy war. This was a revolutionary ruling since it went beyond the traditional interpretations of "defensive jihad," that local Muslims had an obligation to fight a jihad against a non-Muslim occupying force, because it ruled that all Muslims, whether they lived in Brooklyn or Jakarta, had to fight in the Afghan War. Azzam opined, "Expelling the Kuffar [infidels] from our land is *Fard Ayn*, a compulsory duty upon all. . . . We have to concentrate our efforts on Afghanistan and Palestine now, because they have become our foremost problems." Azzam announced his new fatwa during the 1984 Hajj pilgrimage to Mecca.

The same year that he issued the fatwa, Azzam decided to set up a "Services Office" that would coordinate the work of the Arab volunteers who were beginning to arrive in Pakistan to help the war effort and provide them guesthouses to live in Peshawar, the nearest major Pakistani city to the Afghan border. From the beginning Azzam emphasized that the word "service" in "Services Office" was because the Arabs coming to help the Afghan war effort were there to serve the Afghans, not their own interests. And who better to finance this effort than bin Laden, whom Azzam had known for the past four years and with whom he was deeply impressed? Azzam often observed how "pure" bin Laden was, a man who lived "the life of the poor," living like "a Jordanian laborer" with not even a single chair or table in his house, yet if you asked him to help the holy warriors, he would write a check on the spot for one million riyals (more than $250,000).

It was a mutual admiration club. Bin Laden was totally in thrall to Azzam, who was a decade and a half older and was many things that he was not. Azzam was a warfighter, a religious authority, a prolific essayist, and a talented public speaker. In Azzam, bin Laden found the father figure he seemed to have been longing for. Vahid Mojdeh, an Afghan working as a translator at the Services Office, remembers Azzam completely over-shadowing bin Laden. "I never heard bin Laden delivering a speech in Pe-shawar. He was not considered clever or intelligent. Azzam, on the other hand, was a powerful speaker, and a declaimer of poems." Similarly, Faraj Ismail, an Egyptian journalist who covered the Afghan jihad for the Saudi *Al Muslimoon* newspaper, described the relationship between bin Laden and Azzam as "a student to a professor. I felt that Azzam was the religious reference for bin Laden."

Azzam's fatwa brought new recruits from the Muslim world. Essam Deraz, an Egyptian writer who covered the "Afghan Arabs," said "They came to die." This, of course, wasn't necessarily the soundest military strategy since intentional death-seeking is not typically the best tactic to win a war, but these idealistic young Arab recruits were fired by fervor for the holy war; they wanted adventure and in many cases they wanted the glory that came with the death of a martyr.

One of the first recruits was the Algerian Abdullah Anas, who de-scribed his fellow volunteers as young men whose minds were "full of Sylvester Stallone and visions of paradise." Anas read a newspaper in 1984 that reported that a group of ulema—religious scholars, including Abdul-lah Azzam—had issued a fatwa that every Muslim should try and liberate Afghanistan from the atheist Soviets. Anas decided to go to Afghanistan even though he had no idea where Afghanistan was, or how to get there.

In a coincidence that would alter the course of his life, Anas was per-forming the Hajj pilgrimage in Saudi Arabia and as he walked around the sacred site in Mecca, he recognized Azzam. Anas asked him, "Are you Abdullah Azzam? I've read the fatwa. I'm from Algeria and I saw your sig-nature among the ulemas saying that jihad in Afghanistan is a duty. And if I decide to go, what can I do?"

Azzam told him that after two weeks he should go to Islamabad, the capital of Pakistan, and "call me from the airport and I will give you the address to come to my home." Anas stayed at Azzam's house, and at lunch one day a man was sitting on Anas's right. Azzam told him, "This is your brother, Osama." Bin Laden was very shy, very well mannered, and said virtually nothing. This was characteristic of bin Laden during this period; Azzam did all the talking and bin Laden did all the listening,

Anas says he was the fourteenth of the Arabs who arrived in Pakistan to help the Afghan jihad. He wanted to find out what was going on inside Afghanistan, particularly on the more distant battlefronts. Anas volunteered to join a caravan of three hundred Afghan mujahideen, holy warriors, traveling to Mazar-i-Sharif in the north of Afghanistan. The trip took forty days of walking across the mountains of Afghanistan.

For the Arabs it was intensely emotional to travel among the Afghans. When villagers heard that among the caravan of mujahideen there was an Arab, they all came out of their homes to see him because he spoke the language of the Prophet. Anas spoke at village mosques and hundreds would gather to hear him, crying, "*Allah Akbar!*" [God is great!] Anas recounted, "I used to feel that I am an angel. I am walking in the air. I'm doing my duty, making my God happy, helping brother Muslims, and no pressure of life, sitting with the Afghans. These simple people all were loving the Prophet, all loving the Koran, making jihad."

Anas stayed in Mazar-i-Sharif for two months and decided that the Arab participation in Afghanistan was not just about fighting and being martyred, but to find ways to help Afghans from being forced from their homes and becoming refugees in Pakistan. Already the Soviets had dislodged millions of Afghans, creating the largest refugee population since World War II. Anas determined that the Arabs and their wealthy backers had to help build schools and hospitals for the Afghans.

During the first four years of the war bin Laden went back and forth from Saudi Arabia to Pakistan bringing donations to the Afghan factions fighting the Soviets, but he did not set foot in Afghanistan itself, dissuaded by family and friends who told him it was too dangerous. But in 1984 Azzam suggested bin Laden take a look for himself. One of the easier places in Afghanistan to access from Pakistan was Jaji, because a parrot's beak of Pakistani territory made travel into this part of eastern

Afghanistan just a few miles from the Pakistani border relatively easy. This route avoided having to make one of the weeks-long treks by foot that were necessary to reach more distant parts of Afghanistan.

At first bin Laden was afraid to be on the ground in Afghanistan. Azzam regularly took his teenage sons to the Afghan front lines, and one of them remembered that when bin Laden first heard explosions he used to jump and run away, which made Azzam's sons have a good laugh at bin Laden's expense. But once bin Laden reached Jaji, he was appalled by the terrible state of the weapons the Afghans were using and even of their trenches. These discoveries made him feel embarrassed that it had taken him four years to get to the front lines of the holy war. He believed that he could be pardoned for this great sin in the eyes of God only if he were to be "martyred."

While he was in Jaji the Soviets launched an air raid, during which bin Laden said he felt closer to God than ever before. He went back to Saudi Arabia even more fired up by the Afghan cause. During Ramadan he was able to raise more than $5 million from private donors, including eight million riyals (more than $2 million) from one of his half-sisters.

In September 1984 bin Laden agreed with Azzam that he would start paying for the volunteers and their families who were moving to Pakistan to work for the Services Office. Bin Laden started paying around $300,000 a year to the Services Office so that these Muslim recruits from around the world could "join the caravan," the title of one of Azzam's books about the Afghan jihad.

A key project of Azzam and bin Laden's Services Office was *Jihad* magazine, which started publishing in December 1984. The first issue informed readers, "We remind you that the Afghan jihad is a necessity for the Muslims, even if the number of Russian enemies and others are double your number. And, in God's name, you will defeat your enemies, because one of you is superior to ten of your enemies."

The Arabic-language magazine appeared monthly, carrying news of the war in Afghanistan, and it also focused on Arab efforts to help the Afghan jihad. In its first six months the magazine was an amateur production in black-and-white, while subsequent issues were well laid out and featured a wealth of color photographs. The magazine was a vital tool for fundraising and for recruiting Muslim volunteers from around the world for the Afghan jihad. Azzam, a man of immense energy, wrote much of the copy and edited much of the magazine, while bin Laden was content at this stage in his life to take a back seat to Azzam and barely registered in its pages.

Two of the first recruits to work at *Jihad* magazine were Jamal Ismail, a Palestinian student who was studying at Peshawar Engineering University, who translated news items from English for the magazine. Another was Ahmad Zaidan, a Syrian. Both Ismail and Zaidan would later become journalists for major Arab media outlets and would cover the rise of bin Laden as he launched his war against the United States.

Jihad magazine was a powerful tool for recruitment for the Afghan holy war as it was distributed to some fifty countries around the world and was an early example of how jihadists harnessed the most current media format to spread their propaganda. At its height, seventy thousand copies were printed of each issue, many of which went to the United States. Indeed, the Services Office had its U.S. headquarters in Brooklyn, as well as other offices in Boston, Chicago, Phoenix, Tucson, and Washington, DC.

Azzam, backed by bin Laden's money, launched what was effectively the first global jihadist project, bringing Muslims from around the world to aid the Afghan war who were often inspired by what they had read in *Jihad* magazine. This was enabled by an era of relatively cheap air travel, including a 75 percent discount on Saudia airline for Saudis who wanted to support the Afghan jihad.

Jamal al-Fadl, a Sudanese living in Brooklyn in the mid-1980s, was working in a grocery store when he read a copy of *Jihad* magazine and he saw the news about Azzam's fatwa. Fadl left for Pakistan, where he attended training camps, learning how to shoot AK-47s and rocket-propelled grenades and how to handle explosives such as TNT and C4.

Bin Laden, aged twenty-seven, began thinking about solving some of the logistical issues around supplying the Afghan guerrillas fighting in places like Jaji. He decided that his experience in construction in Saudi Arabia might be transferable to Afghanistan. Better roads would allow the mujahideen more maneuverability, and tunnels would allow them to shelter during bombardments and could also function as hospitals. Of course there were major logistical issues involving transporting bin Laden's construction equipment from Saudi Arabia into Pakistan and then on to Afghanistan, but bin Laden enlisted both the Saudi ambassador in Pakistan and the Saudi Red Crescent charitable organization to help him surmount these hurdles.

While he became increasingly involved in the Afghan War, bin Laden continued to work in the family business. In 1982 he was appointed by his older brother Salem to be an executive overseeing the project to renovate the Prophet's Mosque in Medina, the second-holiest site in Islam. Bin Laden moved to the holy city to help supervise the project. Working to renovate the Medina mosque was enormously significant for bin Laden given its special connection to the Prophet.

While invested both in the Afghan war effort and also in the renovations in Medina, bin Laden started thinking about marrying again. He had pronounced views about the proper practice of polygamy, which he had discussed at great length with Jamal Khalifa, his best friend at university. The two friends had agreed that polygamy wasn't about "fun" and "just having women with you to sleep with," but was in fact a solution for a very real social problem, since it was well established, in their view, that there were more women in the world than men. The two friends discussed how their own fathers had practiced polygamy and agreed that they hadn't approached it in a properly religious manner. In the friends' view, to be a true Muslim you should marry only the four wives sanctioned by Islam and then only if you could treat all four of them fairly.

Bin Laden and Khalifa agreed they wouldn't follow in their fathers' footsteps, as each man had married many more than four women and had frequently divorced them. This was a particularly sensitive subject for bin Laden, whose parents had divorced after a brief marriage when bin Laden was only two and whose father, Mohammed, had sired fifty-five children from some twenty wives. Since Mohammed bin Laden never had more than four wives at any one time, he was constantly divorcing the third and the fourth and marrying new ones. Bin Laden believed that was not the Islamic way at all; you had to divide your time and attention fairly between your wives and stick with them.

As his family grew and bin Laden began ruminating about marrying again and having more children, in 1983 he purchased a large building in Jeddah's Aziziyah neighborhood on Wadi Bishah Street, just to the north of the neighborhood where his mother lived. Bin Laden chose to leave his new home undecorated; there were no pictures, the carpet was cheap, and the overall color scheme was gray. This would continue to be bin Laden's favored mode of decor in all of his future homes. In the steaming-hot city of Jeddah, bin Laden wouldn't let the air-conditioning be turned on in his house, nor would he permit the refrigerator to be used, pompously observing that "Islamic beliefs are corrupted by modernization." It's a stance that he would also adopt in other brutally hot climates that he would later live in, such as Sudan and southern Afghanistan.

Bin Laden was quite deliberate about the three women he chose to marry next. All of them claimed descent from the Prophet Mohammed, a subject of great importance to the ultra-orthodox bin Laden, who tried to model every aspect of his life on the Prophet. Unlike his first wife, Najwa, they were all well-educated teachers. When bin Laden increasingly adopted a life of exile, these wives would end up becoming the tutors to his many children.

During Najwa's fifth pregnancy bin Laden raised "an unexpected topic": his plans to take a second wife. Najwa was not thrilled by this suggestion and over the next months they spent many hours discussing the issue. Bin Laden wore her down, arguing that he wanted to have "many children for Islam." Over time Najwa began to accept the idea; her husband wasn't unhappy with his current marriage, it was just that he genuinely wanted to bring more Muslims into the world. Bin Laden told her, "Najwa if you are contented in your heart for me to take a second wife, you will gain in heaven. It is certain that your life will end in Paradise."

In 1983 bin Laden married Khadijah al-Sharif, an educated woman who had taught at a girls' school in Jeddah and was a direct descendant of the Prophet. Najwa didn't attend the wedding ceremony, but over time she and Khadijah became friends. Khadijah bore bin Laden a son, Ali, while Najwa had her fifth son, Osman.

A year after marrying Khadijah, bin Laden took his two wives and six sons on a trip to Peshawar, Pakistan, so they could see for themselves the great jihad project he had embarked upon in neighboring Afghanistan. There he procured a spacious villa for his growing family and he devoted more time than usual to his young sons. He brought the eldest, eight-year-old Abdullah, on one of his jihad excursions to the Afghanistan-Pakistan border. During the broiling Saudi summers, while much of the rest of the Saudi elite was off in London or the South of France, the bin Laden family often returned to Peshawar.

Bin Laden enlisted his first wife, Najwa, in his quest to find his third wife. Together they already had six children, but bin Laden told Najwa that the time was coming when "Islam would need more followers" and he wanted to have more sons and daughters "to carry forth the message of God." To his close male friends bin Laden often repeated a saying attributed to the Prophet Mohammed: "Marry and increase in number because with you I increase the nation [of Muslims]."

He asked Najwa if she would help find him a "suitable wife." Najwa contemplated the matter for a few days and concluded that she would indeed help "for Islam" and that her love for her husband "would live and grow even more." "Guided by God," within a few weeks Najwa found Khairiah Sabar—"a lovely woman from Jeddah," who was very devout and hailed from a wealthy, distinguished family that claimed descent from the Prophet. Unusual for someone from a conservative family in the deeply conservative Saudi Arabia of the mid-1980s, Sabar had an independent career as a specialized teacher of deaf-mute children. Bin Laden married Umm Hamza in 1985, when he was twenty-eight and she was thirty-six, which was a very late age in Saudi Arabia for a woman to get married.

By now bin Laden was becoming increasingly celebrated as a genuine war hero in Saudi Arabia. The six-foot-four scion of one of the richest families in the kingdom with the aquiline features of a Saudi prince and his tales of derring-do from the Afghan holy war made bin Laden quite the catch, even if he did come with the not insignificant baggage of already being married to three other women.

During the war against the Soviets in Afghanistan bin Laden had fought alongside Saad al-Sharif and had formed a close friendship with him. Sharif exerted great effort to persuade his sister Siham to marry bin Laden. When bin Laden proposed marriage to Siham, she was pursuing an MA in religion. She told bin Laden that she would have to complete her education as a condition of accepting his proposal, a request that he acceded to only reluctantly. Siham's parents opposed the match because bin Laden was already thrice married, but she went ahead anyway in 1987 because she believed that bin Laden was truly a hero of jihad.

Bin Laden rarely told anything approximating a joke, but he did tell his closest buddies, "I don't understand why people take only one wife. If you take four wives, you live like a groom." With his requisite four wives bin Laden could now truly live like a groom. And his reputation as a proselytizer of polygamous marriages grew to such an extent that married women tried to keep their husbands away from him as they had no interest in having bin Laden convince them to adopt his cause.

Bin Laden even suggested to Jamal Khalifa, his old university friend, that he take Sheikha bin Laden, one of his half-sisters, as an additional wife. She was deeply religious and she didn't have any full brothers, so bin Laden took a strong fraternal interest in her welfare. In 1986 Khalifa married Sheikha bin Laden, but her family found Khalifa's house in Jeddah unsuitable for her. So Osama gave Khalifa an unexpectedly generous gift; he divided his Jeddah villa by building an internal wall so that Khalifa could have his own quarters for his family.

The same year that he arranged for Sheikha's marriage, bin Laden's once close relationship with his mentor Abdullah Azzam began to fray. The young Saudi militant millionaire was preoccupied with personally fighting the Soviets on the front lines rather than simply supporting the activities of the Afghan mujahideen, which was Azzam's goal. Bin Laden wanted to create a stand-alone Arab force that would hold its ground against Soviet attacks because his recruits were eager to martyr themselves, unlike the Afghans, who had a much more pragmatic approach to fighting; they might leave the battlefront if they faced serious opposition, or sometimes simply because they had to go home to see their families.

Bin Laden's Arab force made scant sense militarily. At any given moment there were at most three hundred Arabs fighting on the front lines in Afghanistan, so from a military standpoint pulling them together would have a negligible impact on the war. After all, there were an estimated 175,000 to 250,000 Afghan fighters on the battlefield.

Abdullah Azzam was opposed to the idea of a separate Arab military unit because he believed the presence of Arabs scattered throughout all of the Afghan factions not only boosted morale but could also teach the Afghans about Islam, aid them with education and medicine, and bring news of the Afghan jihad to wealthy donors in the Middle East. A single Arab military force would end this effort, and in any event could not alter the conduct of the war.

Bin Laden, who had no military expertise, selected the area around Jaji in the mountains of eastern Afghanistan to build a new base—*Al-Qaeda* in Arabic—because it overlooked Soviet positions. Bin Laden's men called the base *Masada*, "the Lion's Den." In this place epic battles would be fought. The Lion's Den was named after a verse by one of the Companions of the Prophet who wrote in the seventh century, "Whoever wishes to hear the clash of swords, let him come to the Lion's Den, where he will find courageous men ready to die for the sake of God." *Osama* also means "lion" in Arabic. This would be his den.

Bin Laden said he hoped that the base would draw Soviet firepower, explaining, "We want the Lions' Den to be the first thing that the enemy faces. Its place as the first camp visible to the enemy means that they will focus their bombardments on us in an extreme manner."

This, of course, made no sense at all from a military perspective, and the Afghan fighters knew this. They had avoided setting up a base in Jaji because it was blocked by heavy snows and ice in the brutal Afghan winters and was buffeted by strong winds, which made it difficult to supply. Also the Afghans were fighting a guerrilla war that focused on hit-and-run operations, and setting up a permanent base in imitation of a conventional army undercut their strategy. Bin Laden wasn't fazed by these logistical and strategic issues. Work began at Jaji on October 24, 1986. He and four of his friends lived in a tent as they began construction on their base. The winter was so intense that water kept in plastic bottles would freeze overnight.

Their number soon grew to sixteen and this group of Saudis, mostly from the holy city of Medina, built shelters underground with bulldozers and diggers. They fashioned an operations room, a weapons storage area, and a food storage facility, which they constructed from nearby trees that they had cut down. These shelters sometimes collapsed, so bin Laden brought in welding equipment that he used himself to fortify the ceilings of the bunkers they had built. They also purchased their first machine gun. Bin Laden had to restrain some of "the brothers" who wanted to immediately launch an operation against Soviet forces. He recalled this as "one of the most beautiful periods of my life." He told his team, "We want this site to be only for the Saudi mujahideen and not for anyone else. We want to stay away from anything that might harm our reputation and the reputation of our families as Saudi mujahideen."

As the number of brothers at Jaji grew to forty, bin Laden asked some of them to go to the arms market in the nearby Pakistani village of Tari Mangal to buy weapons. They purchased AK-47s and a rocket-propelled grenade. Bin Laden's men started mounting small operations against the Soviets and soon there were casualties; young Saudi men who yearned for "martyrdom" were granted their wish.

In January 1987 bin Laden put his military commanders in Afghanistan, the Egyptians Abu Hafs and Abu Ubayda, on his payroll, paying them each 4,500 Pakistani rupees a month (then a little over $250).

When he visited Jaji, Jamal Khalifa was unimpressed by bin Laden's plan to set up a base near a Soviet military post, and he was concerned that his old friend was sending idealistic young Arabs under his command on kamikaze missions. Khalifa went to bin Laden's military commander, Abu Ubayda, a former sergeant in the Egyptian army who had actual battle-field experience, and asked him: "Is this the right place to have this kind of camp?" Abu Ubayda said it was not. He also made it clear that he was following bin Laden's orders, who, after all, was paying his salary.

Khalifa confronted bin Laden, telling him, "Osama, everybody is against this idea. Why are you here? Don't you know that this is very dangerous?"

Bin Laden said, "We came to be in the front."

Khalifa replied, "No, we did not come to be in the front. We came to act as supporters of the Afghans. Every drop of blood bleeds here in this place; God will ask you about it in the hereafter. Everybody is saying this is wrong, so Osama, please leave this place right now."

Everyone in the Jaji base could hear the two old friends arguing loudly.

Khalifa said, "Look, you will leave the place or I will never see you again."

Bin Laden replied, "Do whatever you want."

So Khalifa left and their friendship never recovered.*

Because bin Laden had his own money he could forge ahead with his plans, and he did.

Meanwhile, Osama was also at loggerheads with Azzam over the management of bin Laden's money at the Services Office. Azzam was many things—a guerrilla fighter, a religious scholar, and a prolific writer—but he was not an able administrator. Until 1986 bin Laden had commuted back and forth between Pakistan and Saudi Arabia. Now he decided to live full-time in Peshawar to better oversee the affairs of the Services Office and also to be closer to the action in Afghanistan.

So he set up a home in Hayatabad, a suburb of Peshawar, which was

---

*Years later both Jordan and the U.S. would charge Khalifa with terrorism-related crimes and he would be murdered in mysterious circumstances in Madagascar in 2007.

a fifteen-minute drive from Bait Al-Ansar, the House of the Supporters, the guesthouse for his Arab volunteers. That guesthouse was named after Al-Ansar, the residents of Medina who supported the Prophet Moham-med during his battles. A few blocks away was the American Club, which was one of the only bars in town and which did a brisk business catering to a *Casablanca*-like cast of Western journalists, spies, aid workers, and diplomats, all involved in some fashion in the Afghan War.

When bin Laden made visits back to Saudi Arabia he sometimes saw his old childhood friend Khalid Batarfi, who was now a journalist. Bin Laden tried to persuade Batarfi to go to Afghanistan to cover the war, say-ing, "You can fight with your pen. Come as a journalist and write about us. I'll grant you access to anybody you need." Batarfi was reluctant; he preferred the beach to the battlefield, recalling, "I was more romantic. I was thinking of love. He was thinking of love of God."

Batarfi noticed that bin Laden seemed to be changing. He was be-coming less shy and more assertive, and he started making speeches at mosques and other gathering places. In 1986 he gave his first lecture, which focused on Palestine, long an obsession for him. Bin Laden urged an audience in Jeddah to boycott all U.S. goods, even American apples, because he believed that without the support of the United States, Israel couldn't exist. He banned his own family from drinking Pepsi and Coca-Cola, though some of his children would continue drinking American soft drinks behind his back.

Back in Afghanistan bin Laden kept building up his base in Jaji, so much so that the Soviets began to notice. The inevitable battle of Jaji began on May 12, 1987, and lasted some three weeks of attacks and coun-terattacks. There were around sixty men in the Lion's Den, the command-ers of which were Abu Ubayda and Abu Hafs. On May 23 the Russian shelling became so intense that Abu Ubayda insisted to bin Laden that they needed to retreat. Bin Laden told some of his men to withdraw as they didn't have the training to confront the Russian advance. Some were shocked; they came to die and had built the Lion's Den with their own hands, only now to abandon it? The Russian attack in earnest came four days later with tanks advancing and planes dropping thousand-pound bombs as well as napalm to clear the thickly forested area around the base. Spetsnaz, Russian Special Forces units, assaulted the area. Bin Laden said he had heard that the Russians wanted him taken prisoner, although it seems improbable that the Russians knew who he was.

Abdullah Azzam was also at Jaji, despite his private misgivings about bin Laden's separate Arab military unit. During the battle bin Laden was ill, afflicted with low blood pressure for which he was drinking salted water and receiving injections of glucose from an Egyptian doctor. Azzam told bin Laden to rest, but he refused to do so, staying on the front line.

For bin Laden a key moment in the battle came at 7 a.m. on May 25 when most of his men were still sleeping in the camp because it was Ramadan and they had been up late breaking their fast. He saw a Soviet warplane passing above that had been targeted by a group of Afghan fighters. Under their fire, the plane broke into pieces and crashed nearby. Bin Laden said, "This battle is what gave me the strong will to continue with this war." For bin Laden it would not have been a coincidence that this key moment in the battle took place on the twenty-seventh day of Ramadan, an especially sacred moment in the Muslim calendar, known as "Lailat al Qadr," the Night of Power. Muslims believe that this day is when destiny is decided and the gates of heaven are opened.

Bin Laden always tried to model himself on the Prophet Mohammed, and there he was, fighting the infidels, just like the founder of Islam, also a military commander, who participated in twenty-seven raids against his enemies.

During the battle of the Lion's Den, thirteen of bin Laden's Arab fighters were killed, many of them in their early twenties, along with seventy Afghans. After the Arabs withdrew they were replaced by a much larger force of Afghans of more than two hundred fighters. The Arab sacrifices were applauded by the Afghans, who admired the bravery of bin Laden's men because they had largely stood their ground during the three weeks of attacks and counterattacks. The Russians lost tanks and armored vehicles, and at least two dozen Russians were killed. Victory songs were sung by the mujahideen and the battle of Jaji entered into the realm of mythology among the Afghan Arabs.

Essam Deraz, a forty-year-old former captain in the Egyptian army, decided to document the Afghan War and traveled into Afghanistan multiple times. Bin Laden gave Deraz considerable access so he could photograph and film him and his group. As a teenager bin Laden had abjured pictures and photographs on religious grounds, but now he wanted to star in his own war movie. Cognizant of his own iconography, bin Laden made sure he was filmed and photographed in the caves of Afghanistan. Muslims know that it was in a cave that the Prophet Mohammed had started receiving the first verses of the sacred Koran from Allah.

Deraz noticed that bin Laden was increasingly seen as a leader by the Afghan Arabs, and he was fighting bravely in battles against the Russians. At one point, bin Laden was wounded in the foot, which he treated with herbs.

Those wounds helped make 1987 a critical turning point in bin Laden's life, when he left behind his former role as a donor and fundraiser for the mujahideen and launched his career as a mujahid. Bin Laden felt that his Arab force could deliver an important psychological victory for the Afghans and the entire Muslim world if it stood up to the Soviets. To some degree that happened, because the Afghan Arabs' stand against the Russians at Jaji in 1987 was lionized not only in *Jihad* magazine but also in the mainstream Arab press, turning bin Laden into an authentic war hero and providing a boost to recruitment efforts for Muslims around the world to come to Afghanistan.

A month after the battle *Jihad* magazine wrote an account of it, saying, "Beginning the night of Ramadan, the enemy tried to take over, but every time they tried, our men hit them with weapons. And they tried again for another hit with their commandos, but we hit them with our rocket-propelled grenades. And we saw them retreating with our telescopes. Russia lost many of their well-respected commandos to the mujahideen." A later issue explained that stories about the Jaji battle were a tremendous recruiting device for Arabs: "After the victorious battle of the Lion's Den in 1987 the youths started coming in waves."

Abdullah Anas, who, along with Azzam and bin Laden, was one of the cofounders of the Services Office, estimated that between three thousand to five thousand volunteers showed up between 1987 and 1989. Of that no more than 10 percent fought inside Afghanistan; the vast majority worked in support roles in Pakistan as teachers, accountants, and doctors. Some Saudis even came on a jihad vacation, spending time during the Islamic holidays to support the war effort. "Instead of going to Switzerland they would go spend a few days or weeks with the Afghan refugees; sharing their suffering, bringing some clothes, some money," Anas recalled.

The first journalist from a major Arab media outlet to cover bin Laden was Jamal Khashoggi, who came from the same social milieu as bin Laden. Bin Laden's father had jump-started the business career of Jamal's uncle, Adnan Khashoggi, who would go on to become a multibillionaire. Khashoggi recalled that Osama was just "like many of us who become part of the Muslim Brotherhood movement," but he was even more religious than his contemporaries in the Brotherhood. In late 1987 bin Laden offered Khashoggi the chance of a scoop: to cover the Arabs fighting in Afghanistan. Khashoggi traveled into Afghanistan with bin Laden to Jaji, where he found "a very enthusiastic bunch of Arabs who believed in what they were doing."

Khashoggi published a lengthy article about the Jaji base in the Saudi magazine *Al Majallah* on May 4, 1988, and a similar English-language version appeared in *Arab News* the same day. The story starred bin Laden and how he had built up the Jaji camp that had been attacked by the Russians a year earlier. The stories also featured a photograph of bin Laden in Afghanistan with some of his men, the first time such an image was published. Khashoggi quoted bin Laden saying, "We sometimes spent the whole day in the trenches or in the caves until our ears could no longer bear the sound of the explosions around us. War planes continually shrieked by us and their crazy song of death echoed endlessly." He went on, "It was God alone who protected us from the Russians during their offensive last year. Reliance upon God is the main source of our strength."

Jaji would be bin Laden's first brush with publicity, and over time the shy millionaire would increasingly come to appreciate, and learn the value of, the spotlight. In that sense, the battle of Jaji was, above all, a public relations victory. It did not change the military situation on the ground, particularly as compared with the battles fought by the Afghan military leader Ahmad Shah Massoud. Massoud had resisted several major Soviet offensives against his stronghold in the Panjshir Valley in northern Afghanistan during the 1980s and was the most effective commander during the war.

Bin Laden later referred to the Jaji battle as "going down in history as one of the great battles of contemporary Islamic times." This was an exaggeration. No doubt an intense battle was fought at Jaji. Days after the height of the battle the wire service UPI noted that "Western diplomats reported the movement of an unusually large convoy of 320 vehicles, including Soviet T-62 tanks and 152mm self-propelled guns, heading south from the Afghan capital of Kabul toward the Jaji region." The UPI story went on to quote an Afghan guerrilla leader who said the fighting in Jaji was "the most severe in the current year" and "he had never seen such massive high-altitude bombing in the past seven years." But, as even the Afghan Arabs' own account of the Jaji battle made clear, only thirteen of bin Laden's men were killed, and when the Arabs retreated from the battlefield, a large group of Afghan fighters was sent in to relieve them. The bulk of the fighting and the bulk of the dying during the Jaji battle was done by the Afghans, not by bin Laden's men.

Authoritative histories of the Afghan War rarely mention the battle of Jaji. Yet in bin Laden's own mind his men had played a key role in defeating the Soviet superpower. Bin Laden and his Afghan Arabs were a minor sideshow in a war that was won, in the end, by the sacrifices of at least fifty thousand Afghan fighters who were killed and $3 billion of aid from the CIA. That money was matched dollar for dollar by the Saudi government.

What mattered much more than the Afghan Arabs was the introduction by the CIA of the highly effective Stinger antiaircraft missile. The weapon ended the Soviets' total air superiority and greatly increased the effectiveness and the morale of Afghan fighters. In 1986 Milt Bearden was appointed to be CIA station chief in Pakistan running the agency's war in Afghanistan. Bearden's instructions from President Ronald Reagan's CIA director Bill Casey were simple: "Go out and win. I'll give you a billion dollars. You get the Stingers now, and you get anti-tank stuff. You tell me what you need. The president and I want to try to see if these guys can win." Three years later the Soviets withdrew.

The only significant role that the Afghan Arabs had was in publicizing the Afghan conflict in their own countries, which helped raise large-scale private donations for the Afghans. The CIA estimated that by 1989 Gulf Arabs were donating around $250 million a year for Afghan humanitarian and construction projects, while al-Qaeda's leaders estimated that nongovernmental Arab sources donated $200 million to the Afghan cause over the course of the war.

It's worth mentioning here that there is simply no evidence for the common myth that bin Laden and his Afghan Arabs were supported by the CIA financially. Nor is there any evidence that CIA officials at any level met with bin Laden or anyone in his circle. Yet the notion that bin Laden was a creation of the CIA is widespread. For instance, the American filmmaker Michael Moore has written, "WE created the monster known as Osama bin Laden! Where did he go to terrorist school? At the CIA!" The real problem is not that the CIA helped bin Laden during the 1980s, but that the U.S. government had no idea about his possible significance until 1993, when he first started to appear in internal U.S. intelligence analyses describing him as a financier of Islamist extremist groups.

The notion that the CIA aided the rise of the Afghan Arabs is based on a fundamental misunderstanding of how the agency supported the Afghan War effort. First, it was overseen by a tiny group of CIA officers in Pakistan. Vincent Cannistraro, who helped coordinate CIA support to the Afghans during the mid-1980s, explained there were only six CIA officials in Pakistan at any given time, and they were simply "administrators."

Secondly, CIA officers in Pakistan seldom left the embassy in Islamabad, and rarely even met with the leaders of the Afghan resistance, let alone Arab militants. That's because the CIA officers provided American funding to Pakistan's Inter-Services Intelligence (ISI) agency, which, in turn, decided which among the Afghan mujahideen groups would receive the funding.

Brigadier Mohammad Yousaf, who ran the ISI's Afghan operations, explained that it was "a cardinal rule of Pakistan's policy that no Americans ever become involved with the distribution of funds or arms once they arrived in the country. No Americans ever trained or had direct contact with the mujahideen, and no American official ever went inside Afghanistan." Marc Sageman, a CIA officer who worked on the Afghan "account" in Pakistan during the mid-1980s, recalls "we were totally banned" from going into Afghanistan, for fear that it would hand the Soviets a great propaganda victory if a CIA officer was captured there. The CIA's Milt Bearden says the agency "never recruited, trained or otherwise used Arab volunteers. The Afghans were more than happy to do their own fighting—we saw no reason not to satisfy them on this point." No independent evidence of the CIA supporting al-Qaeda has emerged in the four decades since the end of the anti-Soviet war in Afghanistan.

In short, the CIA had very limited dealings with the Afghans, let alone the Afghan Arabs. There was simply no point for the CIA and the Afghan Arabs to be in contact with each other, since the agency worked through Pakistan's military intelligence agency during the Afghan War, while the Afghan Arabs had their own sources of funding. The CIA did not need the Afghan Arabs and the Afghan Arabs did not need the CIA.

In public relations terms, bin Laden now had a great backstory. A scion of the enormously rich bin Laden family, he had given up a life of wealth and leisure to go to Afghanistan to wage a dangerous, private holy war against the infidel Soviets. There is no record of any of the thousands of Saudi princes fighting in the Afghan holy war, despite the fact that the Saudi royal family awarded themselves the fancy religious title "The Custodian of the Two Holy Mosques" in 1986. Those in Saudi Arabia following the Afghan War believed that bin Laden had "won" the battle of Jaji. The marginal figure in his own family was now a national hero.

The battle at the base in Jaji became the foundation myth for all that followed. Jaji was known by bin Laden's men as *al-Qaeda*, "the Base" in Arabic, and over time that name stuck.

Al-Qaeda was born in the battle of Jaji.

FOUR

AL-QAEDA

The walls of oppression and humiliation cannot be demolished except in a rain of bullets.

—Osama bin Laden

What is more important in world history? The Taliban or the collapse of the Soviet empire? Some agitated Moslems, or the liberation of Central Europe and the end of the Cold War?

—Zbigniew Brzezinski

Since the battle of Jaji in May 1987, the idea of al-Qaeda cemented in bin Laden's mind. As a result of that battle, he and his two Egyptian military commanders, Abu Ubayda and Abu Hafs, became heroes among the Afghan Arabs. They contemplated starting an organization that was devoted to jihad and jihad alone.

As it became clear that the Soviets would likely be withdrawing from Afghanistan, bin Laden, now thirty-one, and increasingly confident in his role as a leader, wanted to preserve his battle-trained warriors to fight in other jihads around the world. Bin Laden told Jamal Khashoggi, the Saudi journalist covering the Afghan War, "The flame of jihad should continue elsewhere, in places like Central Asia. It will be called al-Qaeda."

As bin Laden later recalled in an interview with Al Jazeera television, his military commander, Abu Ubayda, had set up training camps in Afghanistan "during the 1980s. We used to call the training camp 'al-Qaeda' ['the Base']. And the name stayed."

While al-Qaeda as an idea may have existed as early as January 1987 when bin Laden had first put Abu Ubayda and Abu Hafs on his personal payroll, it was further formalized in meetings held in Peshawar during the sweltering summer of 1988. On August 11, 1988, bin Laden, referred to as "the Sheikh," discussed "new military work" with one of his aides. They agreed that 314 "brothers will be trained" by al-Qaeda within six months. The 314 figure was certainly metaphorical since it was also the total number of fighters the Prophet Mohammed led at the Battle of Badr in the year 624, underlining the fervid religious zeal that surrounded the founding of al-Qaeda, which, like so many other actions in bin Laden's life, was supposed to replicate the example of the Prophet. Al-Qaeda, in bin Laden's mind, would go into battle as a Legion of the Prophet.

Abu Ubayda, and Abu Hajir al-Iraqi, al-Qaeda's religious adviser, participated in meetings on August 18 and August 20. There was a notetaker for these meetings. A portion of them covered the "mismanagement and bad treatment in the Services Office." At least one of the participants may have seen this as the main issue under discussion. Azzam was not listed as a participant at any of the meetings, which suggests that there was indeed a lively discussion of the management problem at the Services Office, since they were generally presumed to be Azzam's fault.

The notes record that the overall aim of al-Qaeda was both vague and all-encompassing: "To lift the word of God," and at this stage, nothing suggested that bin Laden intended to start a holy war against the United States. Declaring that "the work of al-Qaeda commenced on September 10, 1988," the notes listed "Sheikh Osama" as the number one attendee at the meetings, and he was only one of two of the nine men who attended the meetings who was given the honorific of "Sheikh" in the notes.

The men at the meeting agreed that prospective recruits would undergo a relatively quick training course at a camp in Pakistan near the Afghan border. Then, following a selection process, "the best brothers" would receive additional military training at "Al-Qaeda Al Askariya," the military base. The notes went on to define "al-Qaeda" as an "organized Islamic group" with a list of membership requirements, and specified an oath of allegiance for new members.

Despite later claims that Ayman al-Zawahiri was critical to the formation of al-Qaeda, there is no evidence that he was present at any of the two days of marathon meetings where the formation of al-Qaeda was discussed. Nor was Zawahiri given any role in the group as a result of those meetings. This shouldn't have been surprising; al-Qaeda saw itself as a military organization and Zawahiri was no warrior.*

Two months before bin Laden started solidifying al-Qaeda as an organized group, his eldest brother died in a plane crash, a distant echo of their father's death in a plane crash in Saudi Arabia two decades earlier. On May 29, 1988, Salem bin Laden, a skilled pilot, crashed an ultralight aircraft he was piloting shortly after takeoff from Kitty Hawk airfield in San Antonio, Texas, dying at age forty-two. Although Salem had not seen much of Osama because he was busy running the family business, Salem's death was a blow. Osama's mother recalls, "His older brother Salem, who was killed in a plane crash in America, was like a father to him." Another relative says that Salem was one of the few people in the world who could have intervened with Osama and made him abandon his increasingly militant path: "If Salem had still been around no one would be writing books about Osama bin Laden."

Salem's body was flown back to Saudi Arabia and he was given the distinct honor of being buried in the holy city of Medina. A massive memorial at the bin Laden family compound in Jeddah took place over the course of two days and all twenty-two of the bin Laden sons, including

---

*Abdullah Anas, a confidant of Azzam's who became his son-in-law, didn't consider Zawahiri a mujahid and, indeed, there doesn't seem to be any evidence that Zawahiri fought in the Afghan War. That view was also shared by Jamal Khashoggi, the Saudi journalist who covered the Afghan jihad, who considered Zawahiri an "insignificant doctor in Peshawar."

Osama, formed a receiving line for the thousands of guests at the funeral. The bin Laden family owed much of their continued good fortune to Salem. It was Salem who had secured a billion-dollar contract in the early 1980s to renovate the Prophet's Mosque in Medina and who had appointed Osama to help manage the project. Following Salem's death, in 1989 Osama received a cash payment from the bin Laden estate of about $8 million, while he also continued to retain an interest in the bin Laden family companies, which amounted to $10 million.

After occupying Afghanistan for almost a decade, on February 15, 1989, the Soviets withdrew from the country. Milt Bearden, who ran the CIA station in Pakistan, sent a cable to top agency officials that simply said in large capital letters: "WE WON."

At CIA headquarters in Northern Virginia, the agency threw itself a party with food and whiskey flowing to celebrate the great victory. Champagne bottles were popped in the White House Situation Room.

But what was won exactly? Certainly, the American strategy in Afghanistan achieved its goal of revealing the Soviet military to be a paper tiger. It was hardly a coincidence that nine months after the Soviets pulled out of Afghanistan, the Berlin Wall came down. The principal goal of American foreign policy over the past four and half decades had been the containment and ultimately the dissolution of the Soviet empire.

The Soviet failure in Afghanistan hastened that goal, but a second-order effect of the Afghan War was the creation of a cadre of thousands of international volunteers who had traveled to Pakistan from around the Muslim world. There, they swapped business cards and imbibed the militant Islamist ideas that were then circulating among the Afghan Arabs. Hundreds of those volunteers also fought inside Afghanistan, gaining valuable battlefield experience and bragging rights, and it was out of this milieu that al-Qaeda was born, a development that went unnoticed at the time.

As the Soviets withdrew, the U.S. embassy in Kabul closed because of concerns about the safety of American diplomats in a post-Soviet Afghanistan. This would turn out to be a blunder. The U.S. was largely blind in Afghanistan during the years of civil war that followed the Soviet with-drawal, out of which emerged the Taliban, which then gave sanctuary to al-Qaeda.

That was all a long way in the future for bin Laden, who was overjoyed by the Soviet withdrawal, which happened to take place on his thirty-second birthday. Fundamentalist Sunni Muslims don't celebrate birth-days, but bin Laden told his first wife, Najwa, that he had just received his most important gift: The war against the Soviets was won. Najwa hoped that her husband would now settle down and return to his life working in the family business and that she would no longer have to constantly worry about his safety. But a quiet life of business, family, and mosque with a pair of comfortable slippers tucked under his bed was not to be bin Laden's destiny.

With the Soviet military gone from Afghanistan, all sides anticipated that the Afghan communist government in Kabul would collapse. Jalala-bad, an Afghan city near the border with Pakistan, was the most obvi-ous place where it was thought that the Afghan mujahideen might win a quick victory, since they could be easily supplied there from neighboring Pakistan.

Bin Laden wanted to show off his new military force and was eager to fight in the Jalalabad battle. He had prepared for this moment by building a crude road suitable for four-wheel-drive vehicles that could transport his men from their base in the Jaji region across the mountains of Tora Bora and down into the plain below to Jalalabad. This seems to have been the first time that bin Laden became familiar with Tora Bora, knowledge that would serve him well almost a decade and a half later when he fled there after the 9/11 attacks.

During early 1989, bin Laden started moving his men into the Ja-lalabad area. The battle for Jalalabad began in earnest on March 5, 1989. Urged on by Pakistan's Inter-Services Intelligence agency, the Afghan mu-jahideen fought to take Jalalabad city, which didn't play to their strengths as a mobile guerrilla force. Instead, the Afghan communist air force bombed them repeatedly and Scud missiles with two-thousand-pound warheads rained down on them. After four months of fighting, the operation to take the city collapsed.

Even *Jihad* magazine, which typically gave supportive accounts of the Afghan Arabs' battlefield exploits, couldn't gloss over this defeat. An issue from the summer of 1989 explained, "The hot fights started in Jalalabad; and Abu Abdullah [bin Laden] took charge of the closest front lines to the enemy and he started attacking with every hero that God gave him. The Arab mujahideen lost eighty fighters and more than one hundred fighters were injured." In another issue the magazine recounted the pain that bin Laden felt at the loss of his men: "Every time he would say good-bye to one holy warrior, a new rocket would come and take another one and it would leave him in pain and sorrow."

In an account that bin Laden gave to Essam Deraz, the Egyptian former military officer who documented the Afghan Arabs, he talked up the heroism of his men in the battle of Jalalabad, but couldn't hide that al-Qaeda sustained heavy losses. Bin Laden told Deraz that the Afghan communist forces had attacked his forces on July 9 with twenty-seven tanks backed by air power and Scud missiles. They attacked on the first day of Eid al-Adha—a major Islamic holiday—because they knew that the Afghan mujahideen would spend the holiday with their families. Bin Laden said that Shafiq, one of the first of his recruits who had built his base at Jaji, "died while operating the 75-millimeter cannon. I was very impacted by his martyrdom. The losses of the enemy were huge, forty-two tanks that were either destroyed or taken as booty. Many Arab fighters fell as martyrs—more Arab martyrs died in these battles than all of the martyrs killed in all the years of the Afghan War."

By his own account bin Laden lost more of his fighters during the Jalalabad battle than in the years of war that had preceded it. The battle illustrated bin Laden's military incompetence. Like his decision to build the permanent base at Jaji two years earlier, it was bin Laden who had pushed his men to take considerable military risks. Among the Arabs in Peshawar, bin Laden was criticized for his decision to throw his fighters into the battle.

Despite bin Laden's loss on the battlefield, militant Egyptians in Peshawar were eager to elevate bin Laden, whom they saw as a useful source of funding and to marginalize Abdullah Azzam, bin Laden's erstwhile mentor. Hassan Abd-Rabbuh al-Surayhi, an early Saudi recruit to the Afghan jihad, observed, "There was friction between the Egyptians and Azzam. They hated him due to differences in theological beliefs and they wanted to give a chance to bin Laden's star to rise."

By now bin Laden was growing closer to militants in Egypt's Jihad Group, which was led by Ayman al-Zawahiri, an Egyptian surgeon. In 1986, he met Zawahiri at a Kuwaiti-funded hospital in Peshawar where bin Laden was giving a lecture. Bin Laden was intrigued by the older, more politically experienced Zawahiri, who had joined a jihadist group at fifteen and had served three years in prison in Egypt. Zawahiri encouraged bin Laden to not only focus on the Afghan jihad, but also imagine the possibilities of overthrowing the regimes in Arab countries such as Egypt.

Zawahiri turned bin Laden against Azzam by speaking about the mismanagement at the Services Office. Zawahiri told Osama Rushdi, an Egyptian dissident living in Peshawar, that Azzam was "an agent of America, an agent of Saudi Arabia." Zawahiri even told other Arabs in Peshawar not to pray with Azzam. Rushdi observed, "That is a grave thing in Islam, because in Islam it is correct to pray with any Muslim." Leaflets were distributed in Peshawar saying Azzam was not a good Muslim. The charges that Azzam was a bad Muslim and a spy may have led to his death.

On November 24, 1989, Azzam, accompanied by two of his sons, was driving to the Mosque of the Martyrs in Peshawar, where he used to preach every Friday. They were driving down a narrow street when a massive bomb exploded by their car. Another son, Hudhayfa Azzam, who was not in the vehicle, said that the blast was so powerful that "my brother Mohammed was found seventeen meters from the car. My father went out of the car directly into the road. My brother Ibrahim went into the electric wires overhead; his hands were found in another area."

The assassination of Azzam was a pivotal moment in bin Laden's increasingly radical journey. Who killed Azzam remains a mystery. The most likely culprits were the Islamist hardliners living in Peshawar who rid themselves of a leader who did not share their enthusiasm for overthrowing Middle Eastern regimes. Azzam was always clear that his only goal was to fight the "infidels" who were occupying Muslim lands, whether in Afghanistan or Palestine. He was opposed to the militants who wanted to bring down the regimes around the Middle East.

Bin Laden was back in Saudi Arabia at the time of Azzam's assassination. It is quite unlikely that bin Laden was involved with Azzam's death since he remained on friendly terms with him. But with Azzam gone, there was little to counter al-Qaeda's militant ideas among the Afghan Arabs.

Around this time al-Qaeda drew up a draft of its by-laws that ran to nineteen pages in Arabic. The by-laws made it clear that the group's sole purpose was to wage jihad "anywhere in the Islamic world" and that it would "not be distracted by relief and aid projects." There was considerable discussion of the duties of the "Military Committee" and the "Security Committee," which included "imprisonment and torture."

Bin Laden personally funded much of al-Qaeda's expenses in its early years while it was based in Pakistan. Monthly salaries for members of al-Qaeda were quoted in Pakistani rupees; married members received 6,500 rupees a month (around $400) and they received 300 rupees a month for each additional child, and in the cases where they had multiple wives, an additional 700 rupees per wife. Cost-of-living increases were pegged at a generous annual rate of 10 percent. Members received a yearly one-month vacation and two additional weeks of sick leave, with extra time off for those who were on the front lines. Bachelors received a free airline ticket home every eighteen months, while married men and their families could get free travel home every two years. Medical treatment was free if provided by a member of the al-Qaeda staff, and in cases where the al-Qaeda team didn't have the requisite medical expertise, permission could be sought from senior management to receive additional free medical treatment outside of al-Qaeda's orbit. For married members of the group, there was a generous furniture allowance of 20,000 rupees (around $1,200), although it was considered a loan that would be deducted from salaries and the furniture had to be returned to al-Qaeda should the member be transferred to another country.

Waging a holy war could get very bureaucratic.

The shy, monosyllabic twenty-two-year-old millionaire who had arrived in Pakistan in 1980 to give donations to the Afghan groups fighting the Soviets was a different man a decade later. With Salem bin Laden and Azzam both dead, the two men who could have possibly deflected him from leading al-Qaeda, bin Laden was free to do as he pleased, especially with the millions of dollars in cash that he had on hand following his oldest brother's death.

Like the Prophet Mohammed, bin Laden now had his own Islamic army and was a leader of men, bloodied in battles that he believed were great victories and had led to the defeat of the Soviets in Afghanistan. He had four wives at home, three of whom claimed descent from the Prophet. They had already given him eleven children, increasing the number of Muslims in the world.

Now bin Laden turned to a grandiose dream: He wanted to overthrow the socialist government in South Yemen, the ancestral home of the bin Ladens.

PART II

WAR WITH THE U.S.

FIVE

RADICAL

Whoever seeks his rights, must eventually find the sword to be his best guide.

—A line of poetry that bin Laden often cited when
asked why he was turning to violence

L
ike many veterans of war, bin Laden found it hard to settle back into an uneventful domestic life when he returned to Saudi Arabia. Going back to work in his family's construction business had none of the glamour and excitement that leading his men into battle in Afghanistan in the name of Allah did.

War changes men. It certainly changed bin Laden; he was now the leader of his own small army of men who had sworn a religious oath of fealty to him. His brother-in-law Jamal Khalifa noticed that bin Laden was different; once he had been a listener, but now he believed he was right about everything.

In early 1990, Khaled Batarfi, bin Laden's childhood friend from Jeddah, saw him at a gathering of a group of intellectuals that met every Friday to discuss politics. Bin Laden was concerned about the Iraqi dictator, Saddam Hussein, predicting that Saddam had regional ambitions and that he would invade Saudi Arabia. Bin Laden told the group, "We should train our people and increase our army and prepare for the day when eventually we are attacked. Saddam can never be trusted."

Bin Laden now saw himself as a leader of some significance, but how could he fulfill his growing sense that he was a man who could shape history in the service of Allah? He started casting about for roles that demonstrated his importance to the Muslim world. Bin Laden believed he could help topple the Afghan communist government that had replaced the Soviets after their withdrawal from Afghanistan, but his efforts to be a player in the Afghan civil war fizzled. Bin Laden thought he could lead a legion of men to defeat Saddam Hussein's army, which invaded Saudi Arabia's neighbor Kuwait in 1990. The Saudi royal family laughed at this ridiculously naive notion. And bin Laden thought he could play a key role in overthrowing the socialist "infidel" government of South Yemen, which the Saudis also blocked him from doing. All of bin Laden's jihadist projects in the early 1990s in Afghanistan, Saudi Arabia, and Yemen were flops.

During the nineteenth century, the magnificent natural port of Aden in southern Yemen was a key stopping-off point during the lengthy sea voyage between the United Kingdom and British-ruled India, but by 1967 the sun had largely set on the empire. The British pulled out of its protectorate in Aden. They were replaced by the People's Democratic Republic of Yemen, a government aligned with the Soviets that now ruled over the Hadhramaut region, where many decades earlier bin Laden's father had been born.

Bin Laden was determined to rid South Yemen of its "infidel" government, which he believed desecrated the sacred land of the Arabian Peninsula. On his deathbed, the Prophet Mohammed decreed that only Islam should reign on the peninsula. Bin Laden believed that socialism was a secular religion that defied the Prophet's ruling.

In early 1990 bin Laden went to see Prince Turki al-Faisal, the head of Saudi intelligence, and proposed that "his mujahideen" overthrow the Marxist regime in South Yemen. Prince Turki, a debonair member of the royal family who had attended boarding school in the States, rejected the plan and was privately incredulous that bin Laden referred to "his mujahideen," as if he were the general of his own personal army.

After the fall of the Berlin Wall, the Marxist government of South

Yemen united with northern Yemen on May 22, 1990. The Saudi government supported this new government. Saudi officials warned bin Laden to desist his revolutionary efforts in Yemen. They also constrained his ability to travel outside the kingdom. It was the beginning of a rift between the Saudi regime and bin Laden, which would only widen in coming years.

That split intensified following Saddam Hussein's invasion of Kuwait on August 2, 1990, which seemed like a prelude for the Iraqi dictator to attack Saudi Arabia. Bin Laden met with key Saudi officials to offer the services of his mujahideen to expel Saddam from Kuwait. The offer made no sense. Saddam was estimated to have an army of a million men, the fourth largest in the world, which was battle-hardened by the decade-long war Iraq had just fought with Iran. Meanwhile bin Laden implausibly claimed that he had tens of thousands of fighters at his disposal in Saudi Arabia and could quickly train tens of thousands more. Prince Turki recalled, "I saw radical changes in his personality as he changed from a calm, peaceful and gentle man interested in helping Muslims, into a person who believed that he would be able to amass and command an army to liberate Kuwait. It revealed his arrogance." King Fahd told the U.S. ambassador to Saudi Arabia, Chas Freeman, about bin Laden's proposal and laughed, saying it was "absolutely ridiculous."

The Saudis turned to their longtime allies, the Americans, for military support. Within months, 500,000 U.S. troops, including women, arrived to defend the Saudi kingdom. Bin Laden opposed the fact that non-Muslims were defending the holy land of Arabia. He believed this contravened the Prophet's deathbed admonition, "Let there be no two religions in Arabia."

Since the mid-1980s bin Laden had often told audiences in the Saudi kingdom that American products should be boycotted because of America's support for Israel. The arrival of a large U.S. army in the kingdom was a transformational event that hardened bin Laden's anti-Americanism into a passionate hatred for the United States.

During the summer of 1990, the Saudi journalist Jamal Khashoggi attended an event in Jeddah where bin Laden claimed that the United States had a secret plan to secularize Saudi Arabia. Bin Laden now risked offending the Saudi monarchy, which had invited the American military into the kingdom.

Since his plans to overthrow the socialist government in Yemen had failed and his offer to fight Saddam Hussein in Kuwait had been summarily rejected, bin Laden turned his focus to Afghanistan, where the withdrawal of the Soviets had not resulted in a united effort by the Afghan warlords to defeat the Afghan communist regime that remained in power. The Afghan factions were fragmented by bickering and fighting, failing to seize the capital, Kabul.

Bin Laden had a poorly conceived plan to seize Kabul, spending considerable sums on the effort. The mujahideen leaders didn't consider bin Laden to have any military expertise, and for good reason: the battle of Jaji was relatively insignificant and the Jalalabad battle had been a debacle. Afghan mujahideen leaders saw bin Laden merely as a money guy, not someone they could rely on for military advice.

Bin Laden wanted to secure Afghanistan for an Islamist government, but an obstacle was the aging Afghan king, Zahir Shah, who lived in exile in Rome and retained considerable popularity and legitimacy among Afghans, who viewed him as a symbol of a time when their country had been at peace. Al-Qaeda's leaders were concerned that the king might be brought back from exile to become the titular head of a new Afghan government.

Paulo Jose de Almeida Santos, a Portuguese convert to Islam and an early al-Qaeda recruit, proposed to kill the Afghan king. Santos was invited to Peshawar to meet bin Laden to discuss how he planned to carry out the assassination of the monarch.

Santos asked bin Laden, "If a woman were to be near the king, and I were to use a bomb or a weapon that could injure or kill the person next to him, would I be allowed to continue?"

Bin Laden replied, "If it were the king's wife, she shares with the king the same responsibilities; she may therefore be eliminated."

Santos then asked, "And if it happened to be a grandson of the king, a child?"

Bin Laden became angry, saying, "We are Muslims, we do not eliminate children! I would rather have the king return and have a civil war
than kill a child!" Bin Laden was sometimes concerned about actions that
he thought might harm the reputation of his followers.

Santos was dispatched to Italy to assassinate the Afghan king. The assassination attempt on November 4, 1991, was the first time that al-Qaeda
engaged in international terrorism. Posing as a journalist Santos entered
the king's heavily guarded villa. After an hour or so of discussion, Santos
grabbed a dagger with an ornate silver handle from Afghanistan that he
had given the king as a gift, and stabbed the seventy-seven-year-old monarch several times. The king had recently been ordered by his doctor to
stop smoking Havana cigars and had switched to Café Crème cigarillos.
A tin of cigarillos was in the king's breast pocket, deflecting the dagger's
blade, saving the monarch from death. The king's security wrestled Santos
to the ground and he was arrested and jailed for ten years in Italy, while
the monarch was hospitalized and later recovered.

Bin Laden had now exhausted his options to significantly influence
Afghanistan, so he decided to launch an entirely new chapter of his life in
the desperately poor country of Sudan. There he would rebrand himself
as a big-deal businessman, while continuing his jihadist activities covertly.
On May 1, 1991, bin Laden was given permission to leave Saudi Arabia for
Pakistan. He would never return to the holy land of Arabia.

Once he was settled in Sudan in the latter half of 1991, bin Laden devoted
much of his energy to helping shore up the fortunes of the new Sudanese
National Islamic Front government, a group of Islamist militants who had
come to power in a coup two years earlier. The deal that bin Laden made
with the government was that he would invest in their poverty-stricken
country and try to persuade other Saudi businessmen to do so as well.
This would help the National Islamic Front establish itself as a functional
Islamist state. For its part, the National Islamic Front would protect bin
Laden and his men.

Bin Laden's half-decade sojourn in Sudan was a pivotal moment in his life; he built the foundations of his anti-American terrorist organization, supporting militants in Somalia and Yemen who were intent on attacking American targets; he made plans to bomb U.S. embassies in Africa; and some of his followers made unsuccessful efforts to acquire weapons of mass destruction. He also became a prominent leader of the Saudi opposition.

At the same time, bin Laden maintained the facade that he was a successful entrepreneur, just like his father. To complete the picture that he was just a prosperous businessman, he summoned his large family to live with him.

Sometime in the latter half of 1991 he departed Pakistan for Sudan, followed a few months later by his four wives and their fourteen children, who flew from Saudi Arabia on a Saudia airlines flight to Khartoum. Bin Laden was at the airport to greet them and they loaded into a convoy of cars with black-tinted windows that took them to their new home, a three-story compound in Riyadh, an upscale neighborhood in Khartoum. Each of his four wives had her own apartment in the compound. As was bin Laden's way, his wives and children were forbidden to use refrigerators or air-conditioning, despite the broiling desert heat of Khartoum, where temperatures routinely go well above 100 degrees.

As a young man bin Laden had trained himself to survive in harsh desert conditions. As he grew older he increasingly embraced the belief that the West might attack the Muslim world, so his family should learn how to survive in the desert. When bin Laden went into the deserts of Sudan on long hikes with his boys, he forbade them to drink water, to make them as "tough" as possible.

Bin Laden also tried to prepare his wives and daughters, taking them all to a desert region outside Khartoum. They were allowed to take only a limited amount of water and food, and shovels. Once they were out in the desert bin Laden instructed his oldest sons to dig hollows in the sand for their family members to sleep in. Even the babies had to sleep in these holes. As the desert night turned cold, he advised his family that in the absence of blankets they should cover themselves with dirt.

Bin Laden had other eccentric, even dangerous, notions that he foisted on his family. He was suspicious of modern medications because they were not available during the era of the Prophet Mohammed. He allowed his children to use only natural remedies. A few of his sons suffered from asthma, which bin Laden said should be treated by breathing through a piece of honeycomb. Needless to say, this did nothing to alleviate their asthma. When bin Laden's sons heard about Ventolin, a common treatment for asthma, they secretly purchased a supply of the medicine and an inhaler.

On the surface, bin Laden led a far more conventional life in Sudan than he had as a holy warrior traveling between Pakistan and Afghanistan. The bin Laden family construction company was building the airport at Port Sudan, the second most important city in the country. After his father's death, one of Osama's half-brothers, Bakr bin Laden, ran the family business and authorized the Saudi Binladin Group to invest $12 million in Sudan with Osama in charge. The exiled bin Laden founded Al Hijra ("the Exile") Construction, which built roads and bridges and employed more than six hundred people. Bin Laden built a new five-hundred-mile-long road from Khartoum to Port Sudan. And at Damazin on the Blue Nile, bin Laden farmed on a massive one-million-acre estate employing four thousand laborers. As a result, bin Laden's Taba Investment Ltd. secured a near-monopoly over Sudan's key agricultural exports of corn, sunflower, and sesame products. He also started a trucking company, a leather company, a tannery that made shoes and purses, a bakery, and a furniture-making business.

He indulged his passion for horses in Khartoum, visiting the racetrack to watch horse racing. When music came over the track's loudspeaker system he blocked his ears with his fingers as music was haram, forbidden.

Bin Laden was keen to display an image of a successful entrepreneur and he gave his first interview to a Western reporter in December 1993. Veteran Middle East correspondent Robert Fisk wrote a story for the British *Independent* newspaper about how bin Laden had presided over the opening ceremony of a portion of the new road that he was building between Khartoum and Port Sudan. He behaved like a munificent sheikh, dressed in a gold-fringed robe, which is worn for special occasions in Saudi Arabia. Villagers thanked him for the new highway, men danced in his honor, and a lamb's throat was cut, all honoring the great sheikh bin Laden.

But behind closed doors, business was more complicated. Bin Laden complained that his businesses were not faring well, claiming that the local workforce was lazy. He told old friends that business in Sudan was "very bad," but that his agenda in Sudan superseded business. He sought to support the Islamist Sudanese government, which in turn was protecting al-Qaeda.

Also, bin Laden's family quietly started falling apart. In 1993 Osama's second wife, Khadijah, asked him for a divorce, saying she hadn't signed up for this life of austerity and hardship in Sudan. Bin Laden respected her wishes and allowed her to return to Saudi Arabia with their three children.

Abdullah, bin Laden's oldest son, also deeply resented that his father was wealthy yet their family lived like peasants without even a refrigerator to preserve their food in the baking Sudanese heat. Aged nineteen, Abdullah left Sudan, the ostensible purpose of which was his impending marriage in Saudi Arabia in 1995, but he never returned to Sudan and he never saw his father again. After Abdullah's departure bin Laden avoided mentioning his oldest son's name.

The success of the bin Laden family businesses depended on the patronage of the Saudi royal family. Osama was now seriously jeopardizing that relationship. A month after a profile of bin Laden appeared in an Egyptian magazine headlined "A Millionaire Finances Extremism in Egypt and Saudi Arabia," Bakr bin Laden began a legal process to expel Osama from the family business. Osama's share of the company was valued at $9.9 million, and was frozen under court supervision.

A procession of bin Laden's family members and old friends from Saudi Arabia made their way to Sudan to persuade him to stop his criticism of the Saudi monarchy and to return home to the kingdom. Hassan Abd-Rabbuh al-Surayhi, who had fought with bin Laden in Afghanistan, met with him in Khartoum.

Surayhi said, "You can run your companies from your country."

Bin Laden confessed that he had a great longing for his homeland: "I am tired. I miss living in Medina. Only God knows how nostalgic I am."

His mother and stepfather also visited him in Sudan in 1993, carrying a message from King Fahd urging him to make peace with the Saudi monarchy and return home. Bin Laden told his mother, "I can sacrifice my life for you, but right now what you are talking to me about is against Islam. I'm fighting against the enemies of Islam and you want that I should announce a ceasefire with the enemies of Islam."

Bin Laden's involvement in Islamist politics not only estranged him from his family in Saudi Arabia, but also put his life at risk. In late February 1994 four gunmen shot at his guesthouse. Fortunately for him, he was not there. When he heard the gunfire, he grabbed his AK-47. Together with his bodyguards and Sudanese security forces, they fought off the gunmen, who were wounded or killed in the firefight. The gunmen were from a group who thought that bin Laden wasn't sufficiently Islamic.

Two months after this assassination attempt, on April 8, 1994, the Saudi government officially stripped him of his citizenship, effectively declaring bin Laden a traitor to his country. Around the same time, Bakr bin Laden issued a terse statement to the media saying that on behalf of "all members of the family" they "regret, denounce and condemn all acts that Osama bin Laden may have committed."

Just days after he was stripped of his citizenship, bin Laden released a statement complaining, "Our money was frozen in foreign bank accounts, a defamation campaign was waged against us in the local and international press, and finally, you attempted to cut our ties with the homeland by confiscating our passports." While he confessed he longed for his home—"God only knows how much we miss our homeland, and there is no other country we long for. How could this not be true, given that it is the cradle of Islam"—he remained unrepentant.

Bin Laden sent lengthy memos attacking the Saudi regime to Khalid al-Fawwaz, a member of al-Qaeda who lived in London, and who in turn faxed them to a large number of recipients in Saudi Arabia. Fawwaz's phone bill sometimes came to more than £10,000 a month because he was blasting out so many faxes to the kingdom.

Communiqués written by bin Laden complained about the vast palaces built by the Saudi royal family using "public money," and sarcastically congratulated King Fahd for breaking "every statistical record in squandering and spending public funds." Another bin Laden communiqué railed against "the Christian women" who were part of the large American army that had arrived in the Saudi kingdom after Saddam Hussein's invasion of Kuwait in 1990.

Another bin Laden screed chastised the Saudis for allowing banks to charge interest, which was against Islam, and he condemned anyone who allowed the practice "an apostate and infidel." Apostasy was the gravest charge to make against the Saudi royal family, who had styled themselves "the Custodian" of the holy cities of Mecca and Medina.

In March 1995, Saudi journalist Jamal Khashoggi traveled to Khartoum, where he spent three days with bin Laden. Khashoggi sensed a change in his old acquaintance, who gave him a tour of his farms. He suggested bin Laden strike a deal with the Saudi regime to return home, and he asked bin Laden to go on the record in an interview declaring that he was opposed to any form of violence against the Saudi government. Bin Laden agreed in principle, but then he wouldn't go on the record and the interview didn't happen. This was the last chance that bin Laden had to reconcile with the Saudi monarchy and to return home. He chose another path.

SIX

"THE HEAD OF
THE SNAKE"

Cruel men believe in a cruel God and use their belief to excuse their cruelty.
—Bertrand Russell

Every Thursday evening, al-Qaeda members gathered at one of bin Laden's farms just outside Khartoum to hear him discuss the group's agenda. The lectures often featured calls for U.S. troops to leave Saudi Arabia, but after President George H. W. Bush sent 28,000 American troops to Somalia in December 1992, there was a new intensity to these discussions.

Somalia was in the middle of a brutal civil war and Bush had sent the soldiers there on a humanitarian mission to feed hundreds of thousands of starving Somalis. But bin Laden viewed their mission as part of a larger American strategy to take over the Muslim world.

Bin Laden told his men, "We have to stop the head of the snake. The snake is America." This was the most important strategic decision bin Laden ever made.* He focused al-Qaeda's attacks on the "head of the

---

*There is no evidence that bin Laden's key strategic decision to target the American "head of the snake" had any input from the Egyptian militant Ayman al-Zawahiri, despite later claims that Zawahiri was really the "brains" behind bin Laden. Indeed, bin Laden did not involve Zawahiri in the planning of his major

snake" because he believed that sufficient violence perpetrated against American targets would result in the withdrawal of the United States from the greater Middle East, which would then lead to the collapse of the U.S.-supported Arab regimes that bin Laden despised.

It was a strategy that made little sense, as the United States would surely follow its own interests and was hardly likely to abandon its substantial role in the Middle East simply because of some terrorist attacks by bin Laden's men. But bin Laden truly believed that the U.S. was weak, just as the former Soviet Union had been, and could absorb only a few blows. Attacking the United States also had the advantage for bin Laden that he could unite the motley coalition of militants from around the Muslim world that were now gathered in Sudan around one big idea that they could all agree on.

He drew inspiration from other terrorist groups that had successfully attacked American targets, such as the Lebanese Hezbollah, which had bombed the Marine barracks in Beirut in 1983, killing 241 American Marines, sailors, and soldiers. Within a few months of the attack the United States pulled out all of its troops from Lebanon. The Marine barracks bombing was very much on bin Laden's mind as he plotted attacks that he believed would result in the United States pulling its troops out of Saudi Arabia.

The first time al-Qaeda mounted an anti-American terrorist operation was in late December 1992 when bombs exploded outside two

---

operations, including the 9/11 attacks. The troika who founded and ran al-Qaeda was bin Laden at the apex and his two key military commanders, Abu Ubayda and Abu Hafs the Egyptian, both of whom had been on bin Laden's payroll since the beginning of 1987. They were bin Laden's men, not Zawahiri's. Meanwhile, Zawahiri's obsessive goal was overthrowing the "near enemy" Egyptian regime, a subject that bin Laden evinced very little interest in and that he rarely discussed in his public statements. Instead, the majority of bin Laden's statements focused on what he described as American and Jewish aggression against Muslims, while his second-most-important topic was his criticism of the Saudi government, in particular for its alliance with the United States.

hotels in Aden, the port city in southern Yemen, which housed around one hundred American servicemen on their way to Somalia for Operation Restore Hope, the humanitarian mission to feed Somalis. The bombs killed a tourist and a hotel worker, but no Americans. Within days of the attacks the Pentagon announced it would no longer use Yemen as a base for American troops transiting to Somalia. While the hotel bombings received little attention at the time, bin Laden viewed them as a victory.

Next bin Laden sent Abu Hafs the Egyptian, a key military commander in al-Qaeda, to Somalia to see how his group might attack the American soldiers deployed in the country. Abu Hafs met with members of the tribe of the Somali rebel leader General Mohamed Farah Aidid, who were fighting against U.S. troops. They discussed how they might perform joint military operations.

In early October 1993 eighteen American soldiers were killed during the course of an intense two-day firefight in Mogadishu on a botched mission to try and snatch Aidid. During the battle rocket-propelled grenades downed two American Black Hawk helicopters. This is not an easy feat since RPGs are designed to be antitank weapons that are shot horizontally. Aidid's men were trained by Arabs who had fought in Afghanistan, who taught the Somalis that the most effective way to shoot down a helicopter with an RPG was to hit the tail rotor. They also positioned themselves on high roofs so they could shoot downward on low-flying helicopters. Within a week of the Mogadishu battle the United States announced plans for the pullout of its troops.

Given the fog of war it's not clear what precise role al-Qaeda played in what became known as the "Black Hawk Down" battle, but in his own mind, bin Laden thought he had won another great victory, first forcing American soldiers to leave Yemen, and now believing that he had some role in forcing them out of Somalia as well.

He boasted that "based on the reports we received from our brothers who participated in the jihad in Somalia, we learned that they saw the weakness, frailty and cowardice of U.S. troops. Only eighteen U.S. troops were killed. Nonetheless, they fled."

Bin Laden was now more convinced than ever that the United States was weak, just as the Soviet Union had been, and that his strategy of attacking American targets was achieving his goal of extirpating the U.S. presence in the Muslim world.

In late 1993 he started planning to bomb the U.S. embassy in Nairobi, Kenya. Bin Laden generally left it up to his team on the ground about the details of the execution of a terrorist operation, but when it came to target selection he often played a hands-on role and sometimes even got into the tactical details of an operation, as he would for both the bombing of the U.S. embassy in Nairobi and the planning for the 9/11 attacks. Bin Laden selected the Nairobi embassy as a target because he believed that the deployment of troops to Somalia was planned there and also that it was a key CIA station. Shown photographs of the embassy and drawing on his considerable expertise in construction, he pointed to the most effective place to position a truck bomb.

On February 26, 1993, Ramzi Yousef led a group of militants to bomb the World Trade Center in New York. Yousef hoped to bring down both towers, but the bomb killed only six people. While bin Laden had no direct role in this attack, he was named as an unindicted co-conspirator because he had come to the attention of the FBI after he had supplied $20,000 to the defense team in a related jihadist terrorism case in New York. Yousef's uncle, Khalid Sheikh Mohammed, who had sent $600 to Yousef's group before the attack, would later oversee the 9/11 operation. The subsequent imprisonment in the United States of the prominent Egyptian cleric "the Blind Sheikh" Omar Abdel Rahman, who was the spiritual guide of many of the 1993 Trade Center plotters, would infuriate leaders of al-Qaeda and provide further rationale for their future anti-American operations.

On November 13, 1995, a car bomb went off outside the Saudi National Guard building in Riyadh, a joint Saudi-U.S. facility. The bomb killed five Americans and two Indians. Four months later Saudi television broadcast the confessions of the four alleged perpetrators before they were executed. One of the bombers said he was influenced by the writings of bin Laden and three of the militants had fought in the Afghan War. Once again, bin Laden had no direct role in an attack, but he was becoming influential among jihadist terrorists who were targeting Americans.

After bin Laden was cut off from his fortune in early 1994, money became tight for al-Qaeda, creating friction. Salaries for members of al-Qaeda in Sudan were reduced. Jamal al-Fadl, a Sudanese member of al-Qaeda, resented that Egyptian members of the group received higher salaries than he did, even though he had been an early member of the organization. As a result, Fadl stole $110,000 from al-Qaeda. Bin Laden discovered that the money was missing and confronted Fadl, who said that he had spent much of it already and could pay back only $25,000.

Bin Laden responded, "I don't care about the money, but I care about you because you are one of the best people in al-Qaeda. We give you everything, when you travel we give you extra money, we pay your medical bill—why did you do that?"

Fadl explained that he resented the high salaries given to the Egyptians. Bin Laden said, "If you need money, you should have come speak with me. I can't forgive you until you give all the money back."

Realizing that he was in great danger, Fadl made a fateful decision that would greatly benefit the U.S. government. During the summer of 1996, Fadl went to the U.S. embassy in neighboring Eritrea to tell U.S. officials what he knew. The CIA station chief was on leave, and the only person there was the chief of administration. She could have very easily said, "Not my job." Instead she asked Fadl to tell her as much as possible.

Fadl said that he was part of a group planning to launch a war against the United States.

The U.S. official asked, "What kind of war?"

Fadl replied, "I don't know, maybe they try to do something inside the United States."

The official cabled back to Washington, "I've got a guy here talking about bin Laden." Fadl's tip to the embassy would be critical for the CIA and FBI; it was the first time that a member of al-Qaeda could describe the inner workings of the organization.

One of Fadl's debriefers was Daniel Coleman, an FBI agent from New Jersey, who habitually dressed in a rumpled tan raincoat. Coleman found Fadl's claim that al-Qaeda was a terrorist organization intent on killing as many Americans as possible to be worrisome and plausible. Another U.S. official who shared Coleman's concern was Michael Scheuer, who led a unit at the CIA investigating bin Laden. In the mid-1990s Coleman and Scheuer were leading members of a tiny club within the U.S. government who understood that al-Qaeda represented a substantial threat to American security.

In 1995 bin Laden's men began following the CIA station chief in Khartoum, Cofer Black, seemingly plotting an assassination attempt. The U.S. ambassador complained to the Sudanese government and the plotters backed off, but U.S. officials in Khartoum continued to learn of threats to their safety. After a spirited debate among CIA officers and State Department officials the decision was made to close the embassy in Khartoum in February 1996. Like the closure of the embassy in Kabul seven years earlier after the Soviets had withdrawn from Afghanistan, this would turn out to be a mistake, since it severed relationships that could have provided much useful intelligence about al-Qaeda's half-decade sojourn in Sudan.

The Sudanese government was now coming under increasing pressure from both the Saudi and U.S. governments to expel bin Laden, but the problem was that neither the Saudis nor the Americans actually wanted to take custody of the al-Qaeda leader. The Saudis told the Sudanese that they did not want to take bin Laden back, ostensibly because they had revoked his citizenship. In the United States there was no indictment against bin Laden so there was no legal basis for holding him.

The de facto leader of the National Islamic Front government in Sudan, Hassan al-Turabi, held intense meetings with bin Laden asking him to leave the country. Bin Laden tried to persuade Turabi that there was no need to expel him, as he hadn't committed any acts against Sudan, and there was no other country that was willing to receive his group.

Turabi told bin Laden he had two options: "Either keep silent or leave the country."

Bin Laden refused to stay silent and so he headed to Afghanistan, a country for which he had a considerable, almost romantic attachment. After all, it was the scene of what he believed to be his great battlefield triumphs and where his men, at least in his own mind, had helped to defeat a superpower.

Before leaving, bin Laden called his beloved mother, Allia. He had always been a dutiful son, kissing her hands and feet when he saw her. Osama knew that his mother had agonized about his trips to the battlefields of Afghanistan during the jihad against the Soviets and now he was returning again to the same country, which was involved in yet another war.

The next day, Allia called her son to tell him that she had had a dream in which Osama was sitting between Jesus and Moses, both of whom are considered prophets in the Islamic faith. In the dream Jesus and Moses turned to Allia to tell her that her son would be protected. "Please do not worry. We have made arrangements for his protection, so let him go wherever he wishes." Allia told bin Laden she no longer feared for his safety and that he should go to Afghanistan "trusting in God." Bin Laden valued dreams, and his mother's became a source of comfort.

However, he was furious about being pushed out of Sudan, which he blamed on the American government. Bin Laden also believed that he had left behind $29 million of investments in Sudan, and he resented the Sudanese government for not compensating him for his losses.

Bin Laden left for Afghanistan, an aggrieved exile. He tried to model himself on the Prophet Mohammed, so he took solace in the memory that the Prophet had also been forced into exile thirteen centuries earlier when he fled the pagans of Mecca to build his perfect Islamic society in the nearby town of Medina.

For bin Laden, Afghanistan was the Medina of the new age.

SEVEN

A DECLARATION OF WAR

Against them make ready your strength to the utmost of your power, in-cluding steeds of war, to strike terror in the enemies of Allah.

—Koran, verse 8:60

Bin Laden departed from Khartoum on a small private jet to Jalalabad in eastern Afghanistan on May 18, 1996. Accompanying him was his fifteen-year-old son, Omar, and two of his top military commanders, Abu Hafs the Egytian and Saif al-Adel.*

In many ways bin Laden's voyage to Jalalabad was a flight into the unknown. Much had changed since al-Qaeda's leader had last visited Afghanistan more than half a decade earlier. Following the fall of the Afghan communist regime in 1992, a brutal civil war had torn the country apart. Rather than the Soviets, it was the Afghans who had destroyed Kabul. Out of the chaos of the civil war had emerged a mysterious group with an innocuous name, *Taliban*, meaning "religious students." The Taliban took over much of Afghanistan, promising a return to law and order under a draconian theocracy.

The Taliban were led by Mullah Omar, a reclusive one-eyed cleric who

---

*Not on the flight to Afghanistan was bin Laden's other key military commander, Abu Ubayda, who was in Africa laying the groundwork for al-Qaeda's attacks on the U.S. embassies in Kenya and Tanzania. He drowned in a ferry accident on Lake Victoria on May 21, 1996, along with hundreds of others, just days after bin Laden had arrived in Afghanistan.

rose from being an obscure village mullah to become the "Commander of the Faithful." Mullah Omar was declared so by a convocation of clerics on April 4, 1996; it was a title that immodestly claimed that Mullah Omar commanded all Muslims around the world.

Two months before bin Laden had returned to Afghanistan, Mullah Omar wrapped himself literally and metaphorically in the "Cloak of the Prophet," a religious relic purported to have been worn by the Prophet Mohammed that had been kept in the southern Afghan city of Kandahar for centuries and had almost never been displayed in public. Mullah Omar took the garment out of storage and, ascending to the roof of a building, draped the cloak on himself before a crowd of hundreds of cheering Taliban.

Despite his title of Commander of the Faithful, the Taliban leader was determinedly provincial; in the years that he controlled Afghanistan he rarely visited Kabul, his own capital, considering it to be Sodom and Gomorrah. Mullah Omar personally distributed money from his treasury like a medieval monarch, issuing his funding orders on small slips of handwritten paper. Mullah Omar's understanding of the outside world was virtually nonexistent. On a rare occasion when he met with a group of Chinese diplomats, they presented him with a small figurine of an animal as a gift. The Taliban leader reacted as if they had handed him a live hand grenade, so acute was his religious aversion to images of living beings.

When the Taliban first emerged in Afghanistan under the leadership of Mullah Omar, they enjoyed quite a high degree of popularity and legitimacy, as they brought order and a measure of peace to a country that had suffered through a decade and a half of war. Initially, the Taliban were also seen as incorruptible and little interested in assuming power for themselves. However, the maxim that "power corrupts and absolute power corrupts absolutely" is an almost perfect description of how the Taliban regime evolved over the years. The Taliban increasingly turned their law-and-order government into a polity that aspired to be a truly totalitarian Islamic state.

They banned music and television, and barred females from schools and jobs. Men were not allowed to shave or trim their beards. Women had to wear the all-enveloping burqa and stay at home unless accompanied by a male relative. The Taliban's edicts were enforced by the religious police of the Ministry for the Promotion of Virtue and the Prevention of Vice, who raced around in pickup trucks looking for malefactors to beat with sticks or take to jail. Vahid Mojdeh, a former Taliban official, said, "The Taliban were ruthless torturers, their most commonly used technique was beating people with electric cables." In Kabul, one of the few diversions available were the public executions in the soccer stadium.

When bin Laden landed at Jalalabad airport he was greeted by commanders from the Younis Khalis faction. They were not part of the Taliban, but were a mujahideen group who had fought against the communists. Based on bin Laden's service to the Afghan jihad, Khalis welcomed bin Laden warmly and gave him housing outside Jalalabad in a neighborhood called Hadda, which bin Laden's men called *Najm-al-Jihad*, the "Star of Jihad."

Bin Laden's "Star of Jihad" compound was spread over two acres, a complex of some seventy-five rooms. Across the road was another large al-Qaeda compound with a secret chamber that extended at least fifty feet underground. Bin Laden came and went using four-wheel-drive vehicles with blacked-out windows, and he didn't hire locals as guards or cooks. Arab guards patrolled his perimeter at night.

He was also given a chunk of land in the Tora Bora mountains, a region he knew from the anti-Soviet jihad when he had built crude roads there to transport his men from Jaji through the mountains to the ill-fated battle of Jalalabad. He decided to split his time between the city of Jalalabad and the mountains of Tora Bora.

Bin Laden was thrilled to be back in Tora Bora, a bone-shattering three-hour drive from Jalalabad up a narrow, rocky mountain road. There he built an Afghan-style mud house for his family, part of which was embedded in a large cave. From bin Laden's house all he could see was his own littl feudal fiefdom; the nearest village was out of sight thousands of feet below down a scree-covered slope. Bin Laden's three wives and their dozen children joined him there in early September 1996. They did not share bin Laden's enthusiasm for Tora Bora, where the only heat in winter was from a wood-burning stove around which the wives and children huddled, shivering during the bitter blizzards. Each wife was given a one-ring gas burner to cook on, and the bin Laden family lived on a subsistence diet of eggs, potatoes, rice, and bread. On rare occasions they might get a can of tuna, which was thrilling for the younger children, who were always hungry.

His first wife, Najwa, was pregnant with their ninth child. She could have complained to her husband about the spartan living conditions as she was expecting a new baby, but after more than two decades of marriage she knew her husband well enough to know that he reveled in having his family live like medieval peasants in his cave-house.

Bin Laden updated the survivalist hikes that he had forced his family to take across the deserts of Sudan and adapted them for the mountains of Afghanistan, taking his older sons on all-day walking expeditions across the valleys and peaks of Tora Bora. He loved these forced mountain marches, telling his sons, "We never know when war will strike. We must know our way out of the mountains." He told visitors to his Tora Bora retreat, "I really feel secure in the mountains. I really enjoy my life when I'm here."

In early July 1996 near Jalalabad bin Laden met once again with Robert Fisk, the reporter for the British *Independent* newspaper, whom he had spoken with three years earlier in Sudan. In this interview bin Laden dropped his "I'm just a businessman" schtick that had been his public posture in Sudan. Surrounded by armed guards carrying submachine guns, he railed against the Saudi monarchy and the U.S. military presence in the Saudi kingdom, occasionally picking his teeth with a piece of miswak wood, as had also been the practice of the Prophet Mohammed.

On August 14, 1996, the U.S. State Department issued an unusual, detailed fact sheet that identified bin Laden as "one of the most significant financial sponsors of Islamic extremist activities in the world today." The

State Department outlined bin Laden's role in the Afghan War, his business interests in Sudan, his attempts to kill American troops in Yemen, and detailed his financial support for militants around the Middle East. It also specifically mentioned the formation of al-Qaeda, which was the first time that the U.S. government had publicly used the term. The State Department noted that Ramzi Yousef, who had masterminded the bombing of the World Trade Center three year earlier, had lived at a bin Laden guesthouse after the attack.

On the same day that the State Department released the bin Laden fact sheet, the *New York Times* ran a front-page story under the headline, "Funds for Terrorists Traced to Persian Gulf Businessmen," that described bin Laden as the financier of "a host of hardline groups from Egypt to Algeria."

A little over a week later bin Laden issued his first public statement that he was at war with the United States. Issued on August 23, it was titled "Declaration of War Against the Americans Occupying the Land of the Two Holy Places [Saudi Arabia]." The declaration was melodramatically datelined, "From the Peaks of the Hindu Kush, Afghanistan," making clear that bin Laden had written the declaration while he was at his cave-house in the mountains of Tora Bora. He had turned one of the rooms of the cave into a simple study lined with wooden bookshelves that were weighed down by multiple treatises on Islamic law. Bin Laden's statement also said that it had been written in *Khorasan*, which was the Arabic name for the Afghan region during the era of the Prophet Mohammed.

The "Declaration of War" celebrated the U.S. withdrawal from Beirut after the Marine barracks bombing in 1983 and a decade later the American withdrawals from Yemen and Somalia. Bin Laden wrote that "the latest and the greatest of these aggressions, incurred by the Muslims since the death of the Prophet, is the occupation of the land of the two Holy Places." He was referring to the presence of tens of thousands of U.S. troops in Saudi Arabia. The statement also attacked the Israelis for the seizure of Palestinian territory in East Jerusalem as a result of the 1967 war. He wrote that "the wound of al-Quds [the Islamic holy site in East

Jerusalem] is like a fire burning in my heart." The declaration demanded that all Muslims help with the forceful expulsion of the Americans and the Jews from Islamic lands. Al-Qaeda's leader criticized those who wouldn't take action: "I reject those who enjoy fireplaces in clubs discussing eternally. . . . The walls of oppression and humiliation cannot be demolished except in a rain of bullets."

Al-Qaeda was now officially at war with the United States, although only a handful of Americans were aware of this yet.

Al-Qaeda's man in London, Khalid al-Fawwaz, received a copy of the declaration of war, which he then gave to Abdel Bari Atwan, the editor of the Arabic newspaper *Al-Quds Al-Arabi*, one of the few independent Arab media outlets that wasn't controlled by the Saudis. Atwan printed the declaration in full, which was quite the scoop: A scion of the fabulously rich bin Laden family was declaring war against the United States!

The Taliban seized Jalalabad on September 12, and bin Laden waited nervously to find out how the new rulers of Afghanistan would react to al-Qaeda basing itself in their country. But he had nothing to fear. A Taliban cabinet minister met with bin Laden in Jalalabad and told him, "We serve the ground on which you walk." Another senior Taliban minister told bin Laden, "God will never be ashamed of you because you are the champion of the oppressed and you have waged holy war alongside the downtrodden." According to senior Taliban officials, bin Laden also ingratiated himself by buying expensive vehicles for Mullah Omar. Where bin Laden had obtained the funding for these gifts isn't clear, because at this point he was cut off from his inheritance and had to leave his assets in Sudan.

Atwan, the editor of *Al-Quds Al-Arabi*, landed the first interview with bin Laden after his embrace by the Taliban. In November Atwan was taken to bin Laden's wintry fastness in Tora Bora, where he had a "really awful" dinner with al-Qaeda's leader and a dozen of his followers. It consisted of rotten cheese, potatoes soaked in cottonseed oil, half a dozen fried eggs, and bread caked with sand. During his two-day stay in Tora Bora, Atwan had a bad case of diarrhea and insects bit him all night in the rudimentary bed that he slept in.

The journalist found bin Laden to be likable, humble, and a good listener, unlike the blustery Arab leaders he had interviewed in the past. Still, bin Laden delivered a tirade at the Americans who were "occupying" Saudi Arabia and were "desecrating" the holy land, and he declared war against the United States. Bin Laden said he even wanted to defeat Americans when it came to agriculture, and made the juvenile boast that he had managed to produce sunflowers that were bigger than any American sunflower.

Atwan asked bin Laden why he wasn't fighting the Israelis, telling him, "You know, you are criticized because of this." Bin Laden seemed surprised by this question and didn't have a good answer for it. He then volunteered that he considered Saddam Hussein, the Iraqi dictator, to be an atheist and that he hated him because of that—an interesting observation considering that seven years later senior George W. Bush administration officials would publicly make the case that bin Laden and Saddam were allied as part of their justification for the impending Iraq War.

Bin Laden took Atwan on an early-morning tour of Tora Bora. It was freezing but when the sun came out the snow-covered mountains were quite beautiful. He showed Atwan the mud houses of his followers where children were playing in the snow; a small al-Qaeda oasis.

Atwan asked bin Laden, "If you are kicked out of Afghanistan one day the way that you were kicked out of Saudi Arabia and Sudan, where will you go?"

Bin Laden replied, "I will go to the mountains of Yemen because it is exactly like Tora Bora. I love the mountains."*

---

*In early 1997 bin Laden sent a small delegation of clerics to Yemen to meet with Sheikh bin Shagea, who controlled a sizable chunk of northern Yemen close to the Saudi border and the endless deserts of the Empty Quarter. The sheikh had met with bin Laden on a couple of occasions in Saudi Arabia during the 1980s, but he had little patience with bin Laden's recent calls for holy war. Along with other tribal sheikhs, Sheikh bin Shagea told the clerics that bin Laden and his men could move to Yemen, but they would have to end "any political or military activities directed against other countries." Sheikh bin Shagea recounted this

After Atwan returned to London, *Al-Quds Al-Arabi* published the interview with bin Laden, in which he frequently spoke of Westerners as "Crusaders," which was an attempt to elevate his status as a great Islamic holy warrior from the Middle Ages on par with Saladin. All the copies of the *Al-Quds Al-Arabi* newspaper with bin Laden's interview sold out within an hour. Atwan believed it was an important interview for bin Laden because he wanted media exposure and to declare war on the Americans to a wide audience in the Arabic-speaking world.

He would have an opportunity to do this again, although it took a few tries. The first try came courtesy of the Taliban. On September 26, 1996, they swept into Kabul. The following day the U.S. State Department spokesman stated, "We've seen some of the reports that they've moved to impose Islamic law in the areas that they control. But at this stage, we're not reading anything into that. On the face of it, nothing objectionable at this stage." Similarly, Robin Raphael, the U.S. assistant secretary of state for South Asia, said of the Taliban two months later, "The real source of their success has been the willingness of many Afghans, particularly Pashtuns, to tacitly trade unending fighting and chaos for a measure of peace and security, even with severer social restrictions."

Hamid Mir was a reporter for *Daily Pakistan*, an Urdu-language newspaper that was popular in Pakistan. He received an invitation to speak to Mullah Omar after he wrote a column saying that American officials were backing the Taliban. Mir met Mullah Omar in Kandahar in December 1996. The Commander of the Faithful was sitting on the floor of a mosque where he served Mir green tea and a modest lunch of potatoes, soup, and bread. Mir was surprised by the lack of lavish ceremony that was typical when he met with Pakistan's leaders.

Mullah Omar told Mir, "Iranian media has created a lot of problems for me. They are quoting your column every day saying Hamid Mir, a famous Pakistani journalist, is saying that Mullah Omar is working for the

---

episode to the author, in northern Yemen, close to the Empty Quarter, in December 2000.

American CIA. I'm not CIA." Mullah Omar repeated again and again that he had nothing to do with the CIA.

He added that he could prove he wasn't a CIA agent, saying, "I have a friend who is a great enemy of America and he is my guest in Afghanistan. Do you know him, Osama bin Laden?"

Mir knew so little about bin Laden that when he was back home in Islamabad, the Pakistani capital, he went to the U.S. embassy and asked the librarian there, "Do you know anything about Mr. bin Laden?" The librarian said, "Please give me in writing how that is spelt." Mir wrote down the name and the librarian provided him with a couple of articles.

Mir wasn't sure if the interview was even worth doing, but he agreed to meet the mysterious Mr. bin Laden in Tora Bora in March 1997. There Mir was subjected to a body search by bin Laden's bodyguards, who put their hands inside his underwear.

Mir was furious, shouting, "You are gays!"

The bodyguards replied, "This is our duty."

They argued back and forth for many minutes until bin Laden finally arrived and said in English, "Sorry Mr. Mir. Sorry Mr. Mir."

Before Mir started his interview, bin Laden read from a file that contained Mir's bank account number, the amount of money in his account, the names of his family members and even of his girlfriend, conveying the message "Don't play any games with me."

Bin Laden said, "You are a journalist. I am a freedom fighter. And I hope you will behave like a journalist, you will not behave like an informer or a spy."

Mir found little depth in bin Laden's thinking. He kept returning to his main grievance: Why were there thousands of U.S. troops in Saudi Arabia? Bin Laden also angrily denounced the Iraqi dictator, Saddam Hussein, calling him a "socialist motherfucker."

When Mir's story was published in Pakistan it made no impact whatsoever as no one then knew who bin Laden was. Mir's editor was puzzled that Mir had spent so much effort to interview bin Laden in Afghanistan, asking him, "Why did you waste so much time and so much energy and space in the newspaper?"

Bin Laden was a news junkie who listened to the BBC World Service on the radio and also watched Al Jazeera on satellite television, the Arabic-language network that had started broadcasting the same year bin Laden had moved to Afghanistan. Bin Laden soon realized that his threats against the United States and his rationales for those threats were going largely unnoticed in the English-speaking world. He began to contemplate whether he should do his first-ever television interview with a British or American network, such as the BBC, CBS, or CNN. Bin Laden believed that he had an Islamic duty to warn his enemies before he attacked them.

Following the release of the State Department fact sheet about bin Laden during the summer of 1996, I tracked down Khalid al-Fawwaz, bin Laden's de facto media adviser in London. I was working as a producer for CNN and asked Fawwaz if the network could do an interview with bin Laden. I was intrigued by the possibility that he might have been in some way responsible for the bombing of the World Trade Center three years earlier. The investigation of the Trade Center attack had an unresolved quality since it was clear that the group of militants who attacked the building had some kind of organized link to the Afghan War. Was bin Laden their leader? I then spent some weeks in London meeting with Fawwaz and other Islamist militants who knew bin Laden. Ultimately, al-Qaeda officials decided that bin Laden's first television interview would be with CNN. The network had a reputation for fairness as a result of the Gulf War seven years earlier, when it had provided round-the-clock coverage of the conflict from inside Iraq.

The CNN team consisted of Peter Arnett, a blunt, courageous war correspondent originally from New Zealand who had won a Pulitzer Prize during the Vietnam War and was key to CNN's coverage of the Gulf War. The cameraman was Peter Jouvenal, a British Army veteran who had made dozens of reporting trips covering the Afghan wars, and I was the producer.

Abu Musab al-Suri accompanied us from London to Afghanistan.

Suri, a Syrian who could have passed as a German because of his red hair and red beard, presented himself as an Islamist journalist who ran the Bureau for the Study of Islamic Conflict and who had long-standing contacts with the Afghan Arabs. Suri said he had lived most of the past fifteen years in the West and had married a Spaniard. This was true, but it was far from the full story, as we would discover almost a decade later. That's when Suri released a public statement saying, "I was honored to know Sheikh Osama since 1988, and I was honored to join al-Qaeda and to work in it until 1992. I also taught in its training camps and other Afghan Arab camps, especially in my area of expertise: explosives, special operations and guerrilla warfare."

Together with Suri we flew from London to Pakistan and then crossed over the Khyber Pass to Jalalabad in eastern Afghanistan, where we checked into the zero-star Spinghar Hotel and waited for a few days. A young man with long hair who described himself as a media adviser to bin Laden came to tell us, "You can't bring any of your equipment; to do the interview we'll give you our own camera." Members of al-Qaeda were concerned about a tracking device being hidden in CNN's camera. They also told us not to bring anything except the clothes we were wearing, including leaving our watches behind. This too was aimed at preventing us from carrying any kind of tracking device.

One evening a van pulled up filled with heavily armed men. We all piled in and were given glasses with pieces of cardboard stuck in them that acted as crude blindfolds and were driven up into the mountains surrounding Jalalabad. By then it was night and we passed through cordons of security. Bin Laden's bodyguards, armed with AK-47s and rocket-propelled grenades, occasionally checked us as we drove slowly up a rocky track into the dark peaks of Tora Bora.

We were told that now was the time to admit if we had a tracking device secreted on our persons and nothing would happen to us. However, if they were to find such a device later on, there would be serious consequences. The cameraman, Peter Jouvenal, interpreted this as meaning, "Your head's going to get chopped off."

At one point bin Laden's men ran some kind of detector up and down our bodies. As it turned out, the detector wasn't working, but al-Qaeda's leaders thought it was important to make the CNN crew believe that it was, which they later joked about with bin Laden.

We arrived at a small plateau in the center of which was a mud building, likely for sheltering sheep in the bitter winters. Inside there were a dozen armed men. After some hours bin Laden appeared out of the darkness walking with the aid of a cane. Al-Qaeda's leader was very tall, rail thin, soft-spoken, and comported himself like a cleric. He had a feline presence, which was quite different from the angry table-thumping revolutionary we expected. Bin Laden shook Jouvenal's hand. It was a limp, cold handshake, sort of like shaking hands with a fish.

Seated on the floor, wearing a camouflage jacket, his AK-47 propped next to him and sipping copious amounts of tea, bin Laden said that he was declaring war against the United States because of the seemingly permanent U.S. military presence in the holy land of Arabia and also because of American support for Israel. During the interview an ambiguous, thin smile sometimes played across bin Laden's face. He said nothing about opposing Western freedoms or values, motivations that would later be ascribed to him by the Bush administration as the reason that he had attacked the United States on 9/11.

Bin Laden took some credit for the Black Hawk Down incident in Somalia four years earlier, saying, "We learned from those who fought there, that they were surprised to see the low morale of the American fighters in comparison with the experience they had with the Russian fighters." He wanted to remind the world that his men had fought the Soviets. He also remained convinced that he had played a key role in the Soviet withdrawal from Afghanistan.

At the end of the interview Peter Arnett asked him, "What are your future plans?"

With a touch of menace bin Laden said, "You'll see them and hear about them in the media, God willing."

His followers hung on his every word, and when they talked about him it was with great reverence for "the Sheikh." During the interview bin Laden had become increasingly fired up about his anger against the United States. When it was finished he observed in English with a smile that he had gotten "hot" during the discussion.

The CNN interview was the first time that bin Laden told Western reporters he was declaring war on the United States, but the story, which aired on May 10, 1997, didn't get much attention, likely because bin Laden was still thought of as a financier of extremism, rather than the leader of a terrorist organization. After all, how much harm could someone do who was based in the remote country of Afghanistan, which the Taliban were doing their best to thrust back into the Middle Ages? In Saudi Arabia authorities confiscated copies of the popular *Al-Hayat* newspaper that had run some quotes from bin Laden from the CNN story.

Taliban ministers started visiting bin Laden in Jalalabad and consulted him about technical issues in their ministries, especially related to agriculture and construction since he had expertise in those areas. They hoped that he might invest in Afghanistan as he had in Sudan, but in reality bin Laden was close to bankruptcy. Through his ministers Mullah Omar also wanted to convey to bin Laden that he should stop doing bellicose media interviews since they were alienating other countries. Bin Laden pretended to agree but continued to do as he pleased. "Control of bin Laden was not easy. His gentle disposition hides a wild horse that no one can control, nor can he control himself," observed Abu Walid al-Misri, who edited the Arabic-language magazine of the Taliban.

Bin Laden wrote to Mullah Omar, making the case that he should be allowed to talk to news organizations and underlining how important he believed the "media war" to be. He told the Taliban leader, "Many international media agencies corresponded with us requesting an interview with us. We believe that this is a good opportunity to make Muslims aware of what is taking place in the land of the two Holy Mosques [Saudi Arabia] as well as what is happening here in Afghanistan. It is obvious that the media war in this century is one of the strongest methods; in fact, its ratio may reach ninety percent of the total preparation for the battles."

Mullah Omar was ostensibly concerned about bin Laden's safety in the city of Jalalabad, which was not as firmly under Taliban control as was Kandahar, the de facto capital of the Taliban in southern Afghanistan. So Mullah Omar invited bin Laden to move to Kandahar, where he would certainly be more secure, but also where the Taliban would have much more ability to block bin Laden from giving incendiary interviews to journalists. The Saudis were one of only three governments in the world that recognized the Taliban, and Mullah Omar had no interest in alienating them as they were also subsidizing his impoverished government.

In early April 1997 bin Laden and his family and the other members of al-Qaeda and their families flew by military plane to Kandahar, some 250 people in total. Mullah Omar offered bin Laden the use of some well-equipped buildings in Kandahar city that were once used by the electricity company, or the use of Tarnak Farms, a former Soviet agricultural station that was now almost totally destroyed by years of war about twenty miles outside Kandahar. There was no running water or plumbing at Tarnak Farms. Bin Laden chose the harsher location, renovating the structures at Tarnak Farms and building some new ones so that the base eventually consisted of eighty buildings and a mosque. Bin Laden also established Al-Farouq training camp for his new recruits.

Al-Qaeda's management structure consisted of a military committee, a public relations committee, a finance committee, an administrative section for its training camps, and even a farming committee, which took care of the group's agricultural pursuits. Each section filed regular reports to the group's leadership on a computer, and bin Laden met regularly with the head of each committee "to discuss their issues," according to Abu Jandal, one of bin Laden's bodyguards who was constantly at his side.

Al-Qaeda was a highly bureaucratic terrorist organization, which was a reflection of bin Laden's background working for his family's company and his undergraduate studies in business administration. A detailed application form that potential recruits had to fill out before they were accepted at one of al-Qaeda's training camps asked them about their education level, religious background, arrival in Afghanistan, military skills, involvement in other jihads, marital status, language skills, and political affiliations. The application form also outlined al-Qaeda's requirements for those entering its camps, including that they agree not to leave before their basic two-month training course was finished and that they not bring any "forbidden items" such as tape recorders, radios, and cameras. They were reminded to pack appropriate running shoes and clothes suitable for paramilitary training.

It was bin Laden who set the group's strategy, and key members of the group had sworn a binding religious oath of obedience to the man they referred to as their "emir," or prince. Below bin Laden were his deputies, who enforced the organization's strict conduct rules and handled the operational details of terrorist plots. They managed all this with a flow of paperwork more reminiscent of an insurance company than a group dedicated to revolutionary jihad.

Bin Laden exercised near-total control over al-Qaeda, whose members had to swear a religious oath personally to him, ensuring blind loyalty. One of bin Laden's men outlined the dictatorial powers that bin Laden exercised over his organization: "If the Shura council at al-Qaeda, the highest authority in the organization, had a majority of 98 percent on a resolution and it is opposed by bin Laden, he has the right to cancel the resolution." The legal, media, and economic committees of al-Qaeda were all set up to service the military committee, and they all followed bin Laden's orders. The men who worked for bin Laden typically requested permission before they spoke with their leader by saying, "Dear prince: May I speak?"

To bin Laden's followers he was truly an extraordinarily charismatic man; someone who they knew had given up a life of luxury to live a life of danger and poverty in the cause of jihad. He slept on the floor, ate little, and showed disarming personal modesty along with an almost freakish religiosity. They also admired that he modeled his life of jihad on the life of the Prophet Mohammed.

His followers described their first encounter with bin Laden as an intense spiritual experience. Bin Laden's bodyguard Abu Jandal described meeting with bin Laden in 1997 as "beautiful" and that he came to look on him "as a father." Shadi Abdallah, a Jordanian who was another of bin Laden's bodyguards, explained bin Laden's attraction: "A very charismatic person who could persuade people simply by his way of talking. One could say that he 'seduced' many young men." John Miller, a correspondent for ABC News who interviewed bin Laden in Afghanistan in 1998, noticed that bin Laden's followers spoke with great excitement about "the Sheikh." Miller observed, "There is that charismatic aura or scent that made people follow him; either you have it or you don't."

When bin Laden wasn't engaged in the affairs of al-Qaeda he enjoyed playing volleyball with his men; typically bin Laden was placed on one team while his military commander Abu Hafs was put on the other because they were both tall and skillful. Bin Laden also occasionally indulged his childhood passion for soccer, but because of pain in his back, which forced him to walk with the help of a cane, he kept that sport to a minimum. And he continued riding whenever he could. Bin Laden loved horses because the Prophet Mohammed had supposedly said, "There is always goodness in horses until the Day of Judgment." He sometimes arranged horse races among his followers, and he would ride for long excursions of up to forty miles without stopping.

Bin Laden continued his practice of taking his wives and children out into the desert to toughen them up. He and his guards drove out from Kandahar for an hour or so while his large family followed in a bus. They stopped in a remote desert region where he taught his wives how to use firearms. He also preached self-reliance to his sons, telling them, "Sons, your father's millions about which you hear are not for your father to use. This money is for the Muslims and I hold it in trust for the cause of God. Not one riyal [the equivalent of 30 cents] of it is for you. Each of you is a man. Let him rely on himself."

One of bin Laden's sons, Saad, once asked his father for a money gift so that he could get married. Bin Laden replied, "This does not concern me. Rely on yourself."

Saad asked, "What should I do?"

Bin Laden replied, "Take this plot of land. Till the land and from the

revenue that you get, save money and get married." Saad followed his father's advice.

It was around this time that bin Laden was joined in Afghanistan by the
Egyptian militant Ayman al-Zawahiri, who would become a key public
face of al-Qaeda and eventually bin Laden's top deputy. But for now, Zawahiri was mostly a supplicant in bin Laden's world. That's because he
had made the ill-fated decision to go to Chechnya, where a small group
of Arabs were fighting the Russians alongside Chechen insurgents. There
Zawahiri hoped to relaunch his organization, the Jihad Group, now that it
too had also been expelled from Sudan.

On December 1, 1996, Zawahiri and two other Egyptian militants
traveled into Russia hoping to reach Chechnya. They were arrested by
Russian police as they had no visas and were put in jail for six months.
The Russians had no idea who they had in custody, and when the militants' case came to trial the three men all lied about their identities, pre-
tending they were businessmen who somehow had become confused
about their location.

Zawahiri was released by his Russian jailers in May 1997 and then
made his way back to Afghanistan, where bin Laden was now the unques-
tioned leader of the Arab militants in the country. Toward the end of the
anti-Soviet jihad when they were both living in Peshawar, bin Laden had
been a political neophyte who was still defending the Saudi royal family, while Zawahiri was already a hardened revolutionary who had served
three years in Egypt's brutal jails. As a result, during the late 1980s Zawahiri had influenced bin Laden's thinking about the need to fight the
"near-enemy" Arab regimes such as Egypt. But now, a decade later, their
relative importance on the "field of jihad" had changed quite dramatically.
Zawahiri was a penniless refugee with virtually no followers, whereas bin
Laden was a well-known jihadist hero the Taliban had appointed to be
responsible for all of the Arabs living in Afghanistan.

But bin Laden found a way to use Zawahiri for his own purposes—to advance his goals instead of those of this fellow jihadist whose focus was not on the United States but on Egypt. Bin Laden released a statement on behalf of the "World Islamic Front," a joint declaration made by himself, Zawahiri, and other militant leaders from Bangladesh, Egypt, and Pakistan on February 22, 1998. The declaration said, "The United States has been occupying the lands of Islam in the holiest of places, the Arabian Peninsula. . . . On that basis, and in compliance with Allah's order, we issue the following *fatwa* to all Muslims: The ruling to kill the Americans and their allies—civilians and military—is an individual duty for every Muslim who can do it in any country in which it is possible to do it." The declaration claimed it was now a *religious duty* for any Muslim to kill American civilians anywhere in the world, which was a sharp amplification of al-Qaeda's rhetoric.

A well-known verse in the Koran, which for believers is the Word of God, commands Muslims to "kill the unbelievers wherever you find them, seize them, besiege them, ambush them." When bin Laden made this formal declaration of war against "the Jews and the Crusaders" he cited this verse at the beginning of his declaration. (The same verse also adds that if the nonbelievers repent and pay a tax to Muslims, then they may be spared, but this caveat did not appear in bin Laden's declaration of war.) Of course, bin Laden's beliefs were not a mainstream view among Muslims, but assertions that Islamist terrorism has nothing at all to do with Islam are as nonsensical as claims that the Crusades had nothing to do with Christian beliefs about the sanctity of Jerusalem.

This declaration of war made no mention of Zawahiri's lifelong goal of overthrowing the "near-enemy" Egyptian regime and instead was focused on bin Laden's "far-enemy" goal of attacking America. Nor did the declaration cite Sayyid Qutb, Zawahiri's key ideological guide, who had made the case in the 1960s that secular Arab regimes should be overthrown. Instead, the declaration cited the medieval Islamic scholar Ibn Taymiyya, who had advanced the idea that jihad was the most important duty of a Muslim after belief in Allah. Bin Laden had co-opted Zawahiri to be part of his holy war against the United States, not the other way around, which was the dominant narrative in the years after the 9/11 attacks.*

Within a day of bin Laden issuing his declaration of war, his adviser in London, Khalid al-Fawwaz, phoned Abdel Bari Atwan, the editor of *Al-Quds Al-Arabi*, saying, "I want to come to you to see you." Fawwaz came with a faxed copy of the fatwa and Atwan looked at it realizing that it was

---

*The urtext for the view that Zawahiri wielded Svengali-like influence over bin Laden was Lawrence Wright's story in *The New Yorker*, "The Man Behind Bin Laden," published a year after the 9/11 attacks. The article asserted that "according to officials in the C.I.A. and the F.B.I., Zawahiri has been responsible for much of the planning of the terrorist operations against the United States." In fact, there is no evidence that Zawahiri had a role in the planning of any of al-Qaeda's major anti-American attacks against the U.S. embassies in Kenya and Tanzania in 1998, the USS *Cole* in Yemen in 2000, and 9/11 itself. Wright went on to win a Pulitzer Prize for his 2006 book, *The Looming Tower*, a book that has many strengths, but that also inflated Zawahiri's role in bin Laden's anti-American jihad. Wright did, however, note in *The Looming Tower* that when Zawahiri merged his small group into al-Qaeda in June 2001, it "was bin Laden's organization, not Zawahiri's." I had also overestimated Zawahiri's importance to bin Laden's thinking in my 2001 book, *Holy War, Inc.* After examining all of the evidence, I have since concluded that Zawahiri was a marginal figure when it came to influencing bin Laden's views, and he played only a minor role in the actions of al-Qaeda in the years leading up to the 9/11 attacks. This view is also shared by Michael Scheuer, who led the bin Laden unit at CIA from 1996 to 1999; by Daniel Coleman, the FBI agent who investigated bin Laden for six years before 9/11; and by the Egyptian dissident Montasser al-Zayyat, who spent years in prison in Egypt with Zawahiri. Zayyat explained, "Osama bin Laden had an appreciable impact on Zawahiri, though the conventional wisdom holds the opposite to be the case. Bin Laden advised Zawahiri to stop armed operations in Egypt and to ally with him against their common enemies: the United States and Israel." This was also the conclusion of Noman Benotman, a former leader of the Libyan Islamic Fighting Group, who knew both bin Laden and Zawahiri, who said it was bin Laden who told Zawahiri, "Forget about the 'near enemy' [the Egyptian government]. The main enemy is the Americans because they dominate the whole area and they're supporting these Arab regimes." Abu Walid al-Misri, an Egyptian living in Afghanistan who knew both bin Laden and Zawahiri well, also says that Zawahiri played only a minor role in al-Qaeda before the 9/11 attacks.

dangerous, as it was claiming a religious basis for murdering Jews and Americans. It was shocking even for Fawwaz, who told Atwan, "I don't know who influenced Osama bin Laden to issue this *fatwa*. This is unacceptable and I am against it."

The text of this fatwa was published in *Al-Quds Al-Arabi* on February 23, 1998. A CIA memorandum noted, "These fatwas are the first from these groups that explicitly justify attacks on American civilians anywhere in the world."

Neither bin Laden nor Zawahiri were scholars of Islamic law eligible to issue fatwas, so bin Laden was thrilled when three months later a group of ulema (clergy) in Afghanistan issued a fatwa ruling that U.S. forces had to move out of the Gulf region. This gave bin Laden some clerical cover for his holy war, and he was quick to endorse the ruling of the Afghan clerics. In a report about this fatwa in *Al-Quds Al-Arabi*, bin Laden said, "the fatwa proves with irrefutable religious evidence that it is impermissible for US forces" to be in Saudi Arabia.

The U.S. State Department report "Patterns of Global Terrorism 1997," released in April 1998, noted that "bin Laden continued to incite violence against the United States." The following month bin Laden issued a statement that seemed to revel in the attention that he and the Taliban were receiving from the U.S. government, saying, "So congratulations to the Taliban government on the medal of honor presented by America through the decision to charge it with sponsoring terrorism."

Around the same time bin Laden issued another statement following the Indian government's successful test of a nuclear weapon at a desert site less than one hundred miles from its border with Pakistan. He wrote, "We call upon the Muslim nation in general, and Pakistan and its army in particular, to prepare for the jihad imposed by Allah and terrorize the enemy by preparing the force necessary. This should include a nuclear force." This was bin Laden's first public statement that Muslims needed to acquire nuclear weapons.

In mid-May, Hamid Mir, the Pakistani journalist, spent two days with bin Laden at his base near Kandahar. He suggested to Mir that he sit in on one of his lectures to dozens of his followers. Bin Laden pasted a map of the Middle East on a big board and asked, "Why are Americans present in Kuwait? Why are Americans present in Yemen? Why are they present in Saudi Arabia? What are they doing in Bahrain?"

Bin Laden answered his own question: "They are there to plunder our oil wealth, and they want to destroy our Holy Land."

The fighters chanted, *"Allah Akbar! Allah Akbar!"* "God is great!" "Death to America!"

One of bin Laden's sons, a teenager, was sitting with his father and a gun was lying in his lap. Mir asked bin Laden, "He is a young boy. Why is he carrying a gun?" Bin Laden said it was his son's decision.

Mir asked the son, "Are you following the footsteps of your father?"

The boy answered very confidently, "No. I am following the footsteps of my Prophet."

Bin Laden told Mir that his father, Mohammed bin Laden, was "very keen that one of his sons should fight against the enemies of Islam. So I am the one son who is acting according to the wishes of his father." Even though bin Laden told his own sons that he had met his father on only five occasions, in bin Laden's mind he was the only son of Mohammed bin Laden who was truly fulfilling his father's wishes.

Mir repeatedly pressed bin Laden with versions of the same question, asking, "How can you prove in the light of Islamic teaching that it's permissible to kill Americans?"

Mir pointed out, "The Koran says that the blood of an innocent non-Muslim is equal to the blood of a Muslim. If you are killing an innocent non-Muslim Christian who is an American citizen, if you are killing an innocent non-Muslim Jew, this is a violation of the Koranic teachings. How can you prove that your fatwa is correct?"

Bin Laden finally said, "Actually, this is not my fatwa. Actually, the fatwa is issued by some very big Islamic scholars. I'm just following that fatwa."

In an attempt to make this case, bin Laden gave Mir a copy of a fatwa by the Blind Sheikh, Omar Abdel Rahman, who was the spiritual leader of a major Egyptian terrorist group. Two years earlier Rahman had been sentenced to life imprisonment in the United States for his role in fomenting terrorist plots in New York City. The fatwa called on Muslims to kill Americans everywhere, stating in Arabic, "If they [the Americans] kill me, which they will certainly do—hold my funeral and send my corpse to my family, but do not let my blood be shed in vain. Rather, extract the most violent revenge. . . . And so all Muslims everywhere: Cut off all relations with [the Americans, Christians, and Jews], tear them to pieces, destroy their economies, burn their corporations, destroy their peace, sink their ships, shoot down their planes and kill them on air, sea, and land. And kill them wherever you may find them."

Sheikh Rahman's fatwa was the first time that a prominent Muslim cleric had given his religious sanction to attacks on American aviation, shipping, and economic targets. The fatwa, with its exhortations to "shoot down their planes," "burn their corporations," and "sink their ships," would turn out to be a slowly ticking time bomb that would explode first on October 12, 2000, when a suicide bombing by members of al-Qaeda blew a hole the size of a small house in the USS Cole in Yemen, killing seventeen American sailors, and then again with even greater ferocity on 9/11.

Like Abdullah Azzam, Sheikh Rahman had a doctorate in Islamic jurisprudence from Al-Azhar University in Cairo, while bin Laden had no standing as a religious scholar. He knew he needed some theological cover for his future campaign against American civilians and only someone with Sheikh Rahman's religious credentials could give him that.

Two weeks after his interview with Mir, on May 26, bin Laden held his first and only press conference. Fourteen journalists attended, and bin Laden made quite an entrance. The moment he stepped out of his vehicle he was surrounded by two dozen bodyguards wearing hoods. As he alighted, gunmen on nearby peaks started frenzied shooting and fired rocket-propelled grenades, an awesome display of firepower that went on for many minutes, lighting up the darkening sky.

Rahimullah Yusufzai, one of the most respected journalists in Pakistan, was attending the press conference and asked the men who were shooting off their weapons if they were part of al-Qaeda. Speaking in Pashto, the local language, the men told Yusufzai that they were not part of al-Qaeda and instead were locals who had been asked to bring their guns and put on this show for the journalists.

Bin Laden told the assembled journalists that he had "formed with many other Islamic groups and organizations in the Islamic world a front called the International Islamic Front to do jihad against the Crusaders and Jews." Zawahiri provided some useful window dressing for the claim of an "International Islamic Front" because even though Zawahiri had only a tiny number of followers, he was still an Egyptian militant living in Afghanistan. He sat prominently by bin Laden's side during the press conference, which bolstered the impression that bin Laden's organization was truly global.

Also at the press conference were two sons of the Blind Sheikh, Omar Abdel Rahman. Rahman's sons distributed what they described as the "will" of their father on laminated cards to several of the journalists. It was the same fatwa that bin Laden had handed to Hamid Mir two weeks earlier that gave religious sanction to the killing of American civilians anywhere in the world.

Bin Laden knew that the planning for the bombings of the two U.S. embassies in Africa—in Kenya and Tanzania—was nearly complete when he held his press conference in late May 1998. He wanted to signal both that he was at war with the United States and that he had the theological justification to carry out that war.

During the press conference he said that there was going to be some sort of action by his group in the near future, saying there would be "some good news in the weeks ahead." The prominent Pakistani newspaper *The News* ran a story about the press conference, describing bin Laden's "choked voice" as he described the "infidel" soldiers deployed by the United States in the holy land of Saudi Arabia.

Mullah Omar was furious when he heard about bin Laden's press conference. The Taliban leader called Rahimullah Yusufzai demanding, "How come Osama bin Laden has given a press conference without my

permission? There can only be one ruler in Afghanistan." Mullah Omar's
anger was shared by a number of leaders in the Taliban movement who
were annoyed that bin Laden's grandstanding threats were interfering
with their efforts for greater acceptance and recognition on the world
stage. Mullah Khakshar, the Taliban's powerful deputy minister of the interior, even proposed to a group of other Taliban leaders that they talk to
Mullah Omar about expelling bin Laden. But it never happened, because
they didn't have the courage to say this to the Taliban leader, who seemed
oddly in thrall to bin Laden.

Mullah Omar himself did ask bin Laden, "Look, can you stop talking
to the media?" Bin Laden replied, "Look, Mecca is the most sacred place
on the face of the earth and I left it and I came here because I want to
express myself. Now, if you want me to keep quiet, I'm going to leave Afghanistan." Bin Laden argued that his stance was sanctioned by the Koran
and the hadith, the sayings of the Prophet. Mullah Omar usually backed
down when bin Laden made these religious arguments to him.

So bin Laden continued his interviews. Around the same time as his
press conference, he also gave an interview in Afghanistan to John Miller
of ABC News, one of the three major American television networks.
Miller spoke to Zawahiri about the need to get some "B roll" shots of bin
Laden that showed him doing something other than just sitting. Zawahiri
said, "This is not like your Sam Donaldson [then the White House correspondent for ABC News] and the president walking through the Rose
Garden. Mr. bin Laden is a very important man."

Miller replied, "We are not just going to put bin Laden on for half an
hour talking. We need to build a story around elements."

Zawahiri said, "Elements, we will get you elements."

When bin Laden arrived for the interview a dozen bodyguards surrounded him. Then suddenly there was a barrage of rockets and tracer
bullets fired up into the night sky. Zawahiri noted, "There is always a great
celebration when Sheikh bin Laden comes." Miller got his elements.

For the ABC News interview bin Laden sat down in front of a map of
the world, which Miller thought was designed to transmit that al-Qaeda

was a worldwide organization and that bin Laden was its leader. As always, bin Laden had his AK-47 with him, which he propped up against the wall during the interview.

Miller asked bin Laden about the killing of American civilians, citing the World Trade Center bombing in 1993. Miller observed, "It's not like fighting the Russians on the field of battle. This is targeting innocents and civilians."

Bin Laden replied, "This is a very strange question coming from an American. Was it not your country that bombed Nagasaki and Hiroshima? Were there not women and children and civilians and noncombatants there? You were the people who invented this terrible game and we as Muslims have to use those same tactics against you."

Bin Laden told Miller, "We believe that the biggest thieves in the world are Americans and the biggest terrorists on earth are the Americans. The only way for us to defend against these assaults is by using similar means. We do not differentiate between those dressed in military uniforms and civilians. They're all targets in this fatwa." A year earlier bin Laden had told CNN that the targets of his fury were U.S. soldiers. Now he declared to an American television correspondent that U.S. civilians were also his targets. In the interview, which aired on ABC on June 10, 1998, bin Laden said, "I predict a black day for America." When he made this prediction, bin Laden knew that al-Qaeda's plans to blow up two U.S. embassies in Africa were very close to completion.

Miller's "fixer" and translator on the trip was Tariq Hamdi, an Iraqi living in the United States who had connections among the Arab veterans of the Afghan War. Unbeknownst to Miller, Hamdi had brought with him to Afghanistan a critical battery for bin Laden's satellite phone, which allowed al-Qaeda's leaders to communicate with members of the group around the globe. While bin Laden was careful not to talk too much on his satellite phone, other al-Qaeda leaders used the phone often, logging hundreds of hours of calls between 1996 and 1998. Khalid al-Fawwaz, bin Laden's representative in London, received the largest number of calls. Bin Laden and his top officials also made more than two hundred calls to Yemen and a smaller number of calls to Pakistan, Saudi Arabia, and Sudan, although none were made to Iraq despite later claims by the Bush administration that al-Qaeda was allied to Saddam Hussein.

By now the Saudis were furious about bin Laden's constant public critiques. In June 1998 the head of Saudi intelligence, Prince Turki, went to Kandahar to meet Mullah Omar to persuade him to hand over bin Laden. Mullah Omar seemed quite amenable to the idea, telling Prince Turki to inform the Saudi king that he wanted to set up a joint Saudi-Afghan commission to arrange procedures for the handover. A senior Taliban official traveled to Saudi Arabia the following month to finalize the details of the commission that would oversee bin Laden's return to the Saudi kingdom.

Bin Laden was very close to being forced to return to his homeland. There he could face a trial for treason, which carried the death penalty.

EIGHT

THE U.S. SLOWLY GRASPS THE THREAT

It is much easier after the event to sort the relevant signals from the ir-relevant signals. After the event, of course, a signal is always crystal clear; we can now see what disaster it was signaling since the disaster has now occurred. But before the event it is obscure and pregnant with conflicting meanings. It comes to the observer embedded in an atmosphere of 'noise,' i.e., in all sorts of information that is useless and irrelevant for predicting the disaster.

— Roberta Wohlstetter, *Pearl Harbor: Warning and Decision*

By the time bin Laden arrived in Afghanistan his followers had al-ready tried to kill American soldiers in Yemen and Somalia. Yet he was virtually unknown to the U.S. government. One of the only Ameri-can officials who understood the threat posed by bin Laden and his men was Gina Bennett, a young intelligence analyst working at the State Department.

Just one week out of the University of Virginia, with a degree in eco-nomics and foreign policy, Bennett started working at the State Depart-ment as a clerk-typist in June 1988. The work involved typing and filing. After a couple months Bennett's boss told her, "Gina, you don't belong here. I'm going to promote you so you can get a job as an intelligence analyst."

Bennett joined the State Department's Bureau of Intelligence and Research, one of the smallest U.S. intelligence agencies. Bennett's first job was as a "terrorism watch officer," working eight-hour shifts during which she monitored intelligence and news media to analyze terrorism trends and to respond to terrorist attacks when they occurred.

On December 21, 1988, a bomb blew up on Pan Am 103 as it flew over Scotland. The jet crashed, killing a total of 270 people on the plane and on the ground, thirty-five of whom were students at Syracuse University. It was the first major terrorist attack on Bennett's watch. She worked with Consular Affairs helping the bereaved families and preparing the State Department's daily updates about the bombing. Bennett recalled, "I was really, really changed by Pan Am 103 because so many of the passengers were students who were just a bit younger than me." Stopping the next terrorist attack became a mission for Bennett. "It's like being a cop who is chasing a serial killer on a cold case. You just can't give it up."

The Berlin Wall fell at the end of 1989 and then the Soviet Union collapsed, but Bennett sensed that there was a menacing legacy of the Cold War—the "Afghan Arabs," who were veterans of the anti-Soviet jihad. Bennett realized that the Afghan Arabs were returning to their home countries such as Algeria, Egypt, and Tunisia, and she noticed that some were joining armed groups. Bennett was particularly struck by an attack in November 1991 by a group of militants on Algerian border guards, six of whom were slaughtered like animals, hacked to death with knives and swords. The Algerian terrorists were dressed in Afghan garb and their leader was named Tayeb el Afghani, "Tayeb the Afghan."

Bennett investigated further and found that thousands of Afghan Arabs had left their home countries to go to Pakistan and Afghanistan during the 1980s, relying on a support network that had funneled men, money, and supplies to the Afghan War. By the early 1990s that network was sending veterans of the Afghan conflict to join militant Islamist groups around the world.

She saw that jihadist violence was becoming worse in Egypt and decided to go to Cairo to discuss with her Egyptian counterparts what they were seeing. Egyptian intelligence officials admitted to Bennett that they hadn't done a good job of tracking volunteers when they had left for Pakistan and Afghanistan during the anti-Soviet jihad. Bennett started writing classified papers about what she was learning. She started hearing about an "Abu Abdullah" guy who was financing some of these Afghan Arabs. Bennett had no idea that she would spend much of the rest of her career focused on this mysterious Abu Abdullah, the nom de guerre of bin Laden. Bennett started researching the bombings of two hotels in Aden, Yemen, in December 1992 that were housing U.S. soldiers on the way to Somalia. Yemeni officials said the attack was financed by an "Osama bin Laden," who was then living in Sudan.

As Bennett was investigating bin Laden and the Afghan Arabs she became pregnant with her first child. Bennett delivered her son on February 23, 1993. Three days later a team assembled by one of the Afghan Arabs, Ramzi Yousef, drove a van into the basement of the World Trade Center and detonated a bomb, killing six people. As investigators began looking into Yousef's group they found that several of them had traveled to Afghanistan or Pakistan to aid in the war against the communists.

Bennett was holding her new baby boy in the hospital when she received a frantic call from her boss, who was almost shouting, "Your people did this! Your people did this!" Her boss was referring to the Afghan Arabs whom Bennett had been tracking for the past couple of years.

At first Bennett had no idea what her boss was talking about, as she was in a great deal of pain from her C-section three days earlier and her painkillers had worn off.

She quickly realized that the Afghan Arabs had spread their holy war, this time to New York City. Sitting on Bennett's desk at the State Department was a draft of a paper that she had started writing that described a movement of mujahideen from more than fifty countries who had gained battlefield experience in Afghanistan and were now joining militant organizations in countries such as Algeria, Bosnia, Egypt, Tajikistan, the Philippines, and Yemen, and even in unexpected locations like Burma.

Bennett took some months off for maternity leave. When she returned to the State Department she resumed work on drafting her paper, which she circulated on August 21, 1993. The paper, titled "The Wandering Mujahidin: Armed and Dangerous," was classified Secret and identified "Usama bin Ladin" as a donor who was supporting Islamic militants in "places as diverse as Yemen and the United States." Bin Laden's funding had also enabled hundreds of Afghan Arabs to resettle in Sudan and Yemen, and he had ideological ties to the Blind Sheikh.

It was the first time that the U.S. government had produced a warning about the dangers of a global jihadist movement led by the mysterious multimillionaire Osama bin Laden. And the warning was not issued by the CIA or the FBI, but by a junior analyst at the State Department.

A week later Bennett published another analysis titled "Saudi Patron to Islamic Extremists," in which she observed that bin Laden had founded a group called "al-Qa'ida in the 1980s." This was the first time that anyone in the U.S. government had identified al-Qaeda as a threat, the existence of which was then a well-kept secret. Bennett named bin Laden as the financier of the bombings of the two hotels in Aden. She described how bin Laden had gathered a group of Afghan War veterans in Sudan who were training to fight in new holy wars and was "financing jihads" around the world, from Pakistan to Thailand.

Bennett knew that what she was describing wasn't considered "normal" in the world of counterterrorism, because this was a case of militants from different countries in a loose alliance operating without the support of any state. Bennett wanted policymakers and the intelligence community to pay attention to this phenomenon, but knew it would be difficult.

In classified papers Bennett described bin Laden as a "financier," as that was the best evidence about him that was then available, but privately she saw him as something more. Bennett was an observant Catholic who understood the power of religious beliefs in someone's life. She thought that bin Laden was a visionary who believed God was on his side and who had a model for political change that was based on his experience in Afghanistan, where men from dozens of countries had put their different interpretations of Islam aside and had fought in Allah's name. They had stayed focused on that fight, and look at what they had achieved: The Soviet Union fell. Bennett believed that bin Laden mythologized this whole movement, not just his own role in it, and thought it was a repeatable model, not only in Afghanistan, but around the world.

Bennett's analysis caught the attention of the State Department's coordinator for counterterrorism, Ambassador Philip Wilcox, who requested a full assessment of the jihadist movement led by bin Laden. The Bureau of Intelligence and Research wrote a twenty-five-page report that was circulated in October 1995 pointing to military training provided by bin Laden at his "farms in Sudan, camps in Afghanistan and facilities around the world from New York to Manila." The assessment urged the closure of bin Laden's training camps in Afghanistan, Pakistan, Sudan, and Yemen and also to find ways to halt his funding of the Afghan Arabs. The report argued that the U.S. government should put pressure on the Sudanese government, which was hosting bin Laden, so he would end his support for Islamist militants around the world.

A month later, in November 1995, Bennett helped establish the "Mujahidin Interagency Working Group" to bring together officials at other agencies such as the CIA and FBI who shared her growing concern about bin Laden and the Afghan Arabs.

One of those officials was Cindy Storer, who had started at the CIA right out of college in 1986. Initially, Storer studied Soviet missile networks. Six years later, at the age of twenty-eight, she was appointed as an analyst on Afghanistan. The U.S. embassy in Kabul had closed three years earlier and the U.S. government was largely blind to what was happening there, which for the vast majority of American officials was not much of a concern, since the Afghan War had served its purpose in helping to deal a final death blow to the Soviet Union.

The counterterrorism priorities at the time were Hezbollah, Iran, and Palestinian terrorist groups, but Storer found a senior analyst, Michael Scheuer, who also shared her concern about the Afghan Arabs. Some of their CIA colleagues thought their focus on the Afghan Arabs was "nuts."

Storer was counseled in one performance review that she was spending too much time on bin Laden. She observed, "When you are the first off the blocks, by definition you are going to be in the minority."

In an era before computer programs could easily perform network analysis, Storer used Excel spreadsheets to chart the connections between militants linked to al-Qaeda. She began to notice that all roads led back to Peshawar, where bin Laden had lived during the late 1980s, concluding that al-Qaeda was a hierarchical organization with bin Laden at the top. Contrary to the conventional wisdom at the time that a "ragtag" bunch of Arabs from different countries wouldn't work together, Storer found that they were cooperating.

By the end of 1995 senior CIA officials began to share Storer's concern about bin Laden. David Cohen was the CIA's director of operations in charge of spying operations, including the Counterterrorist Center. Cohen suggested that the agency set up a "virtual station" focused on bin Laden. This would provide its own sources of funding. This was critical at a time when the "peace dividend" following the fall of the Soviet Union meant that the agency was being starved of resources. In 1995 the CIA trained only twenty-five new officers, the lowest number in its history.

Cohen appointed senior analyst Michael Scheuer to run the new station. Scheuer had considerable knowledge of many of the issues surrounding bin Laden, as he had worked for years on the CIA program that had armed the Afghan resistance. Scheuer was a workaholic with a PhD in history whose full beard, bulging eyes, devout Catholicism, and overall intensity gave him something of the look and vibe of an Old Testament prophet. Even by his own account Scheuer could be "abrasive," a self-assessment that few of his colleagues would have quibbled with. Abrasive he may have been, but Scheuer had a prophetic understanding of bin Laden. Scheuer's mantra was, "This guy's gonna kill several thousand Americans."

Scheuer named the new bin Laden unit "Alec Station," after his son. It was the first time in the CIA's history that a station had been founded to focus on a single individual. Alec Station also housed an operational element that would try and disrupt al-Qaeda by curbing bin Laden's funding.

It would also try to "render"—a euphemism for kidnap—members of his organization to their home countries, where they could be tried and imprisoned (and in some cases tortured).

When Alec Station opened in January 1996 in an office building just a short drive from CIA headquarters, Scheuer wanted to recruit as many women as possible to work with him. He felt that female CIA officials didn't waste time sitting around telling war stories and generally produced better results. If he could have put a sign up at Alec Station saying "no boys need apply" he would have done so. The core of the group under Scheuer began with six women, including Jennifer Matthews, who more than a decade later would be killed by an al-Qaeda suicide bomber in Afghanistan. They called themselves "the Bay" because they all worked together in a set of office cubicles arranged in a bay formation. They were fans of the new TV series *Buffy the Vampire Slayer*, about a group of suburban female teens battling the forces of darkness who then went shopping at the mall. It reminded them a bit of their own lives, battling bin Laden and his men and then going home to their houses in the suburbs.

Scheuer's commitment was so intense that he would arrive at Alec Station at 3:30 in the morning. The members of the bin Laden unit were considered so over-the-top in their trumpeting of their concerns about al-Qaeda that around the CIA they were known as the "Manson family."

Officials from outside agencies were brought in to work at Alec Station, notably FBI special agent Daniel Coleman, who was detailed from the New York City field office of the bureau. Coleman had started at the FBI working on Soviet counterintelligence. The father of five children, Coleman had an avuncular, unthreatening manner, which made him effective when it came to earning the trust of Soviet bloc defectors. It was a skill that would serve him well when he began to handle defectors from al-Qaeda. Coleman always wanted the defectors and repentant terrorists whom he handled to come over to the American side with a smile on their faces.

Known to his colleagues as "the Professor," Coleman had opened the first counterterrorism case against an obscure Saudi financier of terrorism named Osama bin Laden in December 1995. Coleman began work at Alec Station in May 1996.

That same month, Jamal al-Fadl's "walk-in" to the U.S. embassy in Eritrea was a big break for the CIA and FBI officials trying to make sense of bin Laden and his group. Fadl was one of the earliest recruits to al-Qaeda and he knew a great deal about the group, but he wasn't a conventional Islamist militant; Fadl loved to gamble, ogle women, and he never seemed to pray. The FBI agents and CIA officers who dealt with Fadl called him "Junior," and the nickname stuck. They housed Junior at a Residence Inn in New Jersey, where they debriefed him for many months. Junior developed a pronounced taste for waffles with syrup, and he would start pouting if his FBI handlers didn't get him this treat on a regular basis. Eventually, Junior's Sudanese family joined him in New Jersey, and FBI agents would sometimes take them all out to the beach.

According to Junior, al-Qaeda was a bureaucratic organization overseen by bin Laden, to whom members swore a *bayat*, a religious oath of allegiance. Junior gave the FBI the names of key members of al-Qaeda and the roles they played in the group. He told Coleman that despite the fact that he betrayed bin Laden, he loved him because al-Qaeda's leader modeled his life on that of the Prophet Mohammed, even sleeping on his right side in the same manner that the Prophet had slept. Crucially, Fadl also told his FBI handlers that bin Laden's men had trained some of the fighters in Somalia involved in the Black Hawk Down incident three years earlier.

For Coleman that opened an interesting possibility as he contemplated a legal case against bin Laden. With Junior they now had a witness who could testify that bin Laden was leading an organization that was conspiring to attack U.S. military targets.

Under pressure from the Saudi and U.S. governments in mid-May 1996, bin Laden was pushed out of Sudan and headed to Afghanistan. Two months later Gina Bennett published another prescient classified analysis titled "Usama bin Ladin: Who's Chasing Whom?" Bennett predicted that bin Laden "would feel comfortable returning to Afghanistan, where he got his start as a patron and *mujahid* during the war with the former Soviet Union." Bennett went on to forecast that bin Laden's "prolonged stay in Afghanistan where hundreds of Arab mujahidin receive terrorist training and extremist leaders often congregate—could prove more dangerous to US interests in the long run than during his three-year liaison with Khartoum."

Bennett believed that bin Laden would be a bigger threat now that he was reunited with the birthplace of his own mythology: the battlefields of Afghanistan. He had a network of contacts in Pakistan and Afghanistan that he could easily utilize. And he was angry about being forced out of Sudan, where he had invested many millions of dollars, an expulsion that he blamed on the Americans.

Coleman was also worried because there was no plausible cover story for a U.S. official to travel to Afghanistan. At least in Khartoum, an American official such as Coleman could stay at the local Hilton hotel and the burgeoning oil exploration business in the country could provide some plausible cover. In Taliban-controlled Afghanistan there wasn't any international business to speak of and Westerners were exceptionally rare.

Scheuer had a different reaction. CIA officials had worked intensively on Afghanistan during the 1980s, and Scheuer thought that he could reactivate the agency's old network of contacts to help track bin Laden.

· Both Coleman and Scheuer were right. CIA officials did have long-standing connections to a number of the warlords in Afghanistan that they could try and tap again. Yet operating in the country was extraordinarily difficult as the United States did not recognize the Taliban government and Afghanistan was decimated by more than a decade and a half of war.

During the summer of 1997 Coleman got another break in the case against bin Laden. Junior had provided a roadmap about who was in al-Qaeda and how it functioned. Coleman started reviewing phone transcripts of tapped calls made by some of the al-Qaeda members whom Junior had identified, which led him to a house in Nairobi, Kenya. Coleman didn't know it yet, but this was the safe house for a member of al-Qaeda who was plotting to blow up the U.S. embassy there.

Coleman secured a warrant from the Kenyans to search the house. He found an Apple PowerBook laptop. With the help of the CIA, Coleman retrieved a number of deleted documents on the computer, including a letter from a member of al-Qaeda in which he boasted to his superiors about the role that the group had played in training the Somali fighters who had brought down the Black Hawk helicopters in Mogadishu in 1993. This letter was never intended to be made public, and it linked bin Laden to an act of violence against Americans. Junior could testify at trial that bin Laden was trying to target U.S. soldiers in Somalia, while the letter discovered on the laptop in Nairobi was evidence that supported this charge.

The Southern District of New York empaneled a grand jury in Manhattan that started hearing evidence that culminated in a secret, sealed indictment being returned against bin Laden that focused on his incitements of violence against U.S. troops in his various public statements and also on the actions of his followers who had trained Somalis who had fought American soldiers in Mogadishu in 1993.

The CIA secretly began planning to "render" bin Laden and take him from Afghanistan to the United States, where he could be put on trial. A force of thirty Afghan tribal militia members with the ungainly code name of TRODPINT started monitoring bin Laden's movements and began planning a snatch operation.

Scheuer received a cable on May 5, 1998, asserting that the planning for the "rendition is going very well" and describing the plan as "detailed, thoughtful, realistic." The cable also made an important caveat, "Still the odds are iffy—as in any special ops raid of this type."

The plan was for the tribal militia to enter bin Laden's Tarnak Farms compound, kidnap al-Qaeda's leader, take him to a cave outside Kandahar, and hide him there for up to a month so that the American role in his kidnapping would not be immediately obvious. Bin Laden would then be taken across the Afghan border into Pakistan, where a C-130 would fly him to the United States.

The CIA modified a shipping container that could fit into the C-130 plane. Inside the container the agency placed a dentist's chair sized to fit a very tall man on which there were restraints that could be used to tie him down. A retired Special Forces medic was recruited to act as bin Laden's doctor on the plane should he be ill or if he had been wounded during his capture. The plan was that when the plane carrying bin Laden landed in the States, Coleman would enter the shipping container, where he would read bin Laden his rights.

CIA officials ran a final set of rehearsals, selecting June 23, 1998, as the date for the raid on bin Laden's compound. A lot of things had to go right for the plan to work. Bin Laden had three wives, so where did he sleep on any given night? He was also surrounded by scores of members of al-Qaeda, many of whom would be willing to fight to the death to save him.

An important skeptic about the CIA plan was Richard Clarke, who ran the Counterterrorism Security Group at the White House, which gave him considerable clout as a cabinet-level "principal" when the National Security Council convened to discuss any terrorism-related issue. Clarke grew up working-class in Boston, and by smarts and hard work graduated from MIT with a degree in management. A workaholic with the pallor of an official who spent a great deal of time at his desk, Clarke was a master of the arcane politics of the national security bureaucracy in Washington. If Clarke didn't like the plan, it wasn't likely to fly should it ever be presented to the National Security Council.

Clarke considered bin Laden to be a real threat to Americans, but he thought that the CIA operation had little chance of success. The "tribals" would have to climb over Tarnak Farms' ten-foot walls, find bin Laden, and then fight their way out of the compound, which was fortified with machine gun nests and was also full of women and children, a number of whom would surely be killed in any firefight. In Clarke's view the plan would probably fail, leaving a trail of dead bodies in its wake, including civilians.

The Covert Action Review Group, a group of senior officers at the CIA, reviewed the plan and gave it only a 30 percent chance of success. Scheuer disagreed and argued that the odds were higher, maybe 50/50.

George Tenet, the CIA director, was briefed about the operation and also about the misgivings of senior officials. Tenet decided to "turn off" the raid, and the plan was never presented to President Bill Clinton to make any final decision about whether to proceed with it.

On May 29, 1998, Alec Station received an order to stand down from the bin Laden raid, because "the risk of collateral damage was too high" and worries "about the lack of precision in the description of what the tribal assets might encounter in the way of armed resistance." Scheuer was apoplectic that the operation had been canceled. It would not be the last time that he would be disappointed.

Three days earlier bin Laden had abruptly disappeared from Tarnak Farms. He never resumed his semipermanent residence there, making him a much harder target from then on. The same day, bin Laden held the press conference with the group of Pakistani journalists where he declared war on the United States.

NINE

THE WAR BEGINS

War is waged by men; not beasts, or by gods.

—Frederic Manning, novelist-poet of World War I

A t 10:30 a.m. on August 7, 1998, a massive truck bomb blew up outside the U.S. embassy in Nairobi. "The lucky are blinded and the unlucky are dead," was how a federal prosecutor described the blast to a Manhattan jury that heard the case against the embassy bombers. The bomb obliterated the embassy, a five-story building next door to it, and wrecked a twenty-five-story bank building a little farther away, killing 213 people.

The American terrorism scholar Brian Michael Jenkins observed in 1975 that "terrorists want a lot of people watching, and not a lot of people dead." Jenkins meant that terrorists wanted to draw as much attention as possible to their cause, but typically they also wanted to avoid carrying out the kind of mass casualty attacks that might drive away their supporters or turn off fence-sitters. With the embassy attacks bin Laden made it clear that he was playing by a new set of rules: He wanted a lot of people dying and a lot of people watching. An al-Qaeda member had surveyed the embassy in Kenya five years before the bombing. He then reported back to bin Laden, specifically noting that the embassy sat at the intersection of two of the busiest streets in downtown Nairobi, a city of some two million people.

Bin Laden enthusiastically green-lighted the operation. Al-Qaeda members described his leadership method as "centralization of decision and decentralization of execution." Strategic targeting decisions were made by bin Laden, but the planning and execution of attacks were undertaken by his field commanders.

The bomb in Nairobi, a mix of TNT and aluminum nitrate, went off without warning in the middle of the morning on a workday. Al-Qaeda timed the bomb to explode on a Friday morning so that observant Muslims might be attending mosque, while non-Muslims would be at work. Around 10 percent of Kenyans are Muslims, so a number of the victims of the bombing were likely Muslim civilians. Of the 213 people who were killed in the blast, only twelve were Americans.

Nine minutes after the Kenya blast there was another explosion, outside another American embassy in Africa. This one, in Dar es Salaam, Tanzania, killed eleven people. None of them were Americans. Bin Laden's first mass casualty terrorist attacks killed 212 Africans and a dozen Americans. Strangely, the U.S. government didn't use the opportunity to publicly point out that while bin Laden was plotting to kill as many American civilians as possible, he was also willing to murder large numbers of African civilians as well.

The bombs at the embassies exploded on a day of great significance to bin Laden. August 7, 1998, was the eighth anniversary of President George H. W. Bush's order to deploy U.S. troops to Saudi Arabia to defend the country after Saddam Hussein's invasion of Kuwait, bin Laden's original casus belli against the United States.

Bin Laden met with his military commanders at a well-appointed guesthouse in Kabul to celebrate the attacks on the two embassies. Blowing up one American embassy was not an easy feat, but bombing two U.S. embassies almost simultaneously, thousands of miles from al-Qaeda's base in Afghanistan, was something that no terrorist group had ever pulled off before.

Now the whole world knew that bin Laden really was at war with the United States.

Abu Jandal, bin Laden's Yemeni bodyguard, was with his boss as they listened to the news coming in about the high number of casualties in Nairobi.

Abu Jandal asked bin Laden, "Did we need so many victims?"

Bin Laden laughed, saying, "We warned the whole world what would happen to the friends of America." Bin Laden was referring to the fatwas he had issued against the United States in 1996 and 1998.

He then asserted, "We weren't responsible for any victims from the moment we warned."

Abu Jandal had spent some time in Nairobi and he knew there was a sizable Muslim population there. He asked bin Laden, "What about the Muslims?"

Bin Laden replied, "We chose the moment well, because on a Friday at that hour all Muslims should be praying at the mosque."

In his own mind, bin Laden wasn't committing mass murder; rather, he was defending Islam, and if some civilians had to pay a price, so be it. Muslims needed to be defended, yet few others had the courage that he did to do so. Bin Laden also subscribed to a particularly extreme belief, that unless you were a fully committed, fundamentalist Muslim, you had no immunity from being killed in his holy war.

He espoused an ideology of "Binladenism" that claimed to explain the world completely. Such ideologies, whether they are secular like Marxism, or religious like Christianity, share the belief that history has a purpose and that at the End of History the world will be made perfect. Bin Laden believed that this would happen after the installation of Taliban-style regimes stretching across the Muslim world from Indonesia to Morocco. He saw a global conspiracy to destroy true Islam, led by the United States and its puppet allies in the Muslim world. If his utopia were ever to be achieved, he needed to do battle with these evildoers and even kill them. For bin Laden, the ends always justified the means.

Bin Laden was even prepared to sacrifice his own sons in the service of his holy war. Once, after he had given a lecture about "the joys of martyrdom" to a group of al-Qaeda fighters in Afghanistan, he gathered a group of his sons around him, telling them, "My sons, there is a paper on the wall of the mosque. This paper is for men who volunteer to be suicide bombers. Those who want to give their lives for Islam must add their names to the list." One of bin Laden's youngest sons bowed slightly toward his father and ran to the mosque.

The mood was grim at CIA headquarters following the attacks on the two embassies. Among the victims of the Nairobi bombing were two of their own, Molly Hardy, a fifty-one-year-old CIA accounting finance specialist who was a new grandmother, and Tom Shah, a thirty-eight-year-old agency officer who was in Kenya to meet with an Iraqi government source.

CIA director George Tenet held a meeting of senior officials in his conference room on the seventh floor of the agency.

He had a simple question: "Who did this?"

Michael Scheuer was sitting directly opposite Tenet and immediately replied: "This is al-Qaeda, no doubt about it." There was no evidence to prove this yet, but no one contradicted Scheuer. They all knew he was right.

Tenet went to visit Scheuer's team at Alec Station hoping to lift their spirits. The meeting did not go well. One of the women analysts who was close to Scheuer angrily confronted Tenet. "Mr. Director, I hope you know that if you had let us proceed with the plan to capture bin Laden some months ago the attacks on the embassies wouldn't have happened." Tenet blandly replied, "Everyone has a right to their opinion." Tenet agreed with the assessment of senior CIA officers that kidnapping bin Laden likely wasn't going to work given that he was usually surrounded by women and children and by al-Qaeda members willing to fight to the death.

The investigation of the two embassy bombings, known in FBI parlance as KENBOM and TANBOM, caught two lucky breaks that quickly pointed to al-Qaeda's role in the attacks. Mohamed Odeh, one of the plotters, left Kenya on a flight for Karachi, Pakistan, arriving there on August 7. He was detained at the airport because he was traveling on a poorly forged Yemeni passport, with an obviously mismatched picture showing a man with a beard; Odeh had shaved his off so that he would appear less religious. When Pakistani officials asked Odeh about the Nairobi bombing, he admitted he had been involved and started trying to persuade them it was the right thing to do for Islam. Odeh was arrested and sent back to Kenya on August 16, where he confessed his role to FBI agents.

Another of the bombers, Mohamed al-'Owhali, was arrested by Kenyan officials, who picked him up because he did not have proper identification papers. He was immediately handed over to FBI agents. 'Owhali confessed to his role in the bombing over the course of a week of interrogations. The arrests and confessions of Odeh and 'Owhali pointed definitively to al-Qaeda's role in the attacks on the embassies—acts of war against the United States—which American officials believed deserved military retaliation.

President Clinton was eager to respond. He was also in the midst of publicly acknowledging his affair with White House intern Monica Lewinsky. On his annual summer vacation in Martha's Vineyard, Clinton alternated between planning for strikes against al-Qaeda and apologizing to his wife, Hillary. The president was sleeping on the couch.

On August 19 the president was briefed by his advisers about options to hit purported al-Qaeda targets with cruise missiles. The targets in Afghanistan were al-Qaeda training camps. Based on electronic intercepts, officials believed that bin Laden would be visiting the camps the following day. They told Clinton he had to authorize launching the strikes on August 20 if he wanted to kill bin Laden. The officials also selected targets in Sudan including a tannery owned by bin Laden and a Sudanese factory purportedly linked to bin Laden that was supposedly producing the deadly nerve agent VX. Clinton took the tannery off the strike list as it seemed to be purely a civilian target. At 3 a.m. on August 20 he authorized the strikes on the other targets.

The same day Zawahiri spoke with the Pakistani journalist Rahimullah Yusufzai by satellite phone, delivering a statement on bin Laden's behalf. "Bin Laden calls on Muslims to continue jihad against Jews and Americans to liberate their holy places. In the meanwhile, he denies any involvement in the Nairobi and Dar es Salaam bombings."

On August 20 the White House press corps was at Martha's Vineyard expecting a quiet news day. With nothing much to report on, some of the journalists were watching the relatively new movie *Wag the Dog*. In the movie, the U.S. president concocts a fake war with the obscure country of Albania to distract the public's attention from an affair that he was having. Clinton knew he was likely going to take some criticism about his decision to launch the missile strikes, which would surely be compared to *Wag the Dog*, but he authorized the strikes anyway.

Clinton told the journalists at Martha's Vineyard that cruise missiles had been launched at targets associated with bin Laden in Afghanistan and Sudan. The president then flew back to Washington where he spoke from the Oval Office. "Our target was terror. Our mission was clear: to strike at the network of radical groups affiliated with and funded by Osama bin Laden, perhaps the preeminent organizer and financier of international terrorism in the world today."

Khaled Batarfi, bin Laden's childhood friend from Jeddah, was shocked, thinking, "That's our bin Laden? It's amazing someone you grew up with, he was just an ordinary man with some special merits, to then be the enemy number one of the greatest power in the world, it was like: Wow!"

Cruise missiles fired by U.S. Navy ships destroyed al-Qaeda's training camps near Khost in eastern Afghanistan, but bin Laden was elsewhere. He may have realized that an attack was in the offing when he heard the news that American diplomatic personnel from neighboring Pakistan were being evacuated in the days before the strike, and Westerners in Kabul were also being evacuated. Some have suggested that Pakistani officials may have tipped off bin Laden, but there is no evidence for this claim.

The most convincing explanation is that al-Qaeda's leader simply got lucky. The night before the strikes bin Laden had decided to visit the Khost camps, but when he and his entourage reached a crossroad on the journey, bin Laden asked, "Where do you think, my friends, should we go to Khost or Kabul?" Bin Laden's followers urged going on to Kabul to visit their comrades there.

Bin Laden said, "Good idea."

The U.S. missile strikes against the Khost camps occurred the next day, killing seven of bin Laden's followers, half a dozen Pakistanis, and twenty Afghans. The camps were simple affairs made of timber and mud and within two weeks of the strikes they were rebuilt.

Bin Laden now became much more careful about his personal security. In a safe house in Kabul he gave one of his bodyguards a pistol, telling him, "I want to be shot twice in the head rather than being taken prisoner. I must never be taken alive by the Americans. I want to die a martyr and above all never end up in prison." Bin Laden often told his bodyguards, "Martyrdom rather than captivity."

The attacks on the Afghan training camps achieved little, while the strikes on the purported chemical weapons plant in Sudan that was supposedly tied to bin Laden were a debacle. The plant was flattened, but no evidence ever emerged that it was doing anything other than providing half of Sudan's legitimate pharmaceuticals.

The unsuccessful strikes against bin Laden had the unintended consequence of turning him into a global celebrity. The ultra-religious, shy teenager who had been a marginal figure in his own family was now one of the world's most famous men, reviled and celebrated in equal measure. A couple of weeks after the strikes, two instant biographies about bin Laden went on sale in bookshops in Pakistan's capital, Islamabad. Osama also became a common name for sons in Pakistan.

The missile strikes also deeply angered Mullah Omar. The Commander of the Faithful was furious about this violation of Afghan sovereignty, telling a journalist, "It is not only an attack against Osama bin Laden, it is also an attack against the entire people of Afghanistan." Mullah Omar added, "We will never hand him over to anyone and will protect him with our blood."

Bin Laden had anticipated this reaction, as he had lived much of his adult life among the Pashtuns of northwest Pakistan and Afghanistan. The Taliban were overwhelmingly made up of Pashtuns who subscribed to the tribal code of *Pashtunwali*, which is a much older tradition than

Islam. *Pashtunwali* puts a great premium on *malmastiya*, which is the obligation to show hospitality to all visitors, and on *nanawati*, the offering of asylum, which entails being prepared to fight to the death for the person who has taken refuge with you. Mullah Omar's tribal code made it very difficult for him to hand over bin Laden to anyone.

Two days after the strikes, Mullah Omar took the unprecedented step of calling the U.S. State Department himself. He complained about the attacks and gratuitously advised that President Clinton should resign given his current political difficulties over the Lewinsky affair. Mullah Omar also said that he was unaware of any evidence that bin Laden was involved in terrorism.

Three weeks later Taliban official Abdul Hakim Mujahid and the deputy chief of mission at the U.S. embassy in Pakistan met to discuss bin Laden. Mujahid said that Mullah Omar was the key supporter of his continued presence in Afghanistan, while 80 percent of Taliban leaders opposed it. This was the first time that a Taliban official had told a U.S. government representative that the Taliban were, in fact, quite split about what to do about bin Laden. Mujahid said that the Taliban had also once again warned bin Laden not to engage in political activities or to give interviews and they had taken away all his "instruments of communication."

After the strikes on the training camps, I faxed a letter to a man in Afghanistan whom I believed to be a media adviser to bin Laden, asking him for another CNN interview with al-Qaeda's leader. I later learned that the man was, in fact, al-Qaeda's military commander, Abu Hafs the Egyptian. We exchanged faxes and phone calls between the Kabul central post office where Abu Hafs was located and hotels in Pakistan where I was staying. On September 12, 1998, Abu Hafs called me suggesting we meet at the Intercontinental Hotel in Kabul. He also offered up footage of the aftermath of the U.S. cruise missile strikes on al-Qaeda's camps three weeks earlier. Four days later, I received another call from Abu Hafs saying that it was "difficult now" for bin Laden to do another interview with CNN. For the moment, bin Laden was heeding Mullah Omar's pleas to stop his media interviews.

Prince Turki, the head of Saudi intelligence, went back again to Afghanistan on September 19, 1998, and found that Mullah Omar had reversed his decision to hand over al-Qaeda's leader. The Taliban leader was also abusive about the Saudi monarchy, saying that despite all their wealth the Saudis were too weak to defend themselves and were relying on the infidel Americans. Prince Turki was deeply irritated and broke off negotiations. As he was leaving, Prince Turki told Mullah Omar, "One day you will regret this decision and the unfortunate Afghan people will pay the price." Within days the Saudi government, one of only three governments that had recognized the Taliban, cut off diplomatic relations with them.

Despite the fact that he was publicly defending bin Laden, privately Mullah Omar was furious at al-Qaeda's leader. After all, Mullah Omar felt that he was the Commander of the Faithful. Now bin Laden was conducting what amounted to his own foreign policy. So Mullah Omar informed bin Laden he would be visiting him at home, which he had never done before. A dozen black Land Cruisers pulled into bin Laden's compound and out stepped the Commander of the Faithful.

Mullah Omar got to the point quickly, telling bin Laden, "It is best if you leave Afghanistan."

Bin Laden knew that there were very few good options where he could rebase al-Qaeda if he and his men were forced out of Afghanistan. He pleaded, "Sheikh, I spent many years in Afghanistan since I was a young man, fighting for your people. Now we are this large group numbering many hundreds of people. How can we move such a large group?"

Mullah Omar repeated, "The time has come for you and your fighters to leave."

Bin Laden parried, "The Sudanese government allowed me to live there five years. Would you offer me the same courtesy. Will you allow me to stay in Afghanistan for another year and a half?"

Shedding tears, bin Laden then made his best argument. "Sheikh, if you give in to the pressure of infidel governments, your decision will be against Islam."

Mullah Omar hesitated. The Commander of the Faithful could never do something un-Islamic. He told bin Laden that he could stay for another year and a half. It was a fateful decision that would eventually lead to the destruction of Mullah Omar's regime.

Bin Laden had laid on a feast for the Taliban leader and his large entourage. Out came servers bearing whole sheep on platters surrounded by rice, but Mullah Omar abruptly said he wasn't hungry and left. It was a grave insult in Pashtun culture to refuse an offer of hospitality, but bin Laden ignored the slight. He was at the mercy of Mullah Omar and had just been granted an eighteen-month reprieve to think through where he might go next.

Seeking to ingratiate himself, bin Laden made a groveling *bayat* (oath of loyalty) to Mullah Omar as his "Commander of the Faithful." The text of this oath was published in a pro-Taliban outlet in Pakistan on September 15, 1998.

In the months after the attacks on the embassies, al-Qaeda, which relied on donations from sympathizers in the Gulf, Pakistan, and Europe that were funneled to the organization by recruits traveling to Afghanistan, started to run out of money. Bin Laden had been paying each al-Qaeda family $200 a month; he cut the allowance to $50. Wheat was now the only food on the menu for members of al-Qaeda, although some of bin Laden's followers hunted for rabbits to supplement their meager diet. The dire financial situation eased somewhat when bin Laden's son Saad went back to Sudan to marry and sold some of bin Laden's business interests there. He traveled there on a Yemeni passport and smuggled back the proceeds when he returned. While he was living in Afghanistan, bin Laden seems to have recovered around $2 million from the investments that he had made in Sudan.

The Saudis made one more effort to persuade bin Laden to stop his campaign against the United States and the Saudi royal family, sending his beloved mother, Allia, and his stepfather to Afghanistan to see if they might cajole him to abandon his life of militancy. Allia brought some chocolates, a treat that bin Laden's younger children had never seen before, and bin Laden seemed happier than he had been in years. His mother said King Fahd would forgive all if he would return to Saudi Arabia. Bin Laden said he couldn't accept the offer: "This is a principle. I keep it in my heart and I have promised God not to abandon it." In any case, bin Laden didn't believe the assurances of the Saudi government that he wouldn't be thrown in prison or, worse, handed over to the Americans.

Despite his promises to Mullah Omar about keeping a low profile, bin Laden enjoyed the limelight too much to remain silent for long. His rise to global prominence coincided with the rise of the first independent Arab TV news network, Al Jazeera, which started broadcasting in 1996. Bin Laden knew that appearing on Al Jazeera would put him in front of audiences across the Middle East.

Jamal Ismail had started in journalism working for the bin Laden–funded *Jihad* magazine in Peshawar during the mid-1980s and was now Al Jazeera's bureau chief in Pakistan. Al-Qaeda leaders contacted Ismail, who interviewed bin Laden in Afghanistan in December 1998. Seven months later the interview aired as part of an Al Jazeera documentary about bin Laden that received considerable attention in the Arabic-speaking world. In the documentary bin Laden renewed his calls for attacks on the American targets and came close to taking credit for the bombings of the U.S. embassies in Africa, explaining that the Nairobi embassy was the site of a key CIA station.

The following month the Syrian jihadist Abu Musab al-Suri, who had known bin Laden for the past decade and had arranged bin Laden's CNN interview a year and a half earlier, had a change of heart about helping raise bin Laden's profile. He saw the considerable unwanted international pressure the interviews were imposing on the Taliban and sent a memo imploring al-Qaeda's leader to heed Mullah Omar's demands. Suri pointed out that bin Laden was also endangering the other Arabs living in exile in Afghanistan, asking, "What right have you got to destroy our and others' homes?"

But nothing changed and the situation got worse for Mullah Omar. The Saudis had already withdrawn their diplomatic recognition, and in

October 1999 the United Nations threatened to impose sanctions on the Taliban unless they expelled bin Laden. Mullah Omar hoped that bin Laden might just leave Afghanistan of his own free will. At one point in early 1999 Taliban officials even told reporters that bin Laden had "disappeared." This was a case of wishful thinking; bin Laden had absolutely no intention of leaving Afghanistan voluntarily.

Mullah Omar sought independent religious advice about the bin Laden issue from the Ulema (Clergy) Union of Afghanistan. The clerics issued a statement on November 1, 1999, backing bin Laden, saying, "We think that if Osama was surrendered, the Americans would then demand that we do away with the veiling of Afghan women. . . . Surrendering Osama bin Laden is not permitted legally or politically. This act must not be carried out because it would be like declaring war on God." The Commander of the Faithful was never going to declare a war on God.

Still, the possibility of being forced into exile again never left bin Laden's mind during the period between when he had arrived in Afghanistan in 1996, right up to the 9/11 attacks, so he began working on a backup plan. It was centered on Yemen, his family's ancestral home. He started to look for a new wife there after his second wife, Khadijah, divorced him when they were living in Sudan in 1993. He believed that Yemen might prove to be a suitable refuge if he were ever forced out of Afghanistan; marrying a Yemeni wife would give him a safe harbor with her tribe.

According to the eventual matchmaker, a Yemeni cleric close to bin Laden, bin Laden's wife had to be religious and young enough not to feel jealous of bin Laden's other wives. "Young" was understood to mean someone in her teens. The cleric told bin Laden that he had someone in mind to whom he had given religious instruction; she was very pious. Her name was Amal al-Sadah and she was just sixteen.

Bin Laden sent an emissary to speak to Amal's family in her home in Ibb, a small Yemeni city. At first the marriage proposal was framed as coming from a Yemeni businessman, but as the marriage discussions continued the emissary said that the suitor was in fact Osama bin Laden. This didn't elicit much of a reaction as bin Laden wasn't yet a household name.

The family agreed to the marriage because they understood bin Laden to be a good Muslim and a man of means, but they didn't know much more about him.

Amal, a happy, smiling teenager of scant education, consented to the union and bin Laden dispatched one of his bodyguards from Afghanistan with a $5,000 dowry for her. The bodyguard returned with Amal to Kandahar, where she married bin Laden in 2000. By then Amal understood exactly who bin Laden was. When Amal's father visited her in Afghanistan she told him that she wanted to die a martyr's death at bin Laden's side.

Bin Laden's three older wives, Najwa, aged forty-one, Siham, aged forty-three, and Umm Hamza, aged fifty-one, didn't disguise their anger at their husband for marrying someone who was more than two and a half decades younger than him. They had all been led to believe that Amal was an older woman who knew the Koran by heart.

After the attacks on the two U.S. embassies in Africa, CIA officials ramped up their efforts to capture or kill bin Laden, but first they needed authorization to do so from President Clinton. Following the mid-1970s Church Committee congressional investigations into the CIA's assassination program during previous decades, the agency had been forbidden to assassinate enemies of the United States. The law, known as Executive Order 12333, was crystal clear, stating, "No person employed by or acting on behalf of the United States Government shall engage in, or conspire to engage in, assassination."

On Christmas Eve 1998 the Clinton White House produced a highly classified Memorandum of Notification that overrode Executive Order 12333 and authorized the CIA to capture or kill bin Laden. The White House believed it was authorizing the assassination of bin Laden, but the CIA heard something quite different: It heard that bin Laden could be killed only if a capture operation wasn't feasible. But who would make this determination? The Afghan tribal assets hunting bin Laden? Their CIA handlers?

Scheuer felt that his team never received an authorization to kill bin

Laden. This was also the view of Cofer Black, who ran the CIA's Counter-terrorist Center and whom bin Laden's men had marked for assassination back when he was the CIA station chief in Sudan. Black said, "If they wanted us to do that, then they should write it down in a Memorandum of Notification. You know how hard that would be? It would be one line: 'Kill Osama bin Laden. Period. By the President of the United States.'" The CIA's understanding of the White House memorandum was communicated to the Afghan tribal militia, who were told that they were authorized to use lethal force only during the course of a snatch operation.*

Meanwhile, the tribal militia kept supplying leads to the CIA about bin Laden, but the leads often didn't pan out. CIA director George Tenet concluded that the agency needed to think about developing other approaches. He sent a memo to CIA leaders in December, writing, "We must redouble our efforts against Bin Ladin himself, his infrastructure, followers, finances etc. with a sense of enormous urgency. We are at war." The memo urged more work with "liaison services" in other countries who could help track down bin Laden and urged that spy satellites make finding bin Laden "our top priority."

Senior Clinton administration officials never ordered up a formal National Intelligence Estimate about the threat posed by bin Laden and al-Qaeda, which would have involved input from all of the more than a dozen U.S. intelligence agencies. Some U.S. officials, such as Bennett, Clarke, Scheuer, and Tenet, were focused on the bin Laden threat, but a formal government-wide assessment of that threat was never produced or disseminated to policymakers and congressional leaders. If it had been, more senior officials across the U.S. government might have made bin

---

*The memorandum has never been publicly released, so it's hard to ascertain if CIA officials were right to feel that the authorization was ambiguous. The staff director of the 9/11 Commission, the historian Philip Zelikow, and another commission staffer were both allowed to read the memorandum, and they believed it unambiguously instructed that the CIA could kill bin Laden. The CIA's inspector general report on the 9/11 attacks found that CIA officers felt they could kill bin Laden only during a "credible capture operation."

Laden and his followers a priority. Even worse, top officials at agencies and departments such as the FBI and the Pentagon were not aware of the CIA director's call to go on a war footing. So the burden largely fell on the agency: the number of CIA officials working at Alec Station on the bin Laden threat increased to around forty, but this was still not enough for what they believed was an overwhelming workload.

On December 20, 1998, the CIA was tipped off that bin Laden was back in Kandahar and was staying at an al-Qaeda guesthouse. This triggered a debate about whether to fire a cruise missile at bin Laden while he was sleeping. Doubts about the quality of the intelligence and worries about "collateral damage" to civilians and the risks of hitting a nearby mosque all combined to prevent the missile strike from receiving a green light. Pentagon officials estimated that as many as six hundred people might have died in the attack.

On December 21 Scheuer sent an email to another CIA officer saying that he hadn't been able to sleep, writing, "I'm sure we'll regret not acting last night." Scheuer pointed out that this was the third time that the CIA had bin Laden in its sights, and White House officials had "balked each time at doing the job." Scheuer scoffed that those officials had even worried that "some stray piece of shrapnel might hit" a mosque in Kandahar and "'offend' Muslims."

Two months later one of the best potential opportunities to kill bin Laden presented itself. Some Arab princes have a passion for hunting houbara bustards with falcons; the bustard's stringy meat is purported to have aphrodisiac powers. The birds had been hunted to near-extinction in the Gulf, but they remained plentiful in Taliban-controlled Afghanistan. During early February 1999 bin Laden was reported to be visiting a remote bustard-hunting camp in southwestern Afghanistan, turning up for dinner occasionally over the course of a week.

For a cruise missile strike to kill bin Laden it was not good enough to know where he was; you had to know where he would be many hours in the future. The intelligence about bin Laden's whereabouts needed to be passed up the chain to White House officials, who would make the decision whether or not to take the shot. The order to launch the strike then had to be communicated to a U.S. Navy ship in the Arabian Sea, which would launch its cruise missiles. The missiles would then have to fly for a couple of hours to their targets. The whole process could take six hours or more.

Bin Laden's visits to the desert hunting camp seemed to be a real opportunity to take a shot at him as he was going back and forth to the camp over several days. The bustard hunters were not roughing it in the desert; they had brought a tractor-trailer with an enormous air-conditioning system and a tall mast for communications back home. At the camp the CIA had an asset who was able to inform agency officials when bin Laden was coming for dinner. CIA officials told the White House that a chance to mount a strike would present itself on February 11, but nothing happened, despite the fact that the encampment was in the middle of the desert, so there would be a lower risk of collateral damage.

What gave White House officials pause was satellite imagery of an Emirati military C-130 aircraft near the hunting camp; this wasn't just a bunch of Gulfie good ol' boys, but very likely members of the Emirati royal family. Clinton's top counterterrorism official, Richard Clarke, wasn't going to sign off on a strike that would likely incinerate a number of Emirati princes when it wasn't clear that bin Laden was among them. Scheuer fumed about another missed opportunity.*

In Kandahar between May 13 and May 19 bin Laden was seen at a location where the tribal assets could try to capture him or cruise missiles could be launched at him. But this intelligence came only days after

---

*Gary Schroen, the CIA station chief in Pakistan at the time, says of the hunting encampment: "I'm sure we would have gotten bin Laden. Our guys were positive that he was there. Years later, I was at home in Reno and the phone rang, and an American was on the line and he said, 'You don't know me but I was the master falcon handler for that camp in the desert. I want to tell you that not only was bin Laden there, and Zawahiri. The reason they were there was they were invited by those guys, the young Arabs, and they were pledging *bayat* or loyalty to bin Laden and they were giving him cash donations. So you should have taken the shot.'"

a spectacular U.S. intelligence failure: During the course of the American air war over Kosovo, the U.S. had mistakenly bombed the Chinese embassy in Belgrade. Policymakers were understandably leery of authorizing another strike where the intelligence was iffy and there were significant concerns about collateral damage.

Scheuer was apoplectic, writing to a colleague that the Clinton administration had "passed up half a dozen good to excellent chances" to capture or kill bin Laden. He wondered at "their stark fear of attacking a terrorist bent on killing as many Americans as possible." Scheuer also wrote a memo to every senior official he could think of at the CIA telling them that when Americans found out that they had not pushed to kill bin Laden, they would have blood on their hands.

Two weeks later Scheuer was called to a meeting with a senior CIA official, who told him he was being relieved because he was burned out, adding, "But don't worry, you're gonna get a cash award and a medal."

Scheuer told his boss, "If you try to give me a medal and money, they will be back on your desk; if I don't shove them up your ass."

Scheuer's zeal led to his demotion; he was given a make-work job in the CIA library. But Scheuer put his time in the library to good use, quietly working on a lengthy report about bin Laden that would prove quite useful immediately after the 9/11 attacks, when so many officials in the U.S. government suddenly needed to understand him and his organization.

It was only the good instincts of an American customs agent that prevented one of bin Laden's followers from detonating a bomb at Los Angeles Airport (LAX) in the middle of the busy 1999 Christmas holiday season. If the plot had succeeded it would have been the first terrorist attack by al-Qaeda in the United States. Ahmed Ressam, a thirty-two-year-old Algerian, was arrested in Port Angeles, Washington, as he arrived by ferry from Canada on December 14. When Ressam's car rolled off the ferry, U.S. customs inspector Diana Dean thought something about Ressam seemed off. He was taking a long, convoluted route from Canada to the city that he called "Sattle." Was he smuggling drugs? Dean noticed

Ressam's hands were shaking and he was sweating, despite the December chill. In Ressam's car the agents found 130 pounds of explosives, and a search of his apartment in Montreal turned up a map of California with circles around LAX.

Ressam's arrest contributed to an atmosphere of growing alarm in the Clinton administration about possible attacks around the world by al-Qaeda. On December 16, CIA director George Tenet was briefed that "UBL [bin Laden] has planned multiple attacks." National Security Advisor Sandy Berger convened meetings at the White House with top officials every day for a month to ensure that all was being done to prevent bin Laden's followers from striking again.

At the CIA's Counterterrorist Center, Gina Bennett and her colleagues were working around the clock now to piece together the dots of intelligence that could help explain what bin Laden's men were up to. The center, which was in a vault on the ground floor of CIA headquarters, was not a lovely place to work; it smelled like burnt coffee and stale wet pizza with a little bit of body odor and some mouse poop mixed in. In the pre-digital-tools age Bennett—who had joined the CIA three years earlier—drew massive charts on the walls. There was real concern that some of the celebrations of the new millennium were going to turn into bloodbaths. CIA officials were pressing hard to try to disrupt whatever plots were out there.

A group of terrorists in Jordan with ties to bin Laden planned to bomb a Radisson hotel and kill American tourists visiting sites associated with St. John the Baptist on New Year's Eve 1999. The militants were arrested three weeks before they could carry out these attacks. The CIA determined in a Top Secret memorandum that the plot was coordinated by "senior Bin Ladin lieutenant" Abu Zubaydah.

More successful for a group of Pakistani terrorists was the hijacking on December 24 of an Indian Airlines flight. The plane with more than 150 passengers on board was flown to Kandahar, where bin Laden played a key behind-the-scenes role in urging the hijackers to cut the best deal possible for themselves. The Indians eventually agreed to release three militants imprisoned in India, one of whom, Omar Sheikh, would go on to orchestrate the kidnapping and murder of *Wall Street Journal* reporter Daniel Pearl in Pakistan in the months after 9/11. Bin Laden prepared a great feast for the released militants, slaughtering many sheep in their honor.

Unbeknownst at the time to U.S. officials, on January 3, 2000, al-Qaeda also tried to blow up the USS *The Sullivans*, an American warship harbored in Aden, Yemen. That effort failed, but the attackers stayed in Yemen, biding their time for the next target that presented itself.

As their alarm about bin Laden grew, U.S. officials also pursued a diplomatic track to put pressure on the Taliban to expel al-Qaeda's leader or, at a minimum, to get him to cease his terrorist plotting. In January 2000 the counterterrorism coordinator at the State Department, Ambassador Michael Sheehan, a former Special Forces officer who rarely minced words, spoke on the phone to the Taliban foreign minister, Wakil Muttawakil. Sheehan read the foreign minister an unambiguous statement: "We will hold the Taliban leadership responsible for any attacks against U.S. interests by al-Qaeda or any of its affiliated groups."

Muttawakil—who privately was one of bin Laden's most bitter critics—responded using standard Taliban talking points: "We have bin Laden under control. He's not going to do anything else."

Muttawakil also said that bin Laden was a guest of Afghanistan and therefore could not be expelled. He offered that the Taliban could try bin Laden under sharia law if the United States would only provide the evidence that he was behind the embassy bombings in Africa. Sheehan countered that a U.S. court had clearly proven this point already and bin Laden was still plotting additional terrorist attacks.

Sheehan told the Taliban foreign minister a story to illustrate the American position: "If we're neighbors on a block, and you have bin Laden in your basement, and at night he's coming out and setting fire to the other houses on the block and then going back into your basement, you are accountable now, because you are harboring that guy." Sheehan added emphatically, "*We hold you fully accountable* if there is another attack against the U.S."

Khaled Batarfi, bin Laden's childhood friend, points to where they played soccer together, Jeddah, Saudi Arabia.

Courtesy of Peter Bergen.

Jamal Khalifa, bin Laden's best friend at university and brother-in-law, Jeddah, Saudi Arabia.

Credit: Peter Bergen.

Bin Laden family on vacation in Falun, Sweden, 1971.

Credit: Dalmas/Scanpix/Sipa.

Abdullah Azzam, bin Laden's mentor in the 1980s, on the cover of *Jihad* magazine. *Courtesy of Peter Bergen.*

Gina Bennett, the first U.S. government official to warn of bin Laden in a classified memo circulated in 1993. *Copyright Notice: © Center for Creative Photography, Arizona Board of Regents Collection. Credit: Center for Creative Photography, The University of Arizona: David Hume Kennerly Archive.*

Child soldiers in Kabul during the Afghan civil war in 1993. The Taliban emerged out of that war. *Credit: Peter Bergen.*

Bin Laden in the Tora Bora
mountains, Afghanistan, 1996.
US Attorney's Office,
Southern District of New York.

Bin Laden in his cave-house study
in Tora Bora, Afghanistan, 1996.
US Attorney's Office,
Southern District of New York.

Peter Arnett, bin Laden, Peter Bergen, and Peter Jouvenal during bin Laden's
CNN interview, March 22, 1997, in Afghanistan. *Courtesy of Peter Bergen.*

Bin Laden at his first and only press conference in Afghanistan, May 26, 1998. On the right is Abu Hafs the Egyptian, al-Qaeda's military commander. On the left is Ayman al-Zawahiri. *Courtesy of Peter Bergen.*

Bin Laden at a 1998 press conference. On the left is journalist Ismail Khan. On the right is journalist Rahimullah Yusufzai. *Courtesy of Peter Bergen.*

The 9/11 attacks so affected Afghanistan that they became a key image on Afghan carpets. *Credit: Peter Bergen.*

Mary Galligan ran the investigation of the 9/11 attacks with FBI director Robert Mueller. *Courtesy of Mary Galligan.*

A cave in Tora Bora, Afghanistan. *Credit: Peter Bergen.*

Model of the Abbottabad compound by the National Geospatial-Intelligence Agency.
Credit: NGA.

Abbottabad compound model showing the animal pen area where a U.S. Black Hawk made a "hard landing" during the bin Laden raid.
Credit: NGA.

Abbottabad compound, with cows in the animal pen area.

Bin Laden at his Abbottabad compound, watching television.

The squalid interior of the Abbottabad compound.

Greenhouse at the Abbottabad compound.

Bin Laden taping a video,
flubbing a line and laughing.

Bin Laden shortly before
he was killed.

President Barack Obama and his war cabinet watching a drone feed of the bin
Laden raid on May 1, 2011. *White House photo by Pete Souza.*

•   •   •

In Afghanistan in late 1998 Abd al-Rahim al-Nashiri proposed a plan to bin Laden to attack an American warship, which he approved. They decided to focus on Yemen. But Nashiri had difficulty finding U.S. Navy ships to attack on the west coast of the country, so bin Laden instructed him to look for suitable targets in the southern port of Aden.

In keeping with his strategic role, bin Laden recorded a video in which he wore the distinctive, ornate, curved jambiya dagger that is worn by Yemeni men. He had never previously worn this dagger but it was his way of subtly claiming credit for an al-Qaeda attack in Yemen he knew was approaching.

On the sweltering morning of October 12, 2000, two al-Qaeda suicide bombers drove to a beach in Aden where they unloaded a boat packed with some six hundred pounds of explosives. They knew they had only a brief window of time to pull off their mission, as the USS *Cole* would take just a few hours to refuel in Aden.

They pushed off to sea for the fifteen-minute trip to where the *Cole* was berthed. The bombers pulled their small skiff alongside the destroyer. They waved at sailors on the deck of the warship before detonating the charge that would, they believed, send them instantly to Paradise, where they would be attended to by seventy-two virgins. The blast from the bomb blew a hole the size of a house in the reinforced steel hull of the *Cole*, killing seventeen American sailors and inflicting a quarter-billion dollars of damage to the ship.

In Afghanistan when bin Laden heard the news of the *Cole* bombing, he fell to his knees thanking God for the attack. He believed that the Americans would now finally get the message to leave the Arabian Peninsula.

The *Cole* investigation got off to an inauspicious start. Barbara Bodine, the U.S. ambassador to Yemen, wanted the FBI to maintain a small footprint and constantly fretted that the FBI agents on the ground in Yemen were offending Yemeni officials. Relations between Bodine and the lead FBI official in Yemen, John O'Neill, became so tense that she banned him from the country after only two months.

O'Neill was replaced by Mary Galligan as the FBI's on-scene commander for the *Cole* investigation. Two years earlier Galligan had been
on the ground in Tanzania investigating al-Qaeda's attack on the embassy.
As she drove to her hotel in the Yemeni capital, Sanaa, Galligan saw signs
for the Binladin Group construction company everywhere. Arabic graffiti
saying "Death to America! Death to the Jews!" was also ubiquitous. It was
quickly clear to Galligan and her small team of investigators that the *Cole*
attacks were not carried out by some local Yemeni militant group, but
by al-Qaeda. As she received increasingly dire warnings about al-Qaeda's
plans to attack her team, Galligan realized that this was the most hostile
environment in which the FBI had ever worked. Galligan pulled her investigators out of Yemen on June 16, 2001.

Bin Laden certainly expected some kind of American retaliation for
the *Cole* attack. Just days before the bombers struck the *Cole*, he gave a
lecture to his followers telling them there was a strong possibility that
the U.S. would strike soon against al-Qaeda targets. He started moving
unpredictably between half a dozen residences in Kandahar and ordered
the evacuation of the large al-Qaeda compound outside the city. But the
retaliatory attacks never came, despite the fact that blowing up a U.S. warship was a clear act of war.

The Clinton administration, which was about to complete its second
term in office, did nothing to respond to the *Cole* attack. After another
inconclusive meeting at the White House about how to respond to the
bombing, the counterterrorism coordinator at the State Department, Michael Sheehan, exclaimed to his close friend Richard Clarke, "Who the
shit do they think attacked the *Cole*? Fucking Martians? The Pentagon
brass won't let Delta [Special Operations Forces] go get bin Laden. Hell,
they won't even let the Air Force carpet bomb the place. Does al-Qaeda
have to attack the Pentagon to get their attention?"

The incoming George W. Bush administration also did nothing to
respond to the *Cole* bombing. For bin Laden the United States' lack of
response to the *Cole* attack confirmed his view that the Americans were

weak, just like the Soviets. It seemed that he could continue to attack U.S. targets with impunity.

A month after the *Cole* bombing, Ahmad Zaidan, Al Jazeera's bureau chief in Pakistan, received a summons to speak to al-Qaeda's leader in Afghanistan. It was not an interview per se; bin Laden was now careful to observe the letter, if not the spirit, of his agreement with Mullah Omar to stop talking to the media. But it was a chance for bin Laden to take some ownership of the *Cole* bombing with a reporter from the most important Arabic-language TV network. Bin Laden made sure that his military commander, Abu Hafs, told Zaidan privately that al-Qaeda was behind the *Cole* attack.

On January 26, 2001, Zaidan received another invitation to meet with bin Laden in Kandahar. Again bin Laden wanted to take credit for the *Cole* bombing, but he wanted to do so in such a way that he wouldn't be accused of doing an interview. One of bin Laden's media advisers had sent al-Qaeda's leader a long memo months earlier that included this suggestion: Bin Laden should exploit the wedding parties of al-Qaeda members for political purposes by giving "well prepared speeches" and "reading poetry," which would be videotaped and distributed. Those speeches would be all about his mission and achievements, and not about the nuptials. Bin Laden thought this was a good idea. He invited Al Jazeera's Zaidan to cover the wedding party of his son Mohammed to Abu Hafs's daughter.

Bin Laden was very happy at the wedding. He presided over the proceedings while sitting in front of a giant Arabic-language map of the world, which was thirty feet in width and eighteen feet high. The map was intended to signal that bin Laden was now a world leader. Adding to bin Laden's happiness, his mother, Allia, had flown in from Saudi Arabia for the wedding, accompanied by one of his half-brothers, Hassan.

In celebration of the nuptials bin Laden recited a poem in front of the more than four hundred guests. The poem did not celebrate the wedding as much as take credit for the *Cole* attack while two cameras were rolling manned by al-Qaeda's cameramen.

Bin Laden declaimed:

A destroyer: even the brave fear its might.
It inspires horror in the harbor and in the open sea.
She sails into the waves
Flanked by arrogance, haughtiness and false power.
To her doom she moves slowly
A dinghy awaits her, riding the waves.

The wedding guests cheered on bin Laden as he recited his poem, shouting, "*Allah Akbar!* God is great!"

After the wedding party was finished, bin Laden told Zaidan, "Okay, come with me."

Zaidan followed bin Laden into his house, where al-Qaeda's leader told him that he didn't like the way he had recited the poem. "I'm going to deliver it again."

So bin Laden repeated his rendition of the poem, which al-Qaeda's cameramen once again filmed.

Then bin Laden changed his mind, preferring his first rendition of the poem, telling Zaidan, "No, no. The first one was better."

Bin Laden never missed a chance to micromanage his media appearances.

President Clinton was irritated by the limited military options that were available to him to take out bin Laden. The president told his chairman of the Joint Chiefs, General Hugh Shelton, "You know, it would scare the shit out of al-Qaeda if suddenly a bunch of black ninjas rappelled out of helicopters into the middle of their camp." Yet Clinton's generals were reluctant to put "boots on the ground" to hunt bin Laden. First, there was no declaration of war against the Taliban. Second, they saw terrorism as a crime and found it convenient to assume that it was the CIA's job to take on al-Qaeda. The memories of the Black Hawk Down fiasco in Somalia in 1993, in which eighteen American soldiers were killed, were still fresh, so there was considerable risk-aversion at the Pentagon when it came to launching military operations in distant, obscure countries. The Pentagon also demanded high-quality "actionable intelligence" before green-lighting any such operation, which was not easy to secure in Taliban-controlled Afghanistan. The general in charge of Special Operations, Peter Schoomaker, later lamented, "Special Operations were never given the mission. It was very, very frustrating. It was like having a brand-new Ferrari in the garage and nobody wants to race it because you might dent the fender."

In addition to the diplomatic track and the efforts by the Afghan tribal assets to capture or kill bin Laden, Clarke and Sheehan were intrigued by the possibilities of a new tool to hunt al-Qaeda's leader: the Predator drone. For the first time, they had the means to secure real-time intelligence about bin Laden's whereabouts. So they pushed the Air Force and CIA to fly more drones to hunt for bin Laden. Sheehan recalled, "They had more Predators flying around in the Balkans than they had over Afghanistan at that time, which really frustrated me because I was working on both programs and, quite frankly, I thought bin Laden was a much higher priority." The first Predator drone flew over Afghanistan on September 7, 2000. These drones were not armed as yet, but they could linger over potential bin Laden locations for hours.

On the seventh Predator mission over Afghanistan, on September 27, 2000, a drone circling high over Tarnak Farms beamed back images of a tall, white-robed man surrounded by smaller, darker figures who were showing him signs of respect. The Taliban spotted the drone and unsuccessfully scrambled a MiG-21 jet to intercept it. The drone images were greeted with elation by White House officials, who were certain that the tall, white-robed man was bin Laden.

The next step was to arm the drone so it could function as a remote-controlled assassin. No longer would the U.S. have to go through the elaborate and lengthy process of ordering up a cruise missile attack on a suspected bin Laden location. Now the decision to take a shot at bin Laden could be reduced to a fraction of the time. Clarke pounded on the

CIA and Air Force to quickly develop the armed Predator. Hellfire missiles were attached to the drones, but the big question was: Would these missiles themselves simply knock the drone out of the sky when they were fired?

At a desert range at the Naval Air Weapons Station in China Lake, California, the CIA built a crude replica of bin Laden's house at Tarnak Farms. In early June 2001 a Predator drone equipped with a Hellfire missile was fired at the house and successfully destroyed much of its interior. National Security Council official Roger Cressey saw a video of the test and thought, "I can't believe anybody would have survived that." Still, the CIA and Air Force moved slowly to get the armed Predators flying over Afghanistan, wrangling over who would pay for them, particularly if one of the $3 million drones were to crash or was shot down.

During the summer of 2001 bin Laden was plotting what he hoped would be his two greatest victories. Advancing quickly were the plans for the attacks on the U.S. Capitol, the Pentagon, and the World Trade Center. The second plot was to eliminate Ahmad Shah Massoud, the leader of the anti-Taliban forces known as the Northern Alliance. Without Massoud, what remained of the resistance to the Taliban in Afghanistan would collapse. But this was not bin Laden's primary motive for plotting to kill him. If he could get rid of Massoud, the Taliban would have reason to owe bin Laden a favor, and he was soon going to need one. Massoud's assassination would give the Taliban an important gift to compensate them for what bin Laden knew was coming: the spectacular attacks in New York and Washington that surely would pose significant problems for his Taliban hosts.

Bin Laden asked some of his followers: "Who will take it upon himself to deal with Ahmad Shah Massoud for me, because he harmed Allah and His sons?" Two volunteers acquired credentials as "journalists" from the London-based Islamic Observation Center. Bin Laden's men shipped to Afghanistan an old TV camera in which they inserted a bomb. When the two Arab "journalists" arrived for the interview with Massoud on September 9, 2001, Massoud jokingly asked an aide, "Are they going to wrestle with us? Neither looks much like a reporter to me. Perhaps they are wrestlers."

Massoud asked the reporters what kind of questions they had for him. One replied, "We want to know why Commander Massoud said that Osama bin Laden was a murderer and should be sent away from Afghanistan."

Massoud seemed annoyed by this question, but he let it pass, saying he would do the interview but they should make it quick. One of the Arab assassins turned on the camera and a red light flashed on top. The cameraman stepped back from the camera, looked at Massoud, and asked, "Sir, what is the state of Islam in Afghanistan?"

Suddenly, a blue wave of fire and thousands of tiny metal fragments slammed into Massoud. Two pieces of shrapnel pierced his heart, killing him. One of the Arab assassins was killed in the blast. The other was killed by Massoud's men.

Massoud's commanders kept their leader's death a secret as long as they could, knowing that the news of it would devastate morale among his soldiers. Still, bulletins quickly started circulating that Massoud was either wounded or dead.

As was his habit, bin Laden woke early on the morning of September 11, 2001, to say his dawn prayers. He had reasons to be cheerful. He knew from news reports that his men had either wounded or, more likely, killed Massoud. And al-Qaeda was as strong as it had ever been. The group had trained many thousands of militants in its training camps in Afghanistan to fight in jihads around the world, while an elite force of 170 members of al-Qaeda had secretly sworn *bayat* to bin Laden. The *bayat* was modeled after the oath that Muslim tribal leaders had given to the Prophet Mohammed. Bin Laden was now the leader of a major jihad-fighting force, just like the Prophet.

Most important, five days earlier a messenger had arrived from Pakistan to inform bin Laden that the nineteen hijackers in the United States would fly their hijacked planes into their four targets on this day.

TEN

THE ROAD TO 9/11

*One belief, more than any other, is responsible for the slaughter of indi-
viduals on the altars of the great historical ideals.... This is the belief that
somewhere, in the past or in the future, in divine revelation or in the mind
of an individual thinker, in the pronouncements of history or science, or
in the simple heart of an uncorrupted good man, there is a final solution.*
 —Isaiah Berlin, "Two Concepts of Liberty," 1958

The seeds of the 9/11 attacks were planted almost from the moment
that bin Laden first arrived in Afghanistan from Sudan in May 1996.
At bin Laden's simple house in the Tora Bora mountains, which was formed
from a cave in which he had set up a book-lined study, Khalid Sheik Mohammed briefed al-Qaeda's leader about his career as a freelance terrorist.
Khalid Sheik Mohammed, known as KSM, told bin Laden that it was his
nephew, Ramzi Yousef, who had masterminded the World Trade Center
bombing three years earlier. KSM said that he had recently schemed with
his nephew to simultaneously bomb a dozen American planes flying in
Asia. They had even run a test in which they had smuggled a bomb onto a
passenger jet that had blown up, killing a Japanese businessman. And they
had also discussed flying a plane into the CIA's headquarters in Northern
Virginia.

In Tora Bora, KSM pitched an ambitious proposal to bin Laden: Al-
Qaeda would train pilots who would crash planes into buildings in the
United States. Such an attack would require numerous suicide attackers

and also considerable financing, which only al-Qaeda could provide. Bin Laden was initially lukewarm about this proposal, but at the urging of Abu Hafs, his military commander, a couple of years later bin Laden reconsidered the idea. He summoned KSM to meet him in Kandahar during the spring of 1999, and KSM formally joined al-Qaeda. KSM proposed to bin Laden that al-Qaeda members fly small planes packed with explosives into the World Trade Center. Bin Laden suggested the attacks would be far more lethal if they used large passenger jets, observing, "Why do you use an axe when you can use a bulldozer?"

There was more than a touch of Hollywood in KSM's plans for a terrorist spectacular in which he cast himself as the hero. KSM told bin Laden that his plan involved hijacking ten planes, nine of which would crash into buildings on the West and East Coasts. KSM would be on the tenth plane, and after his team had killed all the adult male passengers, KSM himself would emerge from the aircraft to deliver a speech to the media castigating the United States for its support of Israel. Bin Laden ordered KSM to scale back his grandiose plans so that they might have a better chance of succeeding, and also so that they didn't star KSM. Bin Laden was always the star of al-Qaeda's show. He also told KSM not to pursue another element of his plan, which was to simultaneously hijack American planes in East Asia and blow them up at the same time that he was hijacking the planes in the United States. Bin Laden pointed out that it would be difficult to synchronize both the attacks in the United States and the operation in East Asia.

Bin Laden, Abu Hafs, and KSM discussed what American targets to hit. They selected the U.S. Capitol, the Pentagon, and the World Trade Center. Neither Ayman al-Zawahiri nor anyone else was involved in deciding on these targets. Bin Laden personally started picking suicide operatives among them, crucially, four militants who had lived in Germany and who understood how to operate in the West. They included Mohamed Atta, the lead hijacker. Bin Laden told Atta he had to hit the Capitol, Pentagon, and Trade Center, but he could use his own discretion if he wanted to add another target, such as the White House, or the Sears Tower in Chicago, or a nuclear power plant.

Bin Laden told those closest to him in al-Qaeda that he was plotting "an event that will turn the world upside down." But the details of that event, including knowledge of the targets and methods of attack, were known only to bin Laden, Abu Hafs, KSM, and the senior hijackers. Most of the hijackers knew only that they were taking part in a "martyrdom" operation.

After saying his dawn prayers bin Laden sometimes asked members of his entourage about their dreams, which he believed had great significance. One of them told him, "I saw in a dream a tall building in America, and saw *Mukhtar* (the alias of KSM) teaching karate." Bin Laden was worried that the secret would be revealed if everyone started seeing it in their dreams, so he now urged his guards to keep their dreams to themselves.

During the summer of 2000 bin Laden invited key Islamist militant leaders from Egypt, Libya, and Morocco for a summit to discuss the state of the global jihadist militant movement. The meetings took place over the course of a week at bin Laden's Tarnak Farms compound near Kandahar airport. On the first night of the jihadist summit, bin Laden put on a feast for hundreds of guests in a large hall at the compound that featured huge platters of lamb. Bin Laden played the role of host, making small talk with his guests.

The next day the serious discussions began led by bin Laden, Abu Hafs, and Zawahiri. Noman Benotman, a leader of the Libyan Islamic Fighting Group, who was based in London, told the group, "The jihadist movement has failed. We have gone from one disaster to another, like in Algeria, because we haven't mobilized the people." He was referring to the Algerian Civil War, launched by a group of Afghan Arabs in the early 1990s, during which more than 100,000 civilians had died. As a student of Mao, Benotman understood that if you couldn't mobilize a popular movement, you were not going to win an insurgency against a regime that was entrenched in power. In Benotman's view the jihadists had failed at this foundational task in country after country in the Arab world.

Benotman also told bin Laden that his calls to attack the United States were "crazy." Bin Laden and some other al-Qaeda leaders smirked when Benotman said, "America will attack the whole region if you launch another attack against it." Benotman noticed that al-Qaeda's top religious adviser, a Mauritanian cleric known as Abu Hafs al-Mauritania, agreed with him. Even within al-Qaeda's leadership, there were apprehensions about attacking the United States.

While Benotman voiced his strong opposition to attacks on the United States, bin Laden sat next to him, quietly smiling. Bin Laden was generally polite when he was confronted by those who disagreed with him. He had a serene, unshakable belief that the United States was weak and that any American response to an al-Qaeda attack would be limited to cruise missile strikes or an assassination attempt against him.

Bin Laden told the group of militant leaders, "I have one more operation, and after that I will quit. I can't call this one back because that would demoralize the whole organization."

He often pointed to the bombing of the Marine barracks in Beirut in 1983, in which 241 servicemen were killed; in response, the Reagan administration pulled American troops out of Lebanon. Some of bin Laden's younger Saudi followers who had visited the States confirmed to bin Laden his strongly held belief that the country "could not bear two or three strong strikes."

In July 2001 Saif al-Adel, a senior al-Qaeda military commander, and Abu Hafs the Mauritanian told bin Laden that they opposed attacking the United States because they feared the likely American response and were worried that the operation would anger their Taliban hosts. Abu Hafs the Mauritanian was also concerned that killing American civilians could not be justified on religious grounds.

However, bin Laden ruled over al-Qaeda like a medieval monarch, and leaders of the group who were skeptical about the looming attacks in the United States were forced to go along with them. It was an echo of bin Laden's foolhardy decision to build a base at Jaji near a Soviet base in 1987 and his equally impetuous decision two years later to participate in the battle at Jalalabad against the communists.

Abu Hafs the Mauritanian and Saif al-Adel admired bin Laden for his politeness, even with those he disagreed with, but both were aware that he had a significant character flaw: If bin Laden was convinced of something, no one could change his mind. If he encountered opposition to his ideas from any of the leaders of al-Qaeda, bin Laden shopped around until he could find other members of the group who would agree with him.

Bin Laden formally merged Zawahiri's Jihad Group into al-Qaeda in June 2001. There is no evidence that bin Laden ever involved Zawahiri in the planning for the 9/11 operation, which was now in its final stages. Feroz Ali Abbasi, a Ugandan Briton who was then training at an al-Qaeda camp, described the merger as "more like the assimilation" of Zawahiri's group. At this point, Zawahiri's group consisted of just ten men, only five of whom agreed to join al-Qaeda, according to Abu Walid al-Misri, who edited the Taliban's Arabic-language newspaper. Abu Jandal, one of bin Laden's key bodyguards, put the number of Zawahiri's followers at seven Egyptians. This small group was regularly creating problems for others in al-Qaeda, and their wives were always complaining they wanted to go back to Cairo.

During this period al-Qaeda produced for its internal consumption a nine-page typed list of its members, 170 in total. The list started with bin Laden and placed Abu Ubayda as the number two leader in al-Qaeda, noting that he had died in a ferry accident in Lake Victoria in Africa in 1996. Abu Hafs the Egyptian was described as the number two commander. This list didn't mention Zawahiri or any of his aliases. Another, similar document from the same era also listed members of al-Qaeda, putting bin Laden and Abu Hafs the Egyptian as the number one and number two leaders. Again, there was no mention of Zawahiri or any of his aliases. A later detailed account of the inner workings of al-Qaeda by bin Laden's confidential secretary outlined the three tiers of al-Qaeda's top leadership, mentioning twenty names in all, in which Zawahiri's name was conspicuously absent.

When it came to ordering significant attacks by al-Qaeda, it was bin Laden who had to approve them. He would then entrust his military commander, Abu Hafs the Egyptian, with moving forward with the plans for the operation. Before 9/11 Zawahiri was a marginal player in al-Qaeda, despite his role as one of the public faces of the organization.

Bin Laden couldn't resist dropping hints about what he believed would be his greatest triumph. During the summer of 2001 he told important visitors "to expect a near-term attack against US interests." Bin Laden also told trainees at an al-Qaeda camp that twenty "martyrs" were about to embark on suicide operations. "With regard to your brothers who went on a martyrdom operation, they went carrying their souls in their hands and seeking death. We ask God to blind the infidels to them, for in the coming days you will hear news that will delight you."

KSM urged bin Laden to be more circumspect about such remarks, as rumors of the impending attacks on the United States were now starting to circulate widely in the jihadist community in Afghanistan. The rumors even reached lower-level trainees in al-Qaeda's camps such as John Walker Lindh, an American, who heard one of his instructors say that bin Laden was going to carry out twenty suicide operations against the United States and Israel. Feroz Ali Abbasi, the British citizen who was also receiving military training from al-Qaeda, said it was common knowledge around al-Qaeda's camps that an attack against the United States was imminent. The fact that Lindh, a U.S. citizen, and Abbasi, a Briton, both heard about the impending attacks suggests that it was not impossible for Western spies to penetrate al-Qaeda's training camps, but there is no evidence that the CIA was ever able to do so.

Aside from dropping hints about the upcoming attacks, bin Laden signaled that another big attack was imminent when he met in June 2001 with Bakr Atyani, a correspondent for a major Arabic-language TV network, the Middle East Broadcasting Center (MBC). Atyani met bin Laden and Abu Hafs near Kandahar. Bin Laden told Atyani, a Jordanian, that they had prepared a special dish of *mansaf*, a Jordanian lamb stew, in his honor. After the meal, bin Laden said that he couldn't speak on camera because he had promised the Taliban that he would not give any media statements, but al-Qaeda's leaders still wanted to take some ownership of the attacks that they were planning in the United States.

Abu Hafs told Atyani off camera, "In the next few weeks we will carry out a big surprise and we will strike or attack American and Israeli interests." He added ominously, "The coffin business will increase in the United States."

Atyani asked bin Laden, "Would you please confirm that?" Bin Laden said nothing, only smiling.

Atyani considered these threats to be big news, which he relayed to MBC's audience on June 23, 2001.

Atyani's story was picked up around the world, including by *The Washington Post*. The *Post*'s correspondent, Pamela Constable, asked Atyani, "Do you really believe that they are going to do it?"

Atyani told her, "Really Pam, I believe, they're going to do it really, because it sounds serious."

In late August 2001 bin Laden told the leaders of al-Qaeda that the big operation against the United States would take place soon, although he did not elaborate on the targets. Two weeks before the 9/11 attacks, he ordered al-Qaeda's training camps to shut down. Al-Qaeda members and trainees were told "because of the imminent martyrdom operation" they should disperse to the mountains or to major cities such as Kabul and Kandahar so that they would not be easy targets in the event of U.S. air strikes.

As bin Laden's plans to attack New York and Washington moved forward in early 2001 there was a new administration in Washington. On January 20, President George W. Bush was inaugurated. He brought with him a group of senior officials who had spent their professional lives in the shadow of the Cold War. Donald Rumsfeld, Bush's secretary of defense, was secretary of defense under President Gerald Ford, while Vice

President Dick Cheney had been Ford's chief of staff. Bush's national security advisor, Condoleezza Rice, was an expert on the Soviet Union.

Several key Bush administration officials such as Paul Wolfowitz, the number two at the Pentagon, incorrectly believed that the Iraqi dictator Saddam Hussein was behind the 1993 World Trade Center attack. It was a group that firmly believed that states such as Iraq posed the biggest threats to the United States and they had little knowledge of or interest in the threats posed by "non-state actors" such as al-Qaeda.

The attitude that bin Laden and al-Qaeda were not serious national security threats permeated top officials in the Bush administration. During their first weeks in office senior Bush officials convened a National Security Council meeting about the pressing threat posed not by al-Qaeda, but by Iraq. Of the thirty-three meetings of cabinet members held by the Bush administration before the 9/11 attacks, only one was about al-Qaeda. In a White House meeting in April 2001 focused on terrorism, Wolfowitz asked, "I just don't understand why we are beginning by talking about this one man bin Laden?" Attorney General John Ashcroft released a budget memo in May 2001 outlining the top priorities for the Justice Department—terrorism was not among them. At a briefing about al-Qaeda on July 12, 2001, Ashcroft dismissed the threat, telling a top FBI official "I don't want you ever to talk to me about al-Qaeda."

In the early months of the Bush administration it was increasingly obvious that al-Qaeda was responsible for the *Cole* bombing, yet the administration did nothing to respond. At the end of March, a senior counterterrorism official wrote Bush's deputy national security advisor Stephen Hadley an email saying, "We know all we need to know about who did the attack to make a policy decision." Yet Wolfowitz thought that the *Cole* attack was "stale."

During the spring and summer of 2001, the American intelligence system received a series of credible intelligence reports about bin Laden's plans for attacks on American targets. On April 20 a report titled "Bin Ladin Planning Multiple Operations" was circulated by the CIA, followed by another report on May 3, "Bin Ladin Public Profile May Presage

Attack." On May 23 the CIA raised the possibility that al-Qaeda might hijack an aircraft to secure the release of the Blind Sheikh from U.S. prison. A month later the agency issued another report, "Bin Ladin Attacks May Be Imminent." On July 3 the CIA reported that "Planning for Bin Ladin Attacks Continues, Despite Delay." And on August 3 the CIA circulated a warning titled "Threat of Impending al-Qaeda Attack to Continue Indefinitely."

According to Gina Bennett, the fact that some of al-Qaeda's plots had previously failed contributed to a sense among senior American national security officials that the CIA was overplaying the threat. Bennett asked herself, "Maybe we are crazy. Maybe we're wrong?" It was wearing on Bennett and her colleagues. It was a hard summer.

While the CIA did an excellent job of supplying strategic warnings to policymakers about bin Laden's intent to attack the United States, dozens of agency officials made a serious error when they failed to "watch-list" two suspected al-Qaeda terrorists: Nawaf al-Hazmi and Khalid al-Mihdhar. The CIA had been tracking the two militants since they attended a terrorist summit meeting in Malaysia in January 2000. Ten days after the Malaysian meeting Hazmi and Mihdhar flew to California and settled in San Diego, where they lived openly using their true names. The CIA also did not alert the FBI about the identities of the suspected terrorists. Some fifty to sixty agency employees read internal cables about the two al-Qaeda suspects without taking any action. It was only on August 24, 2001, as a result of questions raised by a CIA officer on assignment at the FBI, that the two al-Qaeda members were watch-listed and their names communicated to the bureau. Hamzi and Mihdhar were two of the hijackers on American Airlines Flight 77 that crashed into the Pentagon, killing 189 people.

On July 10 Tenet took the unusual step of calling Rice and asking her for a meeting that same day to discuss the mounting al-Qaeda threats. Fifteen minutes later, Tenet and the head of the CIA's Counterterrorist Center, Cofer Black, were in Rice's White House office. One of Tenet's staff predicted to Rice that the next attack would be "spectacular," adding that "multiple and simultaneous attacks are possible and they will occur with little or no warning."

Rice asked counterterrorism adviser Richard Clarke if he shared this assessment. Clarke buried his head in his hands and said with exasperation, "Yes."

Rice asked Black what should be done. Black replied, "This country needs to go on a war footing *now*." Black slammed his fists on the table for emphasis.

Yet following this meeting, Rice did nothing. Around the time of the new millennium Clinton's national security advisor, Sandy Berger, had convened daily meetings of top national security officials at the White House over the course of a month as they worked to counter threats from bin Laden's followers. In contrast, Rice never urged the national security apparatus to find out more about al-Qaeda.

Bush was on vacation at his ranch in Crawford, Texas, on August 6 when he was given his President's Daily Brief (PDB), which was titled "Bin Ladin Determined to Strike in US." The brief was delivered in the living room of the ranch by Bush's regular CIA briefer, Michael Morell, who had ordered up the PDB because the president sometimes asked him if al-Qaeda could attack the United States.

The brief had been prepared by veteran CIA analyst Barbara Sude, who had tracked al-Qaeda for years. When Sude wrote the brief she was particularly influenced by the fact that Ahmed Ressam, the Algerian militant who had been arrested at the Canadian border with explosives in December 1999, had recently pled guilty to charges that he had planned to bomb Los Angeles International Airport. This showed that bin Laden's followers had already recently tried to mount a mass casualty attack in the United States. And, of course, Afghan Arabs led by Ramzi Yousef had bombed the World Trade Center eight years earlier.

Following the August 6 briefing, President Bush never publicly discussed the threat posed by al-Qaeda until after 9/11, and chose not to interrupt the longest presidential vacation in more than three decades.

Bush's national security cabinet met for the first time to discuss al-Qaeda on September 4, 2001. Clarke sent Rice a personal note before the meeting, writing, "Decision makers should imagine themselves on a future day when . . . hundreds of Americans lay dead in several countries, including the US. . . . What would those decision makers wish that they had done earlier? That future day could happen at any time."

During the summer of 2001 there was no need to have access to any classified information to be alarmed by what al-Qaeda was planning. Al-Qaeda was an early adopter of the latest media technology and during that time the group began distributing its video propaganda via chatrooms on the internet. Al-Qaeda released a two-hour propaganda videotape on which bin Laden seemed to take full responsibility for the USS *Cole* bombing, saying, "Your brothers in Aden hit the *Cole*. They destroyed this destroyer." Toward the end of this tape, bin Laden strongly implied more action against the United States: "The victory of Islam is coming. And the victory of Yemen will continue."

I had spent the past couple of years working on a book about al-Qaeda and I found the group's new videotape alarming, as it seemed to be part of a pattern in which bin Laden presaged forthcoming attacks. On August 17, 2001, I emailed John Burns, the *New York Times's* leading foreign correspondent, saying, "I think there is a major story to be told wrapping around the new bin Laden videotape and the various threats against US facilities in past months which can paint both a compelling picture of the bin Laden organization today, and responsibly suggest that an al-Qaeda attack is in the works."

Burns wrote a story headlined "On Videotape bin Laden Charts Violent Future." Because of an editing dispute, the newspaper did not print a version of Burns's story until a day after the 9/11 attacks.

Bin Laden's first wife, Najwa, had spent the past five years living in grim Taliban-controlled Afghanistan. She was now in her early forties and had given bin Laden eleven children and almost three decades of her life, the past decade of which she had spent with him in exile. Najwa told her husband she wanted out.

Bin Laden eventually agreed to Najwa's request to return to her family in Syria, but he allowed her to take with her only three of their unmarried children, insisting that their eleven-year-old daughter, Iman, and eight-year-old son, Ladin, stay with him. Najwa left Afghanistan with the three children whom bin Laden had allowed her to take on September 7, 2001, only four days before al-Qaeda's attacks on New York City and Washington. They never saw bin Laden again.

The 9/11 hijackers were religious fanatics burning with the belief that they were doing God's will. They believed that their mass murder on the morning of Tuesday, September 11, 2001, was an act of worship. In luggage that the lead hijacker, Mohamed Atta, left in a car at Boston's Logan Airport on the morning of 9/11 was an Arabic document titled "Manual for a Raid." The manual urged the hijackers to invoke God as they entered the aircraft. The hijackers firmly believed that they were replicating the heroic battles fought by the Prophet. The manual made no mention of any of al-Qaeda's political grievances against the United States, nor indeed of grievances against any country, but it did mention the "martyrs'" ascension into heaven a dozen times.

The hijackers flew planes into the twin towers of the World Trade Center, collapsing them both. Another passenger jet severely damaged a wing of the Pentagon. The U.S. Capitol was saved only by the heroism of some of the passengers on United Flight 93 who attacked the hijackers, who then crashed the plane into a field in Pennsylvania. Two thousand nine hundred and seventy-seven people were killed in the attacks.

On the morning of September 11, bin Laden left Kandahar for the mountainous province of Logar in central Afghanistan. His men rigged up a TV satellite receiver, but they found it hard to get a television signal in the mountains, so bin Laden tuned his radio to the BBC's Arabic Service. At about 5:30 in the evening local time, the BBC announcer said, "I have just received this news. Reports from the United States say that an airliner was destroyed upon crashing into the World Trade Center in New York." Bin Laden told his men to "be patient." Soon came the news of a second jet flying into the Trade Center. At an al-Qaeda guesthouse in Kabul "the brothers" gathered around the radio to hear the good news. Some of them went out into the streets to shoot off celebratory gunfire. In Kandahar many of bin Laden's followers stayed up all night, unable to sleep so filled were they with joy.

Because Mullah Omar had banned TV, the Taliban leadership had no access to television news from the United States. Mullah Omar's top aides called an Afghan-American businessman whom they knew to be in Pakistan and asked him to turn on CNN and translate the coverage of the attacks for them. Mullah Omar and his top leaders listened aghast on the other end of the phone as the businessman translated what CNN was reporting.

President Bush learned about the attacks as he was visiting an elementary school in Florida. Bush believed that the U.S. intelligence community had "missed something big." This was, in fact, far from the case. During the spring and summer of 2001 the CIA had flooded senior Bush administration officials' in-boxes with strategic warnings that bin Laden was planning a major operation. As is often the case with such intelligence, the date and location of the operation were unknown. 9/11 was as much a policy failure as anything else since senior Bush administration officials simply didn't see bin Laden as a significant problem. No senior Bush official spoke publicly about the threat from bin Laden and his men, even as the CIA's warnings gathered in intensity during the spring and summer of 2001. Bush administration officials did not take any action against al-Qaeda in Afghanistan; nor did they ask for law enforcement to search for any of bin Laden's men who might be in the U.S.

After his visit to the school in Florida, President Bush was rushed onto Air Force One. The president asked his CIA briefer, Michael Morell, to come and see him in his airborne office. It was Morell who five weeks earlier had briefed the president at his Texas ranch about bin Laden's intent to attack the United States.

Bush asked, "Michael, who did this?"

Morell said that only Iran or Iraq were capable of mounting such a terrorist operation, but neither country had anything to gain by it and each would have plenty to lose if held culpable.

Morell said he was only expressing his personal opinion, but he would "bet my children's future that the trail will lead to Osama bin Laden."

Bush asked, "When will we know?"

Morell said, "It might be soon, and then again it might take some time." Morell explained that it took just a few days to determine that the attacks in Africa against the two U.S. embassies were by bin Laden's men, while it took many weeks to do so in the case of the USS *Cole*.

President Bush vowed to himself, "We're going to find out who did this and kick their ass."

PART III

ON THE RUN

ELEVEN

STRIKING BACK

The tactics took over the strategy.

> —Noman Benotman, one of the leaders of the
> Afghan Arabs, when asked to explain 9/11

Everybody has a plan until they get punched in the mouth.

> —Mike Tyson

On the morning of Tuesday, September 11, 2001, the oppressive heat of the Washington summer was finally beginning to dissipate; the sky was a cloudless, azure blue and the air crystalline clear. Gina Bennett and her friend Cindy Storer, both of whom had been on the bin Laden "account" for as long as anyone at the CIA, were carpooling to the agency's headquarters in McLean, Virginia, which is tucked away behind a screen of trees in a leafy neighborhood of well-appointed mansions.

The whole ride Bennett and Storer were discussing the assassination two days earlier of Ahmad Shah Massoud, the leader of the anti-Taliban resistance in Afghanistan. They debated whether this was a gift from bin Laden to the Taliban's leader, Mullah Omar, and they kept probing the question: Why go to the trouble of assassinating Massoud, if not for some larger reason?

Bennett, who was three months pregnant with her fourth child and was occasionally vomiting due to morning sickness, was at her desk at the CIA's Counterterrorist Center when she heard a plane had flown into the

World Trade Center. She and her colleagues turned on a television and watched the coverage. They saw the second plane fly into the other of the towers at 9:03 a.m. The attacks from bin Laden they had warned about were upon them.

CIA managers told everyone to evacuate the agency's headquarters building, but those in the Counterterrorist Center were told they had to remain at their desks; after all, they knew more about al-Qaeda than anyone else in the government. The Counterterrorist Center team split up, with some officials trying to find the passenger manifests of the hijacked planes. Bennett and her team members tried to work out what the next target of the terrorists could be. They were keenly aware that a cell of militants led by Khalid Sheikh Mohammed had developed a plan six years earlier to fly a plane into CIA headquarters. And there was a hijacked passenger jet hurtling toward Washington, DC.

Michael Scheuer, who had pushed repeatedly to capture or kill bin Laden, was working in a vault at the CIA. Scheuer watched the images of the second plane plowing into the Trade Center. He volunteered to remain in the headquarters building.

As Air Force One flew over the United States it went through zones where the passengers could sometimes view the images of 9/11 on the TV monitors on the plane. The most powerless President Bush ever felt was when he saw the images of people jumping to their deaths from the windows of the Trade Center. There was nothing he could do about it.

Officials at the Counterterrorist Center soon proved that it was indeed al-Qaeda. Within a couple of hours of the attacks, an analyst obtained the passenger manifest for the plane that crashed into the Pentagon at 9:37 a.m. and found that two members of al-Qaeda, Nawaf al-Hazmi and Khalid al-Mihdhar, were on the flight. These were the two terrorists the CIA had been tracking since they had attended a meeting of militants in Malaysia in early 2000. They had then both traveled to the U.S. The news was conveyed to CIA director George Tenet and other senior CIA officials who had evacuated from the agency's headquarters building and were now positioned some distance away at the CIA's printing plant.

John Rizzo, a top CIA lawyer who was still in the headquarters, began scribbling out the language for what he knew would surely come next. The CIA would need a legal finding that updated the ambiguous Memorandum of Notification by the Clinton administration about capturing or killing bin Laden. This new memorandum authorized lethal action against members of al-Qaeda and affiliated groups. President Bush soon signed a new highly classified Memorandum of Notification against bin Laden and his followers. This authorization effectively turned the CIA into a paramilitary organization focused on capturing or killing members of al-Qaeda.

FBI special agent Daniel Coleman had spent the past half-decade of his life working intensively to prevent al-Qaeda from killing Americans. On the morning of 9/11 Coleman was at the FBI's office a block away from the World Trade Center. Bin Laden had succeeded in pulling off an attack that was far worse than even Coleman had imagined. As he was rushing to the Trade Center, Coleman saw a cyclone of dense debris and paper hurtling up the street toward him, accompanied by the loudest noise he had ever heard. This was the South Tower of the Trade Center collapsing at 9:59 a.m. The debris cloud smothered Coleman in ash.

Later that day Coleman was given an important piece of evidence. A Saudi passport had fallen to the street shortly after the first hijacked plane had crashed into the Trade Center, and it was turned in to the FBI. The passport was partially burned and it smelled strongly of kerosene. It belonged to Satam al-Suqami, one of the hijackers.

Coleman's former boss, John O'Neill, who ran the FBI's counterterrorism office in New York City and who played a key role in investigating bin Laden, had recently retired and on August 23, 2001, had taken a new job as head of security at the World Trade Center. O'Neill was killed on the morning of 9/11 at the Trade Center by bin Laden's men, in an attack that he had spent years trying to head off. His body was found in the debris of the collapsed South Tower.

Mary Galligan, who was the FBI's on-scene commander in Yemen during the investigation of the USS *Cole* bombing, was in Oklahoma City on the morning of September 11. Galligan was there to answer lingering questions about the FBI's handling of the bombing of the Oklahoma City Federal Building in 1995, in which 168 people had been killed by far-right domestic terrorists. It had been thus far the most lethal terrorist attack in American history.

Galligan was told to get back to New York City immediately to help run the investigation into the attacks. She hitched a ride on an Air Force C-130 that was transporting pallets of blood to New York for any victims trapped under the wreckage of the Trade Center buildings. Galligan arrived in New York as night fell. On the drive into Manhattan she saw signs on the road announcing, "New York City Is Closed." Galligan had grown up on Long Island and had gone to Fordham University in the Bronx. New York City never closed.

The FBI's main office in Manhattan, just a block from the Trade Center, was unusable, so the bureau had improvised a command center at an FBI garage on 26th Street near the West Side Highway with long wooden tables and a tangled forest of phone lines hanging from the ceiling.

Galligan was put in charge of the investigation of the 9/11 attacks, which was known in FBI parlance as the PENTTBOM case. PENTTBOM would grow into the largest criminal investigation in history. John O'Neill had mentored and promoted Galligan at a time when the FBI was a boys' club. Now Galligan was leading the investigation of the most lethal mass murder in American history, among the victims of which was her former boss. For many years Galligan would carry the mass card from O'Neill's funeral service together with her FBI credentials.

The PENTTBOM case generated half a million leads. Many were not helpful, but one that proved to be key was a tip that came in immediately after 9/11 that a suspicious package was found at JFK Airport addressed to someone in the United Arab Emirates. Inside the package Galligan discovered that $10,000 that had been sent by one of the hijackers to Mustafa al-Hawsawi, al-Qaeda's paymaster for the 9/11 plot.

Galligan's team also immediately focused on a phone number in

Yemen, which they knew from previous investigations had been used by some of the *Cole* bombers to talk to al-Qaeda's leaders in Afghanistan. This phone number provided a road map to several of the 9/11 conspirators, including the two hijackers who were on the jet that crashed into the Pentagon whom the CIA had been tracking for more than a year.

The first meeting at the White House to discuss how to respond to the 9/11 attacks started at 9:30 p.m. on September 11 in the Presidential Emergency Operations Center, a cramped, unadorned space in the White House bunker. Cabinet members were guided by Secret Service officers past thick blast doors and down a long underground tunnel under the East Wing, where the bunker was located. The meeting was short and focused on the damage.

The National Security Council met again on the morning of September 12. Secretary of Defense Donald Rumsfeld and his top deputy Paul Wolfowitz immediately pushed to go to war with Saddam Hussein, having already raised the issue the night before. Bush said, "Wait a minute, I didn't hear a word said about him being responsible for the attack."

Richard Clarke realized with almost a sharp physical pain that Wolfowitz and Rumsfeld were going to try and take advantage of the 9/11 catastrophe to push for the overthrow of Saddam.

That same morning, Jamal Ismail, a correspondent for Abu Dhabi television based in Pakistan who had known bin Laden since the era of the anti-Soviet jihad, received a messenger from al-Qaeda who told him, "Jamal, I came last night in a hurry from Afghanistan."

The messenger read out a statement from bin Laden: "We believe what happened in Washington and elsewhere against Americans was punishment from Almighty Allah. They were good people who have done this. We agree with them." Ismail read the statement over the phone to Abu Dhabi television. Ismail knew that his old acquaintance bin Laden never praised non-Muslims, and he concluded that bin Laden knew the men who had carried out the attacks.

Bin Laden was surprised by how lethal the 9/11 attacks were. He and other al-Qaeda leaders did not calculate that both towers of the

Trade Center would collapse. Bin Laden, who had worked for years in his family's construction business, was the most optimistic among them that the attacks would result in mass casualties, but he thought that the twin towers would collapse only above the points of impact of the two passenger jets.

Two days after the 9/11 attacks, Cofer Black, who ran the CIA's Counterterrorist Center, called together his team of analysts and operators. Black was a big guy who had spent much of his career executing high-risk operations in Africa. When he was the CIA station chief in Khartoum during the mid-1990s Black had helped to capture Carlos the Jackal, then the world's most notorious terrorist. Black had a penchant for the dramatic and gave a speech to Counterterrorist Center officials: "It really pains me to tell you this, but by the time this is all over, we will not all be here. If you remember one thing from this, I'd like it to be, we're the good guys and we're going to win." Black believed that dozens of CIA officers could die in the oncoming war. Black's speech was greeted with silence by the staff, some of whom wept.

CIA officers understood that the mind-set of the agency was going to have to change dramatically, from meeting sources in smoky coffee shops in Vienna to sitting with the leaders of tribal militias on hilltops in Afghanistan.

On Saturday, September 15, Bush's war cabinet met at the presidential retreat at Camp David in Maryland. Rumsfeld wanted to attack more countries other than Afghanistan. If this was to be a truly "global war on terror," why not also attack state sponsors of terrorism such as Iraq, but also Libya and Sudan? Over the next few days Rumsfeld even suggested striking the enemy in some unexpected place "like South America or Southeast Asia."

Rumsfeld's deputy Paul Wolfowitz said there was no way that bin Laden could have pulled off the 9/11 attacks without the support of a state such as Iraq. According to Wolfowitz, Saddam Hussein was at the center of global terrorism and was "the head of the snake." This was a striking locution since it was exactly what bin Laden had started calling the United

States after President Bush's father, George H. W. Bush, had deployed U.S. troops to Somalia nine year earlier.

Cofer Black pushed back on Wolfowitz, saying that the 9/11 attacks were carried out by bin Laden's men and Saddam had nothing to do with them. Wolfowitz countered that bin Laden had met with Iraqi officials when he was living in Sudan. Black pointed out that he was the CIA station chief in Khartoum at the time and while Iraqi officials had indeed met with bin Laden in Sudan in 1995 they wanted al-Qaeda's leader to subordinate himself to Saddam. Bin Laden had no plans to be controlled by a secular dictator like Saddam.

Bush settled the matter saying, "We'll leave Iraq for later," and the subject was dropped, for a time.

The chairman of the Joint Chiefs, General Hugh Shelton, presented two military options to attack bin Laden: cruise missile strikes against targets in Afghanistan, or cruise missile attacks supplemented by manned bombers. There wasn't much enthusiasm for either of these plans, since they seemed like a rehash of what the Clinton administration had already tried against al-Qaeda, to little effect.

Bush said, "We're not going to just pound sand."

Bin Laden and his top deputy, Abu Hafs, had concluded that the likely American response would indeed be another round of cruise missile strikes and perhaps some manned bomber raids. They had conveyed this analysis to Ahmad Zaidan of Al Jazeera, whom bin Laden had known since the late 1980s when Zaidan was covering the anticommunist jihad. Eleven months before the 9/11 attacks, at an al-Qaeda safe house in Kabul, Abu Hafs told Zaidan that he and bin Laden thought that any future U.S. military action against their group would be similar to the air war that the Americans had fought against Serbian forces in Kosovo two years earlier, during which there were no American boots on the ground and no U.S. casualties.

Abu Hafs, a former Egyptian policeman who also had served in the Egyptian military, struck Zaidan as very bright. At six-foot-two, Abu Hafs was almost as tall as bin Laden. Abu Hafs's white hair and full beard was dyed with henna, and he was wearing Taliban-style clothing with a turban. Abu Hafs told Zaidan that any manned bomber raids by the United States against targets in Afghanistan would likely come from bases in neighboring Central Asian countries such as Uzbekistan or Tajikistan, and possibly Pakistan.

A common mistake is to start believing your own bluster and by then both bin Laden and Abu Hafs—who seven years earlier had trained Somalis to fight American soldiers in Somalia—firmly believed that the United States really was a paper tiger. As a result bin Laden gravely underestimated the likely American response to the 9/11 attacks, which was based on his misreading of the U.S. pull-out of troops from Yemen in 1992 and, a year later, the withdrawal of American soldiers from Somalia. The United States had no real interests in either country, so pulling its troops did not represent the strategic setbacks that bin Laden interpreted them to be. Bin Laden's misjudgment of the U.S. response was amplified by the ineffectual U.S. cruise missile attacks aimed at him and his followers in 1998 and the complete lack of American response to the USS *Cole* bombing two years later.

At Camp David, CIA director Tenet handed out thick packets of briefing materials, which outlined a far more impressive war plan than what the Pentagon had put forward. The plan involved sending in a small group of CIA officers, some of whom knew Afghanistan, and have them link up with the leaders of the twenty-thousand-man anti-Taliban militia known as the Northern Alliance. They would then advance on the Taliban and al-Qaeda while calling in massive U.S. air strikes. Tenet also proposed using armed drones to hunt for bin Laden.

On Monday, September 17, at the White House, Bush told his war cabinet, "I want the CIA to get in there first. I buy the idea of you going in first and preparing a way for the military. And the military: I want you to develop a plan to dovetail with what CIA will be doing once it gets in, and develop a plan for more robust military action down the road."

At a briefing for reporters the same day, Bush said of bin Laden,

"There's an old saying out West. As I recall, that said 'Wanted: Dead or Alive.'"

Three days later, before a joint session of Congress, Bush delivered an ultimatum to the Taliban: "Deliver to United States authorities all the leaders of al-Qaeda who hide in your land. . . . These demands are not open to negotiation or discussion. The Taliban must act and act immediately. They will hand over the terrorists, or they will share in their fate."

As Bush was delivering this speech to Congress, Mullah Omar convened seven hundred clerics in Kabul to rule on bin Laden's fate. Mullah Omar did not attend in person, but sent a message that if the United States had evidence of bin Laden's guilt in the 9/11 attacks, it should be handed over to the Taliban and his future would then be decided by a group of Afghan religious scholars. After meetings that lasted for two days, the clerics called on bin Laden to leave Afghanistan voluntarily so that war could be avoided. Bin Laden simply ignored this request.

On September 21, 2001, the Voice of America radio network interviewed Mullah Omar, who said he had no intention of giving up bin Laden: "If we did, it means we are not Muslims; that Islam is finished. If we were afraid of attack, we could have surrendered him the last time we were threatened and attacked."

Similarly, Mullah Omar told leading Pakistani journalist Rahimullah Yusufzai, "I don't want to go down in history as someone who betrayed his guest. I am willing to give my life, my regime; since we have given him refuge, I cannot throw him out now."

Like many devout Muslims, Mullah Omar was a great believer in the significance of dreams. The Commander of the Faithful asked Yusufzai, "Have you been to the White House?"

Yusufzai told him, "Yes, I was there once."

Mullah Omar said, "My brother had a dream that there was a White House in flames. I don't know how to interpret this."

Like bin Laden, Mullah Omar naively believed that the threats coming from Washington were bluster.

Mullah Omar was also discreetly hedging his bets. He authorized his number two, Mullah Osmani, who had long despised bin Laden, to go and meet with Robert Grenier, the CIA station chief in Pakistan. Grenier hoped to use this opportunity to open communication with the Taliban leadership about what to do with bin Laden.

Four days after the 9/11 attacks, Mullah Osmani and Grenier met at a quiet hotel in Quetta, the capital of the remote, vast Pakistani desert province of Balochistan, over the border from the Taliban's Kandahar stronghold in southern Afghanistan. Grenier was greatly encouraged when Mullah Osmani said, "Bin Laden has created a great problem for us. I'm speaking now for the Taliban leadership. We don't particularly like this man. We're concerned about the reaction of you Americans. I will go back and I will discuss this with Mullah Omar."

Meanwhile, bin Laden was publicly issuing blanket denials of any role in the 9/11 attacks. In late September, he told a Pakistani newspaper, "As a Muslim, I try my best to avoid telling a lie. I had no knowledge of these attacks." Bin Laden even absurdly suggested that the attacks might have been carried out by "American Jews who are annoyed with President Bush ever since the elections in Florida and want to take revenge on him."

Grenier met with Mullah Osmani again in Quetta on October 2 and pitched him on the idea of fomenting a coup against Mullah Omar, with the quid pro quo that bin Laden be handed over after the removal of the Taliban leader.

Mullah Osmani mulled over the idea. The cleric suddenly leapt out of his chair and wrapped his arms around Grenier exclaiming, "I'll do it!"

Mullah Osmani was elated and sat down for a hearty meal of mutton and rice with Grenier. In the end, though, the mullah didn't go through with the coup. Grenier thought that perhaps Mullah Osmani just could not conceive of himself replacing the Commander of the Faithful.

While Grenier was trying to fragment the Taliban leadership about what to do about bin Laden, his predecessor as CIA station chief in Pakistan, Gary Schroen, prepared to lead the first CIA team into Afghanistan to foment an anti-Taliban uprising. On 9/11 Schroen, aged fifty-nine, was going through the months-long process of retiring from the agency, having hit mandatory retirement age. Two days after the 9/11 attacks, Cofer Black called Schroen and asked him to be "first in" into Afghanistan.

On September 19, Schroen met with Black to receive his orders. Black told him that he wanted bin Laden and his top deputies killed, saying, "I want to see photos of their heads on pikes. I want bin Laden's head shipped back in a box filled with dry ice. I want to be able to show bin Laden's head to the president."

It was the first time in his three-and-a-half-decade career at the CIA that Schroen had been ordered to kill anyone. Schroen replied, "I don't know where we'll find dry ice in Afghanistan, but I think we can certainly manufacture pikes in the field."

A week later, on September 26, Schroen landed in the Panjshir Valley, in northeastern Afghanistan, at the headquarters of the Northern Alliance, leading a seven-man team code-named JAWBREAKER. They were the first Americans on the ground hunting for bin Laden and his men.

For the second time in two decades the CIA was leading the charge to overthrow a regime in Afghanistan.

At the White House there were intense concerns about the possibility of a "second wave" of attacks. This was amplified by the news on October 5 that a photo editor at the *National Enquirer* in Florida had died after opening an anthrax-laced letter.

Similar anthrax-laced letters eventually killed five people. They all contained the message "DEATH TO AMERICA. DEATH TO ISRAEL. ALLAH IS GREAT." The anthrax attacks had an enormous impact on President Bush's mind-set, as they seemed to be part of a new wave of assaults by terrorists armed with weapons of mass destruction. (The FBI would eventually identify the man behind the anthrax attacks as an American government scientist.)

That same month, on October 23, Bush told his war cabinet that bin Laden "may have a nuclear device." Vice President Dick Cheney said, "We have to intensify the hunt for bin Laden."

Two weeks later bin Laden added to the concerns at the White House when he gave an interview claiming he had access to nuclear weapons. On November 8, the Pakistani journalist Hamid Mir interviewed bin Laden at a house in Kabul. Bin Laden was in a jovial mood and he took Mir to task for a recent appearance he had made on CNN, telling him, "I was watching you on the Larry King show a few days ago and you told Larry King that when Osama bin Laden talks on religion he is not convincing, but when he talks on politics he is very much convincing, so today I will convince you on some religious issues."

Mir said, "You watch the Larry King show?"

Bin Laden replied, "Yes, I am fighting a big war and I have to monitor the activities of my enemy through these TV channels."

Then Mir asked bin Laden to comment on reports he had tried to acquire nuclear and chemical weapons. Al-Qaeda's leader claimed, "We have the weapons as deterrent."

Mir asked, "Where did you get these weapons from?" Bin Laden dismissed the question, responding, "Go to the next question."

After the interview was finished, Mir followed up with Ayman al-Zawahiri, who was sitting with bin Laden. Mir said, "It is difficult to believe that you have nuclear weapons."

Zawahiri said, "It is not difficult. If you have thirty million dollars, you can have these kind of nuclear suitcase bombs from the black market of Central Asia."

In fact, the black market in "nuclear suitcase bombs" was a myth, and while al-Qaeda had acquired radioactive materials, they were not suitable for making any kind of nuclear weapon.

Nine months earlier, Abu Hafs had made similar claims to the Al Jazeera reporter Ahmad Zaidan, telling him that the region surrounding Afghanistan was rife with countries that possessed nuclear weapons or fissile materials, such as the former Soviet Central Asian republics, as well as Iran and Pakistan. Abu Hafs said, "Therefore it is not too difficult for us to acquire these types of weapons."

Abu Hafs knew that his men were trying to acquire chemical weapons from Uzbekistan and to recruit Uzbek military veterans who were "experienced in this sphere." Al-Qaeda's chemical weapons researchers were ordered to "procure necessary face masks, protective clothing and protective footwear" six months before the 9/11 attacks.

Abu Hafs also knew that bin Laden had recently met with Dr. Sultan Bashiruddin Mahmood, a fanatically pro-Taliban nuclear scientist who had helped develop the Pakistani facility that produced enriched fuel for nuclear weapons. In 1999 Pakistani authorities had pushed Mahmood out of the nuclear program because of his extreme religiosity. So, when Mahmood met with bin Laden in Kandahar at a dinner in late 2000, he informed the al-Qaeda leader about what it would take to build a nuclear bomb.

One of bin Laden's men even showed the Pakistani nuclear scientist "fissile material" that al-Qaeda had acquired and hoped to use in a nuclear device. Mahmood quickly recognized that this was only some formerly radioactive waste from a medical facility.

Several weeks after the 9/11 attacks, veteran CIA officer Charles "Sam" Faddis was dispatched from Washington to Islamabad to investigate what exactly had taken place between bin Laden and Mahmood. After an intensive investigation of Mahmood, Faddis concluded that bin Laden had no atomic bomb under construction and Mahmood didn't have the necessary expertise to build such a weapon. Faddis was, however, concerned that someone with Mahmood's connections could have assembled a team of militant Islamist scientists to work with bin Laden.

Privately, bin Laden was more ambivalent about the use of chemical, biological, or nuclear weapons than others in his inner circle. His military commander, Abu Hafs the Egyptian, was a hawk about the issue and sought to press forward with al-Qaeda's amateur research into these weapons. Zawahiri agreed with Abu Hafs. While al-Qaeda's leader believed a nuclear weapon should be used only as a last resort if his group was facing total annihilation, Zawahiri didn't have qualms about the use of such weapons. In any event, the entire discussion was fruitless, as al-Qaeda was never able to acquire fissile material or viable biological weapons. In short, al-Qaeda's research into weapons of mass destruction was limited to crude experiments involving the use of chemical weapons on dogs.

•   •   •

As it became clear that the United States was likely to respond militarily to the 9/11 attacks, bin Laden wrote a letter to Mullah Omar on October 3 to stiffen his resolve, telling the Commander of the Faithful that the United States was on the verge of imploding. Bin Laden claimed that "a recent survey showed that seven out of every ten Americans suffered psychological problems following the attacks on New York and Washington." Al-Qaeda's leader also asserted that any "U.S. campaign against Afghanistan will cause great long-term economic burdens" to the United States, which would follow the Soviet Union's pattern of "withdrawal from Afghanistan, disintegration, and contraction."

Faraj Ismail, a journalist working for a Saudi magazine, interviewed Mullah Omar on October 7 in Kandahar. Mullah Omar said he didn't believe that bin Laden was behind the 9/11 attacks, saying, "I have control over Afghanistan. I'm sure he didn't do it. I believe the perpetrators were from inside the United States itself."

Asked who these perpetrators might be, Mullah Omar spouted an absurd conspiracy theory, asserting that "the investigation has not considered the absence on the day of the incident of four thousand Jews who worked at the World Trade Center."

That same day bin Laden made a surprise appearance on TV networks around the globe; the first time he was seen since the 9/11 attacks. Dressed in a camouflage jacket with a gun propped at his side, bin Laden said that the attacks were revenge for the long-standing Western humiliation of the Muslim world. "There is America, full of fear from its north to its south, from its west to its east. Thank God for that. What America tastes now, is something insignificant compared to what we have tasted for scores of years. Our nation [the Islamic world] has tasted this humiliation and this degradation for more than eighty years."

To preserve his protection by the Taliban, bin Laden took some public ownership of the 9/11 attacks, while still avoiding taking any direct responsibility for them. He emphasized the "humiliation" that Muslims had suffered since the dissolution of the Ottoman Empire after World War I, which was followed by the British and the French carving up much of the Middle East between them.

That night the war began. A CIA-operated armed drone flying over Kandahar fired at Mullah Omar but missed. Mullah Omar was now forced to move constantly, and he made decisions based on the interpretations of his dreams. He told his commanders to keep fighting because the United States would soon be destroyed.

Once the U.S. air raids started, bin Laden left Kandahar for Kabul, calculating it would be safer there as there were fewer Taliban leadership targets and a larger civilian population. Bin Laden sat down with Tayseer Allouni of Al Jazeera for a lengthy interview on October 21. For reasons that Al Jazeera never convincingly explained, the network did not air the interview. Three months later CNN broadcast it without Al Jazeera's permission.

During the interview, bin Laden for the first time explicitly linked himself to the 9/11 attacks. Allouni asked him, "America claims that it has proof that you are behind what happened in New York and Washington. What's your answer?" Bin Laden replied, "If inciting people to do that is terrorism, and if killing those who are killing our sons is terrorism, then let history be our judge that we are terrorists."

Bin Laden gloated as he recounted to the Al Jazeera correspondent the large economic consequences of the attacks. In bin Laden's accounting, Wall Street stocks lost 16 percent of their value, airlines and air freight companies laid off 170,000 employees, and the hotel chain Intercontinental fired 20,000 workers.

Bin Laden reveled in the attention that the 9/11 attacks had given his cause around the world, observing that the hijackers "said in deeds, in New York and Washington, speeches that overshadowed all other speeches made everywhere else in the world. The speeches are understood by both Arabs and non-Arabs; even by the Chinese." Bin Laden understood that the 9/11 attacks were one of the most watched events in human history.

On November 12 a tip about an al-Qaeda convoy passing through Kabul bearing a possible "high-value target" was passed up the chain to

CIA headquarters. A CIA-operated drone followed the convoy to a house in the upscale Kabul neighborhood of Wazir Akbar Khan. An air strike was called in that killed Abu Hafs the Egyptian. It was a real loss for bin Laden, who had relied on Abu Hafs to oversee the group's personnel and terrorist operations. Together they had founded al-Qaeda fourteen years earlier and in recent months they had bound their families together in marriage, when Abu Hafs's daughter had married bin Laden's son Mohammed. Al-Qaeda members were shaken by Abu Hafs's death because he was considered bin Laden's likely successor.

That same day Kabul fell to the U.S.-backed forces of the Northern Alliance. Peter Jouvenal, the British cameraman who had covered Afghanistan extensively since 1980 and had filmed the CNN interview with bin Laden, was the first Westerner to set foot in Kabul as it fell. The residents of Kabul were overjoyed the Taliban were gone. Jouvenal observed, "The problem about the Taliban was they were a lot of ignorant, uneducated people. They became more and more brutal, so people were really fed up."

Ahead of the Northern Alliance's capture of Kabul, bin Laden and his followers fled down the steep, winding road to the eastern Afghan city of Jalalabad.

TWELVE

THE GREAT ESCAPE

So let me be a martyr,
dwelling high in a mountain pass
among a band of knights who,
united in devotion to God,
descend to face armies.

—Osama bin Laden

Indeed, I'm more afraid of our own blunders than of the enemy's devices.

—Pericles

In the months after 9/11 the best chance the United States had to kill bin Laden was in the mountains of Tora Bora in eastern Afghanistan, where he and the core of al-Qaeda had retreated during mid-November. He had been hiding there through most of the holy month of Ramadan.

Some fourteen centuries earlier, during the sacred weeks of Ramadan, the Prophet Mohammed had defeated a force of "infidels" that dwarfed his own at the battle of Badr in 624. Also during Ramadan, at the battle of Jaji in 1987—about fifteen miles from Tora Bora as the crow flies—bin Laden had won what he believed was a great victory when his small group of Arabs had held off a much larger Soviet force. It was from the crucible of the Jaji battle that al-Qaeda had been forged.

At Tora Bora, bin Laden wanted to relive the great Ramadan victories of Badr and Jaji by fighting the Americans. And where better to do it? Bin Laden had built crude roads through the Tora Bora mountains after the battle of Jaji so that his forces could fight in the battle of Jalalabad two years later. It was also where he had built his cave-house in 1996 and had enjoyed breathing the clean, alpine air of the Tora Bora mountains and mapping their terrain. Bin Laden knew the region intimately; he had regularly taken his older sons on twelve-hour hikes through the mountains to toughen them up for just this kind of moment.

Bin Laden also knew that during the anti-Soviet jihad a relatively small group of Afghan holy warriors in Tora Bora had held off significant offensives involving thousands of Russian troops because its mountains and caves were easily defended. And he also understood that Tora Bora backed onto Pakistan's wild, ungoverned tribal regions, which was a perfect place for his followers to escape if this became necessary.

By the time bin Laden arrived in Tora Bora, Abu Hafs, al-Qaeda's cofounder and military commander, had been killed in a U.S. air strike. Bin Laden's other key military commander, Saif al-Adel, who had opposed the 9/11 attacks because he feared the scale of the likely American response, hadn't followed his boss to Tora Bora. So bin Laden turned to Ayman al-Zawahiri to be his deputy at the battle.

In late October bin Laden had sent a group of al-Qaeda members to Tora Bora to begin planning for the battle and to pre-position weapons and ammunition in caves. Their preparations were not extensive. Even Zawahiri, who was always publicly an admirer of bin Laden's acumen, admitted that al-Qaeda had very little ammunition and only one mortar.

Some Western news reports painted the Tora Bora caves as if they were the sophisticated lair of a James Bond villain, with their own hydroelectric power, ventilation system, and living quarters for a thousand men. In fact, the Tora Bora caves were simply caves, just large enough that a group of men could stand up in them.

Ayman Batarfi, an orthopedic surgeon from Yemen, attended the wounded members of al-Qaeda in Tora Bora. He had no medicine and had to perform a hand amputation using a knife, and a finger amputation using scissors. Batarfi thought that bin Laden had made scant plans for the battle and was mostly preoccupied with making his own escape.

In Tora Bora bin Laden said farewell to three of his younger children, who were taken away from the battle zone by one of his followers. He was emotional as they all made their goodbyes, not knowing if they would see each other again.

The very heavy bombing began soon afterward, on the morning of December 3, 2001. "Not a second would pass without a fighter plane passing over our heads day and night," bin Laden recalled later. "American forces were bombing us by smart bombs that weigh thousands of pounds and bombs that penetrate caves." Between December 4 and 7, U.S. bombers dropped 700,000 pounds of ordnance on Tora Bora.

Bin Laden told his three hundred followers to dig trenches to protect themselves from the intense American bombing. It was a distant echo of the Prophet Mohammed's Battle of the Trench in 627, when the Prophet's followers dug a trench around the city of Medina, which had held off their enemies.

A messenger came to Tora Bora to tell Zawahiri that his wife, Azza, and his son Mohammad and daughter Aisha had all been killed in a U.S. air strike. Bin Laden embraced Zawahiri and burst into tears. He could become quite lachrymose about those he regarded as "true" Muslims.

But Zawahiri communicated only stoicism. Through a Taliban official, the journalist Faraj Ismail exchanged messages with him and offered his condolences. Zawahiri replied, "No condolences should be offered for their martyrdom if it was granted to them."

There are few accounts of how al-Qaeda's soldiers fought during this period, although Commander Muhammad Musa, one of the Afghan ground commanders allied to a small group of U.S. Special Operations Forces at the Tora Bora battle, described them as fierce and said that when they were captured, some committed suicide using hand grenades. The Americans began to conclude that the Afghan forces they were allied with were not capable of finishing off bin Laden and his followers. CIA officer Gary Berntsen, who was leading the agency's operations in Afghanistan, wrote a cable on December 2 to CIA headquarters requesting eight hundred elite Army Rangers to block the escape routes of al-Qaeda from Tora Bora. The request made it to General Tommy Franks, who had overall control of the Tora Bora operation, who pushed back, pointing out that U.S. Special Forces allied to local Afghan forces had performed well fighting the Taliban. Indeed, on December 7 the Taliban stronghold of Kandahar had fallen to the forces of the future Afghan president Hamid Karzai aided by an eleven-man Special Forces detachment.

Franks also believed that introducing more troops into Afghanistan would replicate the Soviets' military failure in the country. This analogy was quite misleading. The Soviets occupied Afghanistan for a decade and inflicted a brutal war on the Afghans, killing at least one million of them and forcing a third of the population out of their homes. They had created what was then the largest refugee population in the world. By contrast, the Afghan War was the first time in the history of NATO that all its countries had invoked Article 5, the collective right to self-defense. Plus, the enemy they were pursuing was not beloved by the Afghan population. So sending a force of eight hundred American soldiers into the remote region of Tora Bora for the limited purpose of hunting down bin Laden was hardly replicating the Soviet occupation of Afghanistan.

Was such an American force available that could have been deployed to Tora Bora? Indeed, there was. In late November 2001 Marine Brigadier General Jim Mattis had just led the deepest insertion of Marines into a war zone in U.S. military history. His force of one thousand Marines had seized an abandoned airfield one hundred miles from Kandahar city, the seat of Taliban power. A more gung ho commander leading a more gung ho group of Americans was hard to imagine. In early December Mattis proposed a plan to send his Marines into Tora Bora, where they would set up around-the-clock observation posts on the high ground to cut off any escape routes and would be backed up by rifle companies to pick off retreating members of al-Qaeda. There was no response from the Pentagon to Mattis's plan.

In addition, there were more than one thousand soldiers from the

10th Mountain Division stationed in Afghanistan's neighbor to the north, Uzbekistan. As its name implies, the 10th Mountain specializes in alpine warfare and fighting in cold weather. Yet Franks continued to rely on local Afghan warlords to do the fighting at Tora Bora, supported by American air strikes.

On December 9, a U.S. bomber dropped the most lethal non-nuclear bomb in the U.S. arsenal, a fifteen-thousand-pound device known as a Daisy Cutter, on al-Qaeda's positions in Tora Bora. That night a bomb also landed on bin Laden's bunker. His followers worried that their leader had been killed. But bin Laden was not where he was supposed to be. He had dreamed about a scorpion descending into one of the trenches that his men had dug for him, and so he had moved several hundred feet away from his bunker before it was hit.

By now bin Laden's followers were desperate. The caves they were sheltering in were at nine thousand feet, where the temperature was ten degrees below freezing. The siege was tightening. There was no water, because it was frozen. Snow was falling steadily while a barrage of bombs was landing on them around the clock. Bin Laden himself spoke to his followers, saying, "I am sorry for getting you involved in this battle; if you can no longer resist, you may surrender with my blessing."

Al-Qaeda officials offered a cease-fire and promised that bin Laden would personally surrender. Bin Laden lived in a world that was awash in the signs of the divine, and he took it as a sign of Allah's favor that his enemies accepted this truce. That truce would take place between the 12th and 13th of December 2001, the twenty-seventh day of Ramadan, sacred in the Muslim calendar as the "Night of Power" when the gates of heaven are opened. At the battle of Jaji on this same day in 1987 bin Laden had witnessed a Russian fighter jet miraculously fall out of the sky. Fourteen years later bin Laden was witnessing another miracle; he and many of his men might live to fight another day if they could find a way to escape.

Under the cover of darkness at 11 p.m. on December 12 bin Laden and his followers took advantage of the truce to leave Tora Bora. Bin Laden together with his sons Mohammed and Osman and Zawahiri sneaked out of

Tora Bora, staging one of history's great disappearing acts. Confounding expectations that they would likely flee across the border into Pakistan's tribal regions, they traveled instead to northeastern Afghanistan, where they vanished into the densely forested mountains of Kunar province.

The same day that bin Laden left Tora Bora, General Franks, the commander of the Afghan War, was briefing the plan for the coming Iraq War to Secretary of Defense Rumsfeld. Franks had spent the past week revising the several-hundred-page plan. Rumsfeld was deeply invested in the war against Saddam Hussein, who had nothing to do with the 9/11 attacks, at the very moment that their architect was escaping the Pentagon's grasp. It was one of the most spectacular misjudgments in U.S. military history.

As he fled Tora Bora bin Laden drew up his will. It was a sober document; he knew he had only narrowly cheated death. He wrote, "Oh my wives! You were, after Allah, the best support and the best help; from the first day you knew that the road was full of thorns and mines. As to my children, forgive me because I have given you only a little of my time since I answered the jihad call. I have chosen a road fraught with dangers and for this sake suffered from hardships, embitterment, betrayal, and treachery. I advise you not to work with al-Qaeda."

The leader of al-Qaeda was telling his own children not to join his group, which had been bin Laden's life work for the past decade and a half. It showed bin Laden's downcast state of mind as he hastened from the Tora Bora battlefield.

Soon afterward, on December 14, U.S. signals operators picked up bin Laden's voice on a radio transmission in Tora Bora. It seemed like more of a sermon than bin Laden speaking live to his men, and they concluded it had been prerecorded to help disguise the fact that al-Qaeda's leader had fled.

As it happens, bin Laden had planned his escape carefully. He had paid a local commander, Awal Gul, $100,000 during the first half of November 2001, before the Tora Bora battle began. He trusted Gul because he had taken care of bin Laden's security when bin Laden had lived at Tora Bora in 1996.

Early in the morning of December 13 bin Laden and Zawahiri made their way to Gul's house in Jalalabad, thirty miles north of Tora Bora, where they rested. The next leg of their journey, one hundred miles to the northeast, was to the Shigal district in Kunar province, a valley at five thousand feet surrounded by looming mountains. The region was so remote that there were no paved roads, so bin Laden and Zawahiri rode there by horse. They settled in the hamlet of Khwarr, which was so obscure it didn't appear on maps. It was a perfect place to disappear.

While they were hiding in Kunar province bin Laden and Zawahiri were under the protection of the warlord Gulbuddin Hekmatyar, who was one of the Afghan leaders of the anti-Soviet jihad. During that war bin Laden had sometimes fought alongside Hekmatyar's men, and al-Qaeda's leader had known Hekmatyar for the past decade and a half. Hekmatyar's faction had been a major beneficiary of CIA largesse during the anti-Soviet war, receiving an estimated $600 million of American aid. Yet Hekmatyar and his followers would protect bin Laden from the Americans for much of 2002.

Two weeks after he had escaped from Tora Bora, bin Laden spoke on a videotape that aired on networks around the world. Visibly aged, he did not move his entire left side during the half-hour tape, likely because he was injured during the battle. On the tape bin Laden appeared defeated, saying, "I am just a poor slave of God. If I live or die, the war will continue."

But there was a sense of defeat too on the American side. A week later, on January 4, 2002, Michael Morell, President Bush's CIA briefer who had briefed the president virtually every day for the past year, had the unenviable task of informing Bush that it was the CIA's assessment that bin Laden had escaped from Tora Bora.

Bush rarely raised his voice, but he was now madder than Morell had ever seen him. Bush asked, "How the hell could he have possibly eluded you? What are your plans now?"

Morell had nothing to do with bin Laden's disappearance, but he held his tongue.

Bush then got on a secure video call with Cheney, Rice, and Tenet and the president immediately asked them, "What the hell is this? Michael just told me something about bin Laden getting away?"

Seemingly embarrassed that the man responsible for the 9/11 attacks had slipped their grasp, top officials in the Bush administration later claimed that there was no evidence that bin Laden was at Tora Bora. President Bush said, "If we had ever known for sure where he was, we would have moved heaven and earth to bring him to justice." Rumsfeld claimed, "No one knew for certain that Osama bin Laden was there," adding for good measure that "there was far more to the threat posed by Islamist extremism than one man." Rice asserted, "There were conflicting reports about his whereabouts at the time, and as a result the military did not request additional sources to conduct a strike." Another approach was to simply pretend that the Tora Bora episode had never happened; Cheney didn't mention the battle of Tora Bora at all in his more than five-hundred-page autobiography.

In fact, there was considerable intelligence that bin Laden was in Tora Bora for weeks during the late fall of 2001, which was known to top Bush administration officials at the time and which they even talked about publicly. On ABC News on November 29, 2001, Cheney explained why bin Laden was likely in Tora Bora: "I think he was equipped to go to ground there. He's got what he believes to be fairly secure facilities, caves underground. It's an area he's familiar with. He operated there back during the war against the Soviets in the '80s." Two weeks later Paul Wolfowitz, the number two official at the Pentagon, was asked if bin Laden was in Tora Bora, and he told reporters, "We don't have any credible evidence of him being in other parts of Afghanistan or outside of Afghanistan."

Lieutenant General Michael DeLong, General Franks's top deputy, confirmed in his memoir, "We were hot on Osama bin Laden's trail. He was definitely there when we hit caves. Every day during the bombing, Rumsfeld asked me, 'Did we get him? Did we get him?'" The official history of U.S. Special Operations Command also concluded that bin Laden was at Tora Bora: "All source reporting corroborated his presence on several days from 9–14 December."

If more American forces had been positioned in Tora Bora they certainly would have faced obstacles; the region is large, six miles long and six miles wide, and its peaks rise to fourteen thousand feet. The battle took place during the middle of winter and there were a number of escape routes for bin Laden and his men to flee into Pakistan's tribal regions or elsewhere in Afghanistan. Yet no effort was made to insert additional American forces into Tora Bora, which was quite surprising given that the ruins of the World Trade Center buildings were still smoldering. In the end, there were only around seventy U.S. and British servicemen at Tora Bora, while there were around an estimated one hundred journalists on the ground covering the battle. This demonstrated the timidity of the Pentagon at the time and the inattention of senior Bush administration officials. Bin Laden would go on to lead al-Qaeda for another decade.*

If bin Laden had been captured or killed at Tora Bora, along with many of his key lieutenants, might the subsequent "war on terror" have played out differently? After all, the Afghan War had started because the Taliban would not give up bin Laden, and with bin Laden no longer on the battlefield much of the energy about avenging 9/11 would likely have dissipated. Making the case for the Iraq War would also have been harder if bin Laden had been defeated, since the Bush administration was making his purported connection to Saddam Hussein a reason to invade that country. And a peace deal with the Taliban might have been more achievable in the years immediately after 9/11 if the Taliban's alliance with al-Qaeda was no longer an issue.

---

*Tom Greer was the lead officer for U.S. Special Operations Forces at the Tora Bora battle. In his account of the battle, *Kill Bin Laden*, which Greer wrote using the pen name Dalton Fury, he recalled that there were forty Delta operators from Special Operations Forces, fourteen Green Berets from U.S. Special Forces, six CIA operatives, a few Air Force tactical controllers and signals interceptors, and a dozen British commandos from the Special Boat Service who were at Tora Bora. CNN correspondent Nic Robertson and *Washington Post* correspondent Susan Glasser both covered the Tora Bora battle, and both gave the author similar estimates of the number of journalists who covered it on the ground: circa one hundred.

THIRTEEN

AL-QAEDA REVIVES

Far from being a strategic necessity as the Japanese claimed even after the war, it was a strategic imbecility. One can search military history in vain for an operation more fatal to the aggressor.
— The Japanese attack on Pearl Harbor as described by American historian Samuel Eliot Morison

An internal al-Qaeda after-action report portrayed the 9/11 attacks as a brilliant success because jihadists had for the first time in modern history killed "infidels in their homeland." While some members of al-Qaeda gloated over their victory, in reality, by mid-December 2001 the American campaign in Afghanistan had decimated the group. Bin Laden was certain that the Americans wouldn't wage a ground war in Afghanistan and when they did, al-Qaeda, which for the past half-decade had enjoyed a comfortable sanctuary in Afghanistan, started falling apart. Abu Musab al-Suri, the longtime associate of bin Laden's, estimated that as a result of the U.S. campaign against al-Qaeda after 9/11, 1,600 out of the 1,900 Arab fighters then living in Afghanistan were killed or captured.

As the Americans closed in, bin Laden's family and al-Qaeda's leaders scattered in different directions. While bin Laden made his way to northeastern Afghanistan, much of his family traveled south to Pakistan, along with key members of al-Qaeda. Other leaders of the group fled to Iran, where they were eventually joined by bin Laden's oldest wife, Umm Hamza.

Usually his most reliable cheerleaders, even bin Laden's own family understood the disaster that had befallen them. Bin Laden's fourteen-year-old son, Hamza, addressed his father in a poem that was later published on an al-Qaeda website, saying, "Oh father! I see spheres of danger everywhere I look. How come our home has vanished without a trace? Why is it that we only see barriers along our path? Oh father! Why have they showered us with bombs like rain, having no mercy for a child?"

Bin Laden replied to his son with his own poem, saying, "Pardon me my son, but I can only see a very steep path ahead. A decade has gone by during which we have moved from temporary home to temporary home, and here we are in our tragedy."

One of bin Laden's sons-in-law oversaw the resettlement of three of bin Laden's wives, Amal, Siham, and Umm Hamza, and a number of their children. They fled Afghanistan for Pakistan in November 2001. Amal, aged eighteen, made her way to Karachi, a heaving, chaotic megacity, moving some half-dozen times during the eight months she lived there.

In mid-2002 Amal traveled to Peshawar, the city where bin Laden had founded al-Qaeda a decade and a half earlier, where she reunited with her husband, who had shaved off his distinctive beard. He and Amal traveled by van to Swat in the north of Pakistan, where they settled in a house that had a stream flowing beside it. A mountainous, lush green region of rivers and lakes known as the Switzerland of Pakistan, Swat was a romantic place. There, Amal and bin Laden conceived their second child.

In Swat bin Laden and Amal were under the protection of Ibrahim and Abrar, two brothers who were bin Laden's bodyguards. Both were al-Qaeda loyalists who had grown up in Kuwait, which is why Ibrahim was known as "Abu Ahmed al-Kuwaiti," the father of Ahmed from Kuwait.

In January 2002, the president of Pakistan, General Pervez Musharraf, gave considerable credibility to rumors that had been circulating for years that bin Laden suffered from potentially fatal kidney disease. Musharraf told CNN that bin Laden had taken dialysis machines with him to Afghanistan, but was likely now no longer being treated for his disease.

Musharraf asserted, "I think now, frankly, he is dead, for the reason he is a patient, a kidney patient."

Bin Laden certainly had some health issues, including low blood pressure, a foot injury sustained during the anti-Soviet jihad that forced him to walk with a cane on occasion, and acute inflammation of his vocal cords that had been caused, he claimed, by the effects of inhaling napalm during the anti-Soviet jihad. But rumors of bin Laden's death were much exaggerated, and he was now eager to be back in the spotlight. He knew that the best way to do that was to issue a public statement that functioned as a "proof of life" and also positioned him as the leader of a global jihad against the West.

On the night of November 12, 2002, Ahmad Zaidan, Al Jazeera's bureau chief in Pakistan, received a call telling him to meet at a shopping market in Islamabad as soon as possible. There a man handed Zaidan an audiocassette. Zaidan, who had spent many hours interviewing bin Laden before the 9/11 attacks, played the tape in his car and immediately realized that it was al-Qaeda's leader. This was quite the scoop; proof that bin Laden was alive.

On the tape, bin Laden referenced a string of recent terrorist attacks perpetrated by al-Qaeda or one of its affiliated groups, including the suicide bombings at two nightclubs in Bali in Indonesia a month earlier, which had killed two hundred people, mostly young Western tourists. Al-Qaeda had provided funding for those bombings.

The bin Laden tape aired on Al Jazeera and was picked up by media outlets around the globe. President Bush's national security advisor, Condoleezza Rice, called the president with the unwelcome news of the tape.

Bin Laden saw no visitors while he was living in Swat, with one important exception. In early 2003 Khalid Sheikh Mohammed came and stayed with bin Laden for a couple of weeks. Bin Laden and KSM had plenty of time to catch up and discuss their great 9/11 victory, and KSM was able to brief bin Laden about the plans he had for additional anti-American operations.

Just weeks after KSM's visit to Swat on March 1, 2003, he was arrested in Rawalpindi, 120 miles from bin Laden's hideout. The bin Laden family learned about KSM's arrest while watching Al Jazeera. KSM's capture, coming so recently after his visit to Swat, alarmed bin Laden. His enemies seemed to be closing in. He ordered his family and bodyguards to depart from Swat as soon as practicable.

Before he was handed over to the Americans, KSM told his Pakistani interrogators that bin Laden was alive. Indeed, he was carrying a letter from bin Laden addressed to his family members who were living in Iran. KSM also gave the Pakistanis some useful information about bin Laden's bodyguard using his al-Qaeda alias, "Abu Ahmed al-Kuwaiti," saying that the Kuwaiti had helped bin Laden escape after the battle of Tora Bora. But at the same time KSM tried to throw them off bin Laden's scent, telling the Pakistanis that bin Laden was likely living in Kunar in Afghanistan, which was information that was by then a year out of date.

In the spring of 2003, bin Laden reunited with much of his family in Haripur, a city an hour's drive from the Pakistani capital, Islamabad. For the next two years bin Laden, together with Amal and one of his other wives, Siham, and their son Khalid, as well as bin Laden's two oldest daughters, Miriam and Sumaiya, all lived together in a large, comfortable house in Haripur. Amal bore bin Laden a son and a daughter at a local hospital. She used false identity papers to avoid any awkward questions about why a woman from Yemen was delivering her children in an obscure city in Pakistan.

Mindful of the close call with KSM, bin Laden met with no visitors in Haripur, relying on his two bodyguards to maintain contact with others in al-Qaeda. The bodyguards were careful to never use their cell phones in Haripur, and when they needed to make important phone calls they did so from public call offices in neighboring big cities such as Peshawar.

While bin Laden was moving around northern Pakistan, his oldest wife, Umm Hamza, along with five of his sons and two of his daughters, all fled to Iran in 2002. So too did two key leaders of al-Qaeda, Abu Hafs the Mauritanian, al-Qaeda's religious adviser, and Saif al-Adel, the group's military commander. At first, they lived in houses that were provided by supporters or they rented.

In 2002 the Pentagon began planning an operation to capture or kill some of al-Qaeda's leaders and bin Laden's family members who were hiding out in the Iranian coastal resort town of Chalus, on the Caspian Sea. U.S. Navy SEALs began rehearsing the assault at a location on the Gulf Coast.

The chairman of the Joint Chiefs, General Richard Myers, called off the operation because the information about where bin Laden's family members and al-Qaeda leaders were living in Chalus was unclear. No one wanted a repeat of the debacle in Iran in 1980 when the U.S. military failed to rescue American hostages held at the U.S. embassy in Tehran and eight servicemen were killed in the botched mission.

By April 2003 the Revolutionary Guard, the most militant arm of Iran's military, had rounded up all the members of al-Qaeda and bin Laden's family members who were living in Iran and placed them in a detention center in a military training facility in Tehran.

Over the years bin Laden's family and al-Qaeda's leaders frequently protested their living conditions in Iranian detention, and eventually they were moved to Karaj, a city on the outskirts of Tehran, where they were housed on a base in twelve recently constructed homes that were surrounded by six-foot fences, barbed wire, and cameras. Each house had its own yard and the detainees all had access to a central playground. Eventually they were allowed to watch Al Jazeera and to briefly log on to the internet. Although this new location was certainly a cage, the living conditions had improved for bin Laden's family members and the al-Qaeda officials.

The question of whether the United States missed an opportunity to capture or kill bin Laden during the battle of Tora Bora in December 2001 became an issue in the close 2004 U.S. presidential campaign. During a presidential debate on September 30, 2004, Democratic contender Senator John Kerry said that bin Laden "escaped in the mountains of Tora Bora. We had him surrounded." Vice President Dick Cheney publicly described Kerry's critique of the Tora Bora battle as "absolute garbage." The issue was given added resonance when bin Laden himself suddenly appeared on a videotape that aired on October 29, 2004, only four days before the election. While bin Laden was living in Haripur he recorded a videotape, "Address to the American People," which was delivered to Ahmad Zaidan, Al Jazeera's bureau chief in Pakistan. Zaidan realized he had another big bin Laden scoop; here was al-Qaeda's leader trying to insert himself in the U.S. presidential election, which was just days away.

In the video bin Laden projected a quite different image from his previous TV appearances. Gone was the camouflage-jacketed militant with his AK-47 propped beside him. Instead, bin Laden gave his televised address from behind a desk dressed in the gold robes that Saudis wear for special occasions, his full beard now flecked with white and projecting an image as the Elder Statesman of Jihad. Bin Laden taunted Bush on the video for continuing to read a story about a pet goat to children at the elementary school the president was visiting in Florida as the 9/11 attacks unfolded. He also scornfully dismissed Bush's frequent claim that al-Qaeda had attacked the United States because it hated American freedoms, saying if this was really the case, "Why did we not attack Sweden?"

On the tape bin Laden for the first time took explicit responsibility for 9/11, saying, "We agreed with the leader of the hijackers, Mohamed Atta, to perform all attacks within twenty minutes before Bush and his administration were aware of what was going on." Bin Laden went on to exhort Americans, "Your security is not in the hands of Kerry, or Bush, or al-Qaeda. It is in your own hands and any state that does not violate our security has automatically guaranteed its own," suggesting that al-Qaeda would stop its attacks if U.S. foreign policy in the Muslim world changed.

The most obvious message of the videotape was that bin Laden was not only alive but doing well, dressed as if he was attending a formal wedding in Saudi Arabia. It didn't seem like a tape made by a man cowering in some remote cave. Kerry was quick to point out that "when George Bush had the opportunity in Afghanistan and Tora Bora he didn't choose to use American forces to hunt down and kill Osama bin Laden." President

Bush immediately responded to Kerry's charge, asserting, "My opponent tonight continued to say things he knows are not true. It is especially shameful in the light of a new tape from America's enemy."

The sudden reappearance of bin Laden reminded Americans about the threat posed by al-Qaeda during an election in which terrorism was ranked as a top concern by voters. Even though bin Laden had obviously slipped the grasp of the Bush administration at the battle of Tora Bora, Bush significantly outpolled Kerry on the issue of combating terrorism. Referring to the new bin Laden tape, Bush's campaign manager, Karl Rove, told an aide, "This has the feel of something that's not gonna hurt us at all." Bush narrowly won the election against Kerry.

An unintended, symbiotic relationship developed between bin Laden and Bush. Bush's presidency was transformed by 9/11. Suddenly he was a wartime president, the commander in chief of a "war on terror." Three days after the attacks, Bush found his voice on the smoking debris pile of the World Trade Center, where he promised cheering firefighters and viewers around the world, "I can hear you! I can hear you! The rest of the world hears you! And the people who knocked these buildings down will hear all of us soon!" Bush's favorability ratings went from a lackluster 50 percent before 9/11 to 90 percent in the aftermath of the attacks, the highest rating ever in Gallup's polling of presidents going back to Franklin Delano Roosevelt.

With such levels of public approval, Bush accorded himself greatly expanded executive powers, including the right to hold prisoners incommunicado at secret CIA prisons; the right to use coercive interrogation techniques such as waterboarding; the right to act as judge, jury, and executioner when deploying drone strikes against al-Qaeda suspects; the right to hold prisoners indefinitely at the U.S. naval base at Guantánamo Bay in Cuba; and the right to secretly surveil all Americans' communications.

The biggest right Bush accorded himself—acting in concert with a compliant Congress—was to launch a "preemptive war" against Iraq, a war of choice, rather than of necessity, that reenergized bin Laden's followers and that led to the creation of the most lethal al-Qaeda affiliate in the world, Al-Qaeda in Iraq. Al-Qaeda in Iraq launched a sectarian civil war that years later would spill over into Syria, and the group would eventually evolve into ISIS. The Iraq War also sucked resources and attention from Afghanistan and Pakistan, allowing bin Laden's men to regroup, while creating a new generation of terrorists in the Middle East. Jihadist terrorist attacks in Iraq and elsewhere around the world increased sevenfold following the U.S. invasion of Iraq in March 2003. A bigger gift to bin Laden was hard to imagine.

To make the case for the Iraq War the Bush administration had to convince the American public not only that Saddam Hussein had a functioning weapons of mass destruction program, but also that he had played a role in the 9/11 attacks and that Saddam, working together with bin Laden, could use weapons of mass destruction against Americans.

As we have seen, immediately after the 9/11 attacks senior Bush administration officials were pushing for war with Iraq, and the very same day that bin Laden was fleeing Tora Bora they were meeting to discuss the Iraq War plans.

Within weeks of 9/11, Gina Bennett, the CIA analyst who had first warned of bin Laden almost a decade earlier, was pulled from her job to dig into Saddam's possible involvement in 9/11. Bennett investigated whether there were any substantive links between the Iraqi regime and al-Qaeda. She concluded that Saddam's regime and al-Qaeda were "mutually hostile," an analysis she communicated to Bush administration officials and that was also reflected in a CIA report from June 2002.

In August 2002, Daniel Coleman, the FBI special agent who specialized in al-Qaeda, was called by a staffer in Cheney's office and asked "to review everything" on connections between Iraq and al-Qaeda. Coleman had already reviewed the material twice and had come up empty. In the fall of 2002, Michael Scheuer, the former head of the CIA's bin Laden unit, led a group of analysts who reviewed eighty thousand pages of documents going back more than a decade, looking for al-Qaeda–Iraq links. They found there was no substantive relationship.

Nonetheless, senior Bush administration officials fixated on the connection between Iraq and al-Qaeda. The piece of intelligence that seemed to best make that case was a supposed meeting in Prague between the lead 9/11 hijacker, Mohamed Atta, and an Iraqi agent on April 9, 2001. This story was first put into play by Czech government officials who shortly after 9/11 claimed that Atta had met an Iraqi intelligence official in Prague before flying to the United States.

Mary Galligan led the 9/11 investigation for the FBI, which chased down half a million leads. A key product of that work was a three-hundred-page timeline that painstakingly reconstructed what the hijackers were doing every day that they were in the United States. The FBI found no evidence that Atta was out of the country at the time of his supposed meeting with the Iraqi agent in Prague, while Atta's cell phone records showed that he had made multiple calls in Florida between April 6 and April 11. Galligan met with Paul Wolfowitz, the number two at the Pentagon, on August 8, 2002, to brief him about the purported Atta meeting with the Iraqi agent. Wolfowitz was pushing the theory that Saddam was involved in 9/11 harder than any Bush official. Galligan countered that there were no records of Atta leaving the United States or of him coming back in. In addition, there was no indication of *any* Iraqi involvement in the 9/11 attacks.

Still, top Bush administration officials kept publicly pushing lies. Vice President Cheney told NBC in September 2003 that Iraq "was the geographic base of the terrorists that have had us under assault for many years, most especially on 9/11." Such lies worked. Two years after the 9/11 attacks, seven out of ten Americans believed Saddam had a role in them, despite the fact that the largest criminal investigation in history had found that he had nothing to do with them.

In January 2003, the CIA produced an assessment that concluded that there was no Iraqi "authority, direction and control" over al-Qaeda. Yet the following month Secretary of State Colin Powell spoke at the U.N. Security Council, claiming that Saddam concealed a weapons of mass destruction program and was in league with al-Qaeda. Almost everything

Powell said in his U.N. speech turned out to be false, including his most sensational claim, that Saddam's men had trained two members of al-Qaeda to use biological or chemical weapons. A member of al-Qaeda had provided this information when he was tortured in an Egyptian prison, only to recant it later when he was in American custody.

Six weeks after Powell's speech the U.S. invaded Iraq. Gina Bennett saw that the occupation of Iraq immediately galvanized the global jihadist movement because American soldiers waging a war in the heart of the Middle East seemed to prove all of bin Laden's prophecies: that the Americans were out to control Arab oil and to subjugate Muslims.

On Veterans Day, November 11, 2003, Bennett briefed President Bush and his war cabinet at a meeting in the White House Situation Room, telling them, "Iraq came along at exactly the right time for al-Qaeda," as it had allowed the group to stage a comeback. Religious extremists from around the Muslim world were now pouring into Iraq. At the same meeting, Robert Grenier, the Iraq mission manager at the CIA, told Bush that the United States faced an insurgency in Iraq spearheaded by former officers in Saddam's military in league with jihadists. Bush looked grim; the war had now created an alliance between bin Laden's men and Saddam's.

The leader of al-Qaeda in Iraq was a Jordanian, Abu Musab al-Zarqawi, who beheaded his victims on camera and then uploaded the videos of his murders to the internet. Broadband internet was just taking off as the Iraq War began and Zarqawi adeptly took advantage of it to put the videos of his grisly executions in front of millions of viewers.

Zarqawi also helped plunge Iraq into civil war. In early 2004, the U.S. military intercepted a lengthy letter from Zarqawi to bin Laden in which he proposed provoking a civil war between the Sunnis and the Shia. Bin Laden had shown no interest in this in the past, partly because he knew that his own family members and other al-Qaeda leaders were living in largely Shia Iran. While bin Laden may have privately considered the Shia to be heretics, he had no interest in fomenting a war against them that would distract from his main goal of attacking the Americans. Also, although bin Laden didn't advertise it, his own mother was an Alawite, a branch of Shiism. In the letter to bin Laden, Zarqawi argued that the way for al-Qaeda to prosper in Iraq was to position itself as the protectors of Sunnis in a civil war with the Shia that al-Qaeda itself would provoke. Zarqawi was careful in his letter to give bin Laden due deference, noting that he needed bin Laden's leadership and that "we do not see ourselves as fit to challenge you."

On October 17, 2004, Zarqawi issued an online statement pledging his allegiance to bin Laden, saying, "By God, O sheikh of the mujahideen, if you bid us plunge into the ocean, we would follow you. If you ordered it so, we would obey." Two months later bin Laden responded in an audiotape that aired on Al Jazeera officially anointing Zarqawi as the leader of al-Qaeda in Iraq and urging attacks on any Iraqis who cooperated with the Americans. Al-Qaeda in Iraq would tip the country into a full-blown civil war when it bombed the Golden Mosque in Samarra in February 2006, which was one of the most important Shia shrines in the world.

Despite his oath of allegiance, Zarqawi did not act as if he were under bin Laden's control. Al-Qaeda's leaders sent Zarqawi a letter that was intercepted by U.S. forces in Iraq in July 2005 that advocated Zarqawi end his televised executions, observing, "Among the things which the feelings of the Muslim population who love and support you will never find palatable are the scenes of slaughtering the hostages." The letter also urged Zarqawi to exercise more restraint in his campaign against the Shia. Zarqawi ignored this advice.

On November 9, 2005, Zarqawi's men bombed three hotels in Amman, Jordan—the Grand Hyatt, the Radisson, and the Days Inn—killing scores of Jordanians, most of whom were attending a wedding. It was the kind of attack against Muslim civilians that bin Laden abhorred, since it undercut his claim that al-Qaeda was defending Muslims. A month later al-Qaeda's leaders scolded Zarqawi in another letter for what they euphemistically termed his "lack of precision" in the attacks on the hotels in Amman. They also admonished him "to abstain from making any decision" on matters of substance without consulting first with bin Laden.

But these carefully concealed private tensions between bin Laden and

Zarqawi didn't change the big picture: Al-Qaeda was now back in business, and that was even according to the Bush administration's own 2006 National Intelligence Estimate, which observed that "the Iraq War has become the cause célèbre for jihadists . . . and is shaping a new generation of terrorist leaders and operatives." More suicide attacks were conducted in Iraq between 2003 and 2007 than had taken place in every other country of the world combined since 1981, attacks that were overwhelmingly carried out by al-Qaeda's recruits from around the Muslim world, who killed many thousands of ordinary Iraqi civilians.

The Iraq War had saved al-Qaeda.

FOURTEEN

THE HUNT

He may be dead. He may be seriously wounded. He may be in Afghani-stan; or he may be somewhere else.

—Secretary of Defense Donald Rumsfeld testifying
about bin Laden at a congressional hearing in 2002

For many years he simply vanished.

The CIA's hunt for bin Laden yielded little. There were reported sightings of bin Laden purportedly addressing hundreds of followers in some remote corner of Afghanistan, or rumors of al-Qaeda's leader riding on a horse through the foothills of the Himalayas in northern Pakistan. But they never amounted to anything.

On the second anniversary of 9/11, al-Qaeda released a statement memorializing the attacks, along with footage of bin Laden walking slowly with the help of a wooden staff through steep mountains. CIA analysts thought that region looked like Kunar province in Afghanistan, which was an astute guess since Kunar is where bin Laden had fled after the battle of Tora Bora. Geologists were brought in to determine if the rocks on any of the post-9/11 bin Laden videotapes were particular to any place in Afghanistan or Pakistan. When a bird could be heard chirping on one tape, a German ornithologist was called in to analyze the chirps. None of this forensic work on the tapes ever yielded any useful clues.

•   •   •

More than two years after 9/11, on December 13, 2003, a shadowy Joint Special Operations Command unit known as Task Force 121, led by Rear Admiral Bill McRaven, captured the Iraqi dictator, Saddam Hussein, who was hiding in a "spider hole" near his hometown of Tikrit.

Bush's national security advisor, Condoleezza Rice, excitedly called her stepmother, Clara Rice, telling her, "We got him! We got him!"

Clara Rice told her stepdaughter, "Yeah, maybe so. But it's bin Laden, Condi. Isn't that who you really want?"

After 9/11 the CIA became heavily invested in the manhunting business, and the agency developed an entirely new cadre of analysts known as "targeters," who worked full-time on tracking the leaders and midlevel managers of al-Qaeda and their allies. Their job was to either capture them or kill them in air strikes. Nada Bakos led the group that targeted Abu Musab al-Zarqawi, the brutal leader of al-Qaeda in Iraq and the man most responsible for sparking the sectarian civil war that would rip that nation apart.

A break in the long and winding detective story of how the CIA found bin Laden came in January 2004 when the agency's Counterterrorist Center received intelligence that a Pakistani al-Qaeda courier named Hassan Ghul would be traveling in the Kurdish region of northern Iraq. Ghul was arrested and was found to be carrying two CDs of documents and a notebook full of names and phone numbers. Crucially, Ghul was also carrying the letter from Zarqawi to bin Laden in which he urged that he be given permission to wage a war against Iraq's Shia population. Ghul clearly had recent access to those in bin Laden's inner circle.

Ghul "sang like a tweetie bird. He opened up right away and was cooperative from the outset," according to a CIA official. Ghul told the Kurds that bin Laden was likely living in northwestern Pakistan, with a minimal security apparatus of maybe one or two bodyguards and that he was always with Abu Ahmed al-Kuwaiti, whom he described as bin Laden's "closest assistant" and someone who moved messages for him.

Ghul was subsequently taken to a secret CIA prison in Romania known by the cryptonym BLACK, where he was subjected to a variety of coercive interrogation techniques, such as being kept up for fifty-nine hours straight, which induced hallucinations. The CIA later claimed that Ghul gave up the information about the Kuwaiti as a result of these coercive techniques. Bakos has publicly said Ghul made uncoerced statements about the Kuwaiti while he was in a safe house with his Kurdish interrogators.

Ghul's information dovetailed with information provided by Mohammed al-Qahtani, whom al-Qaeda had groomed to be the twentieth hijacker, but who had been turned back by an immigration official at Orlando airport before he could join the 9/11 plotters. Qahtani was subsequently arrested in Pakistan and sent to Guantánamo, where he was interrogated for forty-eight days, rousted from bed at 4 a.m. for sessions that went on until midnight. He was subjected to beatings and long exposures to low temperatures and loud music, and given drugs and enemas so that his interrogations could continue without interruption. During these interrogations Qahtani lost sixty pounds and was hospitalized twice, treatment that the former federal judge overseeing the military tribunals at Guantánamo concluded was "torture." Qahtani told his interrogators that Abu Ahmed al-Kuwaiti had instructed him how to email covertly with al-Qaeda members and that the Kuwaiti worked as a courier for the group.

But Abu Ahmed al-Kuwaiti was just one of hundreds of names and aliases of al-Qaeda members and associates that CIA officials were learning about during the first couple of years after 9/11, and his real significance wasn't yet understood by the agency.

When Khalid Sheikh Mohammed, the operational planner of 9/11, was arrested in the Pakistani city of Rawalpindi in March 2003, there was considerable excitement at the CIA that his capture might lead to bin Laden. In a CIA prison in northern Poland, KSM was waterboarded 183 times and at one point was kept awake for seven and a half days straight while diapered and shackled. KSM did not confess to the Kuwaiti's key role in al-Qaeda, nor did he tell his interrogators about his recent two-week stay with bin Laden at his hideout in Swat in northern Pakistan.

Instead, KSM told his interrogators that the Kuwaiti had worked only with "primarily low-level members" of al-Qaeda and was now "retired" from al-Qaeda.

In 2005 another al-Qaeda leader in U.S. custody, Abu Faraj al-Libi, was subjected to CIA coercive interrogations and told his interrogators that he didn't know the Kuwaiti, asserting that "Abd al-Khaliq Jan" was the name of bin Laden's courier. CIA officials later concluded that Abd al-Khaliq Jan was a made-up name. Neither KSM nor Libi ever produced any information to their U.S. interrogators that was helpful to the hunt for bin Laden.

Defenders of the CIA's coercive interrogation program pointed to KSM's and Libi's lies about the Kuwaiti as evidence for the efficacy of interrogations, since they had spoken truthfully about other matters as a result of those interrogations. This was a strangely negative way to defend the coercive interrogations: They elicited information that was useful, but never the information about bin Laden. As a matter of logic, this didn't hold much water, but it was a strongly held belief among the CIA officials who defended the coercive interrogation program.

During the summer of 2005 it seemed obvious to Major General Stanley McChrystal that the Iraq War was being lost. Al-Qaeda in Iraq was recruiting up to 150 foreign jihadists a month, many of whom were aspiring suicide bombers. Around one hundred Iraqi civilians were dying every day, some in the most terrible ways, killed by having their skulls drilled in. McChrystal commanded Joint Special Operations Command, known as JSOC ("jay-sock"), a unit so secret that, at the time, it wasn't officially acknowledged to exist. JSOC was a mix of Special Operations Forces from the army—Delta Force—and the navy—SEAL Team Six—that worked with the nation's most skilled helicopter pilots in the 160th Aviation Regiment. McChrystal and his deputy, Rear Admiral Bill McRaven, were both astute observers of military history and also men of action who, unlike most American flag officers, regularly went out on raids with their men.

They hunted for members of al-Qaeda in Iraq and every mission became what McChrystal termed a "fight for intelligence." The intelligence was used to get inside the "decision cycle" of the insurgents so that information picked up on one raid could be used to launch still more raids. JSOC's pace of operation increased exponentially, from around four raids a week in August 2004 to three hundred a month two years later. If there was ever a real lead on bin Laden's location, it would be JSOC that would be ordered to take him down.

In 2005 the bin Laden unit at the CIA was closed, and its analysts and operatives were reassigned to other parts of the Counterterrorist Center, which also changed its name to the Counterterrorism Center. This reflected the fact that CIA officials felt that they were now facing a global jihadist movement that was larger than just one man.

The dedicated bin Laden unit may have shut, but the hunt for al-Qaeda's leader quietly continued. "Tina," a targeting analyst at the CIA, and her team of bin Laden hunters realized that there were an infinite number of possibilities where al-Qaeda's leader could be, so they flipped the question from "Where's bin Laden?" to "Who might be harboring bin Laden?" CIA analysts believed that this group consisted of two dozen people at most.

CIA officials also concluded that bin Laden wasn't meeting anyone in the years after 9/11, because none of the al-Qaeda detainees in custody seemed to have met him, although a number of the detainees had described receiving letters from him through couriers. CIA analysts created a composite of what such a courier would look like. "The Kuwaiti" certainly ticked all the boxes for bin Laden's ideal courier: His family was originally from Pakistan, where bin Laden was likely hiding; he had grown up in Kuwait speaking Arabic; and he was believed to have joined al-Qaeda two years before 9/11.

In September 2005 a classified CIA report on the hunt for bin Laden specifically mentioned Abu Ahmed al-Kuwaiti as an "alleged" courier for al-Qaeda's leader. Two years later a CIA report, "Probable Identification of Suspected Bin Ladin Facilitator Abu Ahmad al-Kuwaiti," noted that more than twenty mid- to high-level detainees had discussed the Kuwaiti's ties to "senior al-Qaeda leaders."

By early 2008 a cable from CIA headquarters explained that targeting the Kuwaiti had become as much a priority for the agency as finding KSM once was. The cable stated that detaining the Kuwaiti should be only a "last resort," as the CIA had had "no success in eliciting actionable intelligence on bin Laden's location." In other words, "Don't arrest the one person in al-Qaeda who might lead us to its leader."

But the Kuwaiti was not going to be easy to find, because he went by numerous aliases, some of them as common as "John Smith" in the English-speaking world, including Mohammad Khan, Bara Khan, and Tariq Khan, while his real name was known to only a few. In 2002 a foreign government passed on to the CIA that the Kuwaiti's real name was Habib al-Rahman, which was somewhat helpful as that turned out to be the name of his deceased brother. An important break for the CIA came in 2007, when a foreign intelligence service told the agency that the Kuwaiti's real name was Ibrahim Saeed Ahmed Abd al-Hamid.

President Bush didn't mention bin Laden much in public, but in private he was preoccupied by finding al-Qaeda's leader, especially as his second term starting winding down. During Bush's last year in office, Michael Hayden was the CIA director. At their regular Thursday-morning meeting at the White House, Bush would look up from his desk and ask Hayden, "So where are we, Mike?"

In 2007, counterterrorism officials at the CIA began to brief Hayden on a new approach; pursuing bin Laden through his courier network. In December 2008, Hayden briefed the president about what the CIA knew about Abu Ahmed al-Kuwaiti, and how he might lead the agency to bin Laden.

After President Barack Obama assumed office, on June 2, 2009, he signed a memo to CIA director Leon Panetta stating, "I direct you to provide me within 30 days a detailed operation plan for locating and bringing to justice" bin Laden. That same month Panetta briefed President Obama about the hunt for bin Laden and presented him with a slide that indicated the Kuwaiti was a possible bin Laden courier.

During 2009 "voice cuts" from the Kuwaiti that had been collected by the National Security Agency (NSA) seven years earlier were matched to voice samples of recent discussions he was having with his associates. Through geolocation technologies the NSA was able to zero in on the Kuwaiti's cell phone in northwestern Pakistan. But the Kuwaiti practiced rigorous operational security and was always careful to insert the battery in his phone and turn it on only when he was at least an hour's drive away from bin Laden's compound.

In August 2010, a Pakistani asset working for the CIA tracked the Kuwaiti to the crowded city of Peshawar. Once the CIA asset had identified the Kuwaiti's distinctive white jeep, the agency was able to track him as he drove from Peshawar to Abbottabad, more than two hours' drive to the east.

On August 27, 2010, the CIA officials leading the hunt for bin Laden briefed Director Panetta that the Kuwaiti was living in Abbottabad in a "fortress." Panetta looked up from some briefing papers he was reading. Intrigued, he asked, "Tell me about this fortress."

The officials told Panetta that the large compound didn't have phone or internet service, which was odd since whoever was living in this large house surely had some money. The officials showed Panetta satellite photos of the compound, which had high walls topped with barbed wire. The main house had few windows, and on the third floor there was a terrace that was enclosed by a high privacy wall.

Panetta asked, "Who puts a privacy wall around a patio?"

"Exactly," replied one of the analysts.

On September 10, 2010, a day before the ninth anniversary of 9/11, Panetta and deputy CIA director Michael Morell met with Obama at the White House.

Panetta said, "Mr. President, it's very preliminary, but we think we have a lead on bin Laden—the best one since Tora Bora."

Using a large photograph of overhead imagery of the compound laid out on a coffee table in the Oval Office, Panetta briefed Obama about the mysterious inhabitants of the Abbottabad fortress who burned their own trash and had no landline phone or internet connection. The National Geospatial-Intelligence Agency (NGA) found that other neighboring houses used regular garbage pickup for their trash.

Obama's top counterterrorism adviser, John Brennan, pressed the CIA for intelligence that contradicted the circumstantial case that bin Laden was living in Abbottabad. CIA officials observed that the inhabitants of the compound kept a dog. Fundamentalist Muslims typically regard dogs as unclean, so this seemed like an important data point. Brennan, an Arabic-speaking intelligence officer who had been tracking bin Laden for fifteen years, pointed out that when al-Qaeda's leader was living in Sudan in the early 1990s, he had kept guard dogs.

While CIA officials were never able to acquire definitive evidence that confirmed that bin Laden was living in Abbottabad, such as an image of his distinctive face, they also never found evidence that undercut the notion that he was living there.

In the early fall of 2010 the CIA set up a safe house in Abbottabad for agents not far from the suspected bin Laden hideout so they could build up a "pattern of life" analysis of the people living there. The CIA agents monitoring the compound, which they referred to as "AC1," short for Abbottabad Compound #1, initially observed only the families of the two bodyguards living there.

After making careful observations, they determined that there was a third family living at the compound, the members of which never seemed to leave. Monitoring the movements of this third family on the compound and the number of garments hung up to dry on clotheslines indicated that this family consisted of several adults and at least nine children, all living in the main building. Were these bin Laden's wives, their adult children, and younger kids? Strangely, this large third family also lived on the most desirable top two floors of the main house, even though the compound was registered in the bodyguard's name, who lived in a small one-bedroom annex near the main building.

On December 14 Panetta and Morell went back to the White House to brief Obama again, this time accompanied by the two CIA officers who were leading the hunt. They explained to Obama that the inhabitants of the compound had gone to great lengths to conceal their identities and had purchased the compound under an assumed name. Aerial surveillance had identified a tall man who never left the compound, but he occasionally walked in tight circles in the garden like a prisoner walking in a prison yard.

The lead CIA officer told Obama: "We call him 'the Pacer.' We think he could be bin Laden."

Obama asked his national security team to start thinking through some military options. In January 2011, Vice Admiral Bill McRaven, who was now the commander of Joint Special Operations Command, traveled to CIA headquarters to meet with the agency's deputy director, Michael Morell, who showed him what intelligence officials knew about the compound using images of the building.

Morell asked McRaven: "If your guys had to take down this compound, how would you do it?"

McRaven saw that the trapezoid-shaped compound was bigger than most of the buildings his teams usually assaulted, but it was still a building typical for the region. McRaven said, "We do this every night. We do it about twenty-five times a night in Iraq, and about ten to twelve times a night in Afghanistan."

During February 2011, the CIA and the military started thinking through the "COAs," Courses of Action, that could be used on the suspected bin Laden compound. The various Courses of Action and updates about the bin Laden intelligence were discussed during seventeen meetings in the Situation Room at the White House. Some were at the "principals" (cabinet) level and involved the president; others were at the "deputies" (sub-cabinet) level. These meetings were conducted in extreme secrecy: No "read-aheads" were circulated and the cameras in the Situation Room were turned off. On the National Security Council agenda these meetings were listed cryptically as "Mickey Mouse meetings."

To help the CIA and military in their planning, a model of the compound measuring four by three feet was constructed by the National Geospatial-Intelligence Agency, which worked off of its detailed satellite imagery of the complex to draw up a blueprint. From this blueprint, model makers spent six weeks creating a model of the compound, accurate down to the trees and bushes on the complex. The final touch was adding two toy cars that represented the white Jeep and red van that the Kuwaiti and his brother drove.

Because the "intel" was so tightly held, at first the planners for any possible helicopter assault on the compound consisted of only McRaven and a navy captain. McRaven was concerned that the compound might be rigged with explosives. And what if bin Laden was wearing a suicide vest? His men had seen many "high-value targets" who would literally sleep in a suicide vest.

The other risk was the Pakistanis. The U.S. intelligence community had a good understanding of Pakistani air defenses and radar systems, none of which were particularly sophisticated. Pakistani fighter jets also had limited night-flying capabilities. But the compound was near Pakistan's equivalent of West Point and a police station. McRaven didn't want to get into a fight with the Pakistani army or police.

The Abbottabad compound was in a neighborhood irrigated by small streams, and the National Geospatial-Intelligence Agency concluded that the water table around the complex was relatively high. Given the high water table, analysts dismissed the notion that bin Laden might escape through an underground tunnel, but they were concerned that he might have some kind of safe room or vault in his house.

CIA director Panetta was briefed by a group of airmen from the 509th Bomb Wing based in Kansas about what it would take to eliminate the one-acre compound. The airmen told Panetta it would necessitate two B-2 bombers, which would each need to drop sixteen two-thousand-pound bombs. These thirty-two bombs would kill anyone inside the compound and also blow up any vaults that might be hidden underneath the building. The bombs, which weighed a total of thirty-two tons, would also almost certainly kill a number of neighbors as well. The airmen estimated there would be fifty to hundred casualties.

It was obvious that the bombing raid would also make it quite unlikely that the CIA could recover any DNA from the site that could prove bin Laden was dead. And carrying out such a raid in the city of a nominal ally would be unprecedented.

By the time of the next principals meeting with Obama in the White House on March 29, the B-2 bombing option had been ruled out. McRaven briefed Obama and his war cabinet about a possible helicopter assault, saying, "We're going to take two helicopters with the main force, which is about twenty-four guys. We are going to fly 162 miles into Abbottabad. We are going to put up small blocking positions. The SEALs are going to land on top of the main building and at the same time come up from the bottom of the building. They will get bin Laden, get back on the helicopters, and come back." McRaven said he was confident the operation could be done, but it could get more complicated when the SEALs departed Abbottabad. They would have to refuel the Black Hawks on their way back to Afghanistan in a remote area of Pakistan given the long distances involved.

McRaven, a six-foot-two Texan in his mid-fifties, physically fit to the point that he seemed to be bursting out of his uniform, inspired confidence in Obama and his team. Vice Admiral McRaven still went out with his men on raids about once a month in Afghanistan, yet he didn't overpromise or engage in any bravado about bringing bin Laden's head back in a box of dry ice.

Obama and McRaven were similar in temperament and they admired each other. They both kept calm in crises and brought a detached, rational mind-set to difficult decisions.

Obama asked McRaven, "Will this plan work?"

McRaven replied, "Mr. President, I need to bring the SEALs in. I need to bring helicopter pilots in. We need to rehearse this. What I can tell you is, when we get to the target we can pull off the raid. But I can't recommend the overall mission itself until I've done the homework."

Obama said, "How long will you need?"

McRaven replied, "About three weeks."

Vice Chairman of the Joint Chiefs General James "Hoss" Cartwright was a cerebral aviator who embraced new technologies and was well regarded by Obama. Cartwright suggested a new option that they should also consider to kill bin Laden: a small experimental drone. Weighing around a dozen pounds, the drone would target only the mysterious Pacer. This would ensure that the SEALs wouldn't have to risk flying into Pakistan, where they might get into a firefight with members of al-Qaeda as well as with Pakistani security forces.

The drone strike also had other attractions since it would be "deniable" and whoever was hiding on the compound likely wouldn't lodge a complaint about it, given the lengths they had gone to disguise their presence there. However, when the tall man thought to be bin Laden went for walks around his compound he was often accompanied by small kids. Also, drones were known to sometimes miss their targets, and even if they hit them, targeted individuals could occasionally survive a strike. Finally, this experimental drone hadn't been used in combat before.

A disadvantage shared by both the bombing raid and the drone strike was that there would be no "SSE"—Sensitive Site Exploitation—which the SEALs had become quite proficient at over the years. When they were "on target," SEAL operators always picked up any cell phones, computers, thumb drives, and "pocket litter," which would later be exploited for intelligence. Clearly, there might be a treasure trove of such intelligence if the target was indeed bin Laden.

McRaven assembled his team to begin rehearsals in North Carolina on April 7. Captain Perry "Pete" Van Hooser, the commander of SEAL Team Six, told two dozen of his best men from Six's Red Squadron that they were going after bin Laden.

At one point, the SEALs asked a lawyer who was attending the rehearsals if the bin Laden operation was an assassination mission. The lawyer replied that "if he is naked with his hands up, you're not going to engage him."

Before the final rehearsal a SEAL officer asked McRaven, "Sir, what are we going to call this operation?"

McRaven had given some thought to this question. The name Neptune Spear seemed appropriate for a Navy SEAL mission, since Neptune, the Roman god of the sea, is usually portrayed carrying a trident spear, the symbol of the SEALs.

The SEALs also rehearsed the entire mission in Nevada—where the elevation and temperature were similar to that of Abbottabad—from nighttime takeoff to the return to base more than three hours later. The rehearsals showed that the operation on the ground in Abbottabad could be conducted in under thirty minutes, which was the window of time the SEALs would likely have before they were interrupted by the arrival of Pakistani security forces. Half an hour was also the window that McRaven had learned from his study of multiple successful Special Operations raids that was the optimal amount of time to perform a mission. After half an hour the element of surprise had largely dissipated and by then enemy forces typically had gathered their wits sufficiently for a counterattack.

Meanwhile, the CIA was still trying to gather additional intelligence about the inhabitants of the Abbottabad compound. The agency recruited Shakil Afridi, a Pakistani doctor, to mount a hepatitis B vaccination program around Abbottabad. The idea was to get access to the compound, take samples of the residents' blood, and then match those with samples of bin Laden family DNA that were in the CIA's possession. Dr. Afridi himself had no idea he was involved in the hunt for bin Laden. Afridi spoke to one of bin Laden's bodyguards at the compound, who told him that no one was home and the plan fizzled.

Despite the lack of any concrete evidence that bin Laden was living on the Abbottabad compound, by April, "Maya," a CIA analyst who had an encyclopedic knowledge of al-Qaeda, was 95 percent certain that bin Laden was living there, while her manager was at 80 percent.

When CIA deputy director Morell briefed Obama he put the odds at 60 percent.

Obama asked, "Why do people have different probabilities?"

"Intelligence is not an exact science," Morell explained. "Those analysts who are at eighty percent have been tracking al-Qaeda in recent years. The folks at the lower end of the range are those who lived through intelligence failures, particularly the Iraq WMD issue." Morell told the president that when it came to the sheer volume of data, "the circumstantial case of Iraq having WMD was actually stronger than the circumstantial case that bin Laden is living in the Abbottabad compound."

In late April, Michael Leiter, the director of the National Counterterrorism Center, put together a small "Red Team" to kick the tires of the bin Laden intelligence.

At the final cabinet meeting with Obama on April 28, Leiter said his team assessed that there was a 40 percent to 60 percent chance that bin Laden was in Abbottabad.

CIA director Leon Panetta interjected incredulously, "Forty percent!"

Leiter pointed out, "That's still thirty-eight percent higher than what we have had in the past ten years."

A discussion of the various percentages ensued in the Situation Room. They implied some type of mathematical rigor, but in reality they were just the best judgments of smart analysts operating with incomplete information. If the decision was made to send SEALs to capture or kill bin Laden, he would either be 100 percent in Abbottabad, or he wouldn't be there at all.

Obama interrupted this discussion, saying, "I know we are trying to quantify these factors as best we can, but ultimately this is a fifty-fifty call. Let's move on."

The Red Team assessment didn't change the opinions of the intelligence veterans in the Situation Room meeting, such as Jim Clapper, the Director of National Intelligence, and Brennan. Both of them knew that the analysts who had spent the longest working on the bin Laden "account" were the most confident that it was indeed al-Qaeda's leader living in the Abbottabad compound. And there didn't seem to be any really good alternative explanation for what was known about the compound.

Obama's top national security officials were worried that a leak might develop about the bin Laden operation as the circle of knowledge about it grew wider every day inside the government and military. They were also concerned that "the Pacer" might simply move. This was in fact a much greater danger than was known at the time, since bin Laden had already agreed with his bodyguards that they could separate as early as July 2011.

Secretary of Defense Robert Gates returned to a point he had made repeatedly during the meetings of Obama's war cabinet, which was the botched rescue attempt of the American hostages held in Iran in 1980 that had contributed to Jimmy Carter being a one-term president. Gates was working for then-CIA director Stansfield Turner as that disaster had unfolded. It was a searing memory. The implication was clear: If the Abbottabad operation failed and SEALs were killed or taken hostage, Obama might also end as a one-term president.

The White House Correspondents' Dinner became the subject of intense discussion in the Situation Room on the evening of Thursday, April 28. The ideal time for the raid was over the weekend of Saturday, April 30, and Sunday, May 1, as these would both be moonless nights in Abbottabad. Should the Abbottabad operation be delayed until after the Correspondents' Dinner only forty-eight hours away on Saturday night? The dinner was the annual get-together of the entire DC press corps, the president and his cabinet, and a sprinkling of quasi-celebrities such as Donald Trump. What if the raid went badly and all of Obama's war cabinet attending the dinner suddenly had to leave?

Hillary Clinton looked up and said succinctly, "Fuck the White House Correspondents' Dinner."

This interjection helped settle the issue. Obama agreed with Clinton: "The only thing driving the 'go' or 'no go' are the mission requirements of the SEALs."

Obama polled his advisers if he should green-light the raid. Panetta was adamant the raid should go forward, saying, "If we don't do it, we will regret it."

John Brennan, a veteran CIA official and Obama's counterterrorism adviser, whose judgment the president greatly trusted, urged a go on the raid.

Clinton weighed the pros and cons of the raid in a long, lawyerly answer, and came down on the side of green-lighting the operation.

General Cartwright, the vice chairman of the Joint Chiefs, advocated for the small drone, while his boss, Admiral Michael Mullen, the chairman of the Joint Chiefs, who had attended the full-dress rehearsal of the raid in Nevada and also knew McRaven well, strongly favored green-lighting the SEAL mission.

Gates was against the raid, and in favor of the small drone strike.

Biden was firmly against the SEAL operation: The risks were too great. He wanted to wait and gather more intelligence.

Gates had worked for every administration going back to Lyndon Johnson and Biden had become a U.S. senator when Obama was eleven. Between them Gates and Biden had more than eight decades of experience working in Washington on national security issues. Their unease about the raid option was sobering.

The meeting in the Situation Room broke up at 7 p.m.

Obama returned to his residence in the White House. After his family went to sleep at ten, Obama mulled his decision carefully, pacing for three hours in the Treaty Room, which functioned as his private office. It seemed like the best chance to get bin Laden in a decade, and he had considerable faith in McRaven and his Special Operations Forces. Obama also remembered the many 9/11 families he had met. The president realized there were also risks in doing nothing: What if "the Pacer" slipped away?

At 8:10 a.m. on Friday, April 29, Obama met with Brennan and his national security advisor, Tom Donilon, in the White House Diplomatic Reception Room. He told them simply: "It's a go."

On Saturday McRaven carefully examined the weather reports coming out of Pakistan. The Black Hawk helicopters would be flying in low at around one hundred feet, which was still high enough to avoid any trees or power lines on a moonless night. But there would be fog in some of the valleys they would be flying through. McRaven knew that if they waited until Sunday, they would be in a better position to conduct the operation. He saw no need to rush to failure.

Taking a break from rehearsing his lines for his speech at the Correspondents' Dinner, on Saturday at 5 p.m.—1:30 a.m. in Afghanistan—Obama called McRaven and asked him, "Bill, what do you think?"

McRaven said, "I don't know, sir. But I do know if he's there we'll get him, and if not, we'll come home."

Obama asked McRaven to relay to his Special Operations Forces that he was proud of them, adding, "Good luck, Bill."

McRaven replied, "Thank you, Mr. President. And thank you for making this tough decision."

Obama signed off, "Thank you, Bill."

FIFTEEN

A LION IN WINTER

The best martyrs are those who stay in the battle line and do not turn their faces away until they are killed.

—Osama bin Laden

As al-Qaeda revived, bin Laden decided to find a permanent home big enough for his growing family to live comfortably alongside his two bodyguards and their families. He chose Abbottabad, a small city in northern Pakistan that was a popular retirement destination for Pakistani military officers. To the north of Abbottabad, the snow-covered mountains of the Himalayas marched in serried ranks toward the Chinese border.

During 2004 and 2005 bin Laden's bodyguard, Abu Ahmed al-Kuwaiti, began assembling parcels of land in Bilal Town, a pleasant Abbottabad neighborhood, paying about $50,000 for them and putting the property in his name. The Kuwaiti then hired an architect to design a compound of two stories with four bedrooms on each floor, each with its own private bathroom. During its construction, a third floor was added.

Bin Laden and two of his wives, six of his children, and his two bodyguards and their families all moved to Abbottabad in August 2005. In Abbottabad bin Laden had another two children with Amal, his youngest wife; Zainab was born in 2006 and Hussain in 2008.

While they were living in Abbottabad, there were also tragedies for the bin Laden family. Bin Laden had married off his daughter Khadija to an al-Qaeda fighter in Afghanistan when she was only twelve, but she had died in 2007 after giving birth in Pakistan's remote tribal regions. Khadija's husband was later killed in a CIA drone strike, so now their four orphaned young children were also all living in the Abbottabad compound along with their grandfather Osama.

Living on the compound, in addition to bin Laden and his three wives and their twelve children and grandchildren, were also the two bodyguards and their wives and seven children, totaling twenty-seven people. The compound was crowded, but bin Laden never left it. One of his bodyguard's daughters asked her father why "the uncle who lived upstairs" never went out to shop at the bazaar. The bodyguard made up a story that this uncle was too poor to buy anything. That seemed plausible since bin Laden lived quite frugally, with only three pairs of lightweight *shalwar kameez*, Pakistani shirts and trousers, for the summer, and another three heavier pairs for the winter. From then on bin Laden was known by the bodyguard's family in Urdu, a local language, as *"miskeen kaka,"* the "poor uncle." One day the bodyguard's family was watching Al Jazeera and the daughter recognized the "poor uncle." After that the TV was turned off and the bodyguards' families stopped interacting with the bin Laden family.

The bodyguards' two Pakistani wives occasionally visited their families in other parts of Pakistan. Following orders from their husbands, the wives lied to their families about where they were living, telling them that they lived in Kuwait. They even brought gifts for their families that they claimed to have purchased in Kuwait to bolster their cover stories.

During his long days at the Abbottabad compound, bin Laden read or listen to nonfiction. His digital library of hundreds of books and reports included Bob Woodward's *Obama's Wars* and the audio version of this author's *The Osama Bin Laden I Know: An Oral History of al-Qaeda's Leader*. Bin Laden was a fan of Michael Scheuer, who had spent years trying to capture or kill him while working at the CIA. After leaving the agency, Scheuer had written books sharply critical of U.S. foreign policy in the Middle East, such as his 2007 book, *Imperial Hubris: Why the West*

Is Losing the War on Terror. Bin Laden also collected books with a conspiratorial bent about the Illuminati and Freemasons and even one that claimed that 9/11 was an "inside job." Bin Laden wanted to understand how his American enemies thought about him, so he built up a significant library of analyses of al-Qaeda by think tanks such as RAND, as well as publicly available U.S. government reports about his group.

On the ground floor of the main house was a room where al-Qaeda's leader relaxed watching TV news. There was a gas heater and an improvised exhaust system made from bits of sheet metal. Here bin Laden watched old videos of himself on television, wrapped in a blanket against the chilly Abbottabad winter.

Bin Laden spent much of his time on the top, third floor in the main house on his Abbottabad compound. Here was his bedroom, the height of which was low for someone as tall as bin Laden. There was a tiny bathroom for his use with no tile on the floor, a cheap shower, and a toilet that he squatted over to use. Off to the side of the bedroom was a small outdoor terrace surrounded by a seven-foot wall, which was high enough to disguise his presence when he walked onto the terrace, which was partially covered by an awning that prevented satellites from taking any overhead imagery of him. Next door to the bedroom was his study; crude bookshelves lined its walls and a large window overlooked the enclosed terrace. It was here that bin Laden composed lengthy letters to his key lieutenants and to his family members.

In Abbottabad, bin Laden settled into the role of attentive family patriarch. In the spring of 2011, he and his wife Siham were planning the marriage of their son Khalid. Bin Laden exchanged a number of letters with the mother of the bride-to-be and excitedly described the impending nuptials, "which our hearts have been looking forward to."

From his Abbottabad hideout bin Laden corresponded at length with his son Hamza, who was one of his seven children who had fled to Iran after the 9/11 attacks and were detained there by the Revolutionary Guard. Hamza wrote a heartfelt letter to his father in July 2009 in which he recalled how he hadn't seen him since he was thirteen, nine years earlier:

"My heart is sad from the long separation, yearning to meet with you. . . . My eyes still remember the last time I saw you when you were under the olive tree and you gave each one of us Muslim prayer beads." Hamza told his father that he was now married to a "pious wife" and had named his first-born son Osama.

Bin Laden was disturbed by the reports he received from Hamza and other members of al-Qaeda about the conditions they lived in while detained in Iran. Hamza wrote his father describing how after years of being held in prison-like conditions without charge, al-Qaeda detainees had staged a violent protest involving sit-ins and burning property. The protests were met with violence.

In the spring of 2010 the Iranian regime finally started releasing bin Laden's family members. Two years earlier, bin Laden's men had kidnapped an Iranian diplomat in Pakistan who was released as part of the prisoner swap.

Two of bin Laden's sons, Osman and Mohammad, both in their midtwenties, were released by the Iranians and were now hiding in Pakistan's tribal regions on the border with Afghanistan. Bin Laden wrote to his sons that he was "longing" to see them, but he regretted that "our security situation does not allow us at this time to be together." One of bin Laden's sons, Saad, had been killed in a CIA drone strike in the tribal regions in 2009, and he wanted to make sure his other sons didn't share this fate. He was also paranoid, worried that the Iranians might have injected his sons with a "shot," writing that such a shot might have been "loaded with a tiny chip" no larger than a "seed of grain" that could track their whereabouts. He had no evidence of this.

In early 2011, as we have seen, his two bodyguards had told bin Laden that they were fed up with all the dangers of protecting the world's most wanted man and they were leaving him in six months. Bin Laden told a top deputy that he needed to find a successor who was a Pakistani who could fit in locally, someone who wasn't wanted for any crime, and who had a valid, official ID card that would enable him to rent or buy a new property for the bin Laden family, since they would have to leave his carefully constructed compound in Abbottabad, which was registered in the name of his bodyguard.

While bin Laden was hiding in Abbottabad he not only was trying to reunite with all of his family that had scattered after the 9/11 attacks, he was also trying to extend al-Qaeda's influence through a network of affiliated groups around the world. Al-Qaeda in Iraq was both the most lethal and high-profile of these affiliates, but the Iraqi group tended to ignore bin Laden's directives.

The leader of Al-Qaeda in Iraq, Abu Musab al-Zarqawi, was the subject of an intense American manhunt and was killed in an American air strike on June 7, 2006. Bin Laden released a dutiful eulogy about him describing Zarqawi as a "hero" and remarking that Zarqawi "had clear instructions to focus his fight on the occupiers, particularly the Americans."

In reality, Zarqawi had completely ignored those "clear instructions" and had killed thousands of ordinary Iraqi civilians. Privately, al-Qaeda officials did not mourn Zarqawi's death.

While al-Qaeda was creating considerable havoc in Iraq, the organization was also regrouping in Pakistan's remote and largely ungoverned tribal regions along the border with Afghanistan, where it started training recruits for attacks in the West. One of them was Mohamed Khan, a second-generation British-Pakistani schoolteacher who took time off from his job in November 2004 for a three-month visit to Pakistan, where he received training from al-Qaeda.

On July 7, 2005, a four-man team of British citizens led by Khan detonated suicide bombs on the London Underground and on a bus, killing fifty-two commuters and themselves. It was the most lethal terrorist attack in British history. Two months after the London bombings, an al-Qaeda videotape of Khan appeared on Al Jazeera, in which he described bin Laden and his deputy, Ayman al-Zawahiri, as "today's heroes." The "7/7" attacks in London were not anywhere near the scale of 9/11, but al-Qaeda had now recovered to the point where it could carry out significant attacks in the West.

Al-Qaeda's leaders hoped to replicate the London bombings with similar attacks on the New York City subway. Three years after the 7/7 at-tacks, Najibullah Zazi, an Afghan-American, and two of his friends from Queens, New York, traveled to Pakistan, where they met with members of al-Qaeda who instructed them how to build hydrogen-peroxide-based bombs. But once he was back in the States, Zazi forgot how to construct the bombs, so he sent a message to an al-Qaeda email account asking for instructions. That account was being monitored by British intelligence officials, who tipped off the Americans. Zazi and his two co-conspirators were arrested in September 2009, around the eighth anniversary of the 9/11 attacks. It was the last time that al-Qaeda's core group in Pakistan made a serious attempt to carry out a mass casualty attack in the United States.

A year later, the Pakistani Taliban, which was allied to al-Qaeda, dis-patched a terrorist to bomb civilian targets in New York City. Pakistani-American Faisal Shahzad had internalized the ideology of Binladenism, that there was a Western-led conspiracy to humiliate Islam and the only appropriate response was holy war. In Pakistan Shahzad was trained by the Taliban in bomb-making. When Shahzad was back in the States, on May 1, 2010, he drove a bomb-laden SUV to Manhattan, parking it in Times Square on a busy Saturday evening. Shahzad set off the bomb, but it didn't detonate properly and he was arrested at JFK Airport.

Bin Laden was determined to maintain as much control over his other affiliates as possible; after all, they had all pledged *bayat* to him, a religious oath of obedience. To ensure that they complied with his orders bin Laden wrote lengthy memos to his top lieutenants covering a wide range of is-sues about overall strategy and personnel. Bin Laden sometimes gave bi-zarre guidance to his followers, complaining that as an American citizen, Shahzad, who had tried to blow up the SUV in Times Square, had broken the oath of allegiance he had sworn to the United States. Bin Laden ex-plained, "We do not want the mujahideen to be accused of breaking an oath." Al-Qaeda's leader kept pressing his lieutenants for more attacks on the United States, but now he was telling them that they couldn't recruit naturalized U.S. citizens to carry out those missions.

In 2006 bin Laden welcomed a new affiliate into the al-Qaeda fold, known as al-Qaeda in the Islamic Maghreb (AQIM), which operated in North Africa. The following year he received a detailed report from his North African affiliate detailing its cash flow and personnel issues.

After an aggressive campaign against al-Qaeda in the Arabian Peninsula (AQAP) by the Saudi government following a spate of terrorist attacks by the group in the kingdom between 2003 and 2005, AQAP rebased itself in neighboring Yemen, where it sometimes controlled significant amounts of territory. The group also distinguished itself by regularly producing a slickly written and colorfully laid out jihadist webzine named *Inspire*; the first issue appeared in July 2010. Bin Laden objected to the content of *Inspire*, which aimed to inspire "lone actor" attacks in the West using such crude tools as welding knives onto a truck and ramming the vehicle into a crowd. Bin Laden was dismayed by such tactics, which he felt didn't reflect well on his followers and in any event wasn't the type of mass casualty attack that he preferred.

An increasingly prominent leader of AQAP was Anwar al-Awlaki. A Yemeni-American cleric, Awlaki became one of the most influential jihadist ideologues in the world because of his tapes about jihad that he delivered in colloquial English and were widely circulated on the internet. Awlaki also played an operational role in AQAP's terrorist plots. For instance, he recruited a Nigerian to wear a bomb that evaded airport security measures. The bomb was concealed in the Nigerian's underwear and he smuggled it onto an American passenger jet on Christmas Day 2009 and detonated the device as the plane was coming in to land in Detroit. Luckily, the bomb didn't explode properly, but it put AQAP on the map as an al-Qaeda affiliate that had the capacity to carry out an anti-American operation. Even though the plot failed, bin Laden admired the audacity of the effort to blow up an American passenger jet.

Bin Laden also continued to instruct his followers through the more than two dozen video- and audiotapes that he released in the years after 9/11. These messages reached untold millions of people around the world, as they typically received considerable media coverage. In his Abbottabad compound bin Laden set up a makeshift TV studio with a neutral backdrop where he practiced his video addresses dressed in formal white Pakistani *shalwar kameez* and a neat, white turban. When he flubbed his lines, he chuckled and rapped his knuckles on a desk to signal that he wanted to do a retake.

Bin Laden's tapes not only instructed al-Qaeda's followers to kill Westerners and Jews, but some also carried specific instructions. On October 19, 2003, bin Laden called for action against Spain because of its troop presence in Iraq, the first time that al-Qaeda's leader had singled out the country. Six months later, jihadist terrorists killed 191 people in Madrid. In December 2004, bin Laden called for attacks on Saudi oil facilities, and a little over a year later, al-Qaeda's Saudi affiliate attacked Abqaiq, the largest oil production facility in the world.

Around the sixth anniversary of 9/11, bin Laden was sharply and publicly attacked by one of his heroes, Salman al-Awdah, a leading Saudi religious scholar. Awdah addressed bin Laden in the media, saying, "My brother Osama, how much blood has been spilt? How many innocent people, children, elderly, and women have been killed in the name of al-Qaeda?"

This was a personal rebuke of bin Laden about his murders of innocent civilians, and it was especially significant because Awdah's sermons against the U.S. military presence in Saudi Arabia following Saddam Hussein's 1990 invasion of Kuwait had helped to turn bin Laden against the United States. Since bin Laden was not a religious scholar himself, he was always especially sensitive about the views of genuine Islamic scholars, particularly those from the holy land of Saudi Arabia.

As he mulled over the critique from Awdah that al-Qaeda was killing mostly Muslim civilians, bin Laden became increasingly focused on the issue. A month after Awdah's critical statement, al-Qaeda's leader did something unprecedented, which was to issue a public apology on an audiotape that aired on Al Jazeera admonishing his holy warriors in Iraq to correct their "mistakes" and curb their fanaticism.

The Libyan dissident Noman Benotman, who had privately warned bin Laden in Afghanistan in 2000 not to attack the United States, now came out publicly with his own strong rebuke of al-Qaeda, calling on the group to end all operations that targeted civilians in the West. Benotman's condemnation of bin Laden received widespread coverage in the Arabic-language press.

The issue of civilian casualties became a major preoccupation in bin Laden's communications to groups allied to al-Qaeda. On August 7, 2010, bin Laden advised members of the Somali terrorist group al-Shabaab ("the Youth") to try to avoid killing civilians, as they were then doing in battles in and around the Somali capital, Mogadishu. Bin Laden also warned al-Shabaab that the group would be better off if it did not declare itself publicly to be part of al-Qaeda for fundraising purposes, because businessmen in the Arab world "who are willing to help the brothers in Somalia" would be more likely to do so if they thought they were not supporting al-Qaeda directly.

Bin Laden was keenly aware that al-Qaeda's brand was in trouble, and during the fall of 2010 he started contemplating a major rebranding of his group. He wrote a long letter outlining his plans to his operational commander, Atiyah. Bin Laden was particularly upset by terrorist operations by al-Qaeda in Iraq that had killed Shia Muslims attending mosques, and attacks by the Pakistani Taliban that had killed military officers worshipping at a mosque. He even encouraged the "Commander of the Faithful," Mullah Omar, to come out publicly to condemn "the serious matter of shedding Muslim blood unjustly," in a letter that bin Laden sent to the Taliban leader on November 5, 2010.

Bin Laden was planning to issue a public declaration that would emphasize the "friendliness" of al-Qaeda in order to "regain the trust" of the Muslim public. He wanted to use the upcoming tenth anniversary of 9/11 as the moment to relaunch al-Qaeda and its affiliated groups, which would collectively commit to no longer engage in local attacks against Muslims in countries such as Iraq, Somalia, and Yemen.

At one of the family meetings at the Abbottabad compound in early April 2011, bin Laden told his wives and daughters that he saw the Arab Spring, which was by then in full bloom, as a propitious moment to revamp al-Qaeda. His family urged bin Laden on, saying, "We need a public statement from you in your usual style with phrases that future generations will memorize, and that will be preserved as your heritage." Bin Laden's family saw him as a world historical figure who could reshape history with a speech.

Bin Laden's proposed rebranding of al-Qaeda did not, however, extend to stopping any planning for terrorist attacks against American targets. He told his key lieutenants he wanted "big effective operations whose impact, God willing, is bigger than that of 9/11."

The Americans always remained bin Laden's main enemy, yet he was unable to successfully carry out an attack in the United States in the decade after 9/11.

For their part, in the decade after 9/11 the CIA and the U.S. military hadn't forgotten who their main enemy was.

SIXTEEN

OPERATION
NEPTUNE SPEAR

People sleep peacefully in their beds at night only because rough men stand ready to do violence on their behalf.

—American columnist Richard Grenier in 1993

It was a simple plan, carefully concealed, repeatedly rehearsed, and exercised with surprise, speed, and purpose.

—Admiral Bill McRaven describing Operation Neptune Spear

On Sunday, May 1, as night fell on Jalalabad in eastern Afghanistan, McRaven addressed his team, saying, "Gentlemen, since 9/11 each one of you has dreamed of being the man on the mission to get bin Laden. Well this is the mission and you are the men. Let's go get bin Laden." There were no smiles or cheers. Some of the SEALs believed that they would die on the mission and had written letters to their wives and children in the event they wouldn't be returning home.

Obama entered the White House Situation Room at 2 p.m. At the same time, eight and a half time zones to the east in Jalalabad at 10:30 p.m., two oddly shaped stealth Black Hawk helicopters took off heading for the Pakistani border.

On the choppers were twenty-three SEALs and a Pakistani-American who spoke the local language, Pashto. If crowds gathered at the Abbottabad compound, he would tell people there was a Pakistani military exercise going on and they should go home. Also on the flight to Abbottabad was a dog named Cairo, who would prevent "squirters" from sneaking out of the compound, sniff out any explosives, and hunt for possible safe rooms.

McRaven's team had built a small, makeshift command center at the Special Operations base in Jalalabad for a dozen officials including the SEAL team commander, the helicopter squadron commander, and representatives from the National Security Agency, the CIA, and the FBI. In the command center McRaven positioned himself inside a purpose-built closet so he could monitor the mission and also simultaneously join a videoconference with Panetta at CIA headquarters. Wearing a headset, McRaven narrated the mission's milestones on the video call. McRaven monitored the assault force on a flat panel display as it moved across the border. The helicopters were followed by a RQ-170 stealth drone flying miles above them transmitting live video back to McRaven and his team.

Half an hour after the Black Hawks had departed Jalalabad, three Chinook CH-47 helicopters took off from the same airfield. This was the backup force. One Chinook loaded with SEALs landed just before reaching the Pakistani border and would act as an additional Quick Reaction Force if there was a large-scale firefight in Abbottabad.

The other two Chinooks filled with SEALs and additional fuel for the Black Hawks flew on into Pakistan to Kala Dhaka, a desolate, mountainous region fifty miles northeast of Abbottabad. The lumbering, bus-like Chinooks were far larger than the Black Hawks and were much more likely to be picked up by Pakistani radar, so McRaven wanted to ensure the Black Hawks were well in the lead, should the Chinooks be detected.

The one-and-a-half-hour flight path for the helicopters was indirect by design. They followed the least risky route, avoiding population centers and taking advantage of any terrain that would mask them from Pakistani radar. As the Black Hawks approached Abbottabad, they flew behind a small mountain range, which shielded them. When the Black Hawks came around this range for their descent into Abbottabad there would be a couple of minutes when the helicopters could be detected by radar. More important, people on the ground in Abbottabad were now likely to hear the noise of the helicopter rotors. McRaven thought this was the moment when thing could get dicey, if people living at the compound heard the noise and loosed off rocket-propelled grenades in response.

At the White House, Obama and his war cabinet monitored the progress of the operation in the Situation Room, but they couldn't see the video feed of the raid supplied by the stealth drone flying high over the Black Hawks and SEALs. That video feed was available only in a small anteroom next door to the Situation Room where one of McRaven's deputies, Brigadier General Brad Webb, had set up communications gear. Vice President Joe Biden drifted into the room to watch the video feed, followed by Secretary of Defense Robert Gates and Secretary of State Hillary Clinton. Obama also popped in, announcing, "I need to watch this." Wearing a windbreaker, the president settled himself into a chair in a corner of the cramped room.

It was a moonless night and the electricity was off in Abbottabad; a nice stroke of luck for the SEALs. Pakistani cities routinely experience "load shedding," or rolling power blackouts.

Two minutes out from the compound, the side door of the first Black Hawk opened, and some of the SEALs started swinging their feet out of the helicopter and getting their fast ropes ready. Thirty seconds out and they could see the compound.

The plan was for one of the Black Hawks to hover over what was suspected to be bin Laden's third-floor bedroom. SEALs would then fast-rope onto the roof of the bedroom and surprise al-Qaeda's leader while he slept. The other Black Hawk would drop another group of SEALs onto the ground near the main building on the compound and they would then advance up the stairs to the third-floor bedroom.

It didn't work out that way. The rehearsals at the replicas of the compound in the States had taken place with chain link fencing standing in for the high concrete walls surrounding the compound. This fencing had allowed the helicopter's rotor wash to dissipate, while the concrete walls amplified it, causing a phenomenon known as "settling with power" during which a helicopter gets caught in the downwash from its own rotors. Higher than expected temperatures in Abbottabad also gave the helicopters less "lift," as the air density was lower because of the elevated temperature. As a result, the first Black Hawk started dropping out of the sky.

McRaven was watching his flat panel display and saw that the Black Hawk was wobbling and clearly losing lift. McRaven thought, "That doesn't look too good." The Black Hawk pilot realized what was happening and took immediate action to bring the helicopter down for a "hard landing."

The SEALs had rehearsed this possibility numerous times. There was a large open space inside the compound walls, which was about a third of an acre where the inhabitants kept cows. The SEALs referred to this area as "the animal pen."

Before the raid McRaven had talked to the Black Hawk pilot several times, who told him, "Sir, unless I am killed instantly, I will be able to land this helicopter in the animal pen."

The Black Hawk pilot made a hard landing in the animal pen. As the helicopter went down, the tail rotor clipped the wall of the compound and got hung up there so the chopper could no longer fly.

Watching the video feed of the helicopter going down, Biden, a practicing Catholic, fingered his rosary beads.

McRaven knew the difference between a crash and a hard landing. The helicopter wasn't on fire and he could see that SEALS were already moving away from the downed chopper.

In his distinctive Texan baritone with no hint of anxiety in his voice, McRaven told Obama's war cabinet, "We will now be amending the mission. My men are prepared for this contingency and they will deal with it."

The second helicopter moved to Plan B, landing outside of the compound instead of hovering over the roof of the third-floor bedroom.

Now awake, bin Laden called to his son Khalid on the floor below, where two of his wives, Umm Hamza and Siham, were sleeping. His youngest wife, Amal, went to check on her five children.

Bin Laden's two oldest daughters, Miriam and Sumaiya, came up from the second floor to be with their father. Together they prayed the Kalima, the Muslim profession of faith, reciting, "There is no God but Allah. Muhammed is the messenger of Allah."

Bin Laden told his daughters, "American helicopters have arrived. You need to leave the room immediately." They refused to leave.

The SEALs moved from the animal pen area toward a one-story building that housed bin Laden's bodyguard Ibrahim and his family. They checked the door, which was locked. One of the SEALs, Matt Bissonnette, placed a small explosive charge on the door. An AK-47 started shooting through the door. Bissonnette and his partner returned fire and everything went quiet.

Bissonnette's partner shouted in Arabic, "Open the door and come out."

The door opened and the bodyguard's wife, Maryam, came out holding a small child, three other children trailing behind her. Ibrahim, her husband, lay dead inside the door.

The SEALs flowed past the annex building onto a lawn area dominated by the main three-story house, which they entered. Now the officials at the White House and at CIA headquarters watching the drone feed could no longer see these SEALs.

Inside the house it was pitch black. Bin Laden's other bodyguard, Abrar, and his wife, Bushra, lived on the ground floor. One of the SEALs shot and killed them both.

Walking through the kitchen, three SEALs moved deeper into the house. Near the back of the house was a stairwell. A massive iron metal gate completely blocked the staircase and access to the upper two floors of the house.

One of the SEALs thought, "Who has a metal door at the bottom of their stairs?" The SEALs put an explosive charge on the gate, blowing it open. They made their way up to the second floor. "Maya," the CIA analyst, had told the SEALs that bin Laden's twenty-three-year-old son, Khalid, was likely living on the second floor.

On the second floor, the SEAL who was "on point" saw a head pop out and disappear quickly around a corner. The point man whispered, "Khalid. Khalid." Hearing his name, Khalid looked back around the edge of the hall and the point man shot him dead. The SEALs stepped over Khalid's body, an AK-47 nearby.

The point man then spotted someone poking his head out of a room on the third floor. He knew immediately it was bin Laden and shot at him. This shot may have wounded al-Qaeda's leader. Following the point man up the stairs were two SEALs, first Robert O'Neill and then Bissonnette.

Bin Laden's youngest wife, Amal, saw an American soldier coming up the stairs aiming his weapon at her husband. She saw a red beam of light, which was the laser sight of the soldier's rifle, but she heard no shot from the silenced weapon. Amal rushed the soldier, who shot her in the calf. She passed out on the bed.

"Maya" had told the SEALs that the women living with bin Laden might be wearing suicide vests. The point man rushed into the third-floor bedroom, and seeing two women swept them up in his arms and pushed them against the back wall. If they had suicide vests he would have absorbed the force of the blasts and protected the other SEALs.

O'Neill and Bissonnette shot bin Laden with a few more rounds.* They were carrying photos of al-Qaeda's leader and it certainly looked like him, although in the photos his beard was gray and in death it was jet black because bin Laden had been applying Just for Men hair dye.

---

*The point man, O'Neill, and Bissonnette were the first three SEALs to assault bin Laden's bedroom. O'Neill has since claimed that he was the shooter who killed bin Laden. Others on the raid team told the author that O'Neill's account wasn't accurate. To determine definitively which of the SEALs killed bin Laden is not possible. All the electricity in the compound and the surrounding neighborhood was off on a moonless night and the SEALs were wearing night vision goggles, which allowed them only limited vision. What is certain is that it was a team effort. As McRaven explained to the author, "It wasn't just the SEAL team and the Night Stalkers [helicopter pilots], it was everybody that has fought in the Iraq and Afghanistan wars after 9/11. And this was why it wasn't important who killed bin Laden. There may have been one person that pulled the trigger, but there were hundreds of thousands of troops behind us."

Bin Laden's two oldest daughters confirmed to the American soldiers that the dead man was their father.

Bin Laden died without putting up a fight. Bissonnette found his guns in his bedroom, an AK-47 and a Makarov pistol. They were sitting on a high shelf above the frame of the door that opened into the room. The chambers of both guns were empty. "He hadn't even prepared a defense," Bissonnette thought.

The raid commander called McRaven on a satellite radio, "For God and country: Geronimo." "Geronimo" was the code name for bin Laden.

McRaven relayed the word "Geronimo" to the White House. McRaven realized he wasn't sure if that meant bin Laden was captured or killed.

McRaven asked the SEAL ground force commander, "Is he EKIA [Enemy Killed in Action]?"

A few seconds later, the answer came back: "Roger, Geronimo EKIA."

McRaven announced to the White House, "Geronimo EKIA."

The president quietly said, "We got him."

McRaven came on the line again to the White House, saying, "Please keep your expectations managed a little here. Most operators when they are on a mission their adrenaline is sky-high. Yes, they are professional, but let's not count on anything until they get back and we have some evidence."

McRaven also pointed out, "We've got SEALs on the ground without a ride."

Bissonnette took photographs of bin Laden's body, while another SEAL gathered DNA samples using cotton swabs that soaked up his blood and saliva.

About twenty-five minutes into the mission, McRaven received a call, "Sir, the SEALs are requesting some additional time on the ground. Sir, they say they found a whole shit-ton of computers and electronic gear on the second floor."

Cognizant that the half-hour point was the ideal time to wrap up this kind of operation, McRaven took a deep breath and said, "Okay, grab as much as you can, but we've got to kind of get moving here."

On the second floor bin Laden had meticulously organized his CDs, DVDs, memory cards, thumb drives, computers, and digital voice recorders. The SEALs stuffed bags with as much as they could, taking ten hard drives, five computers, and around one hundred storage devices such as thumb drives and disks.

At about the forty-minute point McRaven told his team, "Okay guys, I'm getting a little nervous here. Let's go ahead and wrap this thing up."

Outside the compound the Pakistani-American interpreter saw that the noise of the helicopters and gunfire had woken up neighbors, who were now coming out of their houses. Some of them started running toward the compound. The interpreter realized he had to do something. He called at them in Pashto, saying, "This is a government business. If you want to stay alive, don't come. Go back to your house."

Two men kept running toward the compound. A SEAL prepared to shoot. The interpreter tapped the SEAL's shoulder, saying, "Wait." The interpreter cursed at the running men, yelling at them in Pashto, "Go back!" They turned around.

On the feed from the drone officials at the White House and CIA saw four black dots moving from the main building on the compound to the one functioning Black Hawk. These were four SEALs carrying bin Laden's body to the helicopter.

The SEALs were "on target" at Abbottabad for forty-eight minutes, eighteen minutes longer than planned. As a result, they had gathered an immense haul of intelligence, but the city of Abbottabad was now full of blue police lights converging on the compound.

It was time to go. The SEALs did not want the downed Black Hawk's stealth technology and secret avionics to fall into the wrong hands. They packed the downed helicopter with explosives and set a timer so they would blow up the Black Hawk after a couple of minutes. Just as the downed chopper was about to explode, the backup Chinook was coming in and was very close to landing.

An urgent call to the Chinook pilot instructed him, "Break away!" The pilot banked steeply to his right. The Black Hawk blew up at

1:06 a.m. in a massive explosion that threw up a 150-foot mushroom cloud. The Chinook made a sharp turn away from the cloud and debris. The explosion was so close to the Chinook that one of the SEALs could feel its heat inside the helicopter. Operation Neptune Spear had come close to losing another helicopter.

The Chinook came in to land to pick up the remaining SEALS on the ground as well as bin Laden's DNA samples and all the intelligence materials that were retrieved at the compound. Bin Laden's body was placed on the surviving Black Hawk; that way, if the Pakistanis mobilized their air force and shot down one of the helicopters, there was still evidence that bin Laden was dead.

One Chinook flew a direct route back toward Afghanistan. In the surviving Black Hawk the lights in the cockpit were blinking, indicating that it was low on fuel. It headed to get fuel from the second Chinook in Kala Dhaka, the mountainous, remote region northeast of Abbottabad. The refueling took nineteen long minutes.

Escorted by the Chinook the Black Hawk flew toward Afghanistan. The Chinook pilot noticed his electronic warfare displays were lighting up, which meant that Pakistani radar systems were "painting" the Chinook and it was being tracked. An F-16 jet took off from a base in Pakistan and started searching for the Chinook. One of the SEALs started thinking they might all die because there was no way they were going to outmaneuver an F-16.

At 2:26 a.m. the Chinook and Black Hawk entered Afghan airspace. It was the first time that the SEALs had really enjoyed hearing the words "Welcome to Afghanistan."

Admiral McRaven was on video link with the White House when the helicopters landed in Jalalabad. Obama asked, "Bill, can you confirm that it's bin Laden?"

McRaven said, "Mr. President, I can't until I go visually ID the body."

The landing field was about five minutes from where McRaven was positioned. By the time McRaven reached the hangar the SEALs had offloaded the body. McRaven unzipped the body bag, thinking, "He doesn't look terrific." Bin Laden had two rounds in his head.

"Maya," the CIA analyst, looked at bin Laden's body stone-faced, say-ing, "I guess I'm out of a fucking job." And then she walked away.

McRaven had several photos of bin Laden, and when he put them close to the dead man's face, even though his beard was a little shorter in the photos, it was immediately obvious that it was al-Qaeda's leader. McRaven knew bin Laden was about six-foot-four. There was a young SEAL standing nearby, McRaven asked him, "Son, how tall are you?"

The SEAL said, "Well, sir, I'm about six-foot-two."

McRaven said, "Come here, I want you to lie down next to the re-mains here."

The young SEAL said, "I'm sorry, sir. You want me to do what?"

McRaven said, "I want you to lie down next to the remains."

Bin Laden's corpse was a couple inches longer than the young SEAL.

McRaven called Obama, saying, "Mr. President, I can't be certain without DNA that it's bin Laden, but frankly it's probably about a 99 per-cent chance that it is. In fact, I had a young SEAL lie down next to him, and the remains were a little taller."

There was a pause on the other end of the videoconference. Obama said, "Okay, let me get this straight. We had $60 million for a helicopter"—the stealth Black Hawk that had gone down—"and you didn't have $10 for a tape measure?"

Now that the SEALs and bin Laden's body were safely out of Pakistan it was time to tell Pakistan's leaders what had happened.

Obama called Pakistan's president, Asif Ali Zardari, whose wife, Benazir Bhutto, the former Pakistani prime minister, had been assassi-nated by allies of bin Laden four years earlier. Zardari told Obama, "I'm happy because these are the same types of people who killed my wife."

Admiral Mullen called the Pakistani army chief of staff, General Ash-faq Parvez Kayani, the most powerful man in the country, who immedi-ately said "Congratulations." Kayani urged that Obama publicly explain what had happened as soon as possible, saying, "We're not going to be able to manage the Pakistani media without you confirming this. You can explain it to them. They need to understand that this was bin Laden and not just some ordinary U.S. operation."

Photos of bin Laden were transmitted back to the CIA. The two best facial recognition analysts in the agency's Science & Technology division independently assessed the photos. They examined seven facial features, including eyes, nasal openings, and earlobes and estimated that there was a 95 percent chance it was bin Laden.

Obama's first reaction was caution. "We're gonna hold. We will not announce tonight. I'm not going in front of three hundred million Americans with a one in twenty chance of being completely wrong. This is too important."

Obama's advisers weighed in, saying, "This story's not gonna hold. If you wait till morning, it will come out somewhere else."

The photos of bin Laden's body were handed around the Situation Room. When Obama looked at them there was a change in his demeanor. It certainly looked like bin Laden. Obama said that he would make the announcement that night.

Obama called George W. Bush in Dallas to tell him that bin Laden was dead.

Obama also called Bill Clinton, saying, "I assume Hillary's already told you?" She hadn't.

Going outside for the first time in many hours, Obama walked down the colonnade overlooking the Rose Garden toward the White House's East Room where the world's media was waiting. The president could hear chants of "USA! USA! USA!" shouted by the crowds of young Americans who had gathered outside the White House gates. Most of them were children when bin Laden's men had struck on 9/11.

At 11:35 p.m. in the East Room without preamble Obama announced, "Good evening. Tonight, I can report to the American people and to the world that the United States has conducted an operation that killed Osama bin Laden, the leader of al-Qaeda, and a terrorist who's responsible for the murder of thousands of innocent men, women, and children."

SEVENTEEN

AFTER BIN LADEN

Osama has woken up the sleeping bin Ladens.
> —Khaled Khawaja, a Pakistani army officer
> who knew bin Laden during the 1980s

Beware that, when fighting monsters, you yourself do not become a monster, for when you gaze long into the abyss, the abyss gazes also into you.
> —Friedrich Nietzsche

We have seen their kind before. They are the heirs of all the murderous ideologies of the 20th century. By sacrificing human life to serve their radical visions, by abandoning every value except the will to power, they follow in the path of fascism, Nazism and totalitarianism. And they will follow that path all the way to where it ends: In history's unmarked grave of discarded lies.
> —President George W. Bush, speaking to a joint
> session of Congress, September 20, 2001

On the morning of May 2, 2011, technicians at a forensics laboratory at Bagram Air Base in Afghanistan analyzed DNA from bin Laden's corpse. They established that it was definitively al-Qaeda's leader.

That same day bin Laden's body was flown from Afghanistan to the USS *Carl Vinson*, which was cruising in the Arabian Sea off the coast of Pakistan. Following the recitation of Islamic burial prayers, American sailors dropped bin Laden's corpse from the deck of the warship into the ocean. There would be no bin Laden burial site to which his followers could make pilgrimages.

Bin Laden's body sank into the deep, to a watery unmarked grave. He was fifty-four.

Protests about the killing of bin Laden were surprisingly muted. Even in the bustling, crowded cities of Pakistan, where million-man marches were routine, only a few hundred protesters gathered to mourn his passing. Bin Laden hadn't died heroically fighting on a "field of jihad," but in a suburban compound surrounded by his family, putting up no resistance. It was not the heroic martyrdom that bin Laden had urged on so many of his followers.

Obama chose not to release the photographs of bin Laden's dead body with a chunk of his head blown off. The president was concerned that publicizing the gory photos would endanger Americans living overseas. When Obama was pressed about why he wouldn't supply this photographic proof, he dryly observed, "The fact of the matter is you will not see bin Laden walking on this earth again."

On May 6, al-Qaeda itself officially confirmed the "martyrdom" of bin Laden. Two weeks later the group also released an audiotape made by its leader just days before he was killed. On the tape bin Laden celebrated the events of the Arab Spring, saying, "I think that the winds of change will blow over the entire Muslim world, God willing."

Gina Bennett worked night shifts on the CIA's Media Exploitation Task Force, which operated around the clock to translate and assess the 470,000 files recovered in Abbottabad. Many of the files were not germane, such as newspaper articles or cartoons that bin Laden's children were watching, but thousands of pages of documents in Arabic included bin Laden's communications with his key lieutenants and with his affiliated terrorist groups around the world. The files also contained the planning for his new operations.

The mammoth task of sifting through all this was aided by artificial intelligence tools that searched through the three terabytes of data. Using machine translation and text recognition, the artificial intelligence tools picked out key documents in a couple of hours, a process that would have taken months without the technology. Every available Arab linguist in the intelligence community was scooped up to work on the pertinent documents.

The documents contained several surprises. CIA officials thought that the dour Egyptian surgeon Dr. Ayman al-Zawahiri, who was nominally bin Laden's top deputy, was running al-Qaeda on a day-to-day basis. The documents showed that it was, in fact, bin Laden who was still managing his organization, if not micromanaging it. He was also in frequent communication with Atiyah Abd al-Rahman, a forty-year-old Libyan, whom bin Laden corresponded with regularly about matters of strategy and tactics. After analyzing the Abbottabad documents, CIA officials realized that Atiyah was bin Laden's chief operations officer. A CIA drone strike killed Atiyah in Pakistan's tribal regions only four months after bin Laden's death.

The documents showed that bin Laden was deeply involved in approving key personnel decisions and also providing strategic advice to his followers in the Middle East and Africa. When Al-Qaeda in the Arabian Peninsula proffered the Yemeni-American cleric Anwar al-Awlaki as a possible new leader of the group, bin Laden nixed the appointment. The leaders of al-Qaeda in Yemen wondered whether it might be the right time to establish an "Islamic State" in Yemen. Bin Laden told them the moment wasn't ripe and they acceded to his wishes. He urged the Somali terrorist group al-Shabaab not to publicly identify itself as part of al-Qaeda, and the group complied.

While the documents revealed bin Laden to be a hands-on boss, they also showed he was increasingly delusional about al-Qaeda's capacity to carry out large-scale attacks. He wanted his followers to hijack oil tankers and blow them up to send the price of oil high and spook global markets. These kinds of unrealistic plans reminded the Director of National

Intelligence, Jim Clapper, of Hitler in the latter stages of World War II: "He's moving all these army groups around that didn't exist."

There was also porn discovered on the Abbottabad hard drives. Bin Laden had no access to the internet and it seems implausible he would have asked his bodyguards to bring porn to him on thumb drives. The most likely explanation was that bin Laden's bodyguards had purchased secondhand computers for him with the porn already embedded.

Bin Laden died knowing that his great dream of attacking the United States again had failed.

Al-Qaeda did continue to retain a limited capacity to attack the United States after bin Laden's death. Eight years after he was killed, al-Qaeda's branch in Yemen coordinated with a Saudi military officer who was in the United States on a training mission. The officer killed three American sailors at the Pensacola Naval Air Station in Florida on December 6, 2019. But it was a relatively small-scale attack that underlined how much the U.S. campaign against al-Qaeda and its affiliates had damaged them.

In the two decades after 9/11, the Pensacola attack was the only lethal assault in the United States that had a direct connection to a foreign terrorist organization. This was an unpredictable outcome given the widespread fears following 9/11 that there would be a serious second wave of attacks. For many years after 9/11, *Foreign Policy* magazine regularly surveyed around a hundred foreign policy experts; at least two-thirds of whom believed that a 9/11-scale assault was likely within a half-decade. This, of course, never happened. Instead, during the two decades that followed 9/11, there were more than a dozen smaller-scale "homegrown" jihadist attacks carried out by U.S. citizens or legal residents that killed 104 Americans. These homegrown terrorists had no formal connections to al-Qaeda or allied groups, but they were inspired by bin Laden's ideology. While each of these 104 deaths was a tragedy, they were not a national catastrophe on the scale of 9/11.

The United States was insulated from a recurrence of a 9/11-scale attack because bin Laden's decision to carry out the 9/11 operation significantly increased the size, power, and funding of the U.S. national security state, which inflicted great damage on al-Qaeda and its allies overseas with many hundreds of drone strikes and thousands of Special Operations raids. The attacks also fortified America's home defenses. There were only sixteen people on the U.S. "no-fly" list on 9/11. Around the time that bin Laden died there were more than forty thousand and another one million people were on a list that ensured they would be put into secondary screening if they boarded a U.S.-bound flight. In 2001, there were thirty-two task forces where multiple law enforcement agencies worked together to build terrorism cases. That number had more than tripled by the time bin Laden was killed. The attacks also gave birth to the Department of Homeland Security, the National Counterterrorism Center, and the Transportation Security Administration. The U.S. intelligence budget also grew dramatically after 9/11, tripling to around $70 billion by the time the CIA tracked down bin Laden in Abbottabad.

Bin Laden's killing reignited some of the most contentious questions of the "war on terror," such as the extent to which al-Qaeda detainees subjected to harsh interrogations by the CIA had provided useful information. Defenders of the CIA's coercive interrogations were quick to point to bin Laden's death as evidence for their efficacy. The day after bin Laden was killed, the Republican chair of the House Homeland Security Committee, Peter King of New York, told Fox News, "For those who say that waterboarding doesn't work, who say it should be stopped and never used again, we got vital information which directly led us to bin Laden." Four days later George W. Bush's attorney general, Michael Mukasey, wrote in *The Wall Street Journal* that bin Laden was found because of the harsh techniques used against al-Qaeda detainees.

This view was given wide currency by the popular 2012 movie *Zero Dark Thirty*. The director, Kathryn Bigelow, and screenwriter, Mark Boal, received considerable cooperation from the CIA to tell the story of the hunt for bin Laden. *Zero Dark Thirty* was a powerful and dramatic piece of filmmaking and was nominated for five Academy Awards. But the film-makers also presented the film as a form of journalism, asserting in a title card at the beginning that it was "based on first hand accounts of actual events."

The first half-hour of *Zero Dark Thirty* consisted of scenes of an ex-hausted, bloodied al-Qaeda detainee who was strung to a ceiling with ropes; beaten; forced to wear a dog collar while crawling around attached to a leash; stripped naked in front of a female CIA analyst; blasted with heavy metal music so he was deprived of sleep; forced to endure crude waterboardings; and locked in a coffinlike wooden crate. After the de-tainee was systematically abused by his CIA captors he was tricked into believing that he had already inadvertently given up key information about al-Qaeda as a result of the abuse he had undergone. At this point, he started cooperating with his CIA interrogators and told them about "Abu Ahmed al-Kuwaiti," which was, of course, the actual alias used by bin Laden's bodyguard.

But the implication that coercive interrogation techniques were essen-tial to finding bin Laden is wrong. As we have seen, the information about the important role that bin Laden's bodyguard, known as "the Kuwaiti," played for bin Laden was provided by an al-Qaeda detainee before he was subjected to coercive interrogations. A foreign intelligence service later supplied the Kuwaiti's real name. U.S. signals intelligence then tracked the Kuwaiti's phone to a city in Pakistan. That's when CIA agents on the ground there observed him at the Abbottabad compound. It was coercive interrogations that proved unreliable: five key members of al-Qaeda held in CIA custody subjected to them consistently provided misleading infor-mation about the Kuwaiti.

It's worth recalling, however, that the man whom al-Qaeda had groomed to be the twentieth hijacker, Mohammed al-Qahtani, did pro-vide important information about the Kuwaiti during the period that he was subjected to coercive interrogations while held in military custody at Guantánamo. But it's not possible to know what might have been learned from Qahtani under standard questioning, and it is certainly the case that important information from members of al-Qaeda was elicited by FBI agents using such standard questioning techniques.* Beyond all that, coercive interrogations are not, of course, ethical.

Another controversy that bin Laden's death underlined was the ambiguous role that Pakistan played in the fight against jihadists. Was Pakistan an arsonist or a firefighter when it came to jihadist groups? Or both? Before 9/11, Pakistan was one of the few countries that had recognized the Taliban when they had ruled Afghanistan and were sheltering bin Laden. In the years after 9/11 the Pakistanis were helpful to the United States, arresting leaders of al-Qaeda living in Pakistan, who were then handed over to American custody. But Pakistan continued to support jihadist groups allied to al-Qaeda, such as the Haqqani network, a particularly violent wing of the Taliban.

Knowing that bin Laden was killed not far from Pakistan's West Point in a compound where he had lived for half a decade, many believed that bin Laden must have received some support from Pakistani officials or military officers. But there was no evidence supporting this assumption. The night of the bin Laden raid, U.S. officials were monitoring the communications of Pakistan's top military officials, and their bewildered reactions showed that the Pakistanis had no clue about bin Laden's presence in Abbottabad. In addition, in the many thousands of pages of al-Qaeda documents recovered in bin Laden's compound there was nothing to back up the notion that bin Laden was protected by Pakistani officials, or that he was in communication with them. Quite the reverse; the documents described the Pakistani army as "apostates," and bemoaned "the intense

---

*For instance, FBI Special Agent Ali Soufan, using standard interrogation techniques, learned considerable, important information from Abu Jandal, a key bin Laden bodyguard, immediately after 9/11. A year later Soufan also learned of the key role that Khalid Sheikh Mohammed had played in the 9/11 attacks from al-Qaeda's travel facilitator, Abu Zubaydah, using similar standard interrogation techniques.

Pakistani pressure on us." They also included plans for attacks against Pakistani military targets.*

Bin Laden's death also shed light on the nature of the relationship between al-Qaeda and the Taliban. Apologists for the Taliban had claimed that they had spurned al-Qaeda, and that premise was key to the Taliban's long-running peace talks with the United States, which required them to reject al-Qaeda in return for a complete withdrawal of American troops from Afghanistan. But the Abbottabad documents showed al-Qaeda and the Taliban had no intention of cutting off their alliance. In addition to corresponding with the Taliban leader, Mullah Omar, bin Laden kept in touch with Tayeb Agha, a close aide to Mullah Omar, who was a key Taliban negotiator with the Americans. Al-Qaeda also provided considerable funding to the Haqqani network, whose leader, Sirajuddin Haqqani, was appointed to be the number two leader of the Taliban four years after bin Laden was killed. In 2010 al-Qaeda's leaders paid the Haqqanis "a large amount" that they had obtained by kidnapping an Afghan diplomat in Pakistan who was released for a $5 million ransom. The Haqqanis and al-Qaeda also jointly attacked the Bagram Air Base in Afghanistan on May 19, 2010, killing an American contractor and wounding ten soldiers.

The same year al-Qaeda's leaders also gave a large sum from the ransom to the leader of the Pakistani Taliban. Treating him as if he were a subordinate, they warned him to suspend his campaign of attacks against Pakistani mosques and also noted, "We're sending the attached short list

---

*During the summer of 2010 al-Qaeda's leaders did contemplate negotiating a cease-fire with the Pakistani government. Al-Qaeda members reached out to leaders of the Pakistani Taliban who maintained contacts with Pakistan's military intelligence service to see if they could negotiate some kind of truce with the Pakistani government. The deal would be that the Pakistanis would leave al-Qaeda alone and vice versa. Al-Qaeda could then focus on its main goal of attacking American targets. However, bin Laden's deputy who was leading this effort told bin Laden, "As you know, this is just talk!" and nothing came of these discussions.

on what is acceptable and unacceptable on the subject of kidnapping and receiving money."

In short, the Abbottabad documents demonstrated that al-Qaeda and various arms of the Taliban cooperated on military operations and funding, while maintaining their friendly relations. A decade after bin Laden's death, "peace" negotiations continued between the Taliban and the U.S. government, with al-Qaeda always in the background. According to a report by the United Nations, "the Taliban regularly consulted" with al-Qaeda during its negotiations with the United States while guaranteeing that they "would honor their historical ties" with the terrorist group. The U.N. also assessed that the links between al-Qaeda and the Taliban "have remained strong" and "have been continually reinforced by pledges of allegiance" by al-Qaeda's leaders to the leader of the Taliban.

The Abbottabad documents were also helpful in illuminating the real relationship between bin Laden and Iran. As we have seen, much of his entourage, including seven of his children, his beloved oldest wife, Umm Hamza, as well as key leaders of al-Qaeda, fled to Iran after 9/11. They had remained there under various forms of house arrest that ranged from tolerable to grim. Yet there was no evidence in the voluminous documents that al-Qaeda or Iran ever cooperated on any attacks, and there is plenty of evidence of bin Laden's intense distrust of the Iranian regime. That distrust was amplified when bin Laden received a memo from a member of al-Qaeda describing how on March 5, 2010, Iranian Special Forces dressed in black and wearing masks stormed the detention center where his family members and leaders of al-Qaeda were being held. At the detention center, the Iranian soldiers beat the men and women, including members of bin Laden's group, who were protesting their poor living conditions.

One verdict that clearly emerges from the documents is the role that drones had in weakening bin Laden's operation in Pakistan. While bin Laden was living in Abbottabad he regularly wrote his family members and his followers living in the country's tribal regions urging them to move around only on cloudy days when the drones were less effective and to hold any meetings in tunnels where the drones couldn't detect them.

By 2005 most of al-Qaeda's leaders had settled in these remote, largely ungoverned areas bordering Afghanistan because they allowed them some freedom of movement and the ability to train new recruits. But in 2010 President Obama authorized a record number of drone strikes in Pakistan's tribal regions, 122 in total. During the decade after 9/11 two dozen al-Qaeda leaders and midlevel operatives were killed by drones. The papers uncovered after his death show that, as a result, bin Laden was planning to pull all of his followers out of the region and resettle them in other parts of Pakistan or in Afghanistan.

As is often the case with significant historical events, conspiracy theories sprang up about bin Laden's death. In the first days after bin Laden was killed, White House officials made a number of false statements about what had happened, claiming that bin Laden had died in a "firefight" and had used a female as a "human shield." The false statements, typical of the "fog of war," grew out of the confusion surrounding the details of the raid before the SEALs could be properly debriefed. Those falsehoods were soon corrected by the White House, but they helped fuel subsequent conspiracy theories.

The most widely circulated one was put into play by the prominent investigative journalist Seymour Hersh, who early in his career broke the story of the My Lai massacre, during which hundreds of unarmed civilians were killed by U.S. soldiers in Vietnam. In 2015 Hersh published a ten-thousand-word story in the *London Review of Books* asserting that President Obama and many of his top advisers had lied about pretty much everything concerning the bin Laden operation. The story attracted so much attention that the magazine's website crashed.

Hersh asserted that U.S. and Pakistani officials were fully aware that bin Laden lived in Abbottabad, cooperated in his capture, and then engaged in a massive cover-up.* The principal claim that Hersh's article

---

*One of the only journalists who backed up any element of Hersh's story was Carlotta Gall, a reporter for the *New York Times*, whose 2014 book, *The Wrong*

made, which largely relied on the assertions of a single, unnamed retired U.S. intelligence official, was that Pakistan's military had held bin Laden prisoner in Abbottabad for five years and simply made him available to the SEALs on the night of the raid. A Pakistani military official accompanied the SEALs on the raid, the article claimed, and the only shots fired that night were the ones that the SEALs fired to kill bin Laden.

None of this was true. The claim that the only shots fired at the Abbottabad compound were the ones that killed bin Laden ignored the fact that two of bin Laden's bodyguards, one of his sons, and one of the bodyguards' wives were all shot and killed that night. I was the only outside observer to visit the Abbottabad compound before the Pakistani military demolished it. The compound was trashed, littered with broken glass, and

---

Enemy: America in Afghanistan, 2001–2014, was excerpted in the *Times* magazine. Gall wrote that she had been told by a Pakistani source that Pakistan's military intelligence agency "actually ran a special desk assigned to handle bin Laden. It was operated independently, led by an officer who made his own decisions and did not report to a superior. He handled only one person: bin Laden." Many years later, no evidence has emerged to substantiate this claim. After the bin Laden raid this author spoke on the record to President Obama; John Brennan, Obama's top counterterrorism adviser; CIA director Leon Panetta and his chief of staff, Jeremy Bash; Secretary of State Hillary Clinton; Chairman of the Joint Chiefs Admiral Mike Mullen; Vice Chairman of the Joint Chiefs General James Cartwright; Michael Leiter, the director of the National Counterterrorism Center; Nick Rasmussen, senior director for counterterrorism at the National Security Council; Michèle Flournoy, head of policy at the Pentagon; Michael Vickers, the civilian overseer of Special Operations; Tony Blinken, Obama's deputy national security adviser; and Denis McDonough, who held that position before Blinken. These officials had collectively spent many decades working to destroy al-Qaeda, and they were deeply suspicious of Pakistan for its continuing support for elements of the Taliban. All of them said that Pakistani officials had no clue that bin Laden was living in Abbottabad. Indeed, an early debate between senior national security officials at the White House was whether to mount a joint U.S.-Pakistani raid on bin Laden's suspected hideout. This plan was rejected because the officials were concerned that such a joint operation carried the risk that word would leak out about the bin Laden intelligence. This debate would have been moot if the Pakistanis already knew bin Laden was living in Abbottabad.

several areas of it were sprayed with bullet holes where the SEALs had fired at members of bin Laden's entourage and family and where they had also exchanged fire with one of his bodyguards.

Common sense would also tell you that if the Pakistanis were holding bin Laden and the U.S. government had found this out, the easiest path for both countries would not be to launch a U.S. military raid into Pakistan, but instead to hand bin Laden over quietly to the Americans. Indeed, the Pakistanis had done this on several occasions with al-Qaeda leaders captured on their territory. Also, if U.S. officials had found out that the Pakistani officials were hiding bin Laden, they had no incentive to cover it up. After all, relations between the United States and Pakistan were at an all-time low around the time of the bin Laden raid because the Pakistanis had recently imprisoned Raymond Davis, a CIA contractor who had killed two Pakistanis. What did U.S. officials have to lose by saying that bin Laden was being protected by the Pakistanis?

A few months after Hersh's story had appeared, *The New York Times Magazine* doubled down on Hersh's nonsensical piece, publishing its own cover story provocatively titled "What Do We Really Know About Osama bin Laden's Death?" *Times* writer Jonathan Mahler asserted that it was "impossible to know what was true and what wasn't" about bin Laden's death, which was now "floating somewhere between fact and mythology." Really? That could be true only if you ignored dozens of eyewitness accounts about the bin Laden operation and actual reporting about the raid by multiple reporters at . . . *The New York Times*. Journalists at the *Times* were furious that their own deep reporting about the bin Laden operation was being called into question. *Times* reporter Eric Schmitt, who shared in a 2009 Pulitzer for his coverage of Pakistan, told the *Times*'s public editor, "This article has struck a nerve among national security and foreign policy reporters at *The New York Times*, and elsewhere, like few I've seen in my three-plus decades at the paper."

I climbed the stairs to bin Laden's third-floor bedroom in his Abbottabad compound and stepped into the room where he was killed. Looking up at the low ceiling, you could still see the dark patterns of blood that had spurted from bin Laden's head when the bullet fired by a U.S. Navy SEAL had torn through the terrorist leader's face. In the room where bin Laden died, I had expected some kind of frisson, a sensation perhaps akin to exploring Hitler's bunker complex at the end of World War II. Instead, I felt only the futility of bin Laden's self-proclaimed jihad against the United States.

On a personal level, bin Laden had destroyed much of his family. Two of his sons, Saad and Khalid, were killed in U.S. counterterrorism operations, while his daughter Khadija had died in childbirth because she was forced to deliver her baby while on the run in Pakistan's remote tribal regions.* Her husband was then killed in a CIA drone strike. Before 9/11 his wives Khadijah and Najwa had left bin Laden with five of their children because they could no longer bear to live with the dangers and privations that were required by life inside al-Qaeda. Two of bin Laden's adult sons had also left him; his oldest son, Abdullah, was tired of living a pauper's life, while Omar was sickened by his father's death cult. After 9/11, seven of bin Laden's children and his oldest wife, Umm Hamza, all lived under house arrest in Iran for almost a decade. Bin Laden's wife Amal was wounded in the operation that killed her husband, and after the Abbottabad raid Amal and bin Laden's two other wives, Siham and Umm Hamza, were all kept in Pakistani custody for a year.

On a global level, bin Laden's 9/11 attacks set the course of U.S. foreign policy for the first two decades of the twenty-first century and reshaped the Muslim world in ways that bin Laden certainly didn't intend and that few could have predicted in their immediate aftermath. The Authorization for Use of Military Force, which Congress passed days after 9/11, allowed President Bush to "use all necessary and appropriate force against those nations, organizations, or persons he determines planned, authorized, committed, or aided the terrorist attacks that occurred on September 11, or harbored such organizations or persons."

---

*A third son, Hamza bin Laden, would also be killed in a CIA drone strike eight years after bin Laden's death.

This authorization sanctioned "forever wars" that lasted for two decades after 9/11. Three presidents as different from each other as Bush, Obama, and Trump used this same authorization to carry out hundreds of drone strikes against groups such as ISIS, al-Qaeda in the Arabian Peninsula, al-Shabaab, and the Pakistani Taliban. Few of these strikes had any connection to the perpetrators of 9/11. The authorization was also used to justify various types of U.S. military operations in countries around the world, in Afghanistan, Ethiopia, Kenya, Libya, Mali, Nigeria, Pakistan, the Philippines, Somalia, Syria, and Yemen. Hundreds of thousands of combatants and civilians died in those wars. And, of course, 9/11 provided much of the rationale for George W. Bush to invade and occupy Iraq two years later.

This was exactly the opposite of bin Laden's aim with the 9/11 attacks, which was to push the United States out of the greater Middle East, so its client regimes in the region would fall. Instead, new American bases proliferated throughout the region, in Afghanistan, Djibouti, Iraq, Kuwait, Qatar, Syria, and the United Arab Emirates. Meanwhile, al-Qaeda—"the Base" in Arabic—lost the best base it ever had in Afghanistan. Rather than ending American influence in the Muslim world, the 9/11 attacks greatly amplified it.

Bin Laden later put a post facto gloss on the strategic failure of 9/11 by dressing it up as a great success and claiming that the attacks were a fiendishly clever plot to embroil the U.S. in costly wars in the Middle East. Three years after 9/11, bin Laden released a videotape in which he asserted, "We are continuing this policy of bleeding America to the point of bankruptcy." There was no evidence that this was really bin Laden's plan in the run-up to the 9/11 attacks. 9/11 was a great tactical victory for al-Qaeda—the group inflicted more direct damage on the United States in one morning than the Soviet Union had during the Cold War—but ultimately it was a strategic failure for the organization, just as Pearl Harbor was for Imperial Japan.

As a result, bin Laden's heroic status in the Muslim world faded. In the two most populous Muslim nations favorable views of him dropped significantly between 2003 and 2010, from 59 percent to 25 percent in Indonesia, and from 46 percent to 18 percent in Pakistan. The declining support for bin Laden reflected plummeting levels of approval in Muslim countries for al-Qaeda's signature tactic of suicide bombing. In Pakistan support for suicide attacks dropped from 41 percent to only 5 percent in the half-decade before bin Laden's death. The reason for this was simple: After 9/11 suicide bombings by al-Qaeda and allied groups had killed more than ten thousand civilians around the Muslim world from Iraq to Pakistan.

Bin Laden also offered no positive vison of the future other than the appeal of a caliphate that would somehow establish itself after the American defeat in the Middle East. There were no bin Laden hospitals or soup kitchens. Meanwhile, bin Laden's enemies list was extensive and included every Middle Eastern regime, Muslims who didn't share his views, the West in general, Jews, and Christians. Making a world of enemies is never a winning strategy. As Sun Tzu once observed, "Tactics without strategy is the noise before defeat."

Bin Laden's failure to convert spectacular acts of terrorism into real political gains wasn't surprising, since terrorism without relatively narrow political objectives generally fails. Anarchists killed President William McKinley in 1901 and blew up a bomb on Wall Street nineteen years later that killed thirty people, which was the deadliest attack in New York until 9/11. Yet the anarchists achieved nothing with these attacks, and their ideology died out.

During the 1970s and 1980s, Marxist terrorists in Germany known as the Baader-Meinhof Gang killed more than thirty people, a number of whom were prominent German government officials and businessmen, yet they also failed to bring about their political objectives. The same was also true of the Weather Underground, which carried out a campaign of bombings in the United States during the same period.

Indeed, few campaigns of terrorism have succeeded, except those with the goal of forcing the withdrawal of a colonial power. For instance, Zionist terrorism helped to push the British occupiers out of Palestine after World War II, leading to the formation of the state of Israel in 1948.

• • •

Despite bin Laden's overall strategic failure on 9/11, al-Qaeda survived for more than three decades, a feat that few other terrorist groups have managed. Its longevity was partly because bin Laden bequeathed a relatively simple set of ideas to the world that outlived him, including that the cause of the problems in the Middle East was the United States propping up Arab regimes and that ordinary Americans were complicit in this because they paid taxes. Bin Laden also legitimized the use of mass casualty suicide attacks among jihadist groups. In 2002 there was only one suicide attack in Afghanistan; there were 140 suicide operations in 2007.

Killing bin Laden didn't kill his ideas, which lingered on among al-Qaeda's affiliates in Afghanistan, Iraq, North Africa, Pakistan, Somalia, Syria, and Yemen; and they also lived on among Islamist militants around the globe, magnified by the internet, where bin Laden remained an inspirational figure to every new generation of jihadists.

Other waves of terrorism—the anarchist wave at the beginning of the twentieth century; the anticolonial wave in the middle of the twentieth century; and the Marxist wave of the 1970s and 1980s—had burned themselves out after four decades. They collapsed because, in the anticolonial cases, they had achieved their goals, or, in the Marxist case, they ended with the dissolution of the Soviet Union.

Al-Qaeda was part of a fourth wave of religious terrorism driven by Islamist militancy that began in the 1980s with the establishment of Ayatollah Khomeini's regime in Iran and with the arrival of the "Afghan Arabs" fighting the Soviets in Afghanistan. This wave was likely to last longer than previous terrorism waves because it was, in the mind of its believers, sanctioned by God, and it's hard to abolish God. Although only a tiny minority of Muslims subscribed to bin Laden's ideology, there were 1.8 billion Muslims around the world, and there were enough ungoverned spaces in countries such as Afghanistan, Somalia, Syria, and Yemen that al-Qaeda and groups aligned with it would still be able to find recruits and spaces in which to operate. This was not because these groups were strong themselves, but because they preyed on weak hosts.

The weaker the government was in a Muslim-majority country, the more likely it was that al-Qaeda or similar groups would establish themselves there.

The longevity of al-Qaeda can also be explained by its ability to seed itself in countries such as the Philippines, Syria, and Yemen. Above all, al-Qaeda in Iraq eventually morphed into ISIS, which at the height of its power four years after bin Laden's death controlled an area in Iraq and Syria that was the size of Portugal and lorded over some eight million people. ISIS also ran a quasi-state that taxed and extorted its millions of subjects, enabling it to field a terrorist army.

Despite the fact that Zawahiri had been bin Laden's deputy since 2001, it took more than six weeks for the group to announce Zawahiri's ascension to the top spot. And Zawahiri, a black hole of charisma, was not able to prevent a schism that developed between al-Qaeda and ISIS, which formally split in 2014. The split was long in the making, as Al-Qaeda in Iraq had gone its own way for years, largely ignoring al-Qaeda's core in Pakistan when it mounted indiscriminate attacks on Shia civilian targets. But while he was alive bin Laden had been a unifying force, which was certainly not the case with Zawahiri.

It was the first time in its history that al-Qaeda had officially rejected one of its affiliates, and this was not a sign of strength. The core of al-Qaeda was now a jihadist group that operated only in parts of Afghanistan and Pakistan and had no ability to mount attacks in the West, while ISIS was proving the most successful al-Qaeda offshoot. Its seizure of many of Iraq's most important cities, including Mosul in 2014, demonstrated that ISIS had gone from being a terrorist group to an effective insurgent army. Some thirty terrorist groups around the world issued statements of support for ISIS or pledged their allegiance to the group.

Bin Laden was a revered figure in ISIS propaganda, and the group saw itself as his rightful heir. Yet ISIS took bin Laden's ideology of waging jihad against the United States and its puppet allies in the Muslim world in order to install Taliban-style regimes, and updated it significantly, although in a way that bin Laden would have frowned upon. Bin Laden had tried to avoid conflicts with Muslim sects like the Shia, but ISIS reveled in them. After bin Laden's death, sectarianism, also fueled by the Iranian regime and the Gulf States, became the defining feature of conflicts in the Middle East from Syria to Yemen.

Bin Laden's 9/11 attacks also had unpredictable, long-term effects on the politics of the United States. Real estate impresario Donald Trump launched his political career with the lie that President Barack Obama wasn't an American and was secretly a Muslim. This lie was especially potent in the context of 9/11, one of the hinge events of American history. During his presidential campaign Trump often claimed that he had seen "thousands" of Arabs cheering the 9/11 attacks from their rooftops in New Jersey. This was false, but it played well with Trump's base.

Trump's presidential campaign also took place during a wave of mass casualty jihadist terrorist attacks in the West. On November 13, 2015, ISIS terrorists killed 130 people in Paris. Within seven months of the Paris attacks, ISIS-inspired terrorists killed fourteen people at an office in San Bernardino, California, and forty-nine people at an Orlando nightclub. As a result, in the run-up to the 2016 presidential election, just over half of Americans said they were "very" or "somewhat" worried that that they, or a member of their family, would be victims of terrorism. This was the largest number to feel this way since just after 9/11.

Sensing a real political opportunity, Trump called for a "total and complete shutdown" of Muslim immigration to the United States and asserted that many Muslims have "great hatred towards Americans." Polling in early 2016 showed that half of all Americans supported banning Muslims traveling to the United States. Other polls showed terrorism as a top-two issue for Americans, with Trump holding a slight advantage over his Democratic challenger, Hillary Clinton, on the issue.

• • •

When she was an intelligence analyst in her mid-twenties, Gina Bennett was the first official in the U.S. government to grasp the threat posed by bin Laden and his men, and she warned about them in a classified memo she circulated in 1993.

Almost two decades later, on the day that bin Laden was killed, a CIA analyst in her mid-twenties sent Bennett a message saying, "Hey, it was a really bad day for al-Qaeda?"

Bennett replied, "Well, yeah. It's a pretty bad day, but it's definitely not their worst."

Bennett's colleague asked, "What are you talking about? Bin Laden is dead."

Bennet replied, "Well, let me ask you this: Have you ever heard of the Baader-Meinhof Gang?"

The colleague said, "No."

Bennett replied, "Well, someday when one officer in CIA's Counter-terrorism Center says to another officer, 'Have you ever heard of Osama bin Laden or al-Qaeda?' and they say no: That's the worst day."

On that day, bin Laden and al-Qaeda will finally be buried in what President Bush called history's unmarked grave of discarded lies.

A NOTE ON SOURCES

In recent years much has become public that helps to illuminate bin Laden and the inner workings of al-Qaeda. Above all, there are the many thousands of pages of bin Laden's letters and memos that were recovered by U.S. Navy SEALs at bin Laden's compound in Abbottabad in 2011. These materials, which bin Laden never expected to fall into enemy hands, were finally released in full by the Trump administration only in November 2017 and total around 470,000 files. These files help explain the life that bin Laden and his family were leading while they were on the run following the 9/11 attacks, and they also help illuminate how al-Qaeda and its various affiliates functioned after those attacks. They include a handwritten 228-page journal in Arabic that when it was publicly released the CIA incorrectly described as "bin Laden's journal." In fact, it was a bin Laden family journal that recorded the lengthy discussions between bin Laden and his older wives and adult children in the weeks before his death as they debated how he should respond to the Arab Spring.

In 2013 the Abbottabad Commission's 336-page report by senior Pakistani officials was leaked. The commissioners had spent two years investigating bin Laden's decade on the run following 9/11 as well as the operation that killed him, and the report contained a wealth of authoritative information about bin Laden's life as a fugitive and the events surrounding the night that he died, information that was derived from some two hundred interviews, including with three of bin Laden's wives and the wife of one of bin Laden's bodyguards, all of whom had survived the U.S. Navy SEAL operation that killed al-Qaeda's leader. The report was highly critical of the Pakistani government's inaction during the long hunt for bin Laden and its feckless response to the SEAL raid that killed him on its sovereign territory, which gave the report considerable credibility.

There were also other troves of important bin Laden documents; for instance, those recovered by Bosnian authorities in Sarajevo in 2002 that document the early history of al-Qaeda. Also, in Afghanistan I purchased all the back issues of *Jihad* magazine, amounting to many thousands of pages that shed light on the Arabs fighting in Afghanistan against the Soviets during the 1980s.

A number of bin Laden's associates have also published useful memoirs in recent years. I also mined thousands of pages of internal al-Qaeda documents and other materials recovered in countries such as Afghanistan and Iraq and have drawn on relevant criminal cases involving jihadist militants in the United States. The many thousands of pages of U.S. military tribunal proceedings of prisoners who were held or are being held at Guantánamo that were released by WikiLeaks in 2011 were also useful.

The Conflict Records Research Center at the National Defense University and the Combating Terrorism Center at West Point possess important collections of primary materials about al-Qaeda that this book drew upon, while the National Security Archive at George Washington University has a trove of useful U.S. government documents relating to al-Qaeda and the Taliban. I also mined the five-hundred-page 2014 Senate Intelligence Committee Report on the CIA's detention and interrogation program, which brought to light considerable hitherto secret material about the hunt for bin Laden. The minority views and CIA rebuttal to that report were also useful. Documents about al-Qaeda on the FBI and CIA websites, which were released in declassified form in response to Freedom of Information requests, and an extensive selection of public statements by bin Laden and other leaders of al-Qaeda maintained by the Global Terrorism Research Project at Haverford College, were also helpful.

Since 9/11 many hundreds of books of varying quality have been written about aspects of the war between al-Qaeda and the West, the most pertinent of which I drew upon and are listed in the selected bibliography. Multiple former U.S. officials have published memoirs about their roles in that long war, and I have also mined the most useful of those. The Miller Center at the University of Virginia houses an oral history project featuring senior officials of the Bill Clinton and George W. Bush administrations that was also useful.

I first traveled to report in Afghanistan after the attack on the World Trade Center on February 26, 1993, when jihadist terrorists—some of whom had trained in Afghanistan—parked a bomb-laden van in the basement of the Trade Center complex, which they detonated, killing six people. Since then, I have reported on many aspects of the global jihadist movement and have made more than a dozen reporting trips to Afghanistan and Pakistan, countries that are both key to understanding bin Laden and al-Qaeda. On one of those trips I was the only outside observer to be granted access to bin Laden's compound by Pakistani security services and spent a couple of hours touring it on February 10, 2012, which gave me a better understanding of the living conditions of the bin Laden family and also the events of the night when bin Laden was killed. Two weeks after I toured the compound it was demolished by the Pakistani military so it wouldn't become a shrine to bin Laden. I also made repeated reporting trips to other countries that have played important roles in the history of al-Qaeda such as Iraq and Saudi Arabia, in addition to research that I also conducted in Egypt, Jordan, the United Kingdom, and Yemen that helped to illuminate bin Laden's story.

Among the hundreds of interviews that I have drawn upon for the book are more than a dozen with members of bin Laden's inner circle, many of whom I have interviewed on multiple occasions. No other researcher in the West has had this range of access to bin Laden and those who knew him, and many of those bin Laden confidants are no longer available to be interviewed because they have been killed or have disappeared, or are jailed in maximum-security prisons, or have died.

Examples of such men include bin Laden himself, whom I met with in 1997 when I produced his first-ever television interview; bin Laden's brother-in-law and best friend Jamal Khalifa, who was murdered in murky circumstances in Madagascar in 2007; Abu Musab al-Suri, a close bin Laden associate and a leading theorist of jihadism, who disappeared in Pakistan in 2005; Mullah Khaksar, the deputy Taliban interior minister who dealt extensively with bin Laden, who was assassinated in Kandahar in 2006; Khalid al-Fawwaz, a confidant of bin Laden's, who is serving a life sentence in a U.S. maximum-security prison; Jamal Khashoggi, the first mainstream journalist to interview bin Laden, who was murdered by Saudi security officials in Istanbul in 2018; Essam Deraz, who filmed bin Laden in Afghanistan during the late 1980s, who died in Egypt in 2019; and Vahid Mojdeh, a Taliban foreign ministry official tasked to work with al-Qaeda before the 9/11 attacks, who was assassinated by unknown assailants in Afghanistan in 2019.

NOTES

PROLOGUE: HOPES AND DREAMS AND FEARS

xiii *"Targeting the Americans"*: Michael Scheuer, *Imperial Hubris: Why the West Is Losing the War on Terror* (Washington, DC, Potomac Books, 2004), 148.

xiii *It was Amal's turn:* Justice Javed Iqbal et al., "Aljazeera Bin Laden Dossier," 2013, 34, https://www.documentcloud.org/documents/724833-aljazeera-bin-laden -dossier.html.

xiii *only sixteen:* Amal and bin Laden married in 2000. In 2011 she was twenty-eight, according to the card that the U.S. Navy SEALs carried on the bin Laden raid. Christina Lamb, "Revealed: The SEALs' Secret Guide to Bin Laden Lair," *Sunday Times,* May 22, 2011, www.thesundaytimes.co.uk/sto/news/world_news /Asia /article631893.ece. More details about bin Laden's marriage to Amal can be found in chapter 9 of this book and in Mustafa al-Ansari, "Bin Laden's Ye-meni Spouse 'Amal' Will Not Remarry Even if Asked by President Saleh!," *Al Hayat,* June 13, 2011.

xiii *a real love match . . . older wives:* Nassar al-Bahri, *Guarding bin Laden: My Life in al-Qaeda* (London: Thin Man Press, 2013), 155.

xiii *"mature":* Ibid., 156.

xiii *older sons were also angered:* Ibid., 155.

xiii *"dragged round his fourth":* Nasser al-Bahri and Georges Malbrunot, *Dans l'ombre de Ben Laden: Révélations de Son Garde du Corps Repenti* (Neuilly-sur-Seine: Michel Lafon, 2010), 201.

xiv *days after the 9/11 attacks:* Author's interview with Hamid Mir, Islamabad, Paki-stan, March 2005. Mir met bin Laden on November 8, 2011, in Kabul. This is when bin Laden told him about Safia, whom Mir described as "one month" old at the time. See also Peter L. Bergen, *The Osama bin Laden I Know: An Oral His-tory of al-Qaeda's Leader* (New York: Free Press, 2006), 319. See also Hala Jaber, "Finding Osama a Wife," *Sunday Times,* January 24, 2010.

xiv   *Bin Laden explained . . . kill Jews:* Author's interviews with Hamid Mir, Islamabad, Pakistan, May 11, 2002, and March 2005; "Hazrat SAFIYAH BINT ABDUL MUTTALIB (رضئ-الله-تعالی-عنہ /)," Aal-e-Qutub Aal-e-Syed Abdullah Shah Ghazi, accessed January 27, 2021, https://aalequtub.com/hazrat-safiyah-bint-abdul-muttalib.

xiv   *four children:* "Constitution of Joint Investigation Team" (Office of the Inspector General of Police Islamabad, January 19, 2012), https://www.cbsnews.com/htdocs/pdf/JIT_Report_033012.pdf.

xiv   *deaf and dumb:* Iqbal et al., "Abbottabad Commission Report," 45.

xiv   *"witnessed for centuries":* Osama bin Laden, "Letter from UBL to `Atiyatullah Al-Libi 2" (Combating Terrorism Center, April 26, 2011), 2, SOCOM-2012-0000010, https://ctc.usma.edu/harmony-program/letter-from-ubl-to-atiyatullah-al-libi-2-original-language-2/.

xv   *doctorate in child psychology:* Bergen, *The Osama bin Laden I Know,* 123. Wisam al-Turabi, the wife of Hassan al-Turabi, who was the de facto leader of Sudan when bin Laden and his family lived there in the mid-1990s, described Umm Hamza as a "university lecturer." Cathy Scott-Clark and Adrian Levy, *The Exile: The Stunning Inside Story of Osama bin Laden and Al Qaeda in Flight* (New York: Bloomsbury, 2017), 23, describes her as a "child psychologist by profession." Najwa bin Laden, Omar bin Laden, and Jean P. Sasson, *Growing Up bin Laden: Osama's Wife and Son Take Us Inside Their Secret World* (New York: St. Martin's Press, 2009), 52, describes her as "a highly specialized teacher of deaf-mute children." Lawrence Wright, *The Looming Tower* (New York: Alfred A. Knopf, 2006), 82.

xv   *the sixty-two-year-old Umm Hamza:* Umm Hamza was sixty-two, according to the card carried by the U.S. Navy SEALs on the bin Laden operation on May 2, 2011.

xv   *It comforts me to hear your news:* Osama bin Laden, "Letter to Wife," January 3, 2011 (Office of the Director of National Intelligence), Bin Laden's Bookshelf, https://www.dni.gov/files/documents/ubl2016/english/Letter%20to%20wife.pdf.

xvi   *told Umm Hamza that a member:* In a longer draft of the letter from bin Laden to his wife, dated January 3, 2011, 6D87FB2078702BB73C1F1E38C82DC840.

xvi   *worried a tracking chip:* Bin Laden, "Letter to Wife."

xvi   *around $300:* "US Dollar to Pakistani Rupee Spot Exchange Rates for 2011," ExchangeRates.org.uk, accessed January 28, 2021, https://www.exchangerates.org.uk/USD-PKR-spot-exchange-rates-history-2011.html.

xvi   *Bin Laden was specifically worried:* Iqbal et al., "Abbottabad Commission Report," 71. This section also draws on Peter Bergen, "An Isolated Osama bin Laden Struggled to Keep His Bodyguards," CNN, June 2, 2016, https://www.cnn.com/2016/03/01/opinions/osama-bin-laden-letters-bergen/index.html.

xvii   *could no longer rely:* Bin Laden, "Letter to Wife."

xviii *"secure your return":* Ibid.

xviii *He was now under pressure:* Bin Laden letter Task ID 7278, 56202CC8E54A736 D2AA34DEA8EB81492. In another letter bin Laden says the deadline was mid-September 2011. Bin Laden, "Letter from UBL to ˋAtiyatullah Al-Libi 2."

xviii *"it would be good if you informed":* Ibid.

xviii *Umm Hamza decided:* Task Number 25528, Letter to Um Abid-al-Rahman from Umm Hamza, undated, E8FCF24E825FFFFD9B7F5D68258F9497.

xviii *packed:* Bin Laden's family at the compound numbered sixteen people: three wives, five children from Amal, three children from Siham, four grandchildren, and bin Laden himself. The two bodyguards and their families were eleven people.

xix *twenty-eight to sixty-two:* The ages were on the card that the U.S. Navy SEALs carried on the night of the bin Laden raid.

xix *arranging his compound:* Peter Bergen, "A Visit to Osama bin Laden's Lair," CNN, May 3, 2012, https://www.cnn.com/2012/05/03/opinion/bergen-bin-laden-lair /index.html.

xix *drank Avena:* JoNel Aleccia, "What Was in Medicine Chests at bin Laden Compound?," NBC News, May 6, 2011, https://www.nbcnews.com/id/wbna42934673.

xix *copious amounts of olives:* Zawahiri interview with bin Laden's Pakistani biographer, Hamid Mir, in Kabul on November 8, 2001.

xix *"best performance":* Iqbal et al., "Abbottabad Commission Report," 41.

xix *"We have made . . . our weapons":* "Bin Laden's Hard Drive," National Geographic Channel, September 11, 2020, https://www.nationalgeographic.com/tv /movies-and-specials/bin-ladens-hard-drive.

xix *shooting a BB gun:* Ibid.

xix *four separate gas and electricity meters:* Iqbal et al., "Abbottabad Commission Report," 60. This section also draws on Peter Bergen, "Bin Laden's Life on the Run," CNN, July 9, 2013, https://www.cnn.com/2013/07/09/opinion/bergen -abbottabad-report/index.html.

xix *complained of pain . . . never saw a doctor:* Iqbal et al., "Aljazeera Bin Laden Dossier," 48.

xix *cowboy hat:* Ibid., 41.

xx *hidden from even those who lived with him:* Ibid., 49. This section also draws upon Bergen, "Bin Laden's Life on the Run"

xx *his own large family and the eleven members:* Card carried by the Navy SEALs during the May 2, 2011, raid, identifying likely residents of the compound.

xx *Dozens of chickens . . . trellises:* This description is based on the author's observations of the compound and video from the compound released by the CIA in November 2017. See Bergen, "A Visit to Osama bin Laden's Lair"; "Bin Laden's Hard Drive."

xx *women would leave the room:* Iqbal et al., "Abbottabad Commission Report," 48. This section also draws upon Bergen, "Bin Laden's Life on the Run."

xx *obscured her face:* "Bin Laden's Hard Drive."

xx *When one of the bodyguards' young daughters saw video:* Iqbal et al., "Abbottabad Commission Report," 46–47.

xxi *Sometimes couriers were arrested:* For instance, Hassan Ghul, who was arrested in northern Iraq in January 2004 carrying a letter to bin Laden from Abu Musab al-Zarqawi, the leader of al-Qaeda in Iraq. Chapter 14 of this book recounts this episode.

xxi *"poison" . . . might damage their reputation:* Bin Laden, "Letter from UBL to `Atiyatullah Al-Libi 2."

xxi *warning to members . . . chlorine gas:* "Letter from Hafiz Sultan" (Combating Terrorism Center, March 28, 2007), SOCOM-2012-0000011, https://ctc.usma .edu/harmony-program/letter-from-hafiz-sultan-original-language-2/.

xxii *Similarly, bin Laden complained:* Osama Bin Laden, "Letter from UBL to `Atiyatullah Al-Libi 4" (Combating Terrorism Center, n.d.), SOCOM-2012-0000019, https://ctc.usma.edu/harmony-program/letter-from-ubl-to-atiyatullah-al-libi -4-original-language-2; Salman Masod and Alan Cowell, "Mosque Serving Pakistani Military Hit by Attackers," *New York Times*, December 4, 2009, https:// www.nytimes.com/2009/12/05/world/asia/05pstan.html.

xxii *"a new phase":* Nelly Lahoud, "What the Jihadis Left Behind," *London Review of Books*, January 23, 2020, https://www.lrb.co.uk/the-paper/v42/n02/nelly-lahoud /what-the-jihadis-left-behind; *The Osama Bin Laden Files*, 180.

xxii *considered changing the name of his group:* In a memo bin Laden made some suggestions about a new name for his organization: "Monotheism and Jihad Group, Monotheism and Defending Islam Group, Restoration of the Caliphate Group." Al-Qaeda—"the Base" in Arabic—remained the name of the group. "A Suggestion to Change the Name of Al-Qa`ida" (Combating Terrorism Center, n.d.), SOCOM-2012-0000009, https://ctc.usma.edu/harmony-program/a-sugg estion-to-change-the-name-of-al-qaida-original-language-2/.

xxii *killed his son Saad:* Mary Louise Kelly, "Bin Laden Son Reported Killed in Pakistan," NPR, July 22, 2009, https://www.npr.org/templates/story/story.php?story Id=106903109.

xxii *too dangerous for his followers:* Osama bin Laden, "Letter from UBL to `Atiyatullah Al-Libi 3" (Combating Terrorism Center, October 21, 2010), 3, SOCOM-2012-0000015, https://ctc.usma.edu/harmony-program/letter-from -ubl-to-atiyatullah-al-libi-3-original-language-2/.

xxii *122 strikes . . . more than seven hundred militants:* Peter Bergen, David Sterman, and Melissa Salyk-Virk, "America's Counterterrorism Wars: The Drone War in Pakistan," New America, August 13, 2020, https://www.newamerica.org/inter national-security/reports/americas-counterterrorism-wars/the-drone-war-in -pakistan/.

xxiii *Mustafa Abu al-Yazid:* Bin Laden, "Letter from UBL to `Atiyatullah Al-Libi 4"; Eric Schmitt, "American Strike Is Said to Kill a Top Qaeda Leader," *New York Times*, May 31, 2010, https://www.nytimes.com/2010/06/01/world/asia/01 qaeda.html; "Al Qaeda Announces Death of No. 3 Man, Intel Group Says," CNN, June 1, 2010, https://www.cnn.com/2010/WORLD/asiapcf/05/31/afghanistan .qaeda.death/.

xxiii *"distinctive loops that we all know":* Letter to bin Laden from Atiyah, early April 2011, *United States v. Abid Naseer*, Eastern District of New York, government exhibit 421 10-CR-019 (S-4) (RJD).

xxiii *overcast days:* Bin Laden, "Letter from UBL to `Atiyatullah Al-Libi 3," 3. This section draws on Peter Bergen, "A Gripping Glimpse into bin Laden's Decline and Fall," CNN, March 12, 2015, https://www.cnn.com/2015/03/10/opinions /bergen-bin-laden-al-qaeda-decline-fall/index.html.

xxiii *"great accumulated expertise"* . . . *"rough terrain":* Bin Laden, "Letter from UBL to `Atiyatullah Al-Libi 3," 3.

xxiii *To his own son:* Bin Laden, "Letter from UBL to `Atiyatullah Al-Libi 4."

xxiii *"backed off that idea":* "Report on the External Operations," *United States v. Abid Naseer*, Eastern District of New York, government exhibit 421 10-CR-019 (S-4) (RJD).

xxiv *gas up and eat heartily:* "Letter to Nasir al-Wuhayshi" (Combating Terrorism Center, n.d.), SOCOM-2012-0000016, https://ctc.usma.edu/harmony-pro gram/letter-to-nasir-al-wuhayshi-original-language-2/.

xxiv *"dangerous for the environment":* This section draws upon Bergen, "A Gripping Glimpse into bin Laden's Decline and Fall."

xxiv *letter intended to be a pep talk:* Osama bin Laden, "Letter to Our Honored Commander of the Faithful" (Office of the Director of National Intelligence, November 5, 2010), Bin Laden's Bookshelf, https://www.dni.gov/files/documents/ubl 2016/english/Letter%20to%20our%20Honored%20Commander%20of%20 the%20Faithful.pdf.

xxiv *"external operations":* "Report on External Operations" (Office of the Director of National Intelligence, n.d.), Bin Laden's Bookshelf, https://www.dni.gov/files /documents/ubl/english/Report%20on%20External%20Operations.pdf.

xxiv *published cartoons:* Inal Ersan, "Bin Laden Warns EU over Prophet Cartoons," Reuters, March 19, 2008, https://www.reuters.com/article/us-security-binladen /bin-laden-warns-eu-over-prophet-cartoons-idUSN1933824120080320.

xxv *killing President Barack Obama* . . . *Petraeus:* Bin Laden, "Letter from UBL to `Atiyatullah Al-Libi 4."

xxv *Bin Laden told his team not to bother:* Ibid.

xxv *both of them had done interviews with bin Laden:* Robert Fisk, "Talks with Osama bin Laden," *Nation*, September 21, 1998, https://www.thenation.com

/article/archive/talks-osama-bin-laden/; Abdul Bari Atwan, "Inside Osama's Mountain Lair," *Guardian*, November 11, 2001, https://www.theguardian.com /world/2001/nov/12/afghanistan.terrorism1.

xxv *"least biased" of the American TV channels:* "Letter from Adam Gadahn" (Combating Terrorism Center, January 2011), SOCOM-2012-0000004, https:// ctc.usma.edu/harmony-program/letter-from-adam-gadahn-original-lan guage-2/.

xxv *Adam Gadahn . . . grown up in California:* Raffi Khatchadourian, "Azzam the American," *New Yorker*, January 14, 2007, https://www.newyorker.com/maga zine/2007/01/22/azzam-the-american.

xxv *"As for the neutrality . . . with the Sheikh":* "Letter from Adam Gadahn."

xxv *ABC News had interviewed bin Laden:* John Miller, "Interview: Osama bin Laden," *Frontline*, PBS, May 1998, https://www.pbs.org/wgbh/pages/frontline/shows /binladen/who/interview.html#video.

xxv *Siham would often edit:* Mustafa al-Ansari, "Bin Ladin's Brother-in-Law to Al Hayah: 'My Sister Holds PhD: She Differs with Husband Usama Ideologically,'" *Al Hayat* online, May 26, 2011.

xxvi *228-page notebook:* Bin Laden Family Journal, https://www.cia.gov/library/ab bottabad-compound/76/76155EE3B4398AC4814FA69DF33057B3_Journal .original.pdf.

xxvi *"Some analysts do mention al-Qaeda":* Ibid., 5.

xxvi *"Gaddafi is doing our bidding for us":* Ibid., 16, 28, 30, 32.

xxvii *"I agree with him on that":* Ibid., 30.

xxvii *"the biggest obstacle":* Ibid., 68.

xxvii *Khalid . . . asked his father:* Ibid., 29.

xxviii *he had just dreamed of Prince Nayef:* Ibid., 54.

xxviii *a big speech to be released:* Ibid., 39.

xxviii *They firmly believed:* Ibid., 31.

xxviii *"the news is sweeter than honey":* Ibid., 86

xxviii *"The Yemeni president resigned":* Ibid., 141

xxviii *Saleh reneged:* "Reports: Saleh Refuses to Sign Exit Deal," *Al Jazeera*, April 30, 2011, https://www.aljazeera.com/news/2011/4/30/reports-saleh-refuses-to-sign -exit-deal.

xxix *"hold Arab rulers accountable":* Bin Laden Family Journal, 143.

xxix *"Is it going to have a negative impact that this happened without jihad?":* Ibid., 175.

xxix *"needed to hurry":* Ibid., 187.

xxx *twelve-minute audio recording:* Scott Shane, "In Message, Bin Laden Praised Arab Revolt," *New York Times*, May 18, 2011, https://www.nytimes.com/2011/05/19 /world/middleeast/19binladen.html.

xxx   *"tight, its meaning important"*: Bin Laden Family Journal, 224.

xxx   *Bin Laden and Amal were sleeping:* Iqbal et al., "Abbottabad Commission Report," 34–35.

xxx   *Bin Laden quickly told her: "No!":* Ibid.

ONE: SPHINX WITHOUT A RIDDLE?

3   *"sphinx without a riddle"*: Alan Strauss-Schom, *The Shadow Emperor: A Biography of Napoléon III* (New York: St. Martin's Press, 2018), 18.

3   *released in full:* "November 2017 Release of Abbottabad Compound Material," Central Intelligence Agency, November 2017, https://www.cia.gov/library/ab bottabad-compound/index.html; Nancy A. Youssef, "CIA Releases More Documents from bin Laden Raid," *Wall Street Journal*, November 1, 2017, https:// www.wsj.com/articles/cia-releases-more-documents-from-bin-laden-raid -1509575253; Bin Laden's Bookshelf, Office of the Director of National Intelligence, accessed February 3, 2020, https://www.dni.gov/index.php/features/bin -laden-s-bookshelf?start=1.

4   *some verses:* Ahmed Al-Dawoody, "IHL and Islam: An Overview," *Humanitarian Law & Policy*, March 14, 2017, https://blogs.icrc.org/law-and-policy/2017/03 /14/ihl-islam-overview/.

4   *tens of thousands of soldiers:* See, for example, Jeff Schogol, "US-Backed Group in Syria Says It Suffered More Than 11,000 Killed and 21,000 Wounded Fighting ISIS," Task & Purpose, March 25, 2019, https://taskandpurpose.com/news /sdf-casualties-isis-syria/; "Afghanistan's Ghani Says 45,000 Security Personnel Killed Since 2014," BBC, January 25, 2019, https://www.bbc.com/news/world -asia-47005558.

4   *hundreds of thousands:* Neta C. Crawford, "Human Cost of the Post-9/11 Wars: Lethality and the Need for Transparency" (Costs of War Project, November 2018), https://watson.brown.edu/costsofwar/files/cow/imce/papers/2018/Human %20Costs%20C%20Nov%208%202018%20CoW.pdf.

TWO: ZEALOT

7   *"The impression . . . will perish"*: Eric Hoffer, *The True Believer: Thoughts on the Nature of Mass Movements* (New York: Harper & Brothers, 1951), 99.

7   *"death is present"*: Doreen Ingrams, *A Time in Arabia: Life in Hadhramaut* (London: Eland, 2013), 6.

7   *Bin Laden Street:* Author's visit to Hadhramaut and al-Rubat, Yemen, November 3, 2000.

8   *segregation of the sexes:* Andrew Cockburn, "Yemen United," *National Geographic*, April 2000.

8   *as he told his wives and children:* Bin Laden Family Journal, 86, https://www

.cia.gov/library/abbottabad-compound/76/76155EE3B4398AC4814FA69DF33 057B3_Journal.original.pdf.

8 *"poverty and little commerce"*: Freya Stark, *The Southern Gates of Arabia—A Journey in the Hadhramaut* (John Murray: London, 1946), 120.

8 *Slavery . . . European woman:* Ibid., 122.

8 *find work in Egypt . . . Malaysia:* Ibid., 111.

8 *emigrated to what would soon become:* Steve Coll, *The Bin Ladens: An Arabian Family in the American Century* (New York: Penguin, 2014), 26.

8 *displayed his porter's bag:* From a company history of the Saudi Binladin Group, removed from the internet after the 9/11 attacks, described in Peter L. Bergen, *Holy War, Inc.: Inside the Secret World of Osama bin Laden* (New York: Free Press, 2001), p. 46.

8 *skilled bricklayer:* Ibid., 38; Michael Field, *The Merchants: The Big Business Families of Saudi Arabia and the Gulf States* (Woodstock, NY: Overlook Press, 1985), 105.

8 *1931:* From a company history of the Saudi Binladin Group removed from the internet after the 9/11 attacks, described in Bergen, *Holy War, Inc.*, 46.

8 *A year later . . . oil fields:* Bernard Lewis, *The Crisis of Islam: Holy War and Unholy Terror* (New York: Modern Library, 2003), 126.

8 *dropping by frequently:* Coll, *The Bin Ladens*, 39.

9 *an ingenious ramp:* Field, *The Merchants*, 105.

9 *Mohammed stepped in:* Coll, *The Bin Ladens*, 54–55; Field, *The Merchants*, 105.

9 *visiting . . . Latakia, Syria, in 1956:* Coll, *The Bin Ladens*, 73.

9 *Jabaryoun:* Lisa Beyer, "Death Comes for the Master Terrorist: Osama bin Laden (1957–2011)," *Time*, May 2, 2011, http://content.time.com/time/world/article /0,8599,2068858-1,00.html.

9 *The Ghanems were Alawite:* Martin Chulov of *The Guardian* interviewed Allia Ghanem in 2018 and she confirmed that she is from an Alawite family. Martin Chulov, "My Son, Osama: The al-Qaida Leader's Mother Speaks for the First Time," *Guardian*, August 2, 2018, https://www.theguardian.com/world/2018 /aug/03/osama-bin-laden-mother-speaks-out-family-interview.

9 *1957:* Najwa bin Laden, Osama bin Laden's first wife, says Osama bin Laden's birth date was February 15, 1957. Najwa bin Laden, Omar bin Laden, and Jean P. Sasson, *Growing Up bin Laden: Osama's Wife and Son Take Us Inside Their Secret World* (New York: St. Martin's Press, 2009), 301.

9 *The union . . . divorced:* Chulov, "My Son, Osama"; Bin Laden, bin Laden, and Sasson, *Growing Up bin Laden*, 8, 301.

9 *originally from Hadhramaut:* Freya Stark encountered members of the aristocratic Attas family when she was visiting Hadhramaut in the early 1930s. Stark, *The Southern Gates of Arabia*, 113.

9   *like he was his own son . . . and a daughter together:* Bin Laden, bin Laden, and Sasson, *Growing Up bin Laden*, 8.

9   *parrot in a cage:* Bin Laden Family Journal, 10–11.

10   *proudly told the story:* Author's interview with Hamid Mir, Islamabad, Pakistan, March 2005.

10   *$19 million:* Coll, *The Bin Ladens*, 84.

10   *even more ambitious . . . $130 million:* Ibid., 86.

10   *granted the contract . . . mid-1960s:* Ibid., 89–91.

11   *"How many bulldozers" . . . "Can you . . . our land":* Author's interview with Hamid Mir, Islamabad, Pakistan, March 2005.

11   *"it wasn't a military defeat . . . Arab world":* Author's interviews with Essam Deraz, Cairo, Egypt, January 2000 and May 2005.

11   *small-scale raids . . . inciting jihad:* Author's interview with Hudhayfa Azzam, Amman, Jordan, September 13, 2005; Thomas Hegghammer, *The Caravan: Abdallah Azzam and the Rise of Global Jihad* (Cambridge, UK: Cambridge University Press, 2020), 57–60.

11   *On September 3, 1967:* Coll, *The Bin Ladens*, 118–20.

11   *even more subdued:* Bin Laden, bin Laden, and Sasson, *Growing Up bin Laden*, 9, 170.

11   *"mental turmoil":* Ibid., 42; Rahimullah Yusufzai, "Taleban let bin Laden Break His Silence," *The News*, January 6, 1999.

12   *business hung in the balance . . . only twenty-one:* Peter L. Bergen, *The Osama bin Laden I Know: An Oral History of al-Qaeda's Leader* (New York: Free Press, 2006), 9.

12   *just over 2 percent each:* Coll, *The Bin Ladens*, 126–27.

12   *Salem was responsible:* Author's interview with a family member of Salem bin Laden, 2000.

12   *cried for days:* Author's interview with Hamid Mir, Islamabad, Pakistan, March 2005.

12   *trusteeship until they were old enough:* Author's interview with a family member of Salem bin Laden, 2000.

12   *Brian Fyfield-Shayler:* Bergen, *The Osama bin Laden I Know*, p. 8.

12   *"Why did I . . . the other students":* Ibid.

12   *more generous assessment:* Bin Laden Family Journal, 10.

13   *didn't have any key influences:* Ibid.

13   *five occasions:* Bin Laden, bin Laden, and Sasson, *Growing Up bin Laden*, 190.

13   *she wasn't really treated as a member:* Author's interview with a family representative, 2000.

13   *not considered to be truly Saudi:* Mamoun Fandy, *Saudi Arabia and the Politics of Dissent* (New York: St. Martin's Press, 1999), 180.

13   *"a wife of the Koran, but a concubine"*: J. Muñoz, "El Chico Del Círculo," *El Correo*, October 10, 2001, https://www.elcorreo.com/apoyos/especiales/11s/andanzas _juveniles.html.

14   *a bit crazy*: Ibid.

14   *summer as a young teenager*: Bin Laden also told Abdel Bari Atwan, the Palestinian journalist, about his summer studying English in Oxford when he was a young teenager. Atwan interview in Christiane Amanpour, *In the Footsteps of Bin Laden*, CNN, August 23, 2006, produced by Peter Bergen, Cliff Hackel, and Ken Shiffman.

14   *"morally degenerate"*: Bin Laden Family Journal, 10.

14   *Millfield*: Bernard Weinraub, "Rich and Royal Children Mix with Poor at Unusual British School," *New York Times*, July 8, 1971, https://www.nytimes.com /1971/07/08/archives/rich-and-royal-children-mix-with-poor-at-unusual-british-school.html.

14   *Salem quickly adapted*: Author's interview with Salem bin Laden's family member, 2000.

14   *more than a dozen*: Coll, *The Bin Ladens*, 189.

14   *"Desert Bear"*: Author's interview with a family member of Salem bin Laden, 2000.

15   *drunk driving in 1969*: From the Falun police report, author's collection.

15   *"They had so much money" . . . "own plane"*: Bergen, *The Osama bin Laden I Know*, 11–12.

15   *"Salem Bin Laden visited . . . in the past"*: "Arab Celebrity Visit," *Dalarnas Tidningar*, September 7, 1971.

15   *some debate*: Coll, *The Bin Ladens*, 136.

15   *Islamic study session*: Steve Coll, "Young Osama," *New Yorker*, December 4, 2005, https://www.newyorker.com/magazine/2005/12/12/young-osama.

16   *adopted the style and habits of Islamists*: Ibid.

16   *later told his family*: Bin Laden Family Journal, 7.

16   *Jabal al-Arab Street*: Lawrence Wright, *The Looming Tower* (New York: Alfred A. Knopf, 2006), 74; author's visit to the Mushrefah neighborhood in Jeddah, September 5, 2005.

16   *"Goodbye"*: Author's interviews with Khaled Batarfi, Jeddah, Saudi Arabia, September 5 and 9, 2005.

16   *avoided using swear words*: Author's interviews with Khaled Batarfi, Jeddah, Saudi Arabia, September 5 and 9, 2005.

16   *"I cannot . . . strewn everywhere"*: "Message to the American People," in *Al Qaeda in Its Own Words*, Gilles Kepel and Jean-Pierre Milelli, eds. (Cambridge, MA: Belknap Press of Harvard University Press, 2008), 72.

16 *"backward"*: Author's interviews with Khaled Batarfi, Jeddah, Saudi Arabia, September 5 and 9, 2005.

17 *"kind of a lonely guy"*: Ibid.

17 *more listening than talking*: Ibid.

17 *some diversions . . . upholstery*: Ibid.

17 *On these trips . . . not encouraged*: Bin Laden, bin Laden, and Sasson, *Growing Up bin Laden*, 10–14.

17 *Continuing his exceptionally close*: Author's interviews with Khaled Batarfi, Jeddah, Saudi Arabia, September 5 and 9, 2005.

17 *delivered Abdullah . . . another son, Abdul Rahman*: Bin Laden, bin Laden, and Sasson, *Growing Up bin Laden*, 24–25.

17 *deformed head*: Author's interviews with Khaled Batarfi, Jeddah, Saudi Arabia, September 5 and 9, 2005.

17 *likely caused by hydrocephalus*: Cathy Scott-Clark and Adrian Levy, *The Exile: The Stunning Inside Story of Osama bin Laden and Al Qaeda in Flight* (New York: Bloomsbury, 2017), 24.

18 *"did not hate . . . did not love it"*: Bin Laden, bin Laden, and Sasson, *Growing Up bin Laden*, 26.

18 *even took photos*: Author's Interviews with Khaled Batarfi, Jeddah, Saudi Arabia, September 5 and 9, 2005.

18 *"We were like in a zoo"*: Ibid.

18 *good chuckle*: Bin Laden, bin Laden, and Sasson, *Growing Up bin Laden*, 26.

18 *King Abdel Aziz University*: Author's interviews with Jamal Khalifa, Jeddah, Saudi Arabia, September 6 and 9, 2005.

18 *At the age . . . turn it down*: Ibid.

18 *The two friends went riding*: Ibid.

19 *"The persons . . . primary aim"*: Sayyid Qutb, *Milestones* (Sime Books, 1997), 32. For a good discussion of these issues, see Gilles Kepel, *Muslim Extremism in Egypt: The Prophet and Pharaoh* (Berkeley: University of California Press, 2003), 37–55. This section also draws on Bergen, *The Osama bin Laden I Know*, 18.

20 *very literal interpretation of Islam*: Author's Interviews with Jamal Khalifa, Jeddah, Saudi Arabia, September 6 and 9, 2005.

20 *"fierce piety" . . . the family*: Carmen Bin Ladin and Ruth Marshall, *Inside the Kingdom: My Life in Saudi Arabia* (New York: Warner Books, 2004), 3.

20 *Like his father, he ate*: Author's interviews with Khaled Batarfi, Jeddah, Saudi Arabia, September 5 and 9, 2005.

20 *skip graduating*: Author's interviews with Jamal Khalifa, Jeddah, Saudi Arabia, September 6 and 9, 2005.

20 *King Faisal . . . assassinated:* David Hirst, "From the Archive, 26 March 1975: Faisal Murder Puts Mideast Nearer Abyss," *Guardian,* March 26, 1975, https://www.theguardian.com/theguardian/2010/jun/23/archive-faisal-murder-mid east-abyss.

20 *Salem acted as a kind of semiofficial jester:* Author's interview with Salem bin Laden family member, 2000.

21 *diversified into a number of areas:* J. R. L. Carter, *Leading Merchant Families of Saudi Arabia* (London: Scorpion Publications/D. R. Llewellyn Group, 1979), 110–11.

21 *The rebels believed that among their ranks:* Nasir al-Huzaimi, *The Mecca Uprising: An Insider's Account of Salafism and Insurrection in Saudi Arabia,* trans. and ed. David Commins (New York: I. B. Tauris, 2020), 97–98.

21 *bin Ladens brought in equipment:* Coll, *The Bin Ladens,* 226.

21 *Some sixty militants:* "Saudi Arabians Behead 63 for Attack on Mosque," *Washington Post,* October 1, 1980, https://www.washingtonpost.com/archive/politics/1980/01/10/saudi-arabians-behead-63-for-attack-on-mosque/18063a57-ba6f-47e3-bdc0-05c1059b6961/.

21 *"King Fahd defiled . . . by tanks":* Osama bin Laden, audio recording, posted to the jihadist website Al-Qai'ah (The Fortress), located at www.qal3ah.net (no longer operational), on December 16, 2004 (translated by the U.S. government). The source is also quoted in Bergen, *The Osama bin Laden I Know,* 23.

22 *free hand:* Yaroslav Trofimov, *The Siege of Mecca: The 1979 Uprising at Islam's Holiest Shrine* (New York: Anchor Books, 2008), 260–62; David Rundell, *Vision or Mirage: Saudi Arabia at the Crossroads* (New York, I. B. Tauris, 2020). 89.

22 *routinely wearing gloves:* Bin Ladin and Marshall, *Inside the Kingdom,* 120.

THREE: JIHAD

23 *"To stand . . . night prayer":* Abdullah Azzam, *Defense of Muslim Lands, The Most Important Personal Duty,* published in booklet form by Modern Mission Library, Amman, 1984, quoted in Peter L. Bergen, *The Osama bin Laden I Know: An Oral History of al Qaeda's Leader* (New York: Free Press, 2006), 27.

23 *gathering donations:* Basil Muhammad, *The Arab Supporters in Afghanistan* (Jeddah: House of Learning Printing Press, 1991), 25.

23 *sting of occupation firsthand:* Thomas Hegghammer, *The Caravan: Abdallah Azzam and the Rise of Global Jihad* (Cambridge, UK: Cambridge University Press, 2020), 20–21.

23 *launched raids:* Ibid., 57–60.

24 *doctorate in jurisprudence:* Ibid., 77.

24 *offer to teach:* Ibid., 106–7.

24 *fatefully met:* Abdullah Anas and Tam Hussein, *To the Mountains: My Life in Jihad, from Algeria to Afghanistan* (London: Hurst, 2019), 174.

24 *waged against the Soviets*: A key, authoritative history of the "Afghan Arabs" is *The Arab Supporters in Afghanistan* by Basil Muhammad (1991). It was published only two years after the end of the Afghan War and it was based on contemporaneous interviews and primary sources, such as tape recordings made of walkie-talkie traffic during the battles fought by the Arabs in Afghanistan. While sympathetic to their cause, the book also covers the disputes between the Afghan Arabs and it is not hagiographic. Basil Muhammad is a pseudonym for Adel Batterjee.

24 *including in the United States*: Hegghammer, *The Caravan*, 143, 249–51.

24 *Essam al-Ridi*: USA v. Usama bin Laden et al., Southern District of New York, Testimony of Essam al-Ridi, February 14, 2001.

24 *Wael Julaidan*: Author's interview with Wael Julaidan, Jeddah, Saudi Arabia, September 11, 2005.

24 *Signs of the Most Merciful in the Afghan Holy War*: Hegghammer, *The Caravan*, 295.

25 "*Expelling the Kuffar . . . foremost problems*": Azzam, *Defense of Muslim Lands*, quoted in Bergen, *The Osama Bin Laden I Know*, 27.

25 *Azzam announced*: Email correspondence with Thomas Hegghammer, April 2, 2021.

25 "*pure . . . the life of the poor . . . a Jordanian laborer*": Sheikh Abdullah Azzam, *The Lofty Mountain* (London: Azzam Publications, undated), 151, https://issuu .com/lifeways11/docs/the_lofty_mountain_www.islamicline.

26 "*I never heard . . . declaimer of poems*": Author's interview with Vahid Mojdeh, Kabul, Afghanistan, January 2005.

26 "*a student . . . bin Laden*": Author's interview with Faraj Ismail, Cairo, Egypt, June 2005.

26 "*They came to die*": Author's interview with Essam Deraz, Cairo, Egypt, December 2000.

26 *the glory that came*: Anas and Hussein, *To the Mountains*, 155.

26 "*Sylvester Stallone and visions of paradise*": Ibid.; Boudejema Bounoua is Abdullah Anas's real name.

26 *Anas read . . . get there*: Author's interviews with Abdullah Anas, London, United Kingdom, June 15, 17, and 20, 2005; Anas and Hussein, *To the Mountains*, 25, 34–35.

26 "*Are you Abdullah Azzam?*": Author's interviews with Abdullah Anas, London, United Kingdom, June 15, 17, and 20, 2005; Anas and Hussein, *To the Mountains*, 36.

26 "*call me from the airport*": Author's interviews with Abdullah Anas, London, United Kingdom, June 15, 17, and 20, 2005; Anas and Hussein, *To the Mountains*, 36.

26 "*your brother, Osama*": Author's interviews with Abdullah Anas, London, United Kingdom, June 15, 17, and 20, 2005; Anas and Hussein, *To the Mountains*, 38.

27 *very shy:* Author's interviews with Abdullah Anas, London, United Kingdom, June 15, 17, and 20, 2005; Anas and Hussein, *To the Mountains*, 38.

27 *fourteenth of the Arabs:* Author's interviews with Abdullah Anas, London, United Kingdom, June 15, 17, and 20, 2005; Anas and Hussein, *To the Mountains*, 42.

27 *caravan:* Author's interviews with Abdullah Anas, London, United Kingdom, June 15, 17, and 20, 2005; Anas and Hussein, *To the Mountains*, 45.

27 *"Allah Akbar!" . . . "I used to feel . . . making jihad":* Author's interviews with Abdullah Anas, London, United Kingdom, June 15, 17, and 20, 2005.

27 *two months:* Ibid.

27 *largest refugee population since World War II:* Rupert Colville, "The Biggest Caseload in the World," *Refugees Magazine*, June 1, 1997, https://www.unhcr.org/en-us/publications/refugeemag/3b680fbfc/refugees-magazine-issue-108-afghanistan-unending-crisis-biggest-caseload.html.

27 *did not set foot in Afghanistan:* Muhammad, *The Arab Supporters in Afghanistan*, 88–89.

28 *a good laugh:* Azzam interview in Christiane Amanpour, *In the Footsteps of bin Laden*, Part 3, CNN, August 23, 2006, produced by Peter Bergen, Cliff Hackel, and Ken Shiffman, https://www.cnn.com/videos/international/2012/04/26/in-the-footsteps-of-bin-laden-part-3.cnn.

28 *made him feel embarrassed:* Muhammad, *The Arab Supporters in Afghanistan*, 85.

28 *raise more than:* Ibid., 105.

28 *around $300,000:* Essam Deraz gave a figure of $25,000 a month. Author's interview with Deraz, Cairo, Egypt, January 2000.

28 *A key project:* Jihad magazine, issue 1, December 28, 1984, lead article, author's collection.

29 *Jamal Ismail . . . Ahmad Zaidan:* Anas and Hussein, *To the Mountains*, 154. Author's interview with Jamal Ismail, Islamabad, Pakistan, March 2005.

29 *fifty countries . . . seventy thousand copies . . . United States:* A sense of *Jihad* magazine's global distribution can be found in a list of cover prices from fifty countries in an issue from late 1989. Bergen, *The Osama bin Laden I Know*, 33, 36.

29 *headquarters in Brooklyn . . . Washington, DC:* Author's interviews with Abdullah Anas, London, United Kingdom, June 15, 17, and 20, 2005; Anas and Hussein, *To the Mountains*, 116.

29 *75 percent discount:* Author's interview with Jamal Ismail, Islamabad, Pakistan, March 2005.

29 *Jamal al-Fadl:* Bergen, *The Osama bin Laden I Know*, 44; *USA v. Usama bin Laden*, Testimony of Jamal al-Fadl, February 6, 7, 13, and 20, 2001.

30 *appointed by his older brother Salem:* Steve Coll, *The Bin Ladens: An Arabian Family in the American Century* (New York: Penguin, 2008), 252.

30 *Bin Laden moved to the holy city:* Author's interviews with Jamal Khalifa, Jeddah, Saudi Arabia, September 6 and 9, 2005.

30 *"fun" . . . "just having . . . sleep with":* Ibid.

30 *twenty wives:* Ibid.

31 *purchased a large building:* Najwa bin Laden, Omar bin Laden, and Jean P. Sasson, *Growing Up bin Laden: Osama's Wife and Son Take Us Inside Their Secret World* (New York: St. Martin's Press, 2009), 28, 304.

31 *undecorated:* Author's interviews with Khaled Batarfi, Jeddah, Saudi Arabia, September 5 and 9, 2005.

31 *"Islamic beliefs are corrupted":* Bin Laden, bin Laden, and Sasson, *Growing Up bin Laden,* 43.

31 *clamed descent from the Prophet:* Ibid., 293

31 *tried to model every aspect of his life on the Prophet:* Author's interviews with Jamal Khalifa, Jeddah, Saudi Arabia, September 6 and 9, 2005.

31 *"unexpected topic":* Bin Laden, bin Laden, and Sasson, *Growing Up bin Laden,* 49.

31 *"many children for Islam":* Ibid., 50.

31 *"Najwa if you . . . end in Paradise":* Ibid., 50.

31 *Khadijah al-Sharif:* Ibid., 50–51, 304.

32 *trip to Peshawar:* Ibid., 51–52.

32 *"Islam would need more followers" . . . "to carry . . . God":* Ibid., 52.

32 *"Marry and increase in number":* Mustafa al-Ansari, "Bin Ladin's Brother-in-Law to Al Hayah: 'My Sister Holds PhD: She Differs with Husband Usama Ideologically,'" *Al Hayat* online, May 26, 2011.

32 *"suitable wife" . . . "for Islam":* Bin Laden, bin Laden, and Sasson, *Growing Up Bin Laden,* 52.

32 *Khairiah Sabar:* Ibid.

32 *very late age:* "World Marriage Data 2012: Ever Married Men and Women, Singulate Mean Age at Marriage (SMAM)," United Nations, Department of Economics and Social Affairs, Population Division, 2013, http://data.un.org/DocumentData.aspx?id=321#25; "Demography Survey" (General Authority for Statistics, 2016), 24, https://www.stats.gov.sa/sites/default/files/en-demographic-research-2016_2.pdf.

33 *Saad al-Sharif:* Mustafa al-Ansari, "Bin Ladin's Brother-in-Law to Al Hayah: 'My Sister Holds PhD: She Differs with Husband Usama Ideologically.'"

33 *sister Siham:* Ibid.

33 *"I don't . . . like a groom":* Author's interviews with Abdullah Anas, London, United Kingdom, June 15, 17, and 20, 2005.

33 *tried to keep their husbands away:* Mustafa al-Ansari, "Bin Ladin's Brother-in-Law

to Al Hayah: 'My Sister Holds PhD: She Differs with Husband Usama Ideologically.'"

33 *suggested to Jamal Khalifa:* Author's interviews with Jamal Khalifa, Jeddah,
Saudi Arabia, September 6 and 9, 2005.

33 *he divided his Jeddah villa:* Ibid.

33 *began to fray:* Author's interviews with Abdullah Anas, London, June 15, 17, and
20, 2005.

34 *175,000 to 250,000:* Mark Urban, *War in Afghanistan* (London: Palgrave Macmillan, 1988), 244.

34 *Abdullah Azzam was opposed* : Bergen, *The Osama bin Laden I Know*, 6.

34 *Bin Laden, who had no military expertise:* Ibid., 49–54.

34 *"Whoever wishes to hear the clash of swords":* Bruce Hoffman, Fernando Reinares, eds., *The Evolution of the Global Terrorist Threat: From 9/11 to Osama bin
Laden's Death* (New York: Columbia University Press, 2016), 382.

34 *"We want . . . extreme manner":* Bergen, *The Osama bin Laden I Know*, 52.

35 *undercut their strategy:* Anne Stenersen, *Al-Qaida in Afghanistan* (Cambridge,
UK: Cambridge University Press, 2017), 19, 22–23.

35 *The winter was so intense:* Jihad magazine, issue 53, April 1989, "The Martyr
Abu Khalil." This entry gives a sense of the difficult conditions the mujahideen
faced in Jaji.

35 *Their number soon grew to sixteen:* Essam Deraz, *The Battles of the Lion's Den of
the Afghan Mujahideen* (Cairo, 1991).

35 *bin Laden brought in welding equipment:* Muhammad, *The Arab Supporters in
Afghanistan*, 213.

35 *They also purchased their first machine gun:* Deraz, *The Battles of the Lion's Den
of the Afghan Mujahideen*.

35 *Bin Laden had to restrain:* Author's interview with Essam Deraz, Cairo, Egypt,
May 2005.

35 *"one of the most beautiful periods of my life":* Deraz, *The Battles of the Lion's Den
of the Afghan Mujahideen*.

35 *As the number of brothers at Jaji grew:* Muhammad, *The Arab Supporters in Afghanistan*, 270.

35 *In January 1987 bin Laden put his military:* TAREEKOSAMA/34/Tareekh Osama
100, author's collection. A collection of notes and memos recovered by Bosnian
authorities in Sarajevo in 2002 that document the early history of al-Qaeda.

35 *When he visited Jaji, Jamal Khalifa was unimpressed:* Author's interviews with
Jamal Khalifa, Jeddah, Saudi Arabia, September 6 and 9, 2005

36 *Abu Ubayda, a former sergeant:* Author's interview with Essam Deraz, Cairo,
Egypt, May 2005

36 *would charge Khalifa:* Nick Fielding, "Gems, Al-Qaida and Murder: Mystery

over Killing of Osama bin Laden's Friend," *Guardian*, March 1, 2007, https://www.theguardian.com/world/2007/mar/02/alqaida.saudiarabia.

36 *murdered in mysterious circumstances:* "Saudi Relative of bin Laden Killed," Reuters, January 31, 2007, https://www.reuters.com/article/us-saudi-madagascar-murder/saudi-relative-of-bin-laden-killed-idUSL3170124620070131.

36 *Because . . . forge ahead with his plans:* Mustafa Hamid (aka Abu Walid al-Misri) and Leah Farrall, *The Arabs at War in Afghanistan* (London: Hurst, 2015), 94–96; Anas and Hussein, *To the Mountains*, 181–82.

36 *loggerheads with Azzam over the management:* Hamid and Farrall, *The Arabs at War in Afghanistan*, 80.

36 *decided to live full-time in Peshawar:* Ahmad Muaffaq Zaidan, "Bin Laden Revealed," unpublished manuscript, which is based on Zaidan's book in Arabic, *Bin Laden Unmasked* (Beirut, 2015), 93.

36 *Hayatabad:* Ibid.

37 *That guesthouse was named:* Bait-al Ansar was at 61, Syed Jamaluddin Afghani Road in University Town, Peshawar, and *Jihad* magazine was based on the same street at 42, Syed Jamaluddin Afghani Road.

37 *American Club:* This description is based on the author's visits to the club in 1993 and Bob McKerrow, "The American Club Peshawar," *Bob McKerrow—Wayfarer* (blog), May 7, 2012, http://bobmckerrow.blogspot.com/2012/05/american-club-peshawar.html; Karin Brulliard, "Khyber Club's Bartender Had Front-Row Seat to History in Pakistan," *Washington Post*, February 7, 2012, https://www.washingtonpost.com/world/asia_pacific/khyber-clubs-bartender-had-front-row-seat-to-history-in-pakistan/2012/01/27/gIQABx3xvQ_story.html.

37 *"I was more romantic":* Batarfi interview in Christiane Amanpour, *In the Footsteps of bin Laden*, Part 1, CNN, August 23, 2006, produced by Peter Bergen, Cliff Hackel, and Ken Shiffman, https://www.cnn.com/videos/international/2012/04/26/amanpour-footsteps-cnn-part-1.cnn.

37 *even American apples:* Bin Laden Family Journal, https://www.cia.gov/library/abbottabad-compound/76/76155EE3B4398AC4814FA69DF33057B3_Journal.original.pdf, 8–10.

37 *banned his own family from drinking:* Author's interview with Jamal Ismail, Islamabad, Pakistan, March 2005; bin Laden, bin Laden, and Sasson, *Growing Up bin Laden*, 60.

37 *On May 23:* Muhammad, *The Arab Supporters in Afghanistan*, 305–15.

38 *napalm:* Author's interview with Hudhayfa Azzam, Amman, Jordan, September 13, 2005.

38 *glucose:* Deraz, *The Battles of the Lion's Den of the Afghan Mujahideen*.

38 *Azzam told bin Laden to rest:* Author's interview with Hudayafa Azzam, Amman, Jordan, September 13, 2005.

38 *Night of Power:* Bergen, *The Osama bin Laden I Know,* 57.

38 *twenty-seven raids:* David Cook, *Understanding Jihad,* 2nd ed. (Oakland: University of California Press, 2015), 6; Peter Partner, *God of Battles: Holy Wars of Christianity and Islam* (Princeton, NJ: Princeton University Press, 1997), 35.

38 *thirteen of bin Laden's Arab fighters were killed:* Muhammad, *The Arab Supporters in Afghanistan,* 336, 361.

38 *After the Arabs withdrew they were replaced:* Ibid., 361.

39 *Victory songs were sung by the mujahideen:* Ibid., 365.

39 *Essam Deraz, a forty-year-old former captain:* Author interviews with Essam Deraz, Cairo, Egypt, January 2000 and May 2005

39 *in a cave:* "First Revelation—Surah Al-`Alaq (The Clot)," *Quran Reading* (blog), April 6, 2015, http://www.quranreading.com/blog/first-revelation-surah-al-alaq-the-clot/.

39 *Deraz noticed that bin Laden:* Author's interviews with Essam Deraz, Cairo, Egypt, January 2000 and May 2005.

39 *"Russia lost many of their well-respected commandos":* *Jihad* magazine, issue 31, June 1987, "With Our Four Automobiles Against the Warsaw Pact," author's collection.

40 *"After the victorious battle":* *Jihad* magazine, issue 54–55, April–May 1989, "No Turning Back," author's collection.

40 *between three thousand to five thousand:* Author's interviews with Abdullah Anas, London, United Kingdom, June 15, 17, and 20, 2005.

40 *"Instead of . . . some money":* Ibid.

40 *Adnan Khashoggi:* Peter L. Bergen, *Holy War, Inc.: Inside the Secret World of Osama bin Laden* (New York: Free Press, 2001), 44.

40 *"like many of us . . . movement":* Author's interview with Jamal Khashoggi, London, United Kingdom, June 13, 2005.

40 *"a very enthusiastic bunch":* Ibid.

40 *Khashoggi published a lengthy article:* Jamal Khashoggi, "Arab Youths Fight Shoulder to Shoulder with Mujahedeen," *Al Majalah,* issue 430, May 4, 1988.

41 *going down in history: The Lofty Mountain:* Azzam, *The Lofty Mountain,* 77.

41 *"Western Diplomats reported" . . . "the most severe":* Jack Reed, "Soviets Race to Cut Rebel Supply Lines from Pakistan," UPI, June 1, 1987.

41 *own account of the Jaji battle:* Muhammad, *The Arab Supporters in Afghanistan,* 336, 316.

41 *only thirteen:* Ibid., 361.

41 *Authoritative histories . . . rarely mention:* Those include *The Bear Trap* by Brigadier Mohammad Yousaf, the Pakistani general who supplied all of the Afghan fighting groups; *The Bear Went Over the Mountain: Soviet Combat Tactics in*

Afghanistan, which was a compilation of accounts of the war by Soviet military commanders; and *Afghan Communism and Soviet Intervention* by Henry Bradsher, an American journalist. Mohammad Yousaf and Mark Adkin, *Afghanistan—the Bear Trap: The Defeat of a Superpower* (Lahore: Jang Publishers, 1993); Lester W. Grau, ed., *The Bear Went Over the Mountain: Soviet Combat Tactics in Afghanistan* (Ft. Leavenworth, KS: Foreign Military Studies Office, 2005); Henry S. Bradsher, *Afghan Communism and Soviet Intervention* (Oxford: Oxford University Press, 1999).

41 *at least fifty thousand:* Hegghammer, *The Caravan*, 365.

41 *highly effective Stinger antiaircraft missile:* Author's interview with Milt Bearden, Austin, Texas, December 19, 2019.

42 *"Go out and win":* Ibid.

42 *Three years later:* Ibid.

42 *$250 million a year:* Milt Bearden and James Risen, *The Main Enemy: The Inside Story of the CIA's Final Showdown with the KGB* (New York: Random House, 2003), 384.

42 *Arab sources donated $200 million:* Ayman al-Zawahiri, *Knights Under the Banner of the Prophet*, extracts, *Asharq al-Awsat*, December 2, 2001, part 1.

42 *"WE created the monster":* Michael Moore, "Bush, The CIA and the Roots of Terrorism," *AlterNet*, September 14, 2001.

42 *until 1993:* "The Wandering Mujahidin: Armed and Dangerous" (United States Department of State Bureau of Intelligence and Research, *Weekend Edition*, August 21–22, 1993) was the first official U.S. government warning about bin Laden and his followers.

42 *six CIA officials:* A former CIA official also confirms the figure of six. Washington, DC, November 2000.

43 *seldom left . . . receive the funding:* Ibid.

43 *"a cardinal rule":* Yousaf and Adkin, *Afghanistan—the Bear Trap*, 81.

43 *"we were totally banned":* Author's interview with Marc Sageman, Washington, DC, October 18, 2019.

43 *"never recruited . . . on this point":* Author's interview with Milt Bearden, Austin, Texas, December 19, 2019. See also Bearden and Risen, *The Main Enemy*, 257.

43 *CIA did not need:* This section draws on Bergen, *Holy War, Inc.*, 63–75.

43 *"The Custodian of the Two Holy Mosques":* An account of the title bestowed in 1986 can be found here: http://www.princemohammad.org/en/Kingdom-King -Fahd.aspx.

44 *Those in Saudi Arabia:* Author's interviews with Jamal Khalifa, Jeddah, Saudi Arabia, September 6 and 9, 2005; Author's interviews with Khaled Batarfi, Jeddah, Saudi Arabia, September 5 and 9, 2005.

44 *foundation myth*: Olivier Roy, *Globalized Islam: The Search for a New Ummah*, The CERI Series in Comparative Politics and International Studies (New York: Columbia University Press, 2004), 297.

44 *born in the battle of Jaji* : Zaidan, "Bin Laden Revealed," 45.

FOUR: AL-QAEDA

45 *"walls of oppression"*: "Declaration of War," Osama bin Laden, August 1996.

45 *"What is more important"*: "Oui, la CIA Est Entrée en Afghanistan Avant les Russes," *Le Nouvel Observateur*, January 15, 1998, https://www.voltairenet.org /article165889.html. The English translation is from David N. Gibbs, "Review Essay: Afghanistan: The Soviet Invasion in Retrospect," *International Politics* 37, no. 2 (June 2000): 242, https://dgibbs.faculty.arizona.edu/sites/dgibbs.faculty .arizona.edu/files/afghan-ip.pdf.

46 *contemplated starting an organization*: Mustafa Hamid and Leah Farrall, *The Arabs at War in Afghanistan* (London: Hurst, 2015), 98, 111.

46 *"The flame of jihad"*: Author's interview with Jamal Khashoggi, London, United Kingdom, June 13, 2005.

46 *"We used to call . . . the name stayed"*: "Transcript of Bin Laden's October Inter- view," CNN, February 5, 2002, https://edition.cnn.com/2002/WORLD/asiapcf /south/02/05/binladen.transcript/.

46 *personal payroll*: TAREEKOSAMA/34/Tareekh Osama 100, author's collection. A collection of notes and memos recovered by Bosnian authorities in Sarajevo in 2002 that document the early history of al-Qaeda.

46 *On August 11, 1988*: TAREEKHOSAMA/50/Tareekh Osama 122–23, author's collection.

46 *battle of Badr*: Richard A. Gabriel, "Muhammad: The Warrior Prophet," *Military History Quarterly*, Summer 2007, https://www.historynet.com/muhammad-the -warrior-prophet.htm.

46 *At least one of the participants*: Author's interview, Wael Julaidan, Jeddah, Saudi Arabia, September 11, 2005.

46 *Azzam was not listed*: TAREEKHOSAMA/54/Tareekh Osama 127–127a, au- thor's collection.

46 *The notes record that the overall aim of al-Qaeda*: Ibid.

46 *nothing suggested that bin Laden*: Author's interview with Noman Benotman, London, United Kingdom, August 30, 2005.

46 *The men at the meeting agreed that*: Ibid.

47 *Despite later claims that Ayman al-Zawahiri*: See for instance, T. Christian Miller, "Zawahiri: The Alleged Brains Behind bin Laden," *Los Angeles Times*, October 2, 2001.

47 *"like a father to him"*: Khaled Batarfi, "Osama Is Very Sweet, Very Kind, Very

Considerate . . . as His Mother I Love Him and I Will Pray for Him," *Mail on Sunday*, December 23, 2001.

47 *"If Salem had still been around"*: Author's Interview with Salem bin Laden family member, 2000.

47 *Salem's body . . . at the funeral*: Ibid.; Steve Coll, *The Bin Ladens: An Arabian Family in the American Century* (New York: Penguin, 2014), 331–32.

48 *It was Salem who*: Author's Interview with Salem bin Laden family member, 2000.

48 *cash payment . . . retain an interest*: Coll, *The Bin Ladens*, 350; Author's Interview with Salem bin Laden family member, 2000.

48 *"WE WON"*: Milt Bearden and James Risen, *The Main Enemy: The Inside Story of the CIA's Final Showdown with the KGB* (New York: Random House, 2003), 376.

48 *the agency threw itself a party*: George Crile, *Charlie Wilson's War: The Extraordinary Story of How the Wildest Man in Congress and a Rogue CIA Agent Changed the History of Our Time* (New York: Grove Atlantic, 2007), 591.

48 *Champagne bottles were popped*: Author's Interview with David Sedney, Kabul, Afghanistan, December 3, 2019.

48 *U.S. embassy in Kabul closed*: Richard M. Weintraub, "U.S. Closes Its Embassy in Kabul," *Washington Post*, January 31, 1989, https://www.washingtonpost.com /archive/politics/1989/01/31/us-closes-its-embassy-in-kabul/6990e6d9-6eb6 -4468-82c7-b4a93a9101c3/.

49 *overjoyed . . . bin Laden's destiny*: Najwa bin Laden, Omar bin Laden, and Jean P. Sasson, *Growing Up bin Laden: Osama's Wife and Son Take Us Inside Their Secret World* (New York: St. Martin's Press, 2009), 74.

49 *With the Soviet military gone*: Mohammad Yousaf and Mark Adkin, *Afghanistan—the Bear Trap: The Defeat of a Superpower* (Lahore: Jang Publishers, 1993), 228–32.

50 *"The hot fights started"*: *Jihad* magazine, issue 57, July 1989, "Kabul: The Place of Final Battle."

50 *"Every time he"*: *Jihad* magazine, issue 59, September 1989, "The Battle of Jalalabad," 36.

50 *"died while operating the 75-millimeter cannon"*: Essam Deraz, *The Battles of the Lion's Den of the Afghan Mujahideen* (Cairo, 1991).

50 *criticized for his decision*: Hudhayfa Azzam and Osama Rushdi interviews in Christiane Amanpour, *In the Footsteps of bin Laden*, Part 4, CNN, August 23, 2006, produced by Peter Bergen, Cliff Hackel, and Ken Shiffman, https://www .cnn.com/videos/bestoftv/2012/04/26/in-the-footsteps-of-bin-laden-part -4.cnn.

51 *"There was friction"*: Hasin al Bayan interview of Hassan Abd-Rabbuh al-Surayhi, *Asharq al-Awsat*, November 25, 2001.

51 *In 1986, he met:* Author's interview with Jamal Ismail, Islamabad, Pakistan, March 2005; Ayman al-Zawahiri, *Knights Under the Prophet's Banner*, extracts, *Asharq al-Awsat*, December 2001.

51 *Zawahiri encouraged bin Laden:* Author's interview with Faraj Ismail, Cairo, Egypt, June 2005.

51 *"an agent":* Peter L. Bergen, *The Osama bin Laden I Know: An Oral History of al Qaeda's Leader* (New York: Free Press, 2006), 95.

51 *Leaflets were distributed:* Ibid.

51 *November 24, 1989: Jihad* magazine, issue 63, January 1990, "Bloody Friday: The Assassination of Sheikh Abdullah and His Two Sons," author's collection.

51 *"my brother . . . another area":* Author's interview with Hudayfa Azzam, Amman, Jordan, September 13, 2005.

52 *draft of its by-laws:* Ibid. The document is undated but it's likely to have been written after the formal founding of al-Qaeda during the summer of 1988 and before 1992, when al-Qaeda wound up all its operations in Pakistan, since the currency for monthly payments for members and other expenditures is in Pakistani rupees.

52 *Bin Laden personally funded much:* "Al-Qa`ida Bylaws" (Combating Terrorism Center, n.d.), AFGP-2002-600048, https://www.ctc.usma.edu/harmony-program/al-qaida-bylaws-2/.

FIVE: RADICAL

57 *"Whoever seeks his rights":* Khalid Al-Hammadi, "Part 7 of a Series of Interviews with Nasir Ahmad Nasir Abdullah al-Bahri, Alias Abu-Jandal, Formerly the 'Personal Guard' of Al-Qa'ida Leader Usama Bin Ladin," *Al Quds Al-Arabi*, April 2, 2005, FBIS Translated Text, http://gtrp.haverford.edu/static/gtr_site/alqaedawithinpt3.pdf.

57 *Jamal Khalifa noticed:* Author's interviews with Jamal Khalifa, Jeddah, Saudi Arabia, September 6 and 9, 2005.

57 *"We should train . . . never be trusted":* Author's interview with Khaled Batarfi, Jeddah, Saudi Arabia, September 5, 2005.

58 *determined to rid South Yemen . . . Prophet's ruling:* Flagg Miller, *The Audacious Ascetic: What the Bin Laden Tapes Reveal About al-Qa'ida* (New York: Oxford University Press, 2015), 123–33.

58 *"his mujahideen":* Meeting Osama bin Laden, PBS, March 22, 2005, interview with Prince Turki. Prince Turki made a similar point in Christiane Amanpour, *In the Footsteps of bin Laden*, CNN, August 23, 2006, produced by Peter Bergen, Cliff Hackel, and Ken Shiffman.

59 *Saudi government supported:* Steve Coll, *The Bin Ladens: An Arabian Family in the American Century* (New York: Penguin, 2014), 375.

59 *Saudi officials warned:* Jamal Khashoggi, "Former Saudi Intel Chief Interviewed on Saudi-Afghan Tie, Bin Laden—Part 5," *Arab News*, November 8, 2001.

59 *fourth largest:* Thomas A. Keaney and Eliot A. Cohen, *Gulf War Air Power Survey: Summary Report* (Washington, DC: U.S. Government Printing Office, 1993), 251; Sharon Otterman, "IRAQ: Iraq's Prewar Military Capabilities," *Backgrounder* (blog), Council on Foreign Relations, March 19, 2007, https://www.cfr.org/backgrounder/iraq-iraqs-prewar-military-capabilities.

59 *bin Laden implausibly claimed:* Khalid Al-Hammadi, "Part 8 of a Series of Interviews with Nasir Ahmad Nasir Abdullah al-Bahri Alias Abu-Jandal, Formerly the 'Personal Guard' of Al-Qa'ida Leader Usama Bin Ladin," *Al Quds Al-Arabi*, April 2, 2005, FBIS Translated Text, http://gtrp.haverford.edu/static/gtr_site/alqaedawithinpt3.pdf.

59 *"I saw radical . . . arrogance":* Jamal Khashoggi, "Former Saudi Intel Chief Interviewed on Saudi-Afghan Tie, Bin Laden—Part 4," *Arab News*, November 7, 2001.

59 *"absolutely ridiculous":* Chas Freeman interview, *Road to 9/11*, History Channel, Part 2, September 5, 2017.

59 *500,000 U.S. troops:* R. Jeffrey Smith, "U.S. Deployment Expected to Exceed 500,000," *Washington Post*, January 25, 1991, https://www.washingtonpost.com/archive/politics/1991/01/25/us-deployment-expected-to-exceed-500000/13038c4d-574d-4079-b7f5-bead3add3dfa/.

59 *"Let there be no two religions":* Harry Munt, 'No Two Religions': Non-Muslims in the Early Islamic Ḥijāz," *Bulletin of the School of Oriental and African Studies* 78, no. 2 (June 2005): 249–269, https://doi.org/10.1017/S0041977X14001049.

59 *often told audiences:* Bin Laden family journal, 8–10; Essam Deraz interview in Bergen, *The Osama bin Laden I Know*, 110.

59 *Khashoggi attended an event in Jeddah:* Khashoggi interview for Amanpour, *In the Footsteps of Bin Laden*, CNN, August 23, 2006.

60 *turned his focus to Afghanistan:* Author's interview with Wael Julaidan, Jeddah, Saudi Arabia, September 11, 2005.

60 *poorly conceived plan:* Author's interviews with Abdullah Anas, London, United Kingdom, June 15, 17, and 20, 2005.

60 *money guy:* Ibid.; Author's interviews with Haji Deen Mohamed, Jalalabad, Afghanistan, June 2003 and January 16, 2005.

60 *Paulo Jose de Almeida Santos:* Jose Pedro Castanheira of the Portuguese magazine *Expresso* tracked Santos down to a location in East Africa, where he gave an interview about his assassination attempt against the Afghan king in April 2002. This description also draws on Peter L. Bergen, *The Osama bin Laden I Know: An Oral History of al Qaeda's Leader* (New York: Free Press, 2006), 116–20; Paulo Anunciacao, "Bin Laden 'Tried to Kill King,'" *Telegraph*, April 14, 2002,

https://www.telegraph.co.uk/news/worldnews/asia/afghanistan/1390843/Bin
-Laden-tried-to-kill-king.html.

61 *assassination attempt:* Alan Cowell, "Afghans' Ex-King Stabbed in Rome," *New York Times,* November 5, 1991, https://www.nytimes.com/1991/11/05/world
/afghans-ex-king-stabbed-in-rome.html.

61 *May 1, 1991:* This date is from an interview with bin Laden that appeared as "The New Powder Keg in the Middle East" in *Nida Ul Islam,* issue 15, October 1996. It can be found in Osama Bin Laden, *Messages to the World: The Statements of Osama Bin Laden,* ed. Bruce B. Lawrence (London: Verso, 2005), 33.

61 *permission to leave:* Abu Jandal interview with Khalid-al Hammadi, *Al Quds al Arabi,* March 24, 2005.

61 *had come to power in a coup:* Alan Cowell, "Military Coup in Sudan Ousts Civilian Regime," *New York Times,* July 1, 1989, https://www.nytimes.com/1989/07/01
/world/military-coup-in-sudan-ousts-civilian-regime.html.

62 *latter half of 1991: USA v. Usama bin Laden,* indictment, Southern District of New York, November 5, 1998, 12.

62 *few months later:* Najwa bin Laden, Omar bin Laden, and Jean P. Sasson, *Growing Up bin Laden: Osama's Wife and Son Take Us Inside Their Secret World* (New York: St. Martin's Press, 2009), 91–92, 94, 307.

62 *forbidden to use refrigerators or air-conditioning:* Ibid., 115.

62 *forbade them to drink water:* Ibid., 60–61.

62 *hollows in the sand . . . cover themselves with dirt:* Ibid., 99–100.

63 *secretly purchased a supply:* Ibid., 60.

63 *building the airport at Port Sudan:* Coll, *The Bin Ladens,* 397–99; *Al Quds al Arabi,* November, 24, 2001 (part one of a series on bin Laden's life in the Sudan).

63 *$12 million in Sudan:* Osama bin Laden, "In Regard to the Money That Is in Sudan—Bin Laden's Will" (Office of the Director of National Intelligence, n.d.), Bin Laden's Bookshelf, https://www.dni.gov/files/documents/ubl2016/english
/in%20regard%2to%20the%20money%20that%20is%20in%20Sudan.pdf.

63 *six hundred:* from *USA v. Usama bin Laden,* Fadl testimony, February 6, 7, 13, and 20, 2001.

63 *five-hundred-mile-long road:* Robert Fisk, "Anti-Soviet Warrior Puts His Army on the Road to Peace: The Saudi Businessman Who Recruited Mujahedin Now Uses Them for Large-Scale Building Projects in Sudan. Robert Fisk Met Him in Almatig," *Independent,* December 6, 1993, https://www.independent.co.uk/news
/world/anti-soviet-warrior-puts-his-army-road-peace-saudi-businessman-who
-recruited-mujahedin-now-uses-them-large-scale-building-projects-sudan
-robert-met-him-almatig-1465715.html.

63 *farmed on a massive:* Tom Cohen, "Affidavit Provides Rare Glimpse of bin Laden as Employer," *Billings Gazette,* January 12, 2001, https://billingsgazette.com

/news/world/affidavit-provides-rare-glimpse-of-osama-bin-laden-as-employer
/article_35d78cbd-8495-51d3-a93b-e7e13dd62a2a.html.

63   *near-monopoly:* State Department fact sheet on bin Laden, August 14, 1996, author's collection.

63   *also started:* Jamal al Fadl testimony, February 6, 2001, in *USA v. Usama bin Laden.*

63   *visiting the racetrack:* Al Quds al Arabi, November, 24, 2001 (part one of a series on bin Laden's life in the Sudan).

63   *Robert Fisk wrote:* Fisk, "Anti-Soviet Warrior Puts His Army on the Road to Peace."

64   *Khadijah, asked him for a divorce:* Bin Laden, bin Laden, and Sasson, *Growing Up Bin Laden*, 104, 120, 308.

64   *Abdullah . . . deeply resented:* Author's interviews with Abdullah Anas, London, United Kingdom, June 15, 17, and 20, 2005; Bin Laden, bin Laden, and Sasson, *Growing Up bin Laden*, 125–28.

64   *avoided mentioning his oldest son's name:* Nassar al-Bahri, *Guarding bin Laden: My Life in al-Qaeda* (London: Thin Man Press, 2013); Abu Jandal interview with Khalid-al Hammadi, *Al Quds Al Arabi*, March 24, 2005; Bin Laden, bin Laden, and Sasson, *Growing Up bin Laden*, 12.

64   *profile of bin Laden:* "A Millionaire Finances Extremism in Egypt and Saudi Arabia," *Rose al-Yusuf*, May 17, 1993.

64   *legal process to expel Osama . . . $9.9 million:* Coll, *The Bin Ladens*, 405–8.

64   *"You can run . . . your country" . . . "I am tired":* Hasin al Bayan interview of Hassan Abd-Rabbuh al-Surayhi, *Asharq al-Awsat*, November 25, 2001.

64   *"I can sacrifice . . . enemies of Islam":* Hamid Mir, author's interview, Islamabad, Pakistan, May11, 2002.

64   *In late February 1994:* The bin Laden assassination attempt happened after an attack on a mosque just outside Khartoum that killed twenty in early February 1994 and before bin Laden gave an interview to *Al-Quds al Arabi* in early March 1994 that mentioned the assassination attempt. Ali Abd-al-Karim and al-Nur Ahmad al-Nur, "Usama Bin Laden Denies 'Terrorism' Link," *Al-Quds Al-Arabi*, March 9, 1994, https://scholarship.tricolib.brynmawr.edu/bitstream/handle/10066/4733/OBL19940309.pdf?sequence=4&isAllowed=y; "Death Toll in Mosque Attack Rises," UPI, February 6, 1994, https://www.upi.com/Archives/1994/02/06/Death-toll-in-mosque-attack-rises/4274760510800/.

64   *four gunmen shot:* Bergen, *The Osama bin Laden I Know*, 135–36; Bin Laden, bin Laden, and Sasson, *Growing Up bin Laden*, 123–27.

65   *a group who thought:* Author's interviews with Abdullah Anas, London, United Kingdom, June 15, 17, and 20, 2005.

65   *officially stripped him of his citizenship:* Youssef M. Ibrahim, "Saudis Strip Citizenship from Backer of Militants," *New York Times*, April 10, 1994, https://

www.nytimes.com/1994/04/10/world/saudis-strip-citizenship-from-backer-of
-militants.html; "Saudi Stripped of Citizenship for Funding Fundamentalists,"
Guardian, April 11, 1994.

65 *"regret, denounce and condemn"*: Statement from Bakr bin Laden, April 1994,
author's collection.

65 *statement complaining*: Osama bin Laden, "Our Invitation to Give Advice
and Reform," April 12, 1994, Al-Qaeda Statements Index, https://scholarship
.tricolib.brynmawr.edu/bitstream/handle/10066/15196/OBL19940912.pdf
?sequence=4&isAllowed=y.

66 *Bin Laden sent lengthy memos: USA v. Khalid al-Fawwaz*, S7 98 Cr. 1023, exhibit C1.

66 *"public money"*: Communiqué 17, August 3, 1995, Osama bin Laden, Khartoum,
Sudan.

66 *"the Christian women"*: Communiqué 5, *Important Telegram to Our Brothers in
the Armed Forces*, September 19, 1994, Osama bin Laden, Khartoum, Sudan.

66 *"an apostate and infidel"*: Communiqué 11, December 29, 1994, Osama bin
Laden, Khartoum, Sudan.

66 *Khashoggi traveled*: Khashoggi interview in Amanpour, *In the Footsteps of bin
Laden*, CNN, August 23, 2006.

SIX: "THE HEAD OF THE SNAKE"

67 *"Cruel men believe"*: Bertrand Russell, edited by John G. Slater and Peter Köllner,
*The Collected Papers of Bertrand Russell, Volume 11, Last Philosophical Testa-
ment: 1943–68* (London: Routledge, 1997), 88.

67 *Every Thursday evening . . . these discussions: USA v. Usama bin Laden*, Testimony of Jamal al-Fadl, February 6, 2000, 263–70.

67 *28,000 American troops*: Michael Wines, "Mission to Somalia; Bush De-
clares Goal in Somalia to 'Save Thousands,'" *New York Times*, December 5,
1992, https://www.nytimes.com/1992/12/05/world/mission-to-somalia-bush
-declares-goal-in-somalia-to-save-thousands.html.

67 *"We have to stop the head of the snake": USA v. Usama bin Laden*, Testimony of
Jamal al-Fadl, 281.

68 *on bin Laden's mind*: In his plea agreement, Ali Mohamed, a key military trainer
in al-Qaeda, said, "Based on the Marine explosion in Beirut . . . and the American pull-out from Beirut, they will be the same method, to force the United
States out of Saudi Arabia." *USA v. Ali Mohamed*, plea agreement of Ali Mohamed, October 20, 2000, https://cryptome.org/usa-v-mohamed.htm.

68 *the majority of bin Laden's statements*: "What Do Terrorists Want?" James L.
Payne, *Independent Review*, summer 2008, 29–39. In 91 public statements by
bin Laden housed at the Global Terrorism Research Project at Haverford College the U.S. is the number one topic; Egypt ranks number 39.

69 *Their bombs killed:* Associated Press, Sana'a, December 30, 1992, *Washington Post*, Stephen Barr, January 3, 1993.

69 *The Pentagon announced:* Ibid., https://www.washingtonpost.com/archive /politics/1993/01/03/us-stops-using-yemen-support-base/ad0a95cc-2433-4f56 -a8ec-a9b2b5c51b98/.

69 *a victory:* Bin Laden interview with CNN's Peter Arnett, produced by Peter Bergen, March 1997, http://www.anusha.com/osamaint.htm.

69 *Next bin Laden sent Abu Hafs:* In March 1993 Abu Hafs sent a letter to bin Laden saying that he was providing military training to hundreds of Somalis opposed to the U.S. presence who received five weeks of basic training and two to three weeks of advanced training on weaponry such as antitank missiles. In the letter Abu Hafs asked for $64,000 to buy additional military equipment. Bin Laden also sent to Somalia another of his top military commanders, Saif al-Adel, who filed a lengthy report about how al-Qaeda might profit from the local fishing business and also gave his assessment of the leadership skills of al-Qaeda members on the ground in Somalia. "The Early History of al-Qa'ida" (unpublished manuscript, RAND, 2007, author's collection), 92; "A Report from Saif Al-'Adl" (Combating Terrorism Center, January 17, 1994), AFGP-2002-600114, 1, https://ctc.usma .edu/harmony-program/a-report-from-saif-al-adl-original-language-2/.

69 *eighteen American soldiers were killed:* "Black Hawk Down: The Somali Battle That Changed US Policy in Africa," BBC, February 1, 2017, https://www.bbc .com/news/av/magazine-38808175.

69 *trained by Arabs . . . tail rotor:* Mark Bowden, *Black Hawk Down: A Story of Modern War* (New York: Atlantic Monthly Press, 1999), 110.

69 *plans for the pullout:* "The Somalia Mission; Clinton's Words on Somalia: 'The Responsibilities of American Leadership,'" *New York Times*, October 8, 1993, https://www.nytimes.com/1993/10/08/world/somalia-mission-clinton-s-words -somalia-responsibilities-american-leadership.html; Mark Huband, *Warriors of the Prophet: The Struggle for Islam* (Boulder, CO: Westview Press, 1999), 41.

69 *"based on the reports . . . they fled":* Salah Najm, "Usama Bin Ladin, the Destruction of the Base," Al Jazeera, June 10, 1999, FBIS Translated Text, 126, https:// fas.org/irp/world/para/ubl-fbis.pdf.

70 *In late 1993: USA v. Ali Mohamed,* plea agreement of Ali Mohamed, October 20, 2000, https://cryptome.org/usa-v-mohamed.htm.

70 *believed . . . a key CIA station:* Najm, "Usama Bin Ladin, the Destruction of the Base."

70 *pointed to the most effective place: USA v. Ali Mohamed,* plea agreement of Ali Mohamed, October 20, 2000.

70 *Ramzi Yousef:* Ramzi Yousef, FD-302, interview by Special Agent Bradley Garrett, Federal Bureau of Investigation, February 7, 1995, author's collection.

70   *unindicted co-conspirator:* Mary Jo White and Andrew C. McCarthy, "To: All Counsel of Record Re: US v. Omar Ahmad Ali Abdel Rahman, et al. (S5) 93 Cr. 181 (MBM)," February 2, 1995, http://www.danielpipes.org/rr/1995-02-02-usg usa049115235.pdf.

70   *$20,000 to the defense team:* John Miller interview, *Road to 9/11*, Part 1: "Brooklyn Jihad," History Channel, September 2017.

70   *$600:* John Miller, Michael Stone, and Chris Mitchell, *The Cell: Inside the 9/11 Plot, and Why the FBI and CIA Failed to Stop It* (New York: Hyperion, 2002), 122.

70   *Trade Center plotters:* John Miller interview, *Road to 9/11*, Part 1.

70   *car bomb:* "Ambassador: Car Bomb Destroyed Military Building," CNN.com, November 13, 1995, http://edition.cnn.com/WORLD/9511/saudi_blast/11am/.

70   *broadcast the confessions:* Peter L. Bergen, *Holy War, Inc.: Inside the Secret World of Osama bin Laden* (New York: Free Press, 2001), 90.

71   *Salaries . . . reduced:* USA v. Usama bin Laden, Testimony of Jamal al-Fadl, February 6, 2001.

71   *Egyptian members . . . received higher salaries:* USA v. Usama bin Laden, Testimony of Jamal al-Fadl, February 7, 2001, 386, https://web.archive.org/web/2012 0609093043/http://cns.miis.edu/reports/pdfs/binladen/070201. pdf.

71   *$110,000:* Ibid., 383.

71   *Bin Laden discovered . . . pay back only $25,000:* Ibid., 384–87.

71   *"I don't care about the money":* Ibid., 388.

71   *"If you need money":* Ibid.

71   *Eritrea:* Jane Mayer, "Junior: The Clandestine Life of America's Top Al Qaeda Source," *New Yorker*, September 3, 2006, https://www.newyorker.com/magazine /2006/09/11/junior.

71   *"What kind of war?":* USA v. Usama bin Laden, Testimony of Jamal al-Fadl, February 7, 2001, 392.

72   *Daniel Coleman:* Lawrence Wright, *The Looming Tower: Al-Qaeda and the Road to 9/11* (New York: Alfred A. Knopf, 2006), 5. Coleman began debriefing Fadl in November 1996 at a U.S. military base in Germany.

72   *Coleman found Fadl's claim:* Author's interview with Daniel Coleman, Princeton, New Jersey, December 19, 2009.

72   *assassination attempt:* Steve Coll, *Ghost Wars: The Secret History of the CIA, Afghanistan, and bin Laden, from the Soviet Invasion to September 10, 2001* (New York: Penguin, 2005), 271.

72   *close the embassy in Khartoum:* Ibid., 320–22.

72   *neither the Saudis nor the Americans:* According to the 9/11 Commission report, "In late 1995, when bin Ladin was still in Sudan, the State Department and the CIA learned that Sudanese officials were discussing with the Saudi government the possibility of expelling bin Ladin. U.S. Ambassador Timothy Carney

encouraged the Sudanese to pursue this course. The Saudis, however, did not want bin Ladin, giving as their reason their revocation of his citizenship. Sudan's minister of defense, Fatih Erwa, has claimed that Sudan offered to hand bin Ladin over to the United States. The Commission has found no credible evidence that this was so. Ambassador Carney had instructions only to push the Sudanese to expel bin Ladin. Ambassador Carney had no legal basis to ask for more from the Sudanese since, at the time, there was no indictment outstanding." Susan Rice was the senior U.S. State Department official responsible for Africa during this period and in her 2019 book, *Tough Love*, she makes a similar point. Thomas H. Kean and Lee H. Hamilton, "9/11 Commission Report, Chapter 7: The Attack Looms" (National Commission on Terrorist Attacks Upon the United States, August 21, 2004), 110, https://govinfo.library.unt.edu/911/report/911Report _Ch7.htm; Susan E. Rice, *Tough Love: My Story of the Things Worth Fighting For* (New York: Simon & Schuster, 2019), 207–11.

73 *"Either keep silent or leave":* Bin Laden's discussions with Turabi come from Abu Jandal, a Yemeni bodyguard of bin Laden's and a confidant of al-Qaeda's leader. Abu Jandal interview with Khalid-al Hammadi, *Al Quds Al Arabi,* March 24, 2005.

73 *a dream:* Unpublished manuscript by Hamid Mir, "The Story of Osama bin Laden," 14, author's collection.

73 *furious about being pushed out:* Omar bin Laden says that the expulsion from Sudan "hugely embittered" his father, who blamed it largely on the American government. Najwa bin Laden, Omar bin Laden, and Jean P. Sasson, *Growing Up bin Laden: Osama's Wife and Son Take Us Inside Their Secret World* (New York: St. Martin's Press, 2009), 207.

73 *left behind $29 million:* Osama Bin Laden, "In Regard to the Money That Is in Sudan—Bin Laden's Will" (Office of the Director of National Intelligence, n.d.), Bin Laden's Bookshelf, http://www.dni.gov/files/documents/ubl2016 /english/In%20regard%20to%20the%20money%20that%20is%20in%20 sudan.pdf.

SEVEN: A DECLARATION OF WAR

74 *"Against them make ready":* "Verse (8:60)—English Translation," Quranic Arabic Corpus, accessed March 10, 2021, https://corpus.quran.com/translation.jsp ?chapter=8&verse=60.

74 *May 18, 1996:* Robert Fisk, "Arab Rebel Leader Warns the British: 'Get out of the Gulf,'" *Independent,* July 10, 1996, https://www.independent.co.uk/news/long _reads/robert-fisk-osama-bin-laden-saudi-arabia-afghanistan-war-b1561291 .html.

74 *Accompanying him . . . al-Adel:* Najwa bin Laden, Omar bin Laden, and Jean P.

Sasson, *Growing Up bin Laden: Osama's Wife and Son Take Us Inside Their Secret World* (New York: St. Martin's Press, 2009), 139.

75   *"Commander of the Faithful"*: The biography of Mullah Omar by the Cultural Commission of the Islamic Emirate, April 6, 2015; Ahmed Rashid, *Taliban: Militant Islam, Oil and Fundamentalism in Central Asia* (New York: I. B. Tauris, 2000), 41.

75   *"Cloak of the Prophet"*: These four paragraphs draw on Peter Bergen, "The Man Who Wouldn't Hand Over bin Laden to the U.S.," *CNN*, July 29, 2015, https:// www.cnn.com/2015/07/29/opinions/bergen-mullah-omar.

75   *personally distributed money*: Copies of a collection of notes in Pashto from Mullah Omar from 1998 and 1999 ordering the disbursal of funds to other Taliban leaders and officials are in the author's collection.

76   *"the Taliban were ruthless torturers"*: Vahid Mojdeh, *Afghanistan Under Five Years of Taliban Sovereignty*, translated by Sepideh Khalili and Saeed Ganji, author's collection.

76   *public executions in the former soccer stadium*: Sanjeev Miglani, "Taliban Executions Still Haunt Afghan Soccer Field," Reuters, September 12, 2008, https://www .reuters.com/article/us-afghan-stadium/taliban-executions-still-haunt-afghan -soccer-field-idUSSP12564220080913.

76   *Khalis welcomed bin Laden*: Kevin Bell, "Usama Bin Ladin's 'Father Sheikh': Yunus Khalis and the Return of Al-Qa'ida's Leadership to Afghanistan" (Combating Terrorism Center, May 13, 2013), 39–43; Abu Jandal interview with Khalid-al Hammadi, *Al Quds Al Arabi*, March 24, 2005.

76   *"Star of Jihad" compound*: This description of the compound is based upon the author's visits to the Hadda compound in 2005 and 2006.

76   *Bin Laden came . . . perimeter at night*: Author's interview with Safiwullah, a fifteen-year-old boy who like many Afghans has only one name, who lived in the house next door to bin Laden's compound; author's 2005 visit to Hadda.

76   *Afghan-style mud house*: Description is based on author's visit to bin Laden's bombed-out former house in Tora Bora in 2005.

77   *early September 1996*: Bin Laden, bin Laden, and Sasson, *Growing Up bin Laden*, 181–85, 310.

77   *wood-burning stove*: Ibid., 203.

77   *one-ring gas burner*: Ibid., 185.

77   *can of tuna*: Ibid., 186.

77   *pregnant with their ninth child*: Ibid.

77   *"We never know"*: Ibid., 173.

77   *"I really feel secure"*: Author's interview with Abdel Bari Atwan, London, United Kingdom, June 2005.

77 *met once again with Robert Fisk:* Fisk, "Arab Rebel Leader Warns the British: 'Get out of the Gulf.'"

77 *wood:* Robert Fisk, "Bin Laden: 'We are at the start of our military action on America," *Independent,* 28 December 2001.

77 *fact sheet:* State Department fact sheet on bin Laden, August 14, 1996, author's collection.

78 *front-page story:* Jeff Gerth and Judy Miller, "Funds for Terrorists Traced to Persian Gulf Businessmen," *New York Times,* August 14, 1996, https://www.nytimes .com/1996/08/14/world/funds-for-terrorists-traced-to-persian-gulf-business men.html.

78 *"Declaration of War Against the Americans":* "Declaration of War Against the Americans," Compilation of Usama bin Laden Statements, 1994–January 2004, FBIS report, January 2004, 13–28.

78 *simple study:* Author's interview with Abdel Bari Atwan, London, United Kingdom, June 2005.

78 *"the latest and the greatest":* Declaration of War Against the Americans," Compilation of Usama bin Laden Statements, 13–28.

78 *"the wound of al-Quds":* Ibid.

79 *"I reject . . . rain of bullets":* Ibid.

79 *Atwan printed the declaration in full: USA v. Khalid al Fawwaz,* S7 S10 98 Crim. 1023, Deposition of Mr. Abdel Bari Abu Atwan, October 1, 2014, Case 1:98-cr -01023-LAK Document 1869-2.

79 *The Taliban seized Jalalabad:* Rahimullah Yusufzai, "Osama bin Laden: Al Qaeda," in *Most Wanted: Profiles of Terror,* Harinder Baweja, ed. (New Delhi: Lotus Collection, Roli Books, 2002), 24. During the summer of 1996 Khalid al-Fawwaz told Atwan that bin Laden was unsure what the Taliban takeover of Jalalabad portended for al-Qaeda.

79 *"We serve the ground":* 'Umar 'Ab-al Hakim (Abu Mus'ab al-Suri), "Afghanistan, the Taliban, and the Battle for Islam Today," (Combating Terrorism Center, October 1998), AFGP-2002-602383 39, https://ctc.usma.edu/harmony-program /afghanistan-the-taliban-and-the-battle-for-islam-today-original-language-2/.

79 *"God will never be ashamed":* Ibid., 41.

79 *buying expensive vehicles:* Mojdeh, *Afghanistan Under Five Years of Taliban Sovereignty,* 37. Also Author's interview with Mullah Khaksar, Kabul, Afghanistan, January 2005.

79 *Atwan . . . the first interview . . . a wide audience:* Author's interviews with Abdel Bari Atwan, London, United Kingdom, June 2005 and February 14, 2020.

81 *swept into Kabul:* Barbara Crossette, "Kabul Falls to Islamic Militia; Afghans Accuse Pakistan," *New York Times,* September 26, 1996, https://www.nytimes

.com/1996/09/26/world/kabul-falls-to-islamic-militia-afghans-accuse-paki
stan.html.

81 *"We've seen . . . at this stage":* "U.S. Department of State Daily Press Briefing #156, 96-09-27" (U.S. Department of State, September 27, 1996), http://www.hri .org/news/usa/std/1996/96-09-27.std.html.

81 *"The real source":* Ahmed Rashid, *Taliban: Militant Islam, Oil and Fundamentalism in Central Asia* (New York: I. B. Tauris, 2000), 178.

81 *Hamid Mir was a reporter:* Author's interview with Hamid Mir, Islamabad, Pakistan, July 9, 2003.

83 *He began to contemplate:* Author's interview with Khalid al-Fawwaz, London, January 1997.

83 *Abu Musab al-Suri accompanied:* Author's interviews with Abu Musab al-Suri, whose real name is Mustafa Setmariam Nasar, in London, Pakistan, and Afghanistan, March 1997.

84 *That's when Suri released:* On January 25, 2005, Abu Musab al-Suri released a statement to jihadist websites in response to the U.S. government's offer of a $5 million reward for information about his whereabouts. Bergen, *The Osama bin Laden I Know*, 185.

85 *some kind of detector . . . joked about with bin Laden:* Ali H. Soufan and Daniel Freedman, *The Black Banners (Declassified): How Torture Derailed the War on Terror After 9/11* (New York: W. W. Norton, 2020), 99.

85 *bin Laden said that he was declaring war:* A transcript of the interview can be found in Osama Bin Laden, *Messages to the World: The Statements of Osama Bin Laden*, ed. Bruce B. Lawrence (London: Verso, 2005), 46–57. In July 1996 bin Laden alluded to the state of war that existed between al-Qaeda and the United States in an interview with Robert Fisk, without declaring war on the U.S. "Arab rebel leader warns the British: "Get out of the Gulf." The Independent, July 10, 1996.

85 *"We learned from those who fought there":* Ibid., 54.

85 *"future plans" . . . "You'll see them":* Ibid., 56.

85 *His followers hung:* Author observations, near Jalalabad, Afghanistan, March 22, 1997.

86 *May 10, 1997:* Phil Hirschkorn, "Bin Laden the Focus of Embassy Bombing Trial," CNN.com, February 22, 2001, https://www.cnn.com/2001/LAW/02/21 /embassy.bombing.02/.

86 *confiscated copies:* "Paper Confiscated in Saudi for Article on Radical Bin Laden," Associated Press, May 13, 1997.

86 *"Control of":* Abu Walid al-Misri, the editor of *Al Imara* ("The Emirate") magazine, the Arabic-language magazine of the Taliban, whose real name is Mustafa Hamid, "History of the Afghan Arabs," serialized in *Asharq Al-Awsat*, December 8–14, 2004.

86 *"Many international media agencies"*: Osama Bin Laden, "Letter to Mullah Muhammed `Umar from Bin Laden," n.d., (Combating Terrorism Center), AFGP-2002-600321 https://www.ctc.usma.edu/wp-content/uploads/2013/10/Letter-to-Mullah-Mohammed-Omar-from-bin-Laden-Translation.pdf

87 *The Saudis were one of only three governments:* "Who Are the Taliban?," BBC News, February 27, 2020, https://www.bbc.com/news/world-south-asia-11451718

87 *subsidizing:* For instance, a note from Mullah Omar on October 15, 1998, instructed that aid from the Saudis should be paid to Jalaluddin Haqqani, an ally of the Taliban—a total of four million rupees. Copy in author's collection.

87 *flew by military plane to Kandahar:* "Osama bin-Laden Rebases in Taleban Stronghold of Qandahar," *Mideast Mirror*, April 8, 1997; Nassar al-Bahri, *Guarding bin Laden: My Life in al-Qaeda* (London: Thin Man Press, 2013), 63.

87 *former Soviet agricultural:* Author's interview with Michael Scheuer, Washington, DC, December 29, 2009.

87 *Bin Laden chose the harsher location:* Nasser al-Bahri, *Guarding bin Laden*, 79.

87 *Al-Farouq training camp:* Ibid., 80.

87 *"to discuss their issues"*: Abu Jandal, FD-302, Federal Bureau of Investigation, 40–41, author's collection.

88 *flow of paperwork:* This section draws on Peter L. Bergen, *The Longest War: The Enduring Conflict Between America and al-Qaeda* (New York: Free Press, 2011), 89.

88 *"If the Shura council"*: "Substitution for the Testimony of Khalid Sheikh Mohammed," filed in the 2006 trial *USA v. Zacarias Moussaoui*, Eastern District of Virginia, Defendant's Exhibit Cr. No. 1-455-A, http://en.wikisource.org/wiki/Substitution_for_the_Testimony_of_KSM.

88 *The legal, media, and economic:* Nelly Lahoud, "Beware of Imitators: Al-Qa'ida Through the Lens of Its Confidential Secretary" (Combating Terrorism Center, June 4, 2012), 56, 70–71, https://ctc.usma.edu/wp-content/uploads/2012/06/CTC-Beware-of-Imitators-June2012.pdf.

88 *"Dear prince: May I speak?"*: Bin Laden, bin Laden, and Sasson, *Growing Up bin Laden*, 161, 213. This section also draws on Bergen, *The Longest War*, 25.

88 *modeled his life of jihad on the life of the Prophet:* Author's interview with Khaled Batarfi, Jeddah, Saudi Arabia, September 7, 2005.

88 *described meeting with:* Khalid Al-Hammadi, "Series of interviews with Nasir Ahmad Nasir Abdullah al-Bahri, Alias Abu-Jandal, Formerly the 'Personal Guard' of Al-Qa'ida Leader Usama Bin Ladin," *Al Quds Al-Arabi*, April 2, 2005.

89 *"'seduced' many young men"*: Excerpts of Shadi Abdallah's interviews with German authorities that occurred between April 2002 and May 2003: "Summary Interrogation S. Abdalla: UK and European Connections plus Background Al

Tawid/Zarqawi," author's collection. This section also draws on Bergen, *The Longest War*, 25.

89   *spoke with great excitement:* Author's interview with John Miller, Washington, DC, September 2005.

89   *volleyball:* "Interview Maha Elsamnah & Zaynab Khadr," *Frontline,* PBS, February 22, 2004, https:/www.pbs.org/wgbh/pages/frontline/shows/khadr/interviews/mahazaynab.html; Abu Jandal interview in Peter L. Bergen, *The Osama bin Laden I Know: An Oral History of al Qaeda's Leader* (New York: Free Press, 2006), 229.

89   *passion for soccer . . . help of a cane:* Author's interviews with Rahimullah Yusufzai, Peshawar, Pakistan, September 1998 and June 29, 2003.

89   *"goodness in horses":* Based on readings from the Hadīth, as found on Sunnah .com. https://sunnah.com/bukhari:3645; https://sunnah.com/nasai:3561.

89   *He sometimes arranged horse races:* Bahri, *Guarding bin Laden,* 76.

89   *Bin Laden continued his practice of taking his wives:* Khalid Al-Hammadi, "Series of interviews with Nasir Ahmad Nasir Abdullah Al-Bahri, Alias Abu-Jandal, Formerly the 'Personal Guard' of Al-Qa'ida Leader Usama Bin Ladin," *Al Quds Al-Arabi,* April 2, 2005.

89   *He also preached self-reliance to his sons:* Ibid.

90   *On December 1, 1996:* Andrew Higgins and Alan Cullison, "Saga of Dr. Zawahiri Sheds Light on the Roots of Al Qaeda Terror," *Wall Street Journal,* July 2, 2002, https://www.wsj.com/articles/SB1025558570331929960.

90   *a political neophyte:* Author's interview with Jamal Ismail, Islamabad, Pakistan, March 2005.

90   *Zawahiri had influenced bin Laden's thinking:* Montasser al-Zayyat, *The Road to Al-Qaeda: The Story of Bin Laden's Right-Hand Man,* Critical Studies on Islam (London: Pluto Press, 2004), 68; Author's interview with Jamal Ismail, the Palestinian journalist who knew both bin Laden and Zawahiri during this period, Islamabad, Pakistan, 1998. Zayyat also concluded that during the mid-1990s the relationship shifted and it was bin Laden who influenced Zawahiri. Zayyat, *The Road to Al-Qaeda,* 69: "Bin Laden advised Zawahiri to stop armed operations in Egypt and to ally with him against their common enemies: the United States and Israel. His advice to Zawahiri came upon their return to Afghanistan [in 1996], when bin Laden ensured the safety of Zawahiri and the [Egyptian] Islamic Jihad members under the banner of the Taliban."

90   *penniless refugee:* Zayyat, *The Road to Al-Qaeda,* 69–70; Fawaz A. Gerges, *The Far Enemy: Why Jihad Went Global* (Cambridge, UK: Cambridge University Press, 2005), 121.

91   *"The United States has been occupying":* This translation of the declaration can be found in *Messages to the World: The Statements of Osama bin Laden,* which has

excellent, fluid translations of many of bin Laden's key statements. Bin Laden, *Messages to the World*, 58–62.

91 *"wherever you find"*: Ibid., 59.

91 *repent and pay a tax . . . spared*: Ibid., 59fn5.

91 *not a mainstream view*: In Indonesia and Pakistan, the two most populous Muslim nations, favorable views of bin Laden dropped significantly between 2003 and 2010, from 59 percent to 25 percent in Indonesia, and from 46 percent to 18 percent in Pakistan. "Obama More Popular Abroad Than at Home, Global Image of U.S. Continues to Benefit: Chapter 7. Attitudes Toward Extremism Among Muslim Publics," Pew Research Center, June 17, 2010, https://www.pewresearch.org/global/2010/06/17/chapter-7-attitudes-toward-extremism-among-muslim-publics/.

91 *nothing at all to do with Islam*: For instance, Pakistani prime minister Imran Khan: "Imran Khan Says, 'Terrorism Has Nothing to Do with Religion,'" Republicworld.com, September 26, 2019, https://www.republicworld.com/world-news/pakistan-news/imran-khan-says-terrorism-has-nothing-to-do-with-religion.html.

91 *Qutb, Zawahiri's key ideological guide*: In his 2001 autobiography, Zawahiri explained his intellectual debt to Qutb: "Sayyid Qutb's call for loyalty to God's oneness and to acknowledge God's sole authority and sovereignty was the spark that ignited the Islamic revolution against the enemies of Islam at home and abroad. . . . Sayyid Qutb played a key role in directing the Muslim youth to this road in the second half of the twentieth century in Egypt in particular, and the Arab region in general." Ayman al-Zawahiri, *Knights Under the Prophet's Banner*, extracts, *Asharq al-Awsat*, December 2001.

91 *Ibn Taymiyya*: Bin Laden and Lawrence, *Messages to the World*, 61fn9.

92 *"I want to come to see you" . . . "I don't know . . . against it"*: Author's interview with Abdel Bari Atwan, London, United Kingdom, June 2005; *USA v. Khalid al-Fawwaz*, S7 S10 98 Crim. 1023 Deposition of Mr. Abdel Bari Abu Atwan, October 1, 2014, Case 1:98-cr-01023-LAK Document 1869-2.

93 *was published*: "Text of Fatwa Urging Jihad Against Americans," *Al-Quds Al-Arabi*, February 23, 1998, https://fas.org/irp/world/para/docs/980223-fatwa.htm.

93 *"These fatwas . . . in the world"*: Cynthia Storer, "Fatwas or Religious Rulings by Militant Islamic Groups Against the United States" (CIA Counterterrorist Center, February 23, 1998).

93 *issued a fatwa ruling*: The National Commission on Terrorist Attacks Upon the United States (also known as the 9-11 Commission), section 2.1, "A Declaration of War," https://govinfo.library.unt.edu/911/report/911Report_Ch2.htm.

93 *In a report*: *Al-Quds Al-Arabi*, May 14, 1998.

93 *"continued to incite"*: "Patterns of Global Terrorism: 1997" (Department of State

Publication 10535, Office of the Secretary of State, Office of the Coordinator for Counterterrorism, April 1998), https://fas.org/irp/threat/terror_97/mideast.html.

93   *"So congratulations to the Taliban":* Bin Laden statement from May 16, 1998, author's collection.

93   *"We call upon . . . nuclear force":* "Dangers and Signs of the Indian Nuclear Explosions," May 14, 1998, author's collection.

93   *In mid-May, Hamid Mir:* Author's interviews with Hamid Mir, Islamabad, Pakistan, 1998, 2002, 2005, 2006.

94   *his father:* Ibid.

94   *Mir repeatedly pressed:* Ibid.

94   *Omar Abdel Rahman:* "The *Fatwa* of the Prisoner Sheikh Doctor Abdel Rahman," author's collection. In 1996 a pamphlet was published by supporters of Sheikh Rahman in the U.S. titled *My Testimony to History.* In the pamphlet, which shows a photograph of Sheikh Rahman in a wheelchair in a U.S. prison, the cleric is quoted in similar language to the will that was distributed at the press conference in Afghanistan, saying, "Take revenge on whoever kills me. Do not let my blood be shed in vain." Of course, it is possible that Sheikh Rahman, who was incarcerated in American prisons from 1993 until he died in 2017, did not write the fatwa himself, but his incarceration did not prevent him from communicating important messages to his followers through his family or lawyers; for instance, in 1997 he endorsed a cease-fire between the Egyptian government and the terrorist Islamic group. Then in 2000 Sheikh Rahman publicly withdrew his support from that cease-fire. In his 2001 autobiography, Zawahiri approvingly noted that "people of the stature of Omar Abdel Rahman . . . oppose the [cease-fire] initiative." For a further discussion of the Rahman fatwa, see Bergen, *The Osama bin Laden I Know,* 206–9.

94   *Sheikh Rahman's fatwa was the first:* This paragraph draws on Peter Bergen, "The Cleric Who Altered the Course of Modern History," CNN.com, February 19, 2017, https://www.cnn.com/2017/02/19/opinions/9-11-spiritual-guide-dies -bergen.

95   *theological cover:* Sometime in mid-1998, Sheikh Rahman's fatwa to attack American targets began to circulate in one of al-Qaeda's key training camps in Afghanistan. At the Khaldan training camp, Algerian Ahmed Ressam was learning how to make explosives, a skill he would later employ in an ill-fated attempt to bomb Los Angeles International Airport in December 1999. At a subsequent terrorism trial, Ressam testified that while he was at the Afghan training camp he saw "a fatwa issued by Sheikh Omar Abdel Rahman with his picture on it, a piece of paper with his photograph on it." At the trial, Ressam was asked what his understanding of a fatwa was, and he replied: "A fatwa is something that a learned person would come up with. If there is an issue that

people want an opinion on, the religious, learned man would study the issue and pass judgment on whether it was permissible or not." (Bergen, *The Osama bin Laden I Know*, 205). Ressam, like other al-Qaeda foot soldiers, understood that a fatwa from the learned Sheikh Rahman gave them a blanket religious imprimatur to attack and kill Americans.

95 *Fourteen journalists attended:* Rahimullah Yusufzai, "Osama bin Laden: Al Qaeda," in Baweja, ed., *Most Wanted*, 28–29.

95 *awesome display of firepower:* Author's interview with Ismail Khan, Islamabad, Pakistan, September 1998.

95 *Rahimullah Yusufzai, one of the most respected:* Author's interview with Rahimullah Yusufzai, Peshawar, Pakistan, June 29, 2003.

96 *the men told Yusufzai:* Yusufzai, "Osama bin Laden: Al Qaeda," in *Most Wanted: Profiles of Terror*, Harinder Baweja, ed., 28–29.

96 *"formed with many":* Bin Laden and Zawahiri both spoke at the press conference, and appeared on a videotape filmed by an al-Qaeda cameraman. The tape was later discovered in Afghanistan by CNN after the fall of the Taliban. Nic Robertson, "Previously Unseen Tape Shows Bin Laden's Declaration of War," CNN, August 20, 2002, https://www.cnn.com/2002/US/08/19/terror.tape.main/index .html#:~:text=Previously%20unseen%20tape%20shows%20bin%20Laden's%20 declaration%20of%20war,-August%2020%2C%202002&text=%22By%20 God's%20grace%2C%22%20bin,against%20the%20crusaders%20and%20 Jews.%22.

96 *two sons of Blind Sheikh:* Author's interview with Ismail Khan, Islamabad, Pakistan, September 1998.

96 *laminated cards:* Ibid.

96 *"some good news":* Ibid.

96 *"choked voice":* "Bin Ladin Creates New Front Against US, Israel," *The News*, May 28, 1998, FBIS Transcribed Text, 68–69. https://fas.org/irp/world/para/ubl -fbis.pdf.

97 *Mullah Khakshar, the Taliban's powerful:* Author's Interview with Mullah Khakshar, Kabul, Afghanistan, January 2005.

97 *did ask bin Laden:* Author's interview with Ahmad Zaidan, Islamabad, Pakistan, March 2005.

97 *argued that his stance was sanctioned by the Koran:* Unpublished manuscript by Hamid Mir, "The Story of Osama bin Laden," 18, author's collection.

97 *Miller spoke to Zawahiri:* Author's interview with John Miller, Washington, DC, September 2005.

97 *"There is always a great celebration":* John Miller interview, *Road to 9/11*, Part 2, "The Bin Ladens," History Channel, September 5, 2017.

98   *Bin Laden told Miller:* ABC News, *Nightline,* June 10, 1998.

98   *"I predict":* "Timeline of al-Qaida statements," NBC News, April 15, 2004, https://
      www.nbcnews.com/id/wbna4686034.

98   *critical battery:* Affidavit in support of a search warrant of Tariq Hamdi residence
      in Virginia, May 13, 2002, by David Kane, Special Agent, U.S. Customs Service.

98   *used the phone often:* Matthew Aid, "All Glory Is Fleeting: Sigint and the Fight
      Against International Terrorism," in *Twenty-First Intelligence,* ed. Wesley K.
      Wark (London: Routledge, 2008), 87.

98   *In June 1998 . . . to the Saudi Kingdom:* Brian Whitaker, "Taliban Agreed Bin Laden
      Handover in 1998," *Guardian,* November 4, 2001, https://www.theguardian.com
      /world/2001/nov/05/afghanistan.terrorism3.

EIGHT: THE U.S. SLOWLY GRASPS THE THREAT

100 *"It is much easier":* Roberta Wohlstetter, *Pearl Harbor: Warning and Decision*
      (Stanford, CA: Stanford University Press, 1966), 387.

100 *Gina Bennett:* Author's interview with Gina Bennett via FaceTime, February 13,
      2021.

101 *a total of 270 . . . students at Syracuse University:* "History," Syracuse University:
      Remembrance, accessed March 12, 2021, https://remembrance.syr.edu/about/.

101 *"Tayeb the Afghan":* John-Thor Dahlburg, "Algerian Veterans the Nucleus for
      Mayhem," *Los Angeles Times,* August 5, 1996, https://www.latimes.com/archives
      /la-xpm-1996-08-05-mn-31535-story.html.

101 *saw that jihadist violence:* Author's interview with Gina Bennett via FaceTime,
      February 13, 2021.

102 *Several of them had traveled:* Peter Arnett, Peter Bergen, and Richard Macken-
      zie, "CNN Presents: Terror Nation? U.S. Creation?" CNN, 1994.

102 *Bennett was holding her new baby boy:* Author's interview with Gina Bennett.

103 *"The Wandering Mujahidin: Armed and Dangerous":* "The Wandering Muja-
      hidin: Armed and Dangerous" (United States Department of State Bureau of
      Intelligence and Research, *Weekend Edition,* August 21–22, 1993), http://www
      .nationalsecuritymom.com/3/WanderingMujahidin.pdf.

103 *A week later . . . identified al-Qaeda as a threat:* Gina M. Bennett, *National Secu-
      rity Mom: Why "Going Soft" Will Make America Strong* (Deadwood, OR: Wyatt-
      Mackenzie, 2009), 21.

104 *The Bureau of Intelligence and Research:* U.S. State Department Bureau of Intel-
      ligence and Research chronology regarding bin Laden, 1995, author's collec-
      tion.

104 *"Mujahidin Interagency Working Group":* Bennett, *National Security Mom,* 22.

104 *counterterrorism priorities:* Author's interview with Cindy Storer, Washington,
      DC, September 13, 2011.

104   *Storer . . . "the minority"*: Ibid.

105   *In an era before . . . they were cooperating*: Cynthia Storer, "Working with Al-Qaeda Documents: An Analyst's View Before 9/11," in Lorry M. Fenner, Mark E. Stout, and Jessica L. Goldings, eds., *9/11, Ten Years Later: Insights on Al-Qaeda's Past & Future Through Captured Records: Conference Proceedings* (Washington, DC: Conflict Records Research Center, Institute for National Strategic Studies, National Defense University, 2012), 41–43, https://www.google.com/books/edition/9_11_Ten_Years_Later/9ryXNXALLvsC?hl=en&gbpv=0.

105   *Cohen suggested . . . a "virtual station"*: Author's interview with David Cohen, New York City, October 1, 2014.

105   *trained only twenty-five new officers*: Thomas H. Kean and Lee H. Hamilton, "9/11 Commission Report" (National Commission on Terrorist Attacks upon the United States, August 21, 2004), 90, https://govinfo.library.unt.edu/911/report/911Report_Ch7.htm.

105   *Michael Scheuer . . . the Afghan resistance*: Author's interview with Michael Scheuer, Washington, DC, December 29, 2009.

105   *"abrasive"*: Scheuer interview, *Road to 9/11*, Part 2, "The Bin Ladens," History Channel, September 5, 2017.

105   *"This guy's gonna kill"*: Author's interview with Cindy Storer, Washington, DC, September 13, 2011.

105   *"Alec Station," after his son*: Author's interview with Michael Scheuer, Washington, DC, October 1, 2011.

105   *single individual*: Amy B. Zegart, *Spying Blind: The CIA, the FBI, and the Origins of 9/11* (Princeton, NJ: Princeton University Press, 2009), 77.

106   *"no boys need apply"*: Author's interview with Michael Scheuer, Washington, DC, October 1, 2011.

106   *"the Bay"*: Ibid.

106   Buffy the Vampire: Author's interview with Cindy Storer, Washington, DC, September 13, 2011.

106   *3:30 in the morning*: Author's interview with Michael Scheuer, Washington, DC, October 1, 2011.

106   *"Manson family"*: Mark Stout, "The Evolution of Intelligence: Assessments of al Qaeda to 2011," in Fenner, Stout, and Goldings, *9/11, Ten Years Later*, 22.

106   *Daniel Coleman*: The description of FBI Special Agent Daniel Coleman draws upon Henry Schuster, "The Al Qaeda Hunter," CNN, March 2, 2005, https://www.cnn.com/2005/US/03/02/schuster.column/index.html.

107   *Jamal Fadl's . . . big break*: Kean and Hamilton, "9/11 Commission Report," 108.

107   *Fadl loved to gamble . . . "Junior" . . . Residence Inn*: Jane Mayer, "Junior: The Clandestine Life of America's Top Al Qaeda Source," *New Yorker*, September 3, 2006, https://www.newyorker.com/magazine/2006/09/11/junior.

107   *pronounced taste for waffles*: Jack Cloonan interview, *Road to 9/11*, Part 2, "The Bin Ladens," History Channel, September 5, 2017.

107   *Junior's Sudanese family joined him*: Mayer, "Junior: The Clandestine Life of America's Top Al Qaeda Source."

107   *out to the beach*: Mike Anticev interview, *Road to 9/11*, Part 2, "The Bin Ladens," History Channel, September 5, 2017.

107   *modeled his life*: Author's interview with Daniel Coleman, Princeton, New Jersey, December 19, 2009.

107   *had trained*: Cloonan interview, *Road to 9/11*, Part 2, "The Bin Ladens," History Channel, September 5, 2017.

107   *"would feel comfortable" . . . "prolonged stay"*: "Usama bin Ladin: Who's Chasing Whom?," The Bureau of Intelligence and Research, U.S. Department of State, July 18, 1996.

108   *Scheuer had a different reaction*: Michael Scheuer interview, *Road to 9/11*, Part 2, "The Bin Ladens," History Channel, September 5, 2017.

108   *During the summer of 1997 Coleman*: FBI Special Agent Daniel Coleman testimony in *USA v. Usama Bin Laden* on February 21, 2001; Author's interview with Daniel Coleman, Princeton, New Jersey, December 19, 2009.

109   *secured a warrant*: Ibid.

109   *Southern District of New York*: The sealed indictment against bin Laden was returned in June 1998 and unsealed in November 1998. Kean and Hamilton, "9/11 Commission Report," 110. Indictment, *USA v. Usama Bin Laden* (United States District Court, Southern District of New York, November 5, 1998), https://fas .org/irp/news/1998/11/indict1.pdf.

109   *thirty Afghan tribal militia members*: Gary Schroen interview, *Road to 9/11*, Part 2, "The Bin Ladens," History Channel, September 5, 2017.

109   *TRODPINT*: Steve Coll, *Ghost Wars: The Secret History of the CIA, Afghanistan, and bin Laden, from the Soviet Invasion to September 10, 2001* (New York: Penguin, 2005), 371–76.

109   *Scheuer received a cable*: [Excised], " '[Title Excised]' 'Planning for the UBL Rendition Is Going Very Well,' to Michael F. Scheuer, From [Excised], Central Intelligence Agency Email," May 5, 1998 (Approved for Release April 25, 2012), https://www.documentcloud.org/documents/368929-1998-05-05-title-excised -planning-for-the-ubl.html.

109   *The plan was . . . to the United States*: Michael Scheuer and Gary Schroen interviews, *Road to 9/11*, Part 2, "The Bin Ladens," History Channel, September 5, 2017.

109   *Inside the container . . . during his capture*: Michael Scheuer interview, *Road to 9/11*, Part 2, "The Bin Ladens," History Channel, September 5, 2017.

110   *Coleman would enter*: Lawrence Wright, *The Looming Tower* (New York: Alfred A. Knopf, 2006), 266.

110 *June 23, 1998*: Kean and Hamilton, "9/11 Commission Report," 113–14.

110 *Richard Clarke*: The description of Clarke is drawn from Daniel Benjamin and Steven Simon, *The Age of Sacred Terror: Radical Islam's War Against America* (New York: Random House, 2002), 235.

110 *In Clarke's view the plan*: Kean and Hamilton, "9/11 Commission Report," 114; Richard Clarke interview, *Road to 9/11*, Part 2, "The Bin Ladens," History Channel, September 5, 2017.

110 *30 percent chance of success*: Michael J. Morell and Bill Harlow, *The Great War of Our Time: The CIA's Fight Against Terrorism—From al Qa'ida to ISIS* (New York: Twelve, 2015), 17.

110 *50/50*: Michael Scheuer interview, *Road to 9/11*, Part 2, "The Bin Ladens," History Channel, September 5, 2017.

110 *order to stand down*: "OIG Report on CIA Accountability with Respect to the 9/11 Attacks," CIA, 2005, approved for release March 19, 2015, 372–73.

111 *three days earlier*: Ibid., 373.

NINE: THE WAR BEGINS

112 *"War is waged by men"*: Frederic Manning, *The Middle Parts of Fortune*. (Melbourne: Text Publishing Co., 2012), xviii, http://public.ebookcentral.proquest.com/choice/publicfullrecord.aspx?p=844235.

112 *"The lucky are blinded"*: U.S. federal prosecutor Patrick Fitzgerald on May 9, 2001 in *USA v. Usama bin Laden*.

112 *The bomb obliterated*: Louise Lief, *U.S. News and World Report*, August 17, 1998.

112 *"a lot of people watching"*: Brian Michael Jenkins, "New Age of Terrorism," RAND, 2006, https://www.rand.org/content/dam/rand/pubs/reprints/2006/RAND_RP1215.pdf.

112 *new set of rules*: Rex A. Hudson, "The Sociology and Psychology of Terrorism: Who Becomes a Terrorist and Why?" (Federal Research Division: Library of Congress, September 1999), https://fas.org/irp/threat/frd.html.

112 *al-Qaeda member had surveyed*: CIA report on targeting study of U.S. Embassy, Nairobi, on December 23, 1993, p. 3, approved for release April 25, 2012.

113 *"centralization of decision"*: Khalid Al-Hammadi, "Series of Interviews with Nasir Ahmad Nasir Abdullah Al-Bahri, Alias Abu-Jandal, Formerly the 'Personal Guard' of Al-Qa'ida Leader Usama Bin Ladin," *Al Quds Al-Arabi*, April 2, 2005.

113 *went off without warning*: Ambassador Prudence Bushnell in her testimony in *USA v. Usama bin Laden*, March 1, 2001.

113 *timed the bomb*: Nelly Lahoud, "Beware of Imitators: Al-Qa'ida Through the Lens of Its Confidential Secretary" (Combating Terrorism Center, June 4, 2012), 56, https://ctc.usma.edu/wp-content/uploads/2012/06/CTC-Beware-of-Imitators-June2012.pdf.

113 *10 percent of Kenyans:* "Kenya," *The World Factbook*, CIA.gov, accessed March 8, 2021, https://www.cia.gov/the-world-factbook/countries/kenya/#people-and -society.

113 *Nine minutes after:* Peter L. Bergen, *Holy War, Inc.: Inside the Secret World of Osama bin Laden* (New York: Free Press, 2001), 113.

113 *August 7:* "Gulf War Fast Facts," CNN, July 29, 2020, https://www.cnn.com /2013/09/15/world/meast/gulf-war-fast-facts/index.html.

113 *Bin Laden met with his military commanders:* Lahoud, "Beware of Imitators," 23.

114 *"Did we need so many victims?":* Nassar al-Bahri, *Guarding bin Laden: My Life in al-Qaeda* (London: Thin Man Press, 2013), 118. Nasser al-Bahri was the real name of Abu Jandal, bin Laden's Yemeni bodyguard.

114 *Bin Laden also subscribed to:* Author's interview with Noman Benotman, London, August 30, 2005.

114 *prepared to sacrifice his own sons:* Najwa bin Laden, Omar bin Laden, and Jean P. Sasson, *Growing Up bin Laden: Osama's Wife and Son Take Us Inside Their Secret World* (New York: St. Martin's Press, 2009), 263.

115 *Among the victims . . . two of their own:* @CIA, "Molly Hardy, senior finance specialist & new grandmother, was killed in Nairobi," Twitter, August 7, 2018, https://twitter.com/cia/status/1026874573680267266?lang=en; "Al-Qaida Killed Two CIA Officers 13 Years Ago," NPR, May 30, 2011, https://www.npr.org/2011 /05/30/136800353/al-qaida-killed-two-cia-officers-13-years-ago.

115 *"Who did this?" . . . "This is al-Qaeda":* Michael J. Morell and Bill Harlow, *The Great War of Our Time: The CIA's Fight Against Terrorism—From al Qa'ida to ISIS* (New York: Twelve, 2015), 19.

115 *Tenet went to visit:* Ibid., and Fenner, Stout, and Goldings, eds., *9/11, Ten Years Later*, 30.

115 *Tenet agreed:* "OIG Report on CIA Accountability with Respect to the 9/11 Attacks," approved for release March 19, 2015, CIA, 2005, 373.

115 *KENBOM:* Mary Galligan, former FBI/New York Office, Special Agent in Charge, at the 9/11 Museum, New York City, December 6, 2016, interviewed by Clifford Chanin.

115 *He was detained:* Pat Milton, "Inspector Testifies in Embassy Trial," Associated Press, April 2, 2001; Peter Bergen, "Holy Warriors," CNN, November 11, 1998.

116 *When Pakistani officials asked . . . to FBI agents:* Author's interview with Pakistani Interior Minister Mushahid Hussain, Islamabad, Pakistan, October 14, 1998. See also Bergen, *Holy War, Inc.*, 113.

116 *'Owhali, was arrested:* FBI Special Agent Steve Gaudin testimony, March 7, 2001, in *USA v. Usama bin Laden*.

116 *'Owhali confessed:* Affidavit Filed by Daniel J. Coleman in *USA v. Mohamed*

Rashed Daoud Al-'Owhali (United States District Court, Southern District of New York, August 25, 1998), https://fas.org/irp/news/1998/08/98090103_npo.html.

116 *pointed definitively to al-Qaeda's role:* Bergen, *Holy War, Inc.*, 121.

116 *Clinton alternated between planning . . . and apologizing:* Bill Clinton, *My Life* (New York: Vintage, 2005), 803; "Clinton Admits to 'Wrong' Relationship with Lewinsky," CNN, August 17, 1998, https://edition.cnn.com/ALLPOLITICS /1998/08/17/speech/.

116 *on August 20 . . . kill Bin Laden:* Hugh Shelton, Ronald Levinson, and Malcolm McConnell, *Without Hesitation: The Odyssey of an American Warrior* (New York: St. Martin's Press, 2010), 347.

116 *Clinton took the tannery off:* Clinton, *My Life*, 803.

116 *the other targets:* Ibid.

116 *"Bin Laden calls . . . Dar es Salaam bombings":* Rahimullah Yusufzai, "Osama Denies Hand in Embassies Blasts," *The News*, August 21, 1998.

117 *Clinton knew he was likely:* Author's interview with Clinton administration official, 1998.

117 *Clinton told the journalists:* Bill Clinton, "Remarks in Martha's Vineyard, Massachusetts, on Military Action Against Terrorist Sites in Afghanistan and Sudan" (U.S. Government Publishing Office, August 20, 1998), https://www.govinfo.gov /content/pkg/PPP-1998-book2/html/PPP-1998-book2-doc-pg1460.htm.

117 *"Our target was terror":* Bill Clinton, "Address to the Nation on Military Action Against Terrorist Sites in Afghanistan and Sudan" (U.S. Government Publishing Office, August 20, 1998), https://www.govinfo.gov/content/pkg/PPP-1998 -book2/html/PPP-1998-book2-doc-pg1460-2.htm.

117 *"That's our bin Laden?":* Author's interviews with Khaled Batarfi, Jeddah, Saudi Arabia, September 5 and 9, 2005.

117 *Cruise missiles . . . evacuated:* Bergen, *Holy War, Inc.*, 120–23.

117 *Some have suggested that Pakistani officials:* Morell and Harlow, *The Great War of Our Time*, 21.

117 *"Khost or Kabul?":* Bahri, *Guarding bin Laden*, 117.

118 *seven of Bin Laden's followers:* Rahimullah Yusufzai, "World's Most Wanted Terrorist: An Interview with Osama Bin Laden," ABC News, December 22, 1998, https://scholarship.tricolib.brynmawr.edu/handle/10066/4720.

118 *The camps were simple affairs:* Rahimullah Yusufzai, *The News*, Pakistan, September 6, 1998.

118 *"shot twice in the head":* Bahri, *Guarding bin Laden*, 9.

118 *purported chemical weapons plant . . . a debacle:* For a detailed account of this episode, see Bergen, *Holy War, Inc.*, 123–26. Michael Morell, who would rise to become deputy director of the CIA, in his 2015 autobiography, *The Great*

War of Our Time, wrote that there was no evidence that the plant in Khartoum produced chemical weapons. (Morell and Harlow, *The Great War of Our Time*, 21.) The same point is made by Clinton's chairman of the Joint Chiefs of Staff, General Hugh Shelton, in his 2010 autobiography, *Without Hesitation*. (Shelton, Levinson, and McConnell, *Without Hesitation*, 350.)

118 *two instant biographies:* Author's observations in Islamabad, Pakistan, in late August 1998.

118 *common name for sons:* Dexter Filkins, "World Perspective, South Asia; Osama Bin Laden Is Wanted Here Too; Babies and Businesses Are Named After the Suspected Terrorist Who Is a Hero on Pakistan's Frontier for His Battle Against the West," *Los Angeles Times*, July 24, 1999.

118 *deeply angered Mullah Omar:* U.S. Department of State, Cable, "Afghanistan: Taliban's Mullah Omar's 8/22 Contact with State Department," August 23, 1998.

119 malmastiya: David M. Hart, *Guardians of the Khaibar Pass: The Social Organisation and History of the Afridis of Pakistan* (Lahore: Vanguard Books, 1985), 13.

119 nanawati: James W. Spain, *Pathans of the Latter Day* (Karachi: Oxford University Press, 1995), 43.

119 *fight to the death:* Louis Dupree, *Afghanistan* (New Delhi: Rama Publishers, 1994), 126.

119 *calling the U.S.:* U.S. Department of State, Cable, "Afghanistan: Taliban's Mullah Omar's 8/22 Contact with State Department," August 23, 1998.

119 *met to discuss:* U.S. Embassy (Islamabad), Cable, "Afghanistan: Demarche to Taliban on New Bin Laden Threat," September 14, 1998.

119 *On September 12, 1998:* Author correspondence with Au Hafs the Egyptian during September 1998.

120 *September 19, 1998:* Anne Stenersen, *Al-Qaida in Afghanistan* (Cambridge, U.K.: Cambridge University Press, 2017), 80.

120 *Taliban leader was also abusive:* Ibid.

120 *"One day":* Jamal Khashoggi, "Former Saudi Intel Chief Interviewed on Saudi-Afghan Tie, Bin Laden—Part 5," *Arab News*, November 8, 2001

120 *cut off diplomatic relations:* Alex Strick van Linschoten and Felix Kuehn, *An Enemy We Created: The Myth of the Taliban–Al Qaeda Merger in Afghanistan* (Oxford: Oxford University Press, 2012), 165.

120 *Mullah Omar informed Bin Laden . . . might go next:* Bin Laden, bin Laden, and Sasson, *Growing Up bin Laden*, 245–48.

120 *Shedding tears:* Ahmad Muaffaq Zaidan, "Bin Laden Revealed," unpublished manuscript, which is based on Zaidan's book in Arabic, *Bin Laden Unmasked* (Beirut, 2015), 105.

121 *The text of this oath was published . . . September 15, 1998:* Jason Burke, *Al-Qaeda: The True Story of Radical Islam* (London: Tauris, I.B. 2004), 186–87.

121 *In the months after the attacks:* BBC Monitoring Middle East, "Mauritanian Detainee Reveals Post Bin Ladin Al Qaeda Leadership Details," *Al-Akhbar* website, Mauritania, November 28, 2014.

121 *cut the allowance to $50 . . . proceeds when he returned:* Bahri, *Guarding Bin Laden,* 132–34.

121 *$2 million from the investments:* Osama bin Laden, "In Regard to the Money That Is in Sudan—Bin Laden's Will" (Office of the Director of National Intelligence, n.d.), Bin Laden's Bookshelf, https://www.dni.gov/files/documents/ubl2016/english/In%20regard%20to%20the%20money%20that%20is%20in%20Sudan.pdf.

121 *one more effort to persuade:* Bin Laden, bin Laden, and Sasson, *Growing Up bin Laden,* 250–55.

122 *"This is a principle":* "Series of Interviews with Nasir Ahmad Nasir Abdullah Al-Bahri, Alias Abu-Jandal, Formerly the 'Personal Guard' of Al-Qa'ida Leader Usama Bin Ladin," *Al Quds Al-Arabi,* April 2, 2005

122 *In the documentary bin Laden renewed his calls:* Salah Najm, "Usama Bin Ladin, the Destruction of the Base," Al Jazeera, June 10, 1999, 126, FBIS Translated Text, https://fas.org/irp/world/para/ubl-fbis.pdf.

122 *Abu Musab al-Suri:* His real name is Mustafa Setmariam Nasar.

122 *"What right have you got":* Stenersen, *Al-Qaida in Afghanistan,* 74–76, which quotes Abu Musab al-Suri, Letter to Osama bin Laden, July 17, 1998.

123 *United Nations threatened to impose sanctions:* "Security Council Demands That Taliban Turn Over Usama bin Laden to Appropriate Authorities" (United Nations Security Council, Press Release SC/6739, October 15, 1999), https://www.un.org/press/en/1999/19991015.sc6739.doc.html.

123 *told reporters that bin Laden had "disappeared":* "Bin Laden Said to Remain in Afghanistan," CNN.com, February 16, 1999.

123 *"We think . . . war on God":* Stenersen, *Al-Qaida in Afghanistan,* 90–91.

123 *a suitable refuge:* Bahri, *Guarding bin Laden,* 160.

123 *had to be religious:* Hala Jaber, "Finding Osama a Wife," *Sunday Times,* January 24, 2010.

123 *Amal al-Sadah:* Bahri, *Guarding bin Laden,* 155–60.

123 *At first the marriage proposal was framed:* Mustafa al-Ansari, "Bin Laden's Yemeni Spouse 'Amal' Will Not Remarry Even if Asked by President Saleh!," *Al Hayat,* June 13, 2011.

124 *When Amal's father visited her in Afghanistan:* Ibid.

124 *anger:* Bahri, *Guarding bin Laden,* 155.

124 *"No person . . . engage in, assassination":* "Executive Order 12333—United States Intelligence Activities" (National Archives, December 4, 1981), https://www.archives.gov/federal-register/codification/executive-order/12333.html#2.11.

124 *On Christmas Eve 1998 . . . overrode:* Philip Shenon, *The Commission: The Uncensored History of the 9/11 Investigation* (New York: Twelve, 2008), 357.

124 *The White House believed . . . CIA heard something quite different:* Richard Clarke interview, *Road to 9/11*, Part 1, "Brooklyn Jihad," History Channel, September 4, 2017.

124 *who would make this determination?:* John Rizzo, *Company Man: Thirty Years of Controversy and Crisis in the CIA* (New York: Scribner, 2014), 162–63.

124 *Scheuer felt:* Michael Scheuer interview, *Road to 9/11*, Part 2, "The Bin Ladens," History Channel, September 5, 2017.

125 *" 'Kill Osama bin Laden. Period' ":* Cofer Black interview, *Road to 9/11*, Part 2.

125 *CIA's understanding . . . was communicated:* "Draft: DCI Report: The Rise of UBL and Al-Qa'ida and the Intelligence Community Response" (Central Intelligence Agency, March 19, 2004), 47–48, https://www.documentcloud.org /documents/368992-2004-03-19-dci-report-the-rise-of-ubl-and-al.html; "2005 CIA OIG Report on CIA Accountability with Respect to the 9/11 Attacks," 158–60.

125 *"We must redouble our efforts":* "2005 CIA OIG Report on CIA Accountability with Respect to the 9/11 Attacks," 128.

125 *never ordered up a formal National Intelligence Estimate:* "OIG Report on CIA Accountability with Respect to the 9/11 Attacks," 140.

125 *Philip Zelikow:* Shenon, *The Commission*, 357–58; Office of the Inspector General CIA, June 19, 2005, 363

126 *not aware of the CIA director's call:* Ibid., 128.

126 *burden fell on the agency:* "OIG Report on CIA Accountability with Respect to the 9/11 Attacks," 200.

126 *risks of hitting a nearby mosque:* DCI report, "Draft: The Rise of UBL and Al-Qa'ida and the Intelligence Community Response," Central Intelligence Agency, March 19, 2004, 27, https://documentcloud.org/documents/368992-2004-03-19 -dci-report-the-rise-of-ubl-and-al.html.

126 *as many as six hundred people might die:* "OIG Report on CIA Accountability with Respect to the 9/11 Attacks," 375–76.

126 *bustards:* Declan Walsh, "For Saudis and Pakistan, a Bird of Contention," *New York Times*, February 7, 2015, https://www.nytimes.com/2015/02/08/world/for -saudis-and-pakistan-a-bird-of-contention.html.

127 *The whole process could take six hours:* Richard A. Clarke, *Against All Enemies: Inside America's War on Terror* (New York: Free Press, 2004), 199.

127 *tractor-trailer . . . the CIA had an asset:* Michael Scheuer interview, *Road to 9/11*, Part 2.

127 *February 11:* Thomas H. Kean and Lee H. Hamilton, "9/11 Commission Report" (National Commission on Terrorist Attacks Upon the United States, August 21, 2004), 138, https://govinfo.library.unt.edu/911/report/911Report_Ch7.htm.

127 *very likely members of the Emirati royal family*: DCI report, "The Rise of UBL and Al-Qa'ida," p. 27; Kean and Hamilton, "9/11 Commission Report," 138.

127 *Clarke wasn't going to sign off*: Clarke, *Against All Enemies*, 200.

127 *Scheuer fumed . . . missed opportunity*: Michael F. Scheuer, "Your Note," CIA Email to [Excised], May 17, 1999, https://www.documentcloud.org/documents /368949-1999-05-17-your-note-from-michael-f-scheuer-to.html.

127 *"I'm sure we would"*: Gary Schroen interview, *Road to 9/11*, Part 2, History Channel, September 5, 2017.

127 *In Kandahar . . . launched at him*: Michael Scheuer interview, *Road to 9/11*, Part 2.

128 *came only days . . . collateral damage*: "OIG Report on CIA Accountability with Respect to the 9/11 Attacks," 377.

128 *"passed up half a dozen" . . . "their stark fear"*: Michael F. Scheuer, "Your Note," CIA Email to [Excised].

128 *memo to every senior official*: Michael Scheuer interview, *Road to 9/11*, Part 2.

128 *"But don't worry" . . . "If you try"*: Ibid.

128 *make-work job in the CIA library . . . lengthy report*: Michael Scheuer interview with author, Washington, DC, October 1, 2011.

128 *Ahmed Ressam*: Andrew Duffy, "Ressam Part of Terror 'Cell,' Expert Testifies: Montreal Ring Forged and Smuggled Passports, Says French Judge," *Ottawa Citizen*, April 3, 2001; "Bomb Plot Focused on Los Angeles International Airport," Associated Press, May 30, 2001.

128 *Diana Dean*: Josh Meyer, "Border Arrest Stirs Fear of Terrorist Cells in U.S.," *Los Angeles Times*, March 11, 2001; Linda Deutsch, "Prosecutor: Anti-Terrorism Arrest Was a 'Tragedy Averted,'" Associated Press, March 13, 2001.

129 *circles around LAX*: *USA v. Mokhtar Haouari*, No. S400 Cr. 15 (U.S. District Court, Southern District of New York), testimony of Ahmed Ressam, July 5, 2001.

129 *On December 16, 1999*: "'Millennium Threat,' Briefing for DCI" (Central Intelligence Agency, December 16, 1999), https://www.documentcloud.org/docu ments/368958-1999-12-17-millennium-threat-briefing-for-dci.html.

129 *meetings . . . every day for a month*: Amy B. Zegart, *Spying Blind: The CIA, the FBI, and the Origins of 9/11* (Princeton, NJ: Princeton University Press, 2009), 8.

129 *A group of terrorists in Jordan*: Vernon Loeb, "Terrorists' 3-Country Attack Was Thwarted," *Washington Post*, December 24, 2000; "'Millennium Threat,' Briefing for DCI."

129 *Top Secret memorandum*: "Intelligence Report" Counterterrorist Center, November 2, 2000, approved for release April 25, 2012.

129 *hijacking on December 24*: Bergen, *Holy War, Inc.*, 208–12.

130 *Omar Sheikh*: Ibid.

130 *Bin Laden prepared a great feast*: Zaidan, "Bin Laden Revealed," 59.

130 *USS* The Sullivans: Ali H. Soufan and Daniel Freedman, *The Black Banners (Declassified): How Torture Derailed the War on Terror After 9/11* (New York: W. W. Norton, 2020), 227.

130 *"We will hold" . . . "We have bin Laden under control":* Author's interview with Michael Sheehan, New York City, November 21, 2009; Michael A. Sheehan, *Crush the Cell: How to Defeat Terrorism Without Terrorizing Ourselves* (New York: Crown, 2008), 137–38.

131 *al-Nashiri proposed a plan . . . port of Aden:* Kean and Hamilton, "9/11 Commission Report," 152–53.

131 *jambiya dagger:* "Mysterious Land May Hold Clues to Mysterious Man; FBI Combs Ancient Yemen for Insight into Osama Bin Laden," *Dallas Morning News,* November 5, 2000; Soufan and Freedman, *The Black Banners (Declassified),* 158.

131 *sweltering morning:* For a fuller accounting of the *Cole* attack, see Bergen, *Holy War, Inc.,* 167–94.

131 *he fell to his knees:* "Syrian Journalist Recounts Meetings with Bin Ladin in New Book," *Al Quds Al-Arabi,* October 24, 2002.

131 *an inauspicious start:* John F. Burns, "U.S. Aides Say the Yemenis Seem to Hinder Cole Inquiry," *New York Times,* November 1, 2000, https://www.nytimes.com/2000/11/01/world/us-aides-say-the-yemenis-seem-to-hinder-cole-inquiry.html.

131 *banned him from the country:* Robert Kolker, "O'Neill Versus Osama," *New York* magazine, December 17, 2001, https://nymag.com/nymetro/news/sept11/features/5513/.

132 *O'Neill was replaced by Mary Galligan:* Author's interview with Mary Galligan via Zoom, September 23, 2020.

132 *most hostile environment:* For a detailed description of the threat environment, see Garrett M. Graff, *The Threat Matrix: The FBI at War in the Age of Terror* (New York: Little, Brown, 2011), 264–65.

132 *June 16, 2001:* Ibid., 267.

132 *gave a lecture:* Bin Laden delivered this speech on September 27, 2000. "Various Admin Documents and Questions" (Combating Terrorism Center, n.d.), AFGP-2002-801138, https://ctc.usma.edu/harmony-program/various-admin-documents-and-questions-original-language-2/.

132 *"Who the shit":* Clarke, *Against All Enemies,* 224.

133 *a long memo:* Memo from Abu Hadayfa to bin Laden, AFGP-2002-003521, June 21, 2001.

133 *Zaidan received:* Zaidan, "Bin Laden Revealed," 77.

133 *Adding to bin Laden's happiness":* Ibid., p. 76.

134 *"A destroyer: even the brave fear its might"*: "Bin Laden Verses Honor *Cole* Attack," Reuters, March 2, 2001.

134 *"it would scare the shit out of al-Qaeda"*: Kean and Hamilton, "9/11 Commission Report," 189; Daniel Benjamin and Steven Simon, *The Age of Sacred Terror: Radical Islam's War Against America* (New York: Random House, 2002), 322.

134 *Clinton's generals were reluctant*: Richard H. Schultz Jr., "Showstoppers: Nine Reasons Why We Never Sent Our Special Operations Forces After al Qaeda Before 9/11," *Weekly Standard*, January 26, 2004.

135 *"They had more Predators"*: Author's interview with Michael Sheehan, New York City, November 21, 2009.

135 *The first Predator drone . . . September 7, 2000*: Alec Bierbauer and Col. Mark Cooter with Michael Marks, *Never Mind, We'll Do It Ourselves: The Inside Story of How a Team of Renegades Launched a Drone Warfare Revolution* (New York, Skyhorse Publishing, 2021), 93.

135 *the seventh Predator mission*: Richard Whittle, *Predator: The Secret Origins of the Drone Revolution* (New York: Henry Holt, 2014), 157–62.

135 *Clarke pounded on the CIA*: Author's interview with Michael Sheehan, New York City, November 21, 2009.

136 *At a desert range at the Naval Air Weapons*: Richard Whittle, *Predator*, 201–6.

136 *"I can't believe anybody"*: Author's interview with Roger Cressey, Washington, DC, November 24, 2009.

136 *wrangling over who would pay*: Kean and Hamilton, "9/11 Commission Report," 211.

136 *Bin Laden asked*: Youssef al-Aayyiri took control of al-Qaeda's operations in the Gulf region in 2002. *Voice of Jihad*, an al-Qaeda magazine in Saudi Arabia, printed his biography in which he described al-Qaeda's role in Massoud's assassination.

136 *"Are they going to wrestle"*: Gary C. Schroen, *First In: An Insider's Account of How the CIA Spearheaded the War on Terror in Afghanistan* (New York: Presidio Press/Ballantine Books, 2005), 4.

137 *"We want to know"*: Ibid., 4.

137 *a red light . . . "Sir, what is the state"*: Ibid., 5.

137 *Two pieces of shrapnel*: Craig Pyes and William C. Rempel, "Slowly Stalking an Afghan 'Lion,'" *Los Angeles Times*, June 12, 2002, https://www.latimes.com/archives/la-xpm-2002-jun-12-fg-masoud12-story.html.

137 *One of the . . . by Massoud's men*: Schroen, *First In*, 6; Pyes and Rempel, "Slowly Stalking an Afghan 'Lion.'"

137 *kept their leader's death a secret*: Pyes and Rempel, "Slowly Stalking an Afghan

'Lion'"; Author's communication with someone close to Massoud on September 10, 2001.

137 *bulletins quickly started circulating:* "Massoud Is Alive, Says Brother," CNN, September 11, 2001, https://www.cnn.com/2001/WORLD/asiapcf/central/09/10/af ghanistan.masood/.

137 *many thousands of militants:* The 9/11 Commission Report estimates 10,000 to 20,000 people trained in the "bin Ladin supported" Afghan camps between 1996 and 9/11. Kean and Hamilton, "9/11 Commission Report," 67.

137 *elite force of 170 members:* "Top Secret, Names of Individuals," AFGP-2002 800648-001-0049, introduced during trial *USA v. Khalid Al Fawwaz,* 98 Cr. 1023 (LAK), AAL-C-000496, Govt. Exhibit 2201A-T.

137 *The* bayat *was modeled:* "Substitution for the Testimony of Khalid Sheikh Mohammed" (United States District Court, Eastern District of Virginia), 54.

137 *five days earlier a messenger:* Peter L. Bergen, *The Longest War: The Enduring Conflict Between America and Al-Qaeda* (New York: Free Press, 2011), 3–5; "Bin Laden Discusses Attacks on Tape," *Washington Post,* December 13, 2001, https:// www.washingtonpost.com/wp-srv/nation/specials/attacked/transcripts/bin ladentext_121301.html.

TEN: THE ROAD TO 9/11

138 *"One belief, more than any other":* Isaiah Berlin, "Two Concepts of Liberty," in *Four Essays on Liberty* (Oxford: Oxford University Press, 1969).

138 *Khalid Sheikh Mohammed…Northern Virginia:* Thomas H. Kean and Lee H. Hamilton, "9/11 Commission Report" (National Commission on Terrorist Attacks Upon the United States, August 21, 2004), 147–50, 153, https://govinfo.library .unt.edu/911/report/911Report_Ch7.htm.

138 *even run a test:* "Factbox: Attacks on Planes by Qaeda, Like-Minded Groups," Reuters, January 24, 2010, https://www.reuters.com/article/us-security-planes -qaeda/factbox-attacks-on-planes-by-qaeda-like-minded-groups-idUSTRE 60N12A20100124

138 *In Tora Bora . . . formally joined al-Qaeda:* "Substitution for the Testimony of Khalid Sheikh Mohammed," (United States District Court, Eastern District of Virginia), 4, 10, 56.

139 *"Why do you use an axe":* "11 September the Plot and the Plotters" (Central Intelligence Agency Directorate of Intelligence, June 1, 2003), 40044HC, 10, https:// www.documentcloud.org/documents/368989-2003-06-01-11-september-the -plot-and-the.html; Robert S. Mueller III, "Speech at the Global Initiative Nuclear Terrorism Conference Miami, Florida" (FBI.gov, June 11, 2007), https:// archives.fbi.gov/archives/news/speeches/nuclear-terrorism-prevention-is-our -endgame.

139   *ten planes . . . West and East Coasts:* "Substitution for the Testimony of Khalid Sheikh Mohammed," 5.

139   *told KSM not to pursue another element:* Ibid., 6.

139   *They selected the U.S. Capitol . . . World Trade Center:* Kean and Hamilton, "9/11 Commission Report," 155.

139   *Bin Laden personally started picking:* Ibid., 166.

139   *Bin Laden told Atta . . . nuclear power plant in Pennsylvania:* "Substitution for the Testimony of Khalid Sheikh Mohammed," 13.

140   *"an event that will turn the world upside down":* Nasser al-Bahri, *Guarding bin Laden: My Life in al-Qaeda* (London: Thin Man Press, 2013), 177.

140   *sometimes asked . . . about their dreams:* Ibid.

140   *"I saw in a dream":* "Excerpts from the Videotape Transcript," *Washington Post,* December 14, 2001, https://www.washingtonpost.com/archive/politics/2001/12/14/excerpts-from-the-videotape-transcript/16340450-2507-44e9-a0c8-76c91ccaa9b4/.

140   *100,000 civilians:* Charles Trueheart, "Hundreds Die in Massacre Near Algiers," *Washington Post,* August 30, 1997, https://www.washingtonpost.com/archive/politics/1997/08/30/hundreds-die-in-massacre-near-algiers/b6e77248-2e68-4244-86b8-4096ce3de497/.

140   *the jihadists had failed:* Author's interviews with Norman Benotman, London, United Kingdom, 2005, 2010.

141   *bin Laden sat next to him, quietly smiling:* Ibid.

141   *"I have one more operation":* Peter Bergen and Paul Cruickshank, "The Unraveling," *New Republic,* June 11, 2008, https://newrepublic.com/article/64819/the-unraveling.

141   *"could not bear":* Abu Walid al Misri, "The History of the Arab Afghans from the Time of Their Arrival in Afghanistan Until Their Departure with the Taliban," *Al Quds Al-Arabi,* December 8, 2004.

141   *In July 2001 Saif al-Adel:* Ahmad Val Ould Eddin, "Former al Qa'idah Leader Interviewed on Group's Affairs, September Attacks," Al Jazeera via BBC Monitoring, October 18, 2012.

141   *Abu Hafs the Mauritanian was also concerned:* Ibid.

141   *leaders of the group who were skeptical:* Ibid.; Kean and Hamilton, "9/11 Commission Report," 251–52.

142   *If bin Laden was convinced of:* "Letter from Saif al-Adel to Khalid Sheikh Mohammed," June 13, 2002.

142   *Feroz Ali Abbasi:* Feroz Ali Abbasi, Guantánamo Bay Prison Memoirs, 2002–2005, author's collection.

142   *just ten men:* Mustafa Hamid (aka Abu Walid al-Misri) and Leah Farrall, *The Arabs at War in Afghanistan* (London: Hurst, 2015), 278.

142 *seven Egyptians . . . their wives:* Bahri, *Guarding bin Laden,* 212.

142 *During this period al-Qaeda produced:* "The names of Al Qa'eda members," AFGP-20002-600046. The document is undated but it cites the arrest in London of Khalid al-Fawwaz, which occurred in September 1998. It seems to have been written in the months after Fawwaz's arrest as it also records other events that happened to members of al-Qaeda during the year 1998, but it says nothing about events during 1999 or later years.

142 *the inner workings:* Nelly Lahoud, "Beware of Imitators: Al-Qa'ida Through the Lens of Its Confidential Secretary" (Combating Terrorism Center, June 4, 2012), 67–68, https://ctc.usma.edu/wp-content/uploads/2012/06/CTC-Beware-of-Imitators-June2012.pdf.

143 *his military commander:* Bahri, *Guarding bin Laden,* 104.

143 *Bin Laden couldn't resist dropping hints:* Mohammed al-Tariri, "Former Member of al-Qaeda Tells *Al Hayat* About Living Through the Events of 9/11 at the Side of Osama bin Laden," *Al Hayat,* September 20, 2006.

143 *KSM urged Bin Laden:* "Substitution for the Testimony of Khalid Sheikh Mohammed," 31.

143 *John Walker Lindh . . . twenty suicide operations:* FBI Report, "Interview of John Philip Walker Lindh," December 9–10, 2001, author's collection.

143 *Abbasi . . . common knowledge:* Feroz Ali Abbasi, Guantánamo Bay Prison Memoirs, 2002–2005, author's collection.

143 *Aytani met bin Laden:* Peter L. Bergen, *The Osama bin Laden I Know: An Oral History of al Qaeda's Leader* (New York: Free Press, 2006), 285–86.

144 *Al-Qaeda members and trainees were told:* Mohammed al-Tariri, "Former Member of al-Qaeda Tells Al Hayat About Living Through the Events of 9/11 at the Side of Osama bin Laden."

145 *Wolfowitz . . . incorrectly believed:* Peter Bergen, "Armchair Provocateur," *Washington Monthly,* December 1, 2003, https://washingtonmonthly.com/2003/12/01/armchair-provocateur/.

145 *"I just don't understand":* Richard A. Clarke, *Against All Enemies: Inside America's War on Terror* (New York: Free Press, 2004), 231.

145 *Ashcroft released a budget memo:* Garrett M. Graff, *The Threat Matrix: The FBI at War in the Age of Terror* (New York: Little, Brown, 2011), 277.

145 *"I don't want you ever":* Ibid., 279.

145 *"We know all we need":* Kean and Hamilton, "9/11 Commission Report," 509fn180.

145 *"stale":* Ibid., 202.

145 *"Bin Ladin Planning Multiple Operations":* "Transcript of testimony from Former CIA Director of the Counterterrorism Center Cofer Black and Former Acting FBI Director Thomas Pickard to the tenth public hearing of the National

Commission on Terrorist Attacks Upon the United States," *Wall Street Journal*, April 13, 2004.

145 *"Bin Ladin Profile May Presage Attack"*: "Terrorism: Bin Ladin Public Profile May Presage Attack" (Central Intelligence Agency Senior Executive Intelligence Brief, May 3, 2001), https://www.documentcloud.org/documents/369162-2001 -05-03-terrorism-bin-ladin-public-profile.html.

146 *On May 23 the CIA raised the possibility*: "Terrorism: Terrorist Groups Said Co- operating on US Hostage Plot" (Central Intelligence Agency Senior Executive Intelligence Brief, May 23, 2001), https://www.documentcloud.org/documents /369163-2001-05-23-terrorism-terrorist-groups-said.html.

146 *"Bin Ladin Attacks May Be Imminent"*: "International: Bin Ladin Attacks May Be Imminent [Excised]" (Central Intelligence Agency Senior Executive Intelligence Brief, June 23, 2001), https://www.documentcloud.org/documents/369166 -2001-06-23-international-bin-ladin-attacks-may.html.

146 *"Planning for Bin Ladin Attacks Continues, Despite Delay"*: "Terrorism: Plan- ning for Bin Ladin Attacks Continues, Despite Delay [Excised]" (Central Intel- ligence Agency Senior Executive Intelligence Brief, July 2, 2001), https://www .documentcloud.org/documents/369168-2001-07-02-terrorism-planning-for -bin-ladin.html.

146 *"Threat of Impending al-Qaeda Attack to Continue Indefinitely"*: Kean and Ham- ilton, *9/11 Commission Report*, 534fn34.

146 *"Maybe we are crazy"*: Author's interview with Gina Bennett via FaceTime, Feb- ruary 20, 2021.

146 *While the CIA . . . taking any action*: "OIG Report on CIA Accountability with Respect to the 9/11 Attacks," CIA, 2005, approved for release March 19, 2015, xiv, 45–46, 65–69.

146 *On July 10 . . . "Yes"*: George Tenet and Bill Harlow, *At the Center of the Storm: My Years at the CIA* (New York: HarperCollins, 2007), 150–53.

147 *"war footing now"*: Cofer Black interview, *Road to 9/11*, History Channel, Part 3, September 6, 2017.

147 *Rice did nothing*: Ibid.; John McLaughlin interview, *Road to 9/11*.

147 *Berger, had convened daily meetings*: Amy B. Zegart, *Spying Blind: The CIA, the FBI, and the Origins of 9/11* (Princeton, NJ: Princeton University Press, 2007), 8.

147 *"Bin Ladin Determined to Strike in US"*: "Bin Ladin Determined to Strike in US" (Central Intelligence Agency Presidential Daily Brief, August 6, 2001), https:// nsarchive2.gwu.edu//NSAEBB/NSAEBB116/pdb8-6-2001.pdf.

147 *The brief was delivered in the living room*: Michael J. Morell and Bill Harlow, *The Great War of Our Time: The CIA's Fight Against Terrorism—From al Qa'ida to ISIS* (New York: Twelve, 2015), 42–43.

147 *The brief had been prepared . . . Los Angeles International Airport:* Author's interview with Barbara Sude, Washington, DC, December 16, 2009.

147 *recently pled guilty:* Michael Powell and Christine Haughney, "Suspect Admits Plot Targeted Los Angeles," *South Florida Sun Sentinel,* July 4, 2001, https://www.sun-sentinel.com/news/fl-xpm-2001-07-04-0107030926-story.html.

147 *longest presidential vacation:* Laurence McQuillan, "White House to Move to Texas for a While," *USA Today,* August 3, 2001, https://usatoday30.usatoday.com/news/washington/august01/2001-08-03-bush-vacation.htm; Fred Kaplan, "The Out-of-Towner," *Slate,* April 14, 2004, https://slate.com/news-and-politics/2004/04/while-bush-vacationed-9-11-warnings-went-unheard.html.

147 *first time . . . "Decision makers should imagine":* Kean and Hamilton, "9/11 Commission Report," 212.

148 *Najwa had spent the past five years . . .stay with him:* Najwa bin Laden, Omar bin Laden, and Jean P. Sasson, *Growing Up bin Laden: Osama's Wife and Son Take Us Inside Their Secret World* (New York: St. Martin's Press, 2009), 281–83.

149 *September 7:* Ibid., 312.

149 *"Manual for a Raid":* An excellent discussion of the religious zealotry that gripped the hijackers can be found in *The 9/11 Handbook: Annotated Translation and Interpretation of the Attackers' Spiritual Manual,* Hans G. Kippenberg and Tilman Seidensticker, eds., (London: Equinox, 2006).

149 *Two thousand nine hundred and seventy-seven people were killed:* "September 11 Terror Attacks Fast Facts," CNN, updated September 18, 2020, https://www.cnn.com/2013/07/27/us/september-11-anniversary-fast-facts.

149 *On the morning . . . Arabic Service:* Jason Burke, *The 9/11 Wars* (London: Penguin, 2012), 24. Proceedings of a military commission, *USA v. Ali Hamza Ahmad Suliman al Bahlul,* May 7, 2008.

149 *"I have just received this news"* Yosri Fouda and Nick Fielding, *Masterminds of Terror: The Truth Behind the Most Devastating Terrorist Attack the World Has Ever Seen* (New York: Arcade, 2003), 145.

149 *"be patient":* "Former Member of al-Qaeda Tells Al Hayat About Living Through the Events of 9/11 at the Side of Osama bin Laden."

150 *In Kandahar . . . with joy:* "An Exclusive Interview with Adam Yahiye Gadahn," *Resurgence* (Al-Qaeda's English language magazine), Summer 2015, 74.

150 *Because Mullah Omar had banned TV . . . what CNN was reporting:* Kabir Mohabbat and Leah McInnis, *Delivering Osama: The Story of America's Secret Envoy* (Berlin: First Draft Publishing, 2020), 278.

150 *visiting an elementary school . . . "missed something big":* George W. Bush, *Decision Points* (New York: Crown, 2010), 127, 135.

150 *No senior Bush official spoke publicly:* For a fuller discussion of this point, see Peter L. Bergen, *The Longest War: The Enduring Conflict Between America and*

al-Qaeda (New York: Free Press, 2011), 42–55. A Nexis database search of all the newspapers, magazines, and TV transcripts of Condoleezza Rice's statements and writings from the mid-1990s until 9/11 shows that she never mentioned al-Qaeda publicly, and only referred to the threat from bin Laden during a 2000 interview with a Detroit radio station. A Nexis database search of all of deputy defense secretary Paul Wolfowitz's pre-9/11 statements and writings shows he never mentioned al-Qaeda, and referred to bin Laden only once, in the context of the Saudi exile's purported links to Saddam Hussein. A Nexis search for anything that President Bush or Vice President Cheney might have written or said about the threat posed by al-Qaeda and bin Laden similarly comes up empty before 9/11.

150 *The president asked his CIA briefer . . . case of the USS Cole:* This scene is drawn from Morell and Harlow, *The Great War of Our Time*, 55–56.

151 *"kick their ass":* Bush, *Decision Points*, 128.

ELEVEN: STRIKING BACK

155 *"the tactics took over the strategy":* Author's interview with Noman Benotman, London, United Kingdom, August 30, 2005.

155 *"Everybody has a plan":* Mike Beradino, "Mike Tyson Explains One of His Most Famous Quotes," *South Florida Sun Sentinel*, November 9, 2012, https://www .sun-sentinel.com/sports/fl-xpm-2012-11-09-sfl-mike-tyson-explains-one-of -his-most-famous-quotes-20121109-story.html.

155 *On the morning . . . some larger reason?:* Author's interview with Gina Bennett via FaceTime, February 20, 2021.

156 *As Air Force One:* George W. Bush, *Decision Points* (New York: Crown, 2010), 130.

156 *analyst obtained the passenger manifest:* Author's interview with John McLaughlin, Washington, DC, December 7, 2009.

156 *The news was conveyed . . . printing plant:* Ibid.

157 *Memorandum of Notification:* John Anthony Rizzo, *Company Man: Thirty Years of Controversy and Crisis in the CIA* (New York: Scribner, 2014), 172–74. The Memorandum of Notification was signed on September 17, 2001.

157 *The debris cloud smothered Coleman in ash:* Author's interview with Daniel Coleman, Princeton, New Jersey, December 19, 2009.

157 *A Saudi passport had fallen:* Ibid.

157 *August 23:* Ali H. Soufan, *Anatomy of Terror: From the Death of bin Laden to the Rise of the Islamic State* (New York: W. W. Norton, 2017), xiii.

157 *O'Neill was killed on the morning of 9/11:* "FBI Terrorist Fighter's Body Found at WTC," CNN, September 22, 2001, http://edition.cnn.com/2001/US/09/21/vic .body.terror.expert/.

157 *Mary Galligan . . . never closed:* Mary Galligan interview by Clifford Chanin at the 9/11 Museum, New York City, December 6, 2016.

158 *The FBI's main office:* Author's interview with Mary Galligan via Zoom, September 23, 2020.

158 *O'Neill had mentored and promoted:* Author's interview with Mary Galligan via Zoom, October 19, 2020.

158 *Galligan would carry the mass card:* Mary Galligan interview by Clifford Chanin at the 9/11 Museum, New York City, December 6, 2016.

158 *half a million leads . . . paymaster for the 9/11 plot:* Author's interview with Mary Galligan via Zoom, September 23, 2020.

159 *The first meeting at the White House:* Hugh Shelton, Ronald Levinson, and Malcolm McConnell, *Without Hesitation: The Odyssey of an American Warrior* (New York: St. Martin's Press, 2010), 436.

159 *pushed to go to war with Saddam:* Ibid.

159 *"Wait a minute":* "Hugh Shelton Oral History: Transcript" (UVA Miller Center, May 29, 2007), https://millercenter.org/the-presidency/presidential-oral-histo ries/henry-hugh-shelton-oral-history-chairman-joint-chiefs.

159 *Clarke realized with almost a sharp physical pain:* Richard A. Clarke, *Against All Enemies: Inside America's War on Terror* (New York: Free Press, 2004), 30.

159 *"Jamal, I came last night in a hurry":* Author's interview with Jamal Ismail, Islamabad, Pakistan, March 2005.

159 *Bin Laden was surprised:* "Bin Laden Discusses Attacks on Tape," *Washington Post,* Dec. 13, 2001, https://www.washingtonpost.com/wp-srv/nation/specials /attacked/transcripts/binladentext_121301.html.

160 *"It really pains me":* Steve Coll, *Directorate S: The C.I.A. and America's Secret Wars in Afghanistan and Pakistan* (New York: Penguin, 2018), 41–42.

160 *CIA officers understood:* Author's interview with Robert Richer, Washington, DC, October 6, 2011.

160 *Saturday, September 15 . . . why not also attack state sponsors:* Bradley Graham, *By His Own Rules: The Ambitions, Successes, and Ultimate Failures of Donald Rumsfeld* (New York: Public Affairs, 2009), 288.

160 *"like South America or Southeast Asia":* Douglas J. Feith, *War and Decision: Inside the Pentagon at the Dawn of the War on Terrorism* (New York: Harper, 2008), 66.

160 *"the head of the snake":* Robert Draper, *To Start a War: How the Bush Administration Took America into Iraq* (New York: Penguin, 2020), 18–19.

160 *it was exactly what bin Laden had started calling:* USA v. Usama bin Laden, Testimony of Jamal al-Fadl, February 6, 2001, 281.

161 *Cofer Black pushed back . . . no plans to be controlled:* Draper, *To Start a War,* 18–19.

161 *"We'll leave Iraq for later"*: Ibid.

161 *"We're not going to just pound sand"*: Donald Rumsfeld, *Known and Unknown: A Memoir* (New York: Sentinel, 2011), 359.

161 *conveyed this analysis*: Ahmad Muaffaq Zaidan, "Bin Laden Revealed," unpublished manuscript, which is based on Zaidan's book in Arabic, *Bin Laden Unmasked* (Beirut, 2015), 34.

161 *no American boots*: Ibid., 32.

161 *very bright*: Ibid., 34.

162 *thick packets of briefing materials*: Author's interview with John McLaughlin, Washington, DC, December 7, 2009.

162 *a far more impressive war plan*: Karen DeYoung, *Soldier: The Life of Colin Powell* (New York: Vintage, 2007), 351.

162 *twenty-thousand-man anti-Taliban militia*: Bob Woodward, *Bush at War* (New York: Simon & Schuster, 2002), 35.

162 *Tenet also proposed using armed drones*: George Tenet and Bill Harlow, *At the Center of the Storm: My Years at the CIA* (New York: HarperCollins, 2007), 177.

162 *"I want the CIA"*: Author's interview with John McLaughlin, Washington, DC, December 7, 2009.

163 *" 'Wanted Dead or Alive' "*: Kurt Eichenwald, *500 Days: Secrets and Lies in the Terror Wars* (New York: Touchstone, 2012), 79; David Stout, "Bush Says He Wants Capture of Bin Laden 'Dead or Alive,' " *New York Times*, September 17, 2001, https://www.nytimes.com/2001/09/17/national/bush-says-he-wants-capture -of-bin-laden-dead-or-alive.html.

163 *"Deliver to United States authorities"*: "State of the Union: Text of George W. Bush's Speech," *Guardian*, September 21, 2001, https://www.theguardian.com /world/2001/sep/21/september11.usa13.

163 *seven hundred clerics in Kabul to rule*: John F. Burns, "Afghan Clerics Urge bin Laden to Leave; White House Says Unacceptable," *New York Times*, September 20, 2001, https://www.nytimes.com/2001/09/20/international/afghan-cler ics-urge-bin-laden-to-leave-white-house-says.html.

163 *"If we did, it means"*: Transcript: VOA Interview with Taliban Leader," *Washington Post*, September 23, 2001, https://www.washingtonpost.com/wp-srv/na tion/attack/transcripts/omarinterview092301.htm.

163 *"I don't want to go down in history"*: Author's interview with Rahimullah Yusuf-zai, Pakistan, June 29, 2003.

163 *"My brother had a dream"*: Ibid.

163 *were bluster*: Abdul Salam Zaeef, *My Life with the Taliban* (New York: Columbia University Press, 2010), 149.

164 *Mullah Osmani and Grenier met*: Robert L. Grenier, *88 Days to Kandahar: A*

CIA Diary (New York: Simon & Schuster, 2016), 80–86; Author's interview with Robert Grenier, Washington, DC, January 19, 2010.

164 *Bin Laden has created a great problem:* Author's interview with Robert Grenier, Washington, DC, January 19, 2010.

164 *"As a Muslim, I try"* . . . *"American Jews":* "The Al-Qa'idah Group Had Nothing to Do with the 11 September Attacks," Khilafah.com, September 28, 2001. Archived at https://web.archive.org/web/20020111073623/http://www.khilafah .com/1421/category.php?DocumentID=2392.

164 *fifty-nine . . . process of retiring:* Gary C. Schroen, *First In: An Insider's Account of How the CIA Spearheaded the War on Terror in Afghanistan* (New York: Presidio Press/Ballantine Books, 2005), 10, 23.

165 *Cofer Black called . . . "first in"* Ibid., 16.

165 *"heads on pikes" . . . "I don't know where":* Ibid., 39–40.

165 *on September 26 . . . JAWBREAKER:* Ibid., 76–78; Gary Schroen interviewed in Greg Barker, "The Longest War," produced by Peter Bergen and Tresha Mabile (New York: Showtime, 2020).

165 *Similar anthrax-laced letters . . . American government scientist:* "Amerithrax or Anthrax Investigation," FBI.gov, accessed March 26, 2021, https://www.fbi.gov /history/famous-cases/amerithrax-or-anthrax-investigation; "Opening of the Letter to Senator Leahy," FBI.gov, accessed March 26, 2021, https://archives.fbi .gov/archives/about-us/history/famous-cases/anthrax-amerithrax/the-leahy -letter.

165 *enormous impact:* Scott McClellan, *What Happened: Inside the Bush White House and Washington's Culture of Deception* (New York: PublicAffairs, 2008), 108.

165 *"may have a nuclear device":* Richard B. Myers and Malcolm McConnell, *Eyes on the Horizon: Serving on the Front Lines of National Security* (New York: Pocket Books, 2014), 163.

165 *"We have to intensify":* Ibid.

165 *Two weeks later bin Laden added . . . "black market of Central Asia":* This scene is drawn from author's interviews with Hamid Mir, Islamabad, Pakistan, May 11, 2002, March 2005; "Osama Claims He Has Nukes: If US Uses N-Arms It Will Get Same Response," *Dawn*, November 10, 2001, https://www.dawn.com/news /5647/osama-claims-he-has-nukes-if-us-uses-n-arms-it-will-get-same-re sponse.

166 *the black market . . . was a myth:* Robin M. Frost, *Nuclear Terrorism After 9/11* (London: Routledge, 2017), 23.

166 *similar claims:* Zaidan, "Bin Laden Revealed," 93.

167 *"experienced in this sphere" . . . "procure necessary face masks":* Roland Jacquard, *Les Archives Secretes d'Al-Qaida* (Paris: Jean Picollec, 2002), 281.

167 *Dr. Sultan Bashiruddin Mahmood:* Grenier, *88 Days to Kandahar,* 171–72; Peter Baker, "Pakistani Scientist Who Met Bin Laden Failed Polygraphs, Renewing Suspicions," *Washington Post,* March 3, 2002, https://www.washingtonpost.com /archive/politics/2002/03/03/pakistani-scientist-who-met-bin-laden-failed -polygraphs-renewing-suspicions/3a2e3693-b16f-4f92-b868-992b1c51fea9/.

167 *met with bin Laden . . . "fissile material":* Grenier, *88 Days to Kandahar,* 177–78.

167 *Faddis was dispatched:* Author's interview with Charles "Sam" Faddis, Washington, DC, January 20, 2010.

167 *Faddis concluded . . . was, however, concerned:* Ibid.

167 *Privately, bin Laden was more ambivalent:* Abu Walid al Misri, "The History of the Arab Afghans from the Time of Their Arrival in Afghanistan Until Their Departure with the Taliban," *Al Quds Al-Arabi,* December 8, 2004.

167 *Zawahiri didn't have qualms:* Nasser al-Bahri, *Guarding bin Laden: My Life in al-Qaeda* (London: Thin Man Press, 2013), 213.

167 *crude experiments:* For a detailed discussion of this issue, see Peter Bergen, "Al-Qaeda's Quixotic Quest for Weapons of Mass Destruction," in Bergen, *The Longest War: The Enduring Conflict Between America and al-Qaeda* (New York: Free Press, 2011), 214–30.

168 *"a recent survey showed":* Alan Cullison, "Inside Al-Qaeda's Hard Drive," *Atlantic,* September 2004, https://www.theatlantic.com/magazine/archive/2004/09 /inside-al-qaeda-s-hard-drive/303428/. See also Alan Cullison and Andrew Higgins, "Forgotten Computer Reveals Thinking Behind Four Years of Al Qaeda Doings," *Wall Street Journal,* December 31, 2001, https://www.wsj.com/articles /SB100975171479902000.

168 *"great long-term economic burdens":* Ibid.

168 *"I'm sure he didn't do it" . . . "four thousand Jews":* Author's interview with Faraj Ismail, Cairo, Egypt, June 2005; Faraj Ismail, "Taliban Leader Mullah Omar Interviewed, *Al Majalla,* October 14, 2001.

168 *"There is America . . . more than eighty years":* "Text: Bin Laden's Statement," *Guardian* (Translation Supplied by the Associated Press), October 7, 2001, https://www.theguardian.com/world/2001/oct/07/afghanistan.terrorism15; "Recorded Message from Osama Bin Laden," Associated Press, YouTube, July 21, 2015, https://www.youtube.com/watch?v=IHInbQcyg2Y.

169 *A CIA-operated armed drone . . . fired at Mullah Omar:* Chris Woods, "The Story of America's Very First Drone Strike," *Atlantic,* May 30, 2015, https://www.the atlantic.com/international/archive/2015/05/america-first-drone-strike-afghan istan/394463/.

169 *his dreams:* Vahid Mojdeh, *Afghanistan Under Five Years of Taliban Sovereignty,* translated by Sepideh Khalili and Saeed Ganji, author's collection.

169 *"said in deeds"*: Bumiller, "A Nation Challenged: The Evidence; Later Video of
bin Laden May Be Public This Week."

170 *killed Abu Hafs*: Richard Whittle, *Predator: The Secret Origins of the Drone Revolution* (New York: Henry Holt, 2014), 279–87.

170 *It was a real loss . . . shaken by Abu Hafs's death*: Peter L. Bergen, *Manhunt:
The Ten-Year Search for bin Laden from 9/11 to Abbottabad* (New York: Crown,
2012), 39.

170 *"the problem about the Taliban"*: Peter L. Bergen, *The Osama bin Laden I Know:
An Oral History of al Qaeda's Leader* (New York: Free Press, 2006), 323.

TWELVE: THE GREAT ESCAPE

171 *"So let me be a martyr"*: Osama bin Laden, *Messages to the World: The Statements
of Osama Bin Laden*, ed. Bruce Lawrence (London: Verso, 2005), 205.

171 *"more afraid of our own blunders"*: Thucydides, *The Landmark Thucydides: A
Comprehensive Guide to the Peloponnesian War*, ed. Robert B. Strassler (New
York: Free Press, 2008), 83.

172 *Afghan holy warriors in Tora Bora held off*: Author's interview with Dr. Mohamed Asif Qazizanda, Jalalabad, Afghanistan, July 4, 2004.

172 *In late October*: "JTF-GTMO Detainee Assessment," Salman Fouad al-Rabai
(Department of Defense, May 12, 2008), 8, Wikileaks Guantánamo Files,
https://wikileaks.org/gitmo/prisoner/551.html.

172 *only one mortar*: Ayman al-Zawahiri, "Zawahiri Calls for Revenge for Slain Libyan Officials, Remembers Tora Bora" (Al Qaeda Statements Index, July 16, 2014),
https://scholarship.tricolib.brynmawr.edu/bitstream/handle/10066/17140
/ZAW20140716.pdf?sequence=3.

172 *as if they were the sophisticated lair of a James Bond villain*: See for instance the
Times of London graphic described in Edward Jay Epstein, "Fictoid #3: The Lair
of bin Laden," *Edward Jay Epstein.Com* (blog), accessed April 22, 2021, http://
www.edwardjayepstein.com/nether_fictoid3.htm.

172 *simply caves, just large enough*: Author's visits to Tora Bora in 2003 and 2005.

172 *Ayman Batarfi*: Andy Worthington, "The Story of Ayman Batarfi, a Doctor
in Guantánamo," *AndyWorthington* (blog), April 14, 2009, http://www.andy
worthington.co.uk/2009/04/14/the-story-of-ayman-batarfi-a-doctor-in-guan
tanamo/; "JTF-GTMO Detainee Assessment: Ayman Saeed Abdulla Batarfi"
(Department of Defense, April 29, 2008), WikiLeaks Guantánamo Files, https://
wikileaks.org/gitmo/prisoner/627.html.

173 *bin Laden said farewell . . . see each other again*: Ayman al-Zawahiri, "Days with
the Imam," October 19, 2014, Al Qaeda Statements Index, https://scholarship
.tricolib.brynmawr.edu/b3itstream/handle/10066/17025.

173 *"Not a second"*: Bin Laden recounted his experiences at Tora Bora on an audio-tape that aired on Al Jazeera on February 11, 2003.

173 *700,000 pounds of ordnance*: George Tenet and Bill Harlow, *At the Center of the Storm: My Years at the CIA* (New York: HarperCollins, 2007), 226.

173 *three hundred followers:* Three hundred is from an Osama bin Laden audiotape that aired on Al Jazeera on February 11, 2003.

173 *intense American bombing:* Ayman al-Zawahiri, "Zawahiri Recalls Siege, Escape from Tora Bora, Advises Jihadi Media to Stop Promoting Discord Between Fighters," August 15, 2015, Al Qaeda Statements Index, https://schol arship.tricolib.brynmawr.edu/bitstream/handle/10066/17131/ZAW20150815 .pdf?sequence=4.

173 *Battle of the Trench:* Sayyid Ali Sghar Razwy, "The Battle of the Trench," in *A Restatement of the History of Islam and Muslims* (World Federation of Khoja Shia Ithna-Asheri Muslim Communities, n.d.), https://www.al-islam.org/re statement-history-islam-and-muslims-sayyid-ali-asghar-razwy.

173 *A messenger came . . . killed in a U.S. air strike:* Al-Zawahiri, "Days with the Imam."

173 *"No condolences"*: Andrew Higgins and Alan Cullison, "Saga of Dr. Zawahiri Sheds Light on the Roots of al Qaeda Terror," *Wall Street Journal*, July 2, 2002, https://www.wsj.com/articles/SB1025558570331929960.

173 *described them as fierce:* Author's interview with Commander Musa, Jalalabad, Afghanistan, July 2003.

174 *requesting eight hundred elite Army Rangers:* Gary Berntsen and Ralph Pezzullo, *Jawbreaker: The Attack on Bin Laden and Al Qaeda: A Personal Account by the CIA's Key Field Commander* (New York: Crown, 2005), 299; Author's interview with Gary Berntsen, Washington, DC, October 27, 2009.

174 *Tommy Franks . . . pushed back:* Author's interview with Hank Crumpton, Washington, DC, November 6, 2009.

174 *aided by an eleven-man Special Forces detachment:* Greg Barker, *Legion of Brothers*, produced by John Battsek, Peter Bergen, and Tresha Mabile (Atlanta: CNN Films, 2017); Eric Blehm, *The Only Thing Worth Dying For: How Eleven Green Berets Forged a New Afghanistan* (New York: Harper, 2010).

174 *Franks also believed:* "Interview: U.S. Army General Tommy Franks," *Frontline*, PBS, June 12, 2002, https://www.pbs.org/wgbh/pages/frontline/shows/campaign /interviews/franks.html.

174 *deepest insertion:* Dan Lamothe, "Mattis: The man, the myths and the influential general's deep bond with his Marines," *Military Times*, April 15, 2013.

174 *killing at least one million:* Amie Ferris-Rotman, "The Soviet Army Was Driven from Afghanistan 30 Years Ago. Putin's Russia Is Repackaging That Defeat as

a Patriotic Victory," *Washington Post*, February 14, 2019, https://www.wash
ingtonpost.com/world/europe/the-soviet-army-was-driven-from-afghanistan
-30-years-ago-putins-russia-is-repackaging-it-as-a-patriotic-victory/2019/02/1
3/3ff61302-1e6f-11e9-a759-2b8541bbbe20_story.html.

174 *largest refugee population in the world:* Rupert Colville, "The Biggest Caseload
in the World," *Refugees Magazine*, June 1, 1997, https://www.unhcr.org/en-us
/publications/refugeemag/3b680fbfc/refugees-magazine-issue-108-afghani
stan-unending-crisis-biggest-caseload.html.

174 *airfield one hundred miles from Kandahar city:* Jim Mattis and Bing West, *Call
Sign Chaos: Learning to Lead* (New York: Random House, 2019), 69.

174 *Mattis proposed a plan . . . Franks continued to rely:* Ibid., 73–75.

174 *More than one thousand soldiers from the 10th Mountain Division:* Tom Bowman,
"Specialized U.S. Troops Poised in Uzbekistan," *Baltimore Sun*, November 3,
2001, https://www.baltimoresun.com/news/bs-xpm-2001-11-03-0111030123
-story.html.

175 *On December 9 . . . a scorpion:* Peter Bergen, "The Account of How We Nearly
Caught Osama bin Laden in 2001," *New Republic*, December 30, 2009, https://
newrepublic.com/article/72086/the-battle-tora-bora. The scorpion story is from
Global Islamic Media Front, "Profile of the Personal Habits of Usama bin Ladin,"
September 21, 2007.

175 *A fifteen-thousand-pound device:* "U.S. Drops 15,000-lb. Bomb on Taliban," Associated Press, November 5, 2001, https://apnews.com/article/15f9fdb62aeee4b
a227d1d60726576db.

175 *worried that their leader:* Abu Jaafar al-Kuwaiti, an eyewitness to the U.S. air
strikes on Tora Bora in early December 2001, posted to al Qaeda's main website
on the first anniversary of 9/11.

175 *bin Laden's followers were desperate . . . ten degrees below freezing:* Bin Laden
recounted his experiences at Tora Bora on an audiotape that aired on Al Jazeera
on February 11, 2003. The details on the weather come from a Delta operator in
an observation post not far from al-Qaeda positions.

175 *water . . . was frozen:* Zawahiri, "Zawahiri Recalls Siege, Escape from Tora Bora,
Advises Jihadi Media to Stop Promoting Discord Between Fighters."

175 *"I am sorry for getting you involved":* Dalton Fury, *Kill Bin Laden: A Delta Force
Commander's Account of the Hunt for the World's Most Wanted Man* (New York:
St. Martin's Griffin, 2009), 234; John F. Kerry, "Tora Bora Revisited: How We
Failed to Get bin Laden and Why It Matters Today: A Report to Members of the
Committee on Foreign Relations, United States Senate" (United States Senate
Committee on Foreign Relations Majority Staff, S. Rep. 111-35. November 30,
2009), 7.

175 *Al-Qaeda officials offered a cease-fire . . . surrender:* Author's interview with

Adam Khan (a pseudonym), who was being concurrently briefed on bin Laden's transmissions in Tora Bora and was present at the battle, interview by phone, March 1, 2020.

175 *"Night of Power"*: Peter L. Bergen, *The Osama bin Laden I Know: An Oral History of al Qaeda's Leader* (New York: Free Press, 2006), 57, 370.

175 *11 p.m. on December 12 . . . leave Tora Bora*: Zawahiri, "Zawahiri Recalls Siege, Escape from Tora Bora, Advises Jihadi Media to Stop Promoting Discord Between Fighters."

176 *Kunar*: Chris Sands and Fazelminallah Qazizai, *Night Letters: The Secret History of Gulbuddin Hekmatyar and the Afghan Islamists Who Changed the World* (London: Hurst, 2019), 409.

176 *The same day . . . briefing the plan*: Tommy Franks, *American Soldier* (New York: Regan Books, 2004), 329–42.

176 *drew up his will*: Bin Laden's "will," written on December 14, 2001, appeared October 2002 in *Al Majallah* magazine.

176 *signals operators picked up*: Author's interview with Adam Khan (a pseudonym), who was being concurrently briefed on bin Laden's transmissions in Tora Bora, Washington, DC, December 16, 2008; Peter L. Bergen, *The Longest War: The Enduring Conflict Between America and al-Qaeda* (New York: Free Press, 2011), 78.

176 *paid a local commander, Awal Gul . . . place to disappear*: "JTF-GTMO Detainee Assessment: Awal Gul" (Department of Defense, February 15, 2008), WikiLeaks Guantánamo Files, https://wikileaks.org/gitmo/pdf/af/us9af-000782dp.pdf; Sands and Qazizai, *Night Letters*, 417–21. Also Wesley Morgan, *The Hardest Place: The American Military Adrift in Afghanistan's Pech Valley* (New York: Random House, 2021), 43.

177 *known Hekmaytar for the past decade and a half*: Sands and Qazizai, *Night Letters*, 217–18.

177 *major beneficiary of CIA largesse*: Milt Bearden, who was CIA station chief in Pakistan during the late 1980s, and his Pakistani counterpart, ISI Brigadier Mohammad Yousaf, both estimated that 20 percent of CIA funding went to Hekmatyar out of a total of $3 billion that the CIA spent on funding the Afghan resistance. Mohammad Yousaf and Mark Adkin, *Afghanistan—the Bear Trap: The Defeat of a Superpower* (Lahore: Jang Publishers, 1993); 105; Author's interview with Mohammad Yousaf, Karachi, Pakistan, August 6, 1993; Author's interview with Milt Bearden, Washington, DC, September 2000.

177 *unenviable task of informing Bush . . . that bin Laden had escaped*: Michael J. Morell and Bill Harlow, *The Great War of Our Time: The CIA's Fight Against Terrorism—From al Qa'ida to ISIS* (New York: Twelve, 2015), 75–76.

178 *"If we had ever known"*: George W. Bush, *Decision Points* (New York: Crown, 2010), 202.

178 *"No one knew for certain"* . . . *"far more to the threat"*: Donald Rumsfeld, *Known and Unknown: A Memoir* (New York: Sentinel, 2011), 402–3.

178 *"conflicting reports"*: Condoleezza Rice, *No Higher Honor: A Memoir of My Years in Washington* (New York: Crown, 2011), 119.

178 *Cheney didn't mention*: Dick Cheney and Liz Cheney, *In My Time: A Personal and Political Memoir* (New York: Threshold, 2011).

178 *"I think he was equipped"*: "Transcript of Cheney Interview," ABC News, January 6, 2006, https://abcnews.go.com/Primetime/story?id=13218&page=1.

178 *"We don't have any credible evidence"*: *Lou Dobbs Moneyline*, December 10, 2001, http://www.cnn.com/TRANSCRIPTS/0112/10/mlld.00.html.

178 *"We were hot on Osama bin Laden's trail"*: Michael DeLong and Noah Lukeman, *A General Speaks Out: The Truth About the Wars in Afghanistan and Iraq* (St. Paul, MN: Zenith Press, 2007), 57.

178 *"All source reporting corroborated"*: "United States Special Operations Command History" (United States Special Operations Command, 2007), 98, https://fas.org/irp/agency/dod/socom/2007history.pdf.

179 *certainly would have faced obstacles*: Kerry, "Tora Bora Revisited," 4.

179 *still smoldering*: "Ground Zero Stops Burning, After 100 Days," *Guardian*, December 20, 2001, https://www.theguardian.com/world/2001/dec/20/september11.usa.

THIRTEEN: AL-QAEDA REVIVES

180 *"Far from being"*: Samuel Eliot Morison, *History of United States Naval Operations in World War II* (Urbana: University of Illinois Press, 2001), 132.

180 *An internal al-Qaeda after-action report*: "The September 11th Attacks or the Impossible Becoming Possible," n.d., AQ-SHPD-D-001-285, Conflict Records Center, https://911conference.files.wordpress.com/2011/09/aq-shpd-d-001-285.pdf.

180 *Bin Laden was certain*: Camille Tawil, *The Other Face of Al-Qaeda*, November 2010, Quilliam Foundation, interview with Noman Benotman, p. 10.

180 *1,600 out of the 1,900 Arab fighters*: Jim Lacey, ed., *A Terrorist's Call to Global Jihad: Deciphering Abu Musab al-Suri's Islamic Jihad Manifesto* (Annapolis, MD: Naval Institute Press, 2008), 99.

181 *"Oh father! I see spheres of danger"*: Muhammad al Shafi'i, "A Site Close to Al Qaeda Posts a Poem by Bin Laden in Which He Responds to His Son Hamzah," *Asharq al-Aswat*, June 16, 2002.

181 *"a very steep path ahead"*: Ibid.

181 *the resettlement of three of bin Laden's wives*: "JTF-GTMO Detainee Assessment: Salim Hamed" (Department of Defense, September 4, 2008), 3, WikiLeaks Guantánamo Files, https://wikileaks.org/gitmo/pdf/ym/us9ym-000149dp.pdf.

181 *Amal moved . . . some half-dozen times*: "Constitution of Joint Investigation Team" (Office of the Inspector General of Police Islamabad, January 19, 2012), https://www.cbsnews.com/htdocs/pdf/JIT_Report_033012.pdf.

181 *Shaved off*: Justice Javed Iqbal t al., "Abbottabad Commission Report," 2013, 44, https://www.documentcloud.org/documents/724833-aljazeera-bin-laden-dos sier.html.

181 *Amal traveled to Peshawar . . . reunited with her husband*: Justice Javed Iqbal et al., "Abbottabad Commission Report," 2013, 273, https://www.documentcloud .org/documents/724833-aljazeera-bin-laden-dossier.html.

181 *traveled by van to Swat . . . conceived their second child*: Ibid., 44.

181 *under the protection of Ibrahim and Abrar*: Ibid., 45.

181 *"he is dead . . . a kidney patient"*: Oliver Burkeman, "Kidney Failure May Already Have Killed Bin Laden," *Guardian*, January 18, 2002, https://www.theguardian .com/world/2002/jan/19/afghanistan.oliverburkeman.

182 *low blood pressure*: Essam Deraz, *The Battles of the Lion's Den of the Afghan Mujahideen.*

182 *walk with a cane*: Author's observations of bin Laden, March 22, 1997, Jalalabad, Afghanistan.

182 *vocal cords*: Bahri, *Guarding bin Laden*, 74.

182 *Ahmad Zaidan . . . received a call*: Author's interview with Ahmad Zaidan, Islamabad, Pakistan, March 2005.

182 *including the suicide bombings . . . in Bali*: "Official: Voice on Tape Is bin Laden's," CNN, November 13, 2002, https://www.cnn.com/2002/WORLD/meast/11/12 /binladen.statement/.

182 *Al-Qaeda had provided funding*: Simon Elgant, "The Terrorist Talks," *Time*, October 5, 2003, http://content.time.com/time/magazine/article/0,9171,493256,00 .html.

182 *called the president*: Johanna McGeary and Douglas Waller, "Why Can't We Find Bin Laden?," CNN, November 18, 2002, https://www.cnn.com/2002/ALLPOLI TICS/11/18/timep.bin.laden.tm/index.html.

182 *Khalid Sheikh Mohammed came and stayed with bin Laden*: Justice Javed Iqbal et al., "Abottabad Commission Report," 2013, 55.

183 *arrested in Rawalpindi*: "Top al Qaeda Operative Caught in Pakistan," CNN, March 1, 2003, https://www.cnn.com/2003/WORLD/asiapcf/south/03/01/paki stan.arrests/.

183 *while watching Al Jazeera*: Iqbal et al., "Abbottabad Commission Report," 41.

183 *ordered his family*: Ibid., 35.

183 *carrying a letter from bin Laden . . . in Iran*: Author's interview with General Asad Munir, Islamabad, Pakistan, July 19, 2011.

183 *KSM . . . telling the Pakistanis:* Pervez Musharraf, *In the Line of Fire: A Memoir* (New York: Free Press, 2008), 220.

183 *all fled to Iran in 2002:* This information comes from FBI 302 interview with Sulaiman Abu Ghaith on March 6, 2013, who fled to Iran from Afghanistan in 2002. From 2003 to 2013 Abu Ghaith was held by the Iranians with al-Qaeda officials and bin Laden family members. Abu Ghaith married Fatima bin Laden in 2008. http://kronosadvisory.com/Kronos_US_v_Sulaiman_Abu_Ghayth_State ment.pdf.

184 *the Pentagon began planning:* Eric Schmitt and Thom Shanker, *Counterstrike: The Untold Story of America's Secret Campaign Against Al Qaeda* (New York: Times Books, 2012), 31–32.

184 *rounded up . . . moved to Karaj:* Abu Abd al-Rahman Anas al-Subay'i, "Letter Dtd 13 Oct 2010" (Office of the Director of National Intelligence, October 13, 2010), Bin Laden's Bookshelf, https://www.dni.gov/files/documents/ubl/english /Letter%20dtd%2013%20Oct%202010.pdf.

184 *Each house . . . al Qaeda officials:* FBI 302 interview with Sulaiman Abu Ghaith.

184 *"escaped in the mountains of Tora Bora":* "Debate Transcript: The First Bush-Kerry Presidential Debate" (Commission on Presidential Debates, September 30, 2004), https://www.debates.org/voter-education/debate-transcripts/sep tember-30-2004-debate-transcript/.

185 *"absolute garbage":* "Vice President and Mrs. Cheney's Remarks and Q&A in Carroll, Ohio" (George W. Bush White House Archives, October 19, 2004), https://georgewbush-whitehouse.archives.gov/news/releases/2004/10/text /20041020-2.html.

185 *a videotape that aired on October 29, 2004:* "10/29/04: Osama Bin Laden Video Message," ABC News, October 29, 2004, https://abcnews.go.com/Archives /video/oct-29-2004-osama-bin-laden-video-message-11700438; "Full Transcript of bin Ladin's Speech," Al Jazeera, November 1, 2004, archived at https:// web.archive.org/web/20081116092323/http://english.aljazeera.net/archive /2004/11/200849163336457223.html.

185 *"when George Bush had the opportunity":* Jill Zuckman and Mark Silva, "Bush, Kerry Defiant After Threat," *Chicago Tribune,* October 30, 2004, https://www .chicagotribune.com/news/ct-xpm-2004-10-30-0410300189-story.html.

187 *"My opponent tonight":* "Bush Rips Kerry's 'Shameful' Attacks," AFP, October 30, 2004.

187 *ranked as a top concern:* Jeffrey M. Jones, "Terrorism, Economy Rank as Top Election Issues," Gallup News, October 27, 2004, https://news.gallup.com/poll /13798/terrorism-economy-rank-top-election-issues.aspx.

187 *Bush significantly outpolled Kerry:* Ibid.

187 *"This has the feel"*: Robert Draper, *Dead Certain: The Presidency of George W. Bush* (Free Press, 2007), 263.

187 *"I can hear you!"*: "George W. Bush's Bullhorn Speech Still Echoes, 'I Can Hear You! The Rest of the World Hears You,'" Fox 35 Orlando, September 11, 2019, https://www.youtube.com/watch?v=zi2SNFnfMjk.

187 *Bush's favorability ratings went*: David W. Moore, "Bush Job Approval Highest in Gallup History," Gallup News, September 24, 2001, https://news.gallup.com/poll/4924/bush-job-approval-highest-gallup-history.aspx; Stephen Schlesinger, "Bush's Low Ratings Reflect Pre-9/11 Views," *Observer*, April 24, 2006, https://observer.com/2006/04/bushs-low-ratings-reflect-pre911-views/.

188 *increased sevenfold*: Peter Bergen and Paul Cruickshank, "The Iraq Effect: War Has Increased Terrorism Sevenfold Worldwide," *Mother Jones*, March 1, 2007, https://www.motherjones.com/politics/2007/03/iraq-101-iraq-effect-war-iraq-and-its-impact-war-terrorism-pg-1/.

188 *pulled from her job ... "mutually hostile"*: Author's interview with Gina Bennett via FaceTime, February 13, 2021.

188 *CIA report*: "Iraq and al-Qa'ida: Interpreting a Murky Relationship," CIA, June 21, 2002.

188 *already reviewed the material ... come up empty*: Author's interview with Daniel Coleman, Princeton, New Jersey, December 19, 2009.

188 *reviewed eighty thousand pages*: Author's interview with Michael Scheuer, Washington, DC, December 29, 2010.

188 *Mary Galligan led*: Author's interview with Mary Galligan via Zoom, September 23, 2020.

188 *three-hundred-page timeline*: "9/11 Chronology Part 01 of 02" (FBI, November 14, 2003), https://vault.fbi.gov/9-11%20Commission%20Report/9-11-chronology-part-01-of-02/view; "9/11 Chronology Part 02 of 02" (FBI, November 14, 2003), https://vault.fbi.gov/9-11%20Commission%20Report/9-11-chronology-part-02-of-02.

188 *Galligan met with Paul Wolfowitz*: Author's interview with Mary Galligan via Zoom, September 23, 2020.

188 *Wolfowitz was pushing the theory*: Peter Bergen, "Armchair Provocateur," *Washington Monthly*, December 1, 2003, https://washingtonmonthly.com/2003/12/01/armchair-provocateur/.

188 *"was the geographic base"*: "Transcript for Sept. 14: EXCLUSIVE: Vice President Dick Cheney, in His First Sunday Interview in Six Months, Discusses the War in Iraq," NBC News, September 14, 2003, https://www.nbcnews.com/id/wbna3080244.

188 *seven out of ten Americans believed*: Dana Milbank and Claudia Deane, "Hussein

Link to 9/11 Lingers in Many Minds," *Washington Post*, September 6, 2003, https://www.washingtonpost.com/archive/politics/2003/09/06/hussein-link -to-911-lingers-in-many-minds/7cd31079-21d1-42cf-8651-b67e93350fde/.

188 *"authority, direction and control"*: George Tenet and Bill Harlow, *At the Center of the Storm: My Years at the CIA* (New York: HarperCollins, 2007), 357. For a detailed account of the Bush administration's campaign to link Saddam Hussein and al-Qaeda, see Peter Bergen, "Building the Case for War with Iraq," in *The Longest War: The Enduring Conflict Between America and al-Qaeda* (New York: Free Press, 2011), 131–52.

188 *Powell spoke at the U.N.*: "'A Policy of Evasion and Deception': Transcript of U.S. Secretary of State Colin Powell's Speech to the United Nations on Iraq," *Washington Post*, February 5, 2003, https://www.washingtonpost.com/wp-srv /nation/transcripts/powelltext_020503.html.

189 *tortured in an Egyptian*: Bergen, *The Longest War*, 146–47; "Committee Study of the Central Intelligence Agency's Detention and Interrogation Program" (Senate Select Committee on Intelligence, December 13, 2012), 141fn857, https:// fas.org/irp/congress/2014_rpt/ssci-rdi.pdf.

189 *"Iraq came along"*: Tenet and Harlow, *At the Center of the Storm*, 435, 438. Two other participants in the meeting: interviews with the author.

189 *insurgency in Iraq*: Robert L. Grenier, *88 Days to Kandahar: A CIA Diary* (New York: Simon & Schuster, 2016), 368.

189 *In early 2004 . . . a lengthy letter*: "Zarqawi Letter: February 2004 Coalition Provisional Authority English Translation of Terrorist Musab al Zarqawi Letter Obtained by United States Government in Iraq" (U.S. Department of State, February 2004), https://2001-2009.state.gov/p/nea/rls/31694.htm; "Letter May Detail Iraqi Insurgency's Concerns," CNN, February 10, 2014, https://www.cnn .com/2004/WORLD/meast/02/10/sprj.nirq.zarqawi/.

190 *"By God, O sheikh"*: Abu Musab al-Zarqawi, "Zarqawi's Pledge of Allegiance to Al-Qaeda: From Mu'asker al-Battar, Issue 21," December 15, 2004, Al Qaeda Statements Index, https://scholarship.tricolib.brynmawr.edu/bitstream/handle /10066/4757/ZAR20041017P.pdf?sequence=3&isAllowed=y.

190 *bin Laden responded*: "Osama Bin Laden to the Iraqi People," December 30, 2004, Al Qaeda Statements Index, https://scholarship.tricolib.brynmawr.edu /bitstream/handle/10066/4802/OBL20041227P.pdf?sequence=3&isAllowed=y.

190 *"Among the things"*: Ayman al-Zawahiri, "Zawahiri's Letter to Zarqawi" (Combating Terrorism Center, July 9, 2005), https://ctc.usma.edu/harmony-program /zawahiris-letter-to-zarqawi-original-language-2/.

190 *On November 9, 2005*: Hassan M. Fattah and Michael Slackman, "3 Hotels Bombed in Jordan; At Least 57 Die," *New York Times*, November 10, 2005,

https://www.nytimes.com/2005/11/10/world/middleeast/3-hotels-bombed-in
-jordan-at-least-57-die.html.

190 *scolded Zarqawi:* 'Atiyah 'Abd al-Rahman, "Atiyah's Letter to Zarqawi," December 12, 2005, Combating Terrorism Center, https://ctc.usma.edu/harmony-program/atiyahs-letter-to-zarqawi-original-language-2/.

191 *More suicide attacks were conducted:* Assaf Moghadam, *The Globalization of Martyrdom: Al Qaeda, Salafi Jihad, and the Diffusion of Suicide Attacks* (Baltimore: Johns Hopkins University Press, 2009), 251.

191 *from around the Muslim world:* In 2008 the U.S. military assessed that al-Qaeda in Iraq's foreign recruits were responsible for up to 90 percent of the suicide attacks in Iraq. (Jim Michaels, "Foreign Fighters Leaving Iraq, Military Says," *USA Today*, March 21, 2008, http://www.usatoday.com/news/world/iraq/2008-03-20-fighters_N.htm.) Similarly, Mohammed Hafez, the author of the authoritative study *Suicide Bombers in Iraq* (Washington, DC: United States Institute of Peace Press, 2007), found that of the 139 "known" suicide bombers in Iraq, fifty-three were from Saudi Arabia and only eighteen were Iraqi, while the rest came from other Arab countries and even Europe. (Author correspondence with Mohammed Hafez, December 14, 2009.) The Israeli academic Reuven Paz also found that of the 154 fighters identified as "martyrs" in Iraq on jihadist forums, 61 percent were Saudi, and the rest were from a variety of other Middle Eastern countries (quoted in Susan Glasser, "'Martyrs' in Iraq Mostly Saudis," *Washington Post*, May 15, 2005). The most extensive suicide campaign in modern history was conducted in Iraq largely by foreigners animated by the deeply held religious belief that they had to liberate a Muslim land from the "infidel" occupiers.

FOURTEEN: THE HUNT

192 *"He may be dead":* "Senate Hearing 107-801: Conduct of Operation Enduring Freedom," United States Senate Committee on Armed Services, July 31, 2002, https://www.govinfo.gov/content/pkg/CHRG-107shrg83471/html/CHRG-107shrg83471.htm.

192 *never amounted:* Author's interview with Michael Scheuer, Washington, DC, October 1, 2011.

192 *Al-Qaeda released a statement:* "New Purported bin Laden Tape Raises Fear of New Attacks," CNN, September 11, 2003, https://www.cnn.com/2003/WORLD/meast/09/10/binladen.tape/.

192 *CIA analysts thought:* Author's interview with senior counterterrorism official, Washington, DC, December 2011.

192 *this forensic work:* Author's interview with Michael Scheuer, Washington, DC, October 1, 2011.

193 *Captured the Iraqi dictator*: William H. McRaven, *Sea Stories: My Life in Special Operations* (New York: Grand Central Publishing, 2019), 200–13.

193 *"Isn't that who you really want?"*: Elisabeth Bumiller, *Condoleezza Rice: An American Life: A Biography* (New York: Random House, 2007), 229.

193 *Nada Bakos*: Nada Bakos and Davin Coburn, *The Targeter: My Life in the CIA, Hunting Terrorists and Challenging the White House* (New York: Little, Brown and Company, 2019), 209.

193 *In January 2004 . . . two CDs of documents*: Stanley A. McChrystal, *My Share of the Task: A Memoir* (New York: Portfolio/Penguin, 2013), 120.

193 *Carrying the letter*: "Bin Laden calls on Zarqawi to attack U.S." *New York Times*, March 1, 2005.

193 *a notebook full of names*: Bakos and Coburn, *The Targeter*, 218–19.

193 *"sang like a tweetie bird"*: "Committee Study of the Central Intelligence Agency's Detention and Interrogation Program" (Senate Select Committee on Intelligence, December 13, 2012), 130fn767, 371fn2090, https://fas.org/irp/congress /2014_rpt/ssci-rdi.pdf.

193 *Ghul told the Kurds . . . "closest assistant"*: Bakos and Coburn, *The Targeter*, 295–96; "Committee Study of the Central Intelligence Agency's Detention and Interrogation Program," 130–31, 384, 396.

194 *BLACK . . . fifty-nine hours straight*: "Committee Study of the Central Intelligence Agency's Detention and Interrogation Program," 132.

194 *Bakos has publicly said*: "CFR and HBO Screening of the New HBO Documentary *Manhunt*," Council on Foreign Relations, April 16, 2013, https://www.cfr .org/event/cfr-and-hbo-screening-new-hbo-documentary-manhunt.

194 *Interrogated for forty-eight days*: Bergen, *The Longest War*, 107.

194 *Ghul's information dovetailed*: "JTF-GTMO Detainee Assessment: Maad Al-Qahtani" (Department of Defense, October 30, 2008), 9, WikiLeaks Guantánamo Files, https://wikileaks.org/gitmo/prisoner/63.html.

194 *"torture"*: Qahtani handwritten, undated statement, 2033A in GTMO, pp. 2–5, https://www.washingtonpost.com/wp-dyn/content/article/2009/01/13/AR2009 011303372.html; Bob Woodward, "Guantanamo Detainee Was Tortured, Says Official Overseeing Military Trials," *Washington Post*, January 14, 2009.

194 *northern Poland*: Adam Goldman, "The Hidden History of the CIA's Prison in Poland," *Washington Post*, January 23, 2014, https://www.washingtonpost.com/world /national-security/the-hidden-history-of-the-cias-prison-in-poland/2014/01/23 /b77f6ea2-7c6f-11e3-95c6-0a7aa80874bc_story.html?tid=a_inl_manual.

194 *waterboarded 183 times*: "Committee Study of the Central Intelligence Agency's Detention and Interrogation Program," 85–93, 493–94.

195 *"primarily low-level members"*: Ibid., 387, fn 2190,399.

195 *subjected to CIA coercive interrogations*: Ibid., 146–48.

195 *didn't know the Kuwaiti:* Ibid., 388fn2190.

195 *"Abd al-Khaliq Jan":* "JTF-GTMO Detainee Assessment: Abu al-Libi" (Department of Defense, September 10, 2008), 5, WikiLeaks Guantánamo Files, https://wikileaks.org/gitmo/prisoner/10017.html.

195 *a made-up name:* "Committee Study of the Central Intelligence Agency's Detention and Interrogation Program," 398fn2244.

195 *a strongly held belief:* See, for instance, Jose A. Rodriguez Jr. and Bill Harlow, *Hard Measures: How Aggressive CIA Actions After 9/11 Saved American Lives* (New York: Threshold, 2013), 110–11.

195 *up to 150:* McChrystal, *My Share of the Task,* 171.

195 *one hundred Iraqi civilians:* Bergen, *The Longest War,* 160.

195 *went out on raids:* James Kitfield, *Twilight Warriors: The Soldiers, Spies, and Special Agents Who Are Revolutionizing the American Way of War* (New York: Basic Books, 2016); Peter L. Bergen, *Manhunt: The Ten-Year Search for bin Laden from 9/11 to Abbottabad* (New York: Crown, 2012), 166.

196 *to three hundred a month: American War Generals* produced by Peter Bergen, Simon Epstein, and Tresha Mabile (Washington, DC: National Geographic, 2014), interview with Stanley McChrystal by author.

196 *the bin Laden unit at the CIA was closed:* Author's interview with Philip Mudd, Washington, DC, June 2, 2011.

196 *flipped the question:* "Tina," CIA targeting analyst, *Revealed: The Hunt for Bin Laden,* exhibition at the 9/11 Museum, New York City.

196 *two dozen people at most:* "Tina," CIA targeting analyst, *The Hunt for Bin Laden* (New York: History Channel, May 2, 2021).

196 *"Probable Identification of":* "Minority Views of Vice Chairman Chambliss Joined by Senators Burr, Risch, Coats, Rubio, and Coburn: Committee Study of the Central Intelligence Agency's Detention and Interrogation Program" (Senate Select Committee on Intelligence, December 5, 2014), 73fn390, https://www.feinstein.senate.gov/public/_cache/files/d/b/db587bbf-f52d-47eb-b90c-a60ff3f92484/B184465DC41EB54A90B740167B0BA173.sscistudy3.pdf; CIA Intelligence Assessment, "Al-Qa'ida Watch. Probable Identification of Suspected Bin Ladin Facilitator Abu Ahmad al-Kuwaiti," November 23, 2007, 2.

197 *"last resort":* "Committee Study of the Central Intelligence Agency's Detention and Interrogation Program," 400.

197 *Mohammad Khan:* Author's interview with local resident, Abbottabad, Pakistan, July 21, 2011.

197 *Bara Khan, and Tariq Khan:* Author's interview with Pakistani military intelligence official, February 2012, Islamabad, Pakistan.

197 *Habib al-Rahman:* "Committee Study of the Central Intelligence Agency's Detention and Interrogation Program," 382, fn2155, 399.

197 *Ibrahim Saeed Ahmed Adb al-Hamid*: Leon Panetta and Jim Newton, *Worthy Fights: A Memoir of Leadership in War and Peace* (New York: Penguin, 2015), 293.

197 *"So where are we, Mike"*: "Interview with Michael V. Hayden," George W. Bush Oral History Project (Charlottesville, VA: UVA Miller Center, November 20, 2012), 41, http://web1.millercenter.org/poh/transcripts/hayden_michael_2012 _1120.pdf.

197 *In December 2008, Hayden briefed*: Michael Vincent Hayden, *Playing to the Edge: American Intelligence in the Age of Terror* (New York: Penguin, 2016), 329.

197 *"I direct you"*: Ken Dilanian, "In Finding Osama bin Laden, CIA Soars from Distress to Success," *Los Angeles Times*, May 8, 2011, https://www.latimes.com /nation/la-xpm-2011-may-08-la-na-bin-laden-cia-20110508-story.html; Mike Allen, "How bin Laden Mission Went Down," *Politico*, May 2, 2011, https:// www.politico.com/story/2011/05/how-bin-laden-mission-went-down-054093.

198 *a slide that indicated*: Panetta and Newton, *Worthy Fights*, 291.

198 *"voice cuts"*: "Committee Study of the Central Intelligence Agency's Detention and Interrogation Program," 381fn2147.

198 *Kuwaiti practiced rigorous operational security*: Author's interview with Pakistani intelligence official, Islamabad, Pakistan, July 2011.

198 *In August 2010 . . . drive to the east*: Author's interview with senior U.S. intelligence official, 2011.

198 *distinctive white jeep*: Author's interview with Pakistani intelligence official, Islamabad, Pakistan, 2012; CIA photograph of the jeep on display at the 9/11 Museum, New York City, https://www.911memorial.org/learn/resources/digital -exhibitions/digital-exhibition-revealed-hunt-bin-laden/president-considers.

198 *"Tell me about this fortress"*: Panetta and Newton, *Worthy Fights*, 294.

198 *"Who puts a privacy wall"*: Michael J. Morell and Bill Harlow, *The Great War of Our Time: The CIA's Fight Against Terrorism—From al Qa'ida to ISIS* (New York: Twelve, 2015), 147.

199 *garbage pickup*: Letitia Long, former Director, National Geospatial-Intelligence Agency, *The Hunt for Bin Laden*, History Channel, May 2, 2021.

199 *had kept guard dogs*: Author's interview with John Brennan, Washington, DC, December 6, 2011.

199 *the CIA set up a safe house*: Author's interview with U.S. counterterrorism officials.

199 *"AC1"*: Bergen, *Manhunt*, 167.

199 *third family*: Author's Interview with U.S. official.

199 *desirable top two floors*: Morell and Harlow, *The Great War of Our Time*, 152.

200 *On December 14 Panetta and Morell*: Author's interview with Leon Panetta, February 16, 2012, The Pentagon, Virginia.

200 *"We call him 'the Pacer' "*: Barack Obama, *A Promised Land* (New York: Crown, 2020), 679.

200 *Obama asked:* John O. Brennan, *Undaunted: My Fight Against America's Enemies, at Home and Abroad* (New York: Celadon, 2020), 229.

200 *"If your guys had"*: Author's interview with William McRaven, Austin, Texas, December 19, 2019.

200 *"Mickey Mouse meeting"*: Morell and Harlow, *The Great War of Our Time*, 150.

201 *six weeks:* Catherine Herridge, "Inside the Model Shop Behind bin Laden Raid," CBS News, September 13, 2020, https://www.msn.com/en-us/news/world/inside-the-model-shop-behind-bin-laden-raid/vi-BB18ZEs.

201 *of only McRaven:* Author's interview with William McRaven, Austin, Texas, December 19, 2019.

201 *Pakistani air defenses:* Author's interviews with U.S. intelligence officials, 2011.

201 *neighborhood irrigated by small streams:* This description is based on author's visit to the Abbottabad compound on February 12, 2012, and an earlier visit to Abbottabad on July 20, 2011.

201 *National Geospatial-Intelligence Agency concluded:* Author's interviews with U.S. intelligence officials, 2011.

201 *the 509th Bomb Wing:* Panetta and Newton, *Worthy Fights*, 311.

202 *ruled out:* Ibid., 312.

202 *"We're going to take two helicopters"*: Author's interview with William McRaven, Austin, Texas, December 19, 2019.

202 *more complicated:* Obama, *A Promised Land*, 682.

202 *need to refuel:* McRaven, *Sea Stories*, 301.

202 *McRaven, a six-foot:* Author's interview with William McRaven, Austin, Texas, December 19, 2019; Peter Bergen, "The Man Who Hunted bin Laden, Saddam and the Pirates," CNN, August 31, 2014, https://www.cnn.com/2014/08/30/opinion/bergen-mcraven-special-forces-influence/index.html.

202 *"Will this plan work?"*: Author's interview with William McRaven, Austin, Texas, December 19, 2019.

203 *"About three weeks"*: McRaven, *Sea Stories*, 294–95.

203 *a small experimental drone:* Morell and Harlow, *The Great War of Our Time*, 159.

203 *a dozen pounds:* Author discussions with participants in the White House meetings that discussed the drone option, Washington, DC, 2011.

203 *This would ensure:* Obama, *A Promised Land*, 683.

203 *small kids:* McRaven, *Sea Stories*, 293.

203 *April 7:* Panetta and Newton, *Worthy Fights*, 313.

203 *two dozen of his best men:* Will Chesney and Joe Layden, *No Ordinary Dog: My*

Partner from the SEAL Teams to the Bin Laden Raid (New York: St. Martin's Griffin, 2021), 211.

203 *"if he is naked"*: Mark Owen and Kevin Maurer, *No Easy Day: The Firsthand Account of the Mission That Killed Osama Bin Laden: The Autobiography of a Navy SEAL* (New York: Dutton, 2016), 177.

204 *Neptune Spear*: Author's interview with William McRaven, Austin, Texas, December 19, 2019.

204 *in Nevada*: Author's interviews with U.S. intelligence officials.

204 *Half an hour was also the window*: William H. McRaven, *Spec Ops: Case Studies in Special Operations Warfare: Theory and Practice* (New York: Presidio Press, 1996), 20.

204 *Shakil Afridi*: Iqbal et al., "Abbottabad Commission Report," 2013, 108–16.

204 *"Maya"*: Panetta and Newton, *Worthy Fights*, 315.

204 *60 percent*: Morell and Harlow, *The Great War of Our Time*, 161.

204 *"Why do people have different probabilities?"*: Bergen, *Manhunt*, 133.

205 *"Red Team"*: McRaven, *Sea Stories*, 305.

205 *didn't change the opinions*: Author's interviews with James Clapper, Virginia, April 25, 2016; John Brennan, Washington, DC, December 6, 2011.

205 *"Let's move on"*: Obama, *A Promised Land*, 685.

205 *worried that a leak*: Morell and Harlow, *The Great War of Our Time*, 162.

206 *bin Laden had already agreed with his bodyguards*: Bin Laden letter, Task ID 7278, undated.

206 *Gates returned to a point*: Ben Rhodes, *The World as It Is: A Memoir of the Obama White House* (New York: Random House, 2018), 128.

206 *a searing memory*: Robert M. Gates, *Duty: Memoirs of a Secretary at War* (New York: Alfred A. Knopf, 2014), 541.

206 *"Fuck the White House Correspondents' Dinner"*: Jonathan Allen and Amie Parnes, *HRC: State Secrets and the Rebirth of Hillary Clinton* (New York: Crown, 2014), 235. Clinton confirms the anecdote in Hillary Rodham Clinton, *Hard Choices* (New York: Simon & Schuster, 2014), 182.

206 *"If we don't do it"*: Panetta and Newton, *Worthy Fights*, 319.

207 *broke up at 7 p.m.*: Author's interview with Tony Blinken, Washington, DC, November 3, 2011.

207 *risks were too great*: Author's interviews with multiple participants in the White House meeting, Washington, DC, 2011.

207 *in the Treaty Room*: Mark Bowden, *The Finish: The Killing of Osama bin Laden* (New York: Atlantic Monthly Press, 2012), 207.

207 *considerable faith . . . slipped away*: Author's interview with President Barack Obama, White House Situation Room, April 28, 2016.

207 *one hundred feet*: Black Hawk pilot interview, *The Hunt for Bin Laden*, History Channel, May 2, 2021.

208 *if they waited until Sunday*: Peter Bergen, *"We Got Him": President Obama, Bin Laden, and the Future of the War on Terror*, CNN, May 2, 2016; Author's interview with William McRaven, Austin, Texas, December 19, 2019.

208 *"Bill, what do you think?"*: McRaven, *Sea Stories*, 305.

FIFTEEN: A LION IN WINTER

209 *"The best martyrs"*: Nelly Lahoud, *The Jihadis' Path to Self-Destruction* (London: Hurst, 2010), 192.

209 *$50,000 for them*: "Pakistani Owner of bin Laden's Hideaway Aided Him," Associated Press, May 4, 2011, https://cnycentral.com/news/political/pakistani-owner-of-bin-ladens-hideaway-aided-him.

209 *third floor*: Author's interview with the architect of the compound, Junaid Younis, Abbottabad, Pakistan, July 20, 2011.

209 *Bin Laden and two of his wives*: Justice Javed Iqbal et al., "Abbottabad Commission Report," 2013, 157, https://www.documentcloud.org/documents/724833-aljazeera-bin-laden-dossier.html.Abbottabad.

209 *had another two children*: Ibid. 45.

210 *Living on the compound*: Card carried by the Navy SEALs during the May 2, 2011, raid that identified likely residents of the compound. Christina Lamb, "Revealed: The SEALs' Secret Guide to Bin Laden Lair," *Sunday Times*, May 22, 2011, www.thesundaytimes.co.uk/sto/news/world_news/Asia /article631893.ece.

210 *"the uncle who lived upstairs"*: Iqbal et al., "Abbottabad Commission Report," 47.

210 *lied to their families*: Ibid., 49.

210 *books and reports*: Bin Laden's Bookshelf, Office of the Director of National Intelligence, accessed February 3, 2020, https://www.dni.gov/index.php/features /bin-laden-s-bookshelf?start=1.

210 *audio version*: Author's interview with Nelly Lahoud, New York City, February 10, 2020.

211 *a gas heater and an improvised exhaust system*: Author's visit to the Abbottabad compound, February 12, 2012.

211 *Here bin Laden watched*: Video released by U.S. government. May 7, 2011.

211 *third floor in the main house*: Author's visit to the Abbottabad compound, February 12, 2012.

211 *"which our hearts have been"*: Osama bin Laden, "Letter to Um Abd-Al-Rahmand Dtd 26 April 2011" (Office of the Director of National Intelligence), Bin Laden's Bookshelf, https://www.dni.gov/files/documents/ubl/english/Letter%20to%20Um%20Abd-al-Rahman%20dtd%202026%2020April%202011.pdf.

212 *"My heart is sad"*: Hamzah Bin Laden, "Letter from Hamzah to Father Dtd July 2009," (Office of the Director of National Intelligence), Bin Laden's Bookshelf, https://www.dni.gov/files/documents/ubl/english/Letter%20from%20Hamzah %20to%20father%20dtd%20July%202009.pdf.

212 *prison-like conditions . . . a violent protest*: Nelly Lahoud, "Al-Qaeda and Iran: The Bond That Does Not Exist," Lobe Log, July 5, 2019, https://lobelog.com/al -qaeda-and-iran-the-bond-that-does-not-exist/.

212 *kidnapped an Iranian*: "Iran Says Rescues Diplomat Kidnapped in Pakistan," Reuters, March 30, 2010, https://www.reuters.com/article/us-pakistan-iran/iran -says-rescues-diplomat-kidnapped-in-Pakistan-idUKTRE62T10T20100330.

212 *prisoner swap*: Author's interview with Pakistani intelligence officials, July 2011.

212 *"our security situation"*: Osama bin Laden, "Letter to Sons 'Uthman and Mu-hammad," (Office of he Director of National Intelligence, dated 02 Safar 1432 (January 7, 2011) Bin Laden's Bookshelf, https://www.dni.gov/files/documents /ubl2017/english/Letter%20to%20sons%20Uthman%20and%20Muhammad .pdf.

212 *"a tiny chip"*: Ibid.

212 *valid, official ID card:* "Letter from UBL to 'Atiyatullah Al-Libi 4" (Combating Terrorism Center, n.d.), SOCOM-2012-0000019, https://www.ctc.usma.edu/wp -content/uploads/2013/10/Letter-from-UBL-to-Atiyatullah-Al-Libi-4-Transla tion.pdf.

213 *air strike on June 7, 2006:* Nada Bakos and Davin Coburn, *The Targeter: My Life in the CIA, Hunting Terrorists and Challenging the White House* (New York: Little, Brown and Company, 2019), 275–80.

213 *"clear instructions to focus"*: Mark Oliver, "Praise for Zarqawi in New 'Bin Laden' Broadcast," *Guardian*, June 30, 2006, https://www.theguardian.com/world/2006 /jun/30/alqaida.terrorism.

213 *did not mourn:* "Letter from Adam Gadahn," late January 2011 (Combating Ter-rorism Center, I), SOCOM-2012-0000004, https://ctc.usma.edu/harmony-pro gram/letter-from-adam-gadahn-original-language-2/.

213 *Mohamed Khan:* Shiv Malik, "My Brother the Bomber," *Prospect*, June 30, 2007, https://www.prospectmagazine.co.uk/magazine/my-brother-the-bomber-mo hammad-sidique-khan.

213 *training from al-Qaeda:* Luke Harding and Rosie Cowan, "Pakistan Militants Linked to London Attacks," *Guardian*, July 18, 2005, https://www.theguardian .com/uk/2005/jul/19/july7.pakistan.

214 *the last time*: For a full account of this episode, see Peter Bergen, *United States of Jihad: Who Are America's Homegrown Terrorists and How Do We Stop Them?* (New York: Crown, 2016), 113–23.

214 *Shahzad:* For a full account of this episode, see ibid., 123–30.

215 *al-Qaeda in the Islamic Maghreb:* "ABDELMALEK DROUKDEL," United Nations Security Council, April 17, 2018, https://www.un.org/securitycouncil/sanctions /1267/aq_sanctions_list/summaries/individual/abdelmalek-droukdel.

215 *a detailed report:* "Addendum to the report of the Islamic Maghreb," August 2007, https://www.dni.gov/files/documents/ubl2017/english/Addendum%20to %20the%20report%20of%20the%20Islamic%20Maghreb.pdf.

215 *aggressive campaign:* See, generally, Thomas Hegghammer, *Jihad in Saudi Arabia: Violence and Pan-Islamism Since 1979* (Cambridge, UK: Cambridge University Press, 2010).

215 *significant amounts of territory:* Joana Cook, " 'Their Fate Is Tied to Ours': Assessing AQAP Governance and Implications for Security in Yemen" (London: ICSR, October 2019), https://icsr.info/wp-content/uploads/2019/10/ICSR-Re port-Their-Fate-is-Tied-to-Ours-Assessing-AQAP-Governance-and-Implica tions-for-Security-in-Yemen.pdf.

215 *Awlaki:* On Awlaki and his role in inspiring and organizing plots, see Alexander Meleagrou-Hitchens, *Incitement: Anwar al-Awlaki's Western Jihad* (Cambridge, MA: Harvard University Press, 2020); Bergen, *United States of Jihad*; Scott Shane, *Objective Troy: A Terrorist, a President, and the Rise of the Drone* (New York: Tim Duggan Books, 2015).

215 *bin Laden admired the audacity:* Bin Laden to Uthman, 2010 Task ID 7531.

215 *more than two dozen:* Simon Jeffrey, "Timeline: The al-Qaida Tapes," *Guardian,* June 30, 2006, https://www.theguardian.com/alqaida/page/0,12643,839823,00 .html.

216 *makeshift TV studio . . . retake:* This description is based on videos recovered in the Abbottabad compound seen by the author.

216 *called for action against Spain:* "Al-Jazeera Airs Purported bin Laden Audio-tapes," CNN, October 19, 2003, http://edition.cnn.com/2003/WORLD/meast /10/18/binladen.tape/index.html; Elizabeth Nash, "Madrid Bombers 'Were In-spired by Bin Laden Address,' " *Independent,* November 7, 2006, https://www .independent.co.uk/news/world/europe/madrid-bombers-were-inspired-by -bin-laden-address-423266.html.

216 *In December 2004:* Simon Henderson, "Al-Qaeda Attack on Abqaiq: The Vulnerability of Saudi Oil," PolicyWatch 1082 (Washington Institute for Near East Policy, February 28, 2006), https://www.washingtoninstitute.org/policy-analysis /al-qaeda-attack-abqaiq-vulnerability-saudi-oil.

216 *"My brother Osama":* Quoted in Turki al-Saheil, "Reaction to Salman al-Awdah's bin Laden letter," *Asharq al-Awsat,* September 18, 2007.

216 *always especially sensitive:* Just weeks after the 9/11 attacks bin Laden asked a Saudi visitor in Afghanistan, "What is the stand of the mosques?." "Bin Laden Discusses Attacks on Tape," *Washington Post,* December 12, 2001. https://www

.washingtonpost.com/wp-srv/nation/specials/attacked/transcripts/binladen
text_121301.html.

216 *a public apology:* "Bin Laden Issues Iraq Message," Al Jazeera, October 23, 2007,
https://www.aljazeera.com/news/2007/10/23/bin-laden-issues-iraq-message;
Fawaz Gerges, *The Rise and Fall of al-Qaeda* (New York: Oxford University
Press, 2011), 110, 120.

217 *Noman Benotman:* Peter Bergen and Paul Cruickshank, "The Unraveling," *New
Republic,* June 11, 2008, https://newrepublic.com/article/64819/the-unraveling.

217 *advised members:* Osama bin Laden, "Letter from Usama Bin Laden to Mukhtar
Abu al-Zubayr" (Combating Terrorism Center, August 7, 2010), SOCOM-
2012-0000005, https://ctc.usma.edu/harmony-program/letter-from-usama-bin
-laden-to-mukhtar-abu-al-zubayr-original-language-2/.

217 *better off if it did not declare:* Ibid.

217 *long letter outlining his plans:* Osama bin Laden, "Letter from UBL to Atiyatullah Al-Libi 4" (Combating Terrorism Center, n.d.), SOCOM-2012-0000019,
https://ctc.usma.edu/harmony-program/letter-from-ubl-to-atiyatullah-al-libi
-4-original-language-2/.

217 *"the serious matter of shedding Muslim":* Letter from bin Laden to Mullah Omar,
November 5, 2010. Osama bin Laden, "Letter to Our Honored Commander
of the Faithful" (Office of the Director of National Intelligence, November 5,
2010), Bin Laden's Bookshelf, https://www.dni.gov/files/documents/ubl2016
/english/Letter%20to%20our%20Honored%20Commander%20of%20the%20
Faithful.pdf.

217 *"regain the trust":* "Letter from UBL to 'Atiyatullah Al-Libi 4" (Combating Terrorism Center, n.d.), SOCOM-2012-0000019, https://ctc.usma.edu/harmony
-program/letter-from-ubl-to-atiyatullah-al-libi-4-original-language-2./

218 *"We need a public statement":* Bin Laden Family Journal, https://www.cia.gov
/library/abbottabad-compound/76/76155EE3B4398AC4814FA69DF33057B3
_Journal.original.pdf, 123.

218 *did not, however, extend:* Bin Laden, "Letter from UBL to Atiyatullah Al-Libi 4," 6.

218 *"big effective operations":* Bin Laden to Sheikh Yunis, n.d. *United States v. Abid
Naseer,* government exhibit 433 10-CR-019 (S-4) (RJD).

SIXTEEN: OPERATION NEPTUNE SPEAR

219 *"People sleep peacefully":* Richard Grenier, "Perils of Passive Sex," *Washington
Times,* April 6, 1993.

219 *"a simple plan":* Author's interview with William McRaven, Austin, Texas, December 19, 2019.

219 *"each one of you has dreamed":* William H. McRaven, *Sea Stories: My Life in
Special Operations* (New York: Grand Central Publishing, 2019), 314.

219 *Some of the SEALs believed:* SEAL #5, SEAL Team Six, *The Hunt for Bin Laden*, (New York: History Channel, May 2, 2021); Phil Bronstein, "The Man Who Killed Osama bin Laden . . . Is Screwed," *Esquire*, February 11, 2013, https://www.esquire.com/news-politics/a26351/man-who-shot-osama-bin-laden-0313/.

219 *2 p.m.:* Barack Obama, *A Promised Land* (New York: Crown, 2020), 693.

219 *twenty-three SEALs:* Ibid.

219 *a Pakistani-American:* McRaven, *Sea Stories*, 302.

220 *Cairo:* Will Chesney and Joe Layden, *No Ordinary Dog: My Partner from the SEAL Teams to the Bin Laden Raid* (New York: St. Martin's Griffin, 2021), 209–36.

220 *In the command center McRaven:* Author's interview with William McRaven, Austin, Texas, December 19, 2019.

220 *three Chinook CH-47:* Ibid.

220 *The one-and-half-hour:* Aviation planner and Chinook pilot #1, Operation Neptune Spear, *The Hunt for Bin Laden*, History Channel, May 2, 2021.

221 *McRaven thought:* Author's interview with William McRaven, Austin, Texas, December 19, 2019.

221 *Vice President Joe Biden drifted:* Author's interview with Michael Leiter, Washington, DC, August 29, 2011.

221 *"I need to watch this":* Obama, *A Promised Land*, 694.

221 *moonless night:* Author's interview with William McRaven, Austin, Texas, April 25, 2016.

221 *Two minutes out:* Aviation planner and Chinook pilot #1, Operation Neptune Spear, *The Hunt for Bin Laden*, History Channel, May 2, 2021.

222 *"That doesn't look too good":* Author's interview with William McRaven, Austin, Texas, December 19, 2019.

222 *The SEALS had rehearsed:* Lead planner, Operation Neptune Spear, and captain, U.S. Navy SEAL, *The Hunt for Bin Laden*, History Channel, May 2, 2021.

222 *third of an acre:* Author's observations on visit to the Abbottabad compound, February 12, 2012.

222 *"the animal pen":* Author's interview with William McRaven, Austin, Texas, April 25, 2016.

222 *fingered his rosary beads:* Peter L. Bergen, *Manhunt: The Ten-Year Search for bin Laden from 9/11 to Abbottabad* (New York: Crown, 2012), 220.

222 *"We will now be amending":* Author's interview with senior Obama administration official, Washington, DC, 2011.

222 *bin Laden called to his son:* Justice Javed Iqbal et al., "Abbottabad Commission Report," 2013, 157, https://www.documentcloud.org/documents/724833-aljazeera-bin-laden-dossier.html.Abbottabad, 35.

223 *"American helicopters have arrived":* Ibid.

223 *Matt Bissonnette, placed:* Mark Owen, an alias for Matt Bissonnette, interview

with Scott Pelley, *CBS 60 Minutes*, produced by Henry Schuster, CBS, September 24, 2012, https://www.cbsnews.com/news/seals-first-hand-account-of-bin -laden-killing/; SEAL #4, *The Hunt for Bin Laden*, History Channel, May 2, 2021.

223 *could no longer see:* Author's interview with senior Obama administration official, Washington, DC, 2011.

223 *A massive iron metal gate:* Author's observations at the Abbottabad compound, February 12, 2012.

223 *"Who has a metal door":* SEAL #4, *The Hunt for Bin Laden*, History Channel, May 2, 2021.

223 *had told the SEALS:* Mark Owen, *60 Minutes.*

224 *"Khalid, Khalid":* Ibid.

224 *an AK-47 nearby:* Mark Owen and Kevin Maurer, *No Easy Day: The Firsthand Account of the Mission That Killed Osama Bin Laden: The Autobiography of a SEAL* (New York: Dutton, 2016), 233.

224 *knew immediately it was bin Laden:* Author's interview with William McRaven, Austin, Texas, April 25, 2016.

224 *This shot may have wounded:* Peter Bergen, "Did Robert O'Neill Really Kill Bin Laden?," CNN, November 4, 2014, https://www.cnn.com/2014/11/04/opinion /bergen-seals-bin-laden-killing.

224 *the bed:* Iqbal et al., "Abbottabad Commission Report," 35.

224 *If they had:* Owen and Maurer, *No Easy Day*, 236.

224 *Just for Men:* Author's observations of Just for Men bottle in bin Laden's bedroom at the Abbottabad compound, February, 12, 2012; Owen and Maurer, *No Easy Day*, 247.

225 *two oldest daughters confirmed:* Iqbal et al., "Abbottabad Commission Report," 36.

225 *"He hadn't even prepared a defense":* Owen and Maurer, *No Easy Day*, 248–49.

225 *"Geronimo":* Author's interview with William McRaven, Austin, Texas, April 25, 2016.

225 *photographs . . . blood and saliva:* Owen and Maurer, *No Easy Day*, 244.

225 *"Sir, the SEALs are requesting":* McRaven, *Sea Stories*, 321.

225 *"grab as much as you can":* Author's interview with William McRaven, Austin, Texas, December 19, 2019.

226 *meticulously organized:* Owen and Maurer, *No Easy Day*, 247.

226 *ten hard drives, five computers:* "Details of Raid on bin Laden Compound Unfold," CNN, May 4, 2011, http://edition.cnn.com/2011/WORLD/asiapcf/05/03 /bin.laden.dead/.

226 *"I'm getting a little nervous":* Author's interview with William McRaven, Austin, Texas, April 25, 2016.

226 *"This is a government business"*: Government interpreter, *The Hunt for Bin Laden*, History Channel, May 2, 2021.

226 *On the feed*: McRaven, *Sea Stories*, 323.

226 *forty-eight minutes*: Author's interview with William McRaven, Austin, Texas, April 25, 2016.

226 *"Break away!"* Chinook helicopter pilot #1, *The Hunt for Bin Laden*, History Channel, May 2, 2021.

226 *1:06 a.m.*: Iqbal et al., "Abbottabad Commission Report," 54.

227 *150-foot mushroom cloud*: Chinook helicopter pilot #1 and SEAL #4, *The Hunt for Bin Laden*, History Channel, May 2, 2021.

227 *The Chinook came in*: SEAL #3 and Chinook helicopter pilot #1, *The Hunt for Bin Laden*, History Channel, May 2, 2021.

227 *nineteen long minutes*: Author's interview with William McRaven, Austin, Texas, April 25, 2016.

227 *2:26 a.m.*: Iqbal et al., "Abbottabad Commission Report," 54.

227 *"Welcome to Afghanistan"*: SEAL #3, *The Hunt for Bin Laden*, History Channel, May 2, 2021.

227 *"Bill, can you confirm"*: Peter Bergen, *"We Got Him": President Obama, Bin Laden, and the Future of the War on Terror*, CNN, May 2, 2016; Author's interview with William McRaven, Austin, Texas, April 25, 2016.

228 *"out of a fucking job"*: Robert O'Neill, *The Operator* (New York: Scribner, 2017), 317.

228 *"Mr. President, I can't be certain"*: Peter Bergen, *"We Got Him": President Obama, Bin Laden, and the Future of the War on Terror*, CNN, May 2, 2016; Author's interview with William McRaven in Austin, Texas, April 25, 2016.

228 *Obama called Pakistan's*: Author's official interview with senior Obama administration official, Washington, DC, 2011.

228 *Admiral Mullen called*: Ibid.

229 *Science & Technology*: Author's interview with senior Obama administration official in the Situation Room during the bin Laden operation, Washington, DC, 2011.

229 *"We're gonna hold"*: Ibid.

229 *Obama called George W. Bush*: Obama, *A Promised Land*, 696.

229 *called Bill Clinton*: Ibid.

229 *She hadn't*: Hillary Rodham Clinton, *Hard Choices* (New York: Simon & Schuster, 2014), 182.

229 *could hear chants*: Obama, *A Promised Land*, 697.

229 *"Tonight, I can report"*: Barack Obama, "Remarks by the President on Osama Bin Laden" (White House, Office of the Press Secretary, May 2, 2011), https://

obamawhitehouse.archives.gov/the-press-office/2011/05/02/remarks-presi
dent-osama-bin-laden.

SEVENTEEN: AFTER BIN LADEN

230 *"Osama has woken up"*: Author's interview with Khalid Khawaja, Islamabad, Pakistan, July 2004.

230 *"Beware that, when fighting monsters"*: Friedrich Wilhelm Nietzsche, *Beyond and Good and Evil* (Macmillan, 1907), 97.

230 *"We have seen their kind before"*: "State of the Union: Text of George W. Bush's Speech," *Guardian*, September 21, 2001, https://www.theguardian.com/world /2001/sep/21/september11.usa13.

230 *definitively al-Qaeda's leader:* Craig Whitlock and Barton Gellman, "To Hunt Osama bin Laden, Satellites Watched over Abbottabad, Pakistan, and Navy SEALs," *Washington Post*, August 29, 2013, https://www.washingtonpost.com /world/national-security/to-hunt-osama-bin-laden-satellites-watched-over -abbottabad-pakistan-and-navy-seals/2013/08/29/8d32c1d6-10d5-11e3-b4cb -fd7ce041d814_story.html.

230 *USS* Carl Vinson: "A V-22 Carried bin Laden to the Vinson," Military.Com, August 2, 2011, https://www.military.com/defensetech/2011/08/02/a-v-22-car ried-bin-laden-to-the-vinson; Nicholas Schmidle, "Getting bin Laden," *New Yorker*, August 1, 2011, https://www.newyorker.com/magazine/2011/08/08 /getting-bin-laden.

231 *only a few hundred:* In Quetta, Pakistan, a Taliban stronghold, for instance. "Hundreds Join Quetta Rally to Honour bin Laden," *Express Tribune*, May 3, 2011, https://tribune.com.pk/story/161126/hundreds-join-first-rally-to-honour -bin-laden."

231 *"The fact of the matter"*: "Obama: Bin Laden Will Not Walk This Earth Again," *60 Minutes*, CBS, May 5, 2011, https://www.cbsnews.com/news/obama-bin-laden -will-not-walk-this-earth-again/.

231 *On May 6:* Elizabeth A. Harris, "Al Qaeda Confirms Bin Laden's Death," *New York Times*, May 6, 2011, https://www.nytimes.com/2011/05/07/world/asia/07 qaeda.html.

231 *"I think that the winds"*: Jason Burke, "Osama bin Laden Praises Arab Spring in Posthumously Released Tape," *Guardian*, May 19, 2011, https://www.theguardian .com/world/2011/may/19/osama-bin-laden-tape-posthumous-arab-spring.

231 *Gina Bennett worked night shifts:* Author's interview with Gina Bennett via Facetime, February 20, 2021.

232 *three terabytes:* "(U) What Does the Death of Usama bin Laden Mean?" (NSA SIDtoday, May 17, 2011), *Intercept*, https://theintercept.com/docu ment/2015/05/18/sidtoday-interview-ubl/. For a sense of just how mammoth

a task analyzing a terabyte of data is, see Kelly Brown, "A Terabyte of Storage Space: How Much Is Too Much?," *The Information Umbrella* (blog), July 8, 2014, https://aimblog.uoregon.edu/2014/07/08/a-terabyte-of-storage-space-how -much-is-too-much/.

232 *artificial intelligence tools:* David Vergun, "AI Gleaned Information About Emerging Threats, Future Plots From bin Laden Raid," Defense News, U.S. Department of Defense, https://www.defense.gov/Explore/News/Article/Article /2234142/ai-gleaned-information-about-emerging-threats-future-plots-from -bin-laden-raid/.

232 *Every available Arabic linguist:* Author's interview with James Clapper, Virginia, April 25, 2016.

232 *CIA officials thought:* Michael J. Morell and Bill Harlow, *The Great War of Our Time: The CIA's Fight Against Terrorism—From al Qa'ida to ISIS* (New York: Twelve, 2015), 176.

232 *A CIA drone strike killed Atiyah:* Mark Mazzetti, "C.I.A. Drone Is Said to Kill Al Qaeda's No. 2," *New York Times*, August 27, 2011, https://www.nytimes.com /2011/08/28/world/asia/28qaeda.html.

232 *bin Laden nixed the appointment:* Letter from Usama Bin Laden to Atiyatullah Al-Libi (Combating Terrorism Center, August 27 26, 2010), SOCOM-2012-0000003.

232 *moment wasn't ripe:* Letter addressed to "Abu Basir," undated, (Nasir al-Wuhayshi, leader of al-Qaeda in the Arabian Peninsula) SOCOM-2012-0000016.

232 *not to publicly identify itself:* Osama bin Laden, "Letter from Usama Bin Laden to Mukhtar Abu Al-Zubayr" (Combating Terrorism Center, August 7, 2010), SOCOM-2012-0000005, https://ctc.usma.edu/harmony-program/letter-from -usama-bin-laden-tomukhtar-abu-al-zubayr-original-language-2/.

232 *to hijack oil tankers:* Damien Pearse, "Al-Qaida Hoped to Blow Up Oil Tankers, Bin Laden Documents Reveal," *Guardian*, May 20, 2011, https://www.theguard ian.com/world/2011/may/20/al-qaida-oil-tankers-bin-laden.

233 *"He's moving all these army groups":* Author's interview with James Clapper, Virginia, April 25, 2016.

233 *There was also porn:* "Bin Laden's Hard Drive," National Geographic Channel, September 11, 2020), https://www.nationalgeographic.com/tv/movies-and-specials /bin-ladens-hard-drive.

233 *believed that a 9/11:* Foreign Policy and the Center for American Progress, "The Terrorism Index," August 18, 2008, http://www.americanprogress.org/issues /2008/08/pdf/time_series.pdf, p.[[tk]]

233 *104 Americans:* New America's "Terrorism in America" database, accessed April 22, 2021, https://www.newamerica.org/in-depth/terrorism-in-america/what- threat-united-states-today/.

234 *thousands of Special Operations raids:* U.S. Special Operations carried out more than two thousand raids in Afghanistan and Iraq in 2010 alone, according to Admiral Eric Olson, the commander of U.S. Special Operations Command, speaking with Martha Raddatz of ABC News at the Aspen Security Forum, July 29, 2011, Aspen, Colorado. "Counterterrorism, Navy SEALs, and Osama Bin Laden," C-SPAN, https://www.c-span.org/video/?300735-1/counterterror ism-navy-seals-osama-bin-laden.

234 *fortified America's home defenses:* This section draws upon Peter Bergen, "Time to Declare Victory: Al Qaeda Is Defeated," CNN, June 27, 2012, https://security .blogs.cnn.com/2012/06/27/time-to-declare-victory-al-qaeda-is-defeated -opinion/.

234 *"no-fly" list:* Steve Kroft, "Unlikely Terrorists on No Fly List," *60 Minutes*, CBS, October 5, 2006, https://www.cbsnews.com/news/unlikely-terrorists-on-no-fly -list/.

234 *In 2001 there were . . . tripled:* Robert S. Mueller III, "Statement Before the Senate Committee on Homeland Security and Governmental Affairs" (FBI, September 13, 2011), https://archives.fbi.gov/archives/news/testimony/ten-years-after -9-11-are-we-safer.

234 *The U.S. intelligence budget:* Steven Aftergood, "Intelligence Budget Data," Federation of American Scientists, accessed April 13, 2021, https://fas.org/irp/budget/.

234 *"For those who say":* Bill O'Reilly. "The World Without Bin Laden; The Death of a Terrorist; Inside the Navy Seal Operation," *The O'Reilly Factor* (Fox News, May 3, 2011).

234 *Michael Mukasey, wrote:* Michael B. Mukasey, "The Waterboarding Trail to bin Laden," *Wall Street Journal*, May 6, 2011, https://www.wsj.com/articles/SB1000 1424052748703859304576305023876506348.

235 *"based on first hand accounts":* Steve Coll, "'Disturbing' & 'Misleading,'" *New York Review*, February 7, 2013, https://www.nybooks.com/articles/2013/02/07 /disturbing-misleading-zero-dark-thirty/; *Zero Dark Thirty*, directed by Kathryn Bigelow, 2012.

235 *The first half-hour:* This paragraph draws on Peter Bergen, "'Zero Dark Thirty': Did Torture Really Net bin Laden?," CNN, December 11, 2012, https://www.cnn .com/2012/12/10/opinion/bergen-zero-dark-thirty.

236 *For instance:* This is all laid out in detail in Ali H. Soufan and Daniel Freedman's 2011 book, *The Black Banners (Declassified): How Torture Derailed the War on Terror After 9/11* (New York: W. W. Norton).

236 *Quite the reverse:* Letter to bin Laden from Atiyah, June 19, 2010, *USA v. Abid Naseer*, Easter District of New York, government exhibit 421, 10-CR-019 (S-4) (RJD) https://kronosadvisory.com/Abid.Naseer.Trial_Abottabad.Documents_Exhib its.403.404.405.420thru433.pdf.

237 *Apologists for the Taliban*: A book-length apologia for the Taliban that seeks to downplay their alliance with al-Qaeda is Alex Strick van Linschoten and Felix Kuehn, *An Enemy We Created: The Myth of the Taliban–Al Qaeda Merger in Afghanistan* (Oxford: Oxford University Press, 2012).

237 *Taliban leader, Mullah Omar:* Osama bin Laden, "Letter to Our Honored Commander of the Faithful" (Office of the Director of National Intelligence, November 5, 2010), Bin Laden's Bookshelf, https://www.dni.gov/files/documents/ubl 2016/english/Letter%20to%20our%20Honored%20Commander%20of%20 the%20Faithful.pdf.

237 *Tayeb Agha:* Letter to bin Laden from Atiyah, early April 2011, *USA v. Abid Naseer*, Eastern District of New York, government exhibit 431 10-CR-019 (S-4) (RJD), 5. (This letter was misdated by a U.S. government translator as May 5, 2011, which was four days after bin Laden's death. But it is correctly dated in the Islamic calendar as "Early Jamadi al-Awwal 1432," which corresponds to early April 2011.) There is also another letter to bin Laden from Atiyah, June 19, 2010, that also mentions "a letter from Tayeb Agha, the friend of Amir Al Mo'mineen [Mullah Omar]," *USA v. Abid Naseer*, government exhibit 421, 10-CR-019 (S-4) (RJD).

237 *Taliban negotiator:* Mujib Mashal, "Taliban Envoy Breaks Silence to Urge Group to Reshape Itself and Consider Peace," *New York Times*, October 31, 2016, https://www.nytimes.com/2016/11/01/world/asia/afghanistan-taliban-peace-talks.html.

237 *"a large amount":* Letter to bin Laden from Atiyah, early April 2011, *USA v. Abid Naseer*, government exhibit 431, 10-CR-019 (S-4) (RJD).

237 *$5 million:* Letter to bin Laden from Atiya, June 19, 2010, *USA v. Abid Naseer*, government exhibit 421, 10-CR-019 (S-4); Matthew Rosenberg, "C.I.A. Cash Ended Up in Coffers of Al Qaeda," *New York Times*, March 14, 2015, https://www.nytimes.com/2015/03/15/world/asia/cia-funds-found-their-way-into-al -qaeda-coffers.html.

237 *Bagram Air Base:* Letter to bin Laden from Atiyah, June 19, 2010, *USA v. Abid Naseer*, government exhibit 421, 10-CR-019 (S-4) (RJD); Dexter Filkins, "Taliban Suicide Strikes Fail at U.S. Air Base Near Afghan Capital," *New York Times*, May 19, 2010, https://www.nytimes.com/2010/05/20/world/asia/20bagram.html.

237 *large sum:* Letter to bin Laden from Atiyah, early April 2011, *USA v. Abid Naseer*, government exhibit 431, 10-CR-019 (S-4) (RJD).

238 *what is acceptable and unacceptable:* Letter to the leader of the Pakistani Taliban, Hakimullah Mahsud, December 3, 2010, SOCOM-2012-0000007, https://ctc.usma .edu/harmony-program/letter-to-hakimullah-mahsud-original-language-2/.

238 *"would honor their historical ties":* Dian Triansyah Djani, "Eleventh Report of the Analytical Support and Sanctions Monitoring Team, May 19, 2020, http:// cdn.cnn.com/cnn/2020/images/06/01/n2011060.pdf.

238 *relationship between bin Laden and Iran:* For an authoritative discussion of this

issue, see Nelly Lahoud, "Al-Qaïda's Contested Relationship with Iran" (New America, September 2018), https://d1y8sb8igg2f8e.cloudfront.net/documents/Al-Qaidas_Contested_Relationship_with_Iran_2018-08-20_151707.pdf.

238 *when bin Laden received a memo:* Abu Abd al-Rahman Anas al-Subay'i, "Letter Dtd 13 Oct 2010" (Office of the Director of National Intelligence, October 13, 2010), Bin Laden's Bookshelf, https://www.dni.gov/files/documents/ubl/english/Letter%20dtd%2013%20Oct%202010.pdf.

239 *122 in total:* Peter Bergen, David Sterman, and Melissa Salyk-Virk, "America's Counterterrorism Wars: The Drone War in Pakistan," New America, August 13, 2020, https://www.newamerica.org/international-security/reports/americas-counterterrorism-wars/the-drone-war-in-pakistan/.

239 *two dozen:* Peter L. Bergen and Daniel Rothenberg, eds., *Drone Wars: Transforming Conflict, Law, and Policy* (New York: Cambridge University Press, 2015), 32–33.

239 *false statements:* Mark Landler and Helene Cooper, "New U.S. Account Says Bin Laden Was Unarmed During Raid," *New York Times*, May 3, 2011, https://www.nytimes.com/2011/05/04/world/asia/04raid.html.

239 *ten-thousand-word:* Seymour M. Hersh, "The Killing of Osama bin Laden," *London Review of Books*, May 21, 2015, https://www.lrb.co.uk/the-paper/v37/n10/seymour-m.-hersh/the-killing-of-osama-bin-laden.

239 *Hersh asserted:* For more on Hersh's bin Laden story, see Peter Bergen, "Was There a Cover-Up in bin Laden Killing?," CNN, May 20, 2015, https://www.cnn.com/2015/05/11/opinions/bergen-bin-laden-story-a-lie.

240 *all shot and killed:* Justice Javed Iqbal et al., "Aljazeera Bin Laden Dossier," 2013, https://www.documentcloud.org/documents/724833-aljazeera-bin-laden-dossier.html.Abbottabad, 3.

241 *sprayed with bullet holes:* Author's visit to the Abbottabad compound, Pakistan, February 12, 2012.

241 *Raymond Davis:* Mark Mazzetti, "How a Single Spy Helped Turn Pakistan Against the United States," *New York Times*, April 9, 2013, https://www.nytimes.com/2013/04/14/magazine/raymond-davis-pakistan.html.

241 *"What Do We Really Know":* Jonathan Mahler, "What Do We Really Know About Osama bin Laden's Death?," *New York Times Magazine*, October 15, 2015, https://www.nytimes.com/2015/10/18/magazine/what-do-we-really-know-about-osama-bin-ladens-death.html. For more on how the *New York Times Magazine* covered Hersh's bin Laden story, see Peter Bergen, "The New York Times Triples Down on Bizarre bin Laden Story," CNN, October 24, 2015, https://www.cnn.com/2015/10/24/opinions/bergen-times-triples-down-bin-laden-story, which this section draws upon.

241 *were furious:* Margaret Sullivan, "Baquet on Bin Laden Story: Critics 'Reading

It Wrong,'" *Opinion Pages* (blog), *New York Times*, October 21, 2015, https://publiceditor.blogs.nytimes.com/2015/10/21/baquet-on-bin-laden-story-critics-reading-it-wrong.

241 *I climbed the stairs:* Author's visit to the Abbottabad compound, February 12, 2012. This section draws on "A visit to Osama bin Laden's lair," Peter Bergen, CNN.com, May 3, 2012 https://www.cnn.com/2012/05/03/opinion/bergen-bin-laden-lair.

242 *Two of his sons:* Zeke Miller, "White House Says bin Laden Son Killed in US Operation," Associated Press, September 14, 2019, https://apnews.com/article/107bb5b28f1c434b91c154e765a80350; Mary Louise Kelly, "Bin Laden Son Reported Killed In Pakistan," NPR, July 22, 2009, https://www.npr.org/templates/story/story.php?storyid=106903109.

242 *his daughter Khadija:* Cathy Scott-Clark and Adrian Levy, *The Exile*, 287

242 *Amal was wounded:* Iqbal et al., "Aljazeera Bin Laden Dossier," 35.

242 *Pakistani custody for a year:* Mark Memmott, "Almost One Year After Bin Laden's Death, Pakistan Deports His Family," *The Two-Way* (blog), NPR, April 27, 2012, https://www.npr.org/sections/thetwo-way/2012/04/27/151510644/almost-one-year-after-bin-ladens-death-pakistan-deports-his-family.

242 *Authorization for Use of Military Force:* Gregory D. Johnsen, "60 Words and a War Without End: The Untold Story of the Most Dangerous Sentence in U.S. History," *BuzzFeed*, January 16, 2014, https://www.buzzfeed.com/gregorydjohnsen/60-words-and-a-war-without-end-the-untold-story-of-the-most.

243 *various types of U.S. military operations:* George Petras, Karina Zaiets, and Veronica Bravo, "Exclusive: US Counterterrorism Operations Touched 85 Countries in the Last 3 Years Alone," *USA Today*, February 26, 2021, https://www.usatoday.com/in-depth/news/2021/02/25/post-9-11-us-military-efforts-touched-85-nations-last-3-years/6564981002/.

243 *Hundreds of thousands of combatants and civilians:* Neta C. Crawford, "Human Cost of the Post-9/11 Wars: Lethality and the Need for Transparency" (Costs of War Project, November 2018).

243 *clever plot to embroil:* "Bin Laden: Goal Is to Bankrupt U.S.," CNN, November 1, 2004, https://www.cnn.com/2004/WORLD/meast/11/01/binladen.tape/.

243 *views of him dropped significantly:* "Obama More Popular Abroad Than at Home, Global Image of U.S. Continues to Benefit: Chapter 7. Attitudes Toward Extremism Among Muslim Publics," Pew Research Center, June 17, 2010, https://www.pewresearch.org/global/2010/06/17/chapter-7-attitudes-toward-extremism-among-muslim-publics/.

244 *only 5 percent:* "Muslim Publics Share Concerns About Extremist Groups," Pew Research Center, September 10, 2013, https://www.pewresearch.org/global/2013/09/10/muslim-publics-share-concerns-about-extremist-groups/.

244 *More than ten thousand*: Michael Schmidt, "Suicide Bombs in Iraq Have Killed 12,000 Civilians, Study Says," *New York Times*, September 2, 2011.

244 *"Tactics without strategy"*: "Strategy without tactics is the slowest route to victory. Tactics without strategy is the noise before the defeat," philosiblog, 4 May 2011, https://philosiblog.com/2011/05/04/strategy-without-tactics-is/.

244 *More than thirty people*: "Who Were Germany's Red Army Faction Militants?," BBC, January 19, 2016, https://www.bbc.com/news/world-europe-3535 4812#:~:text=The%20BBC%20News%20website%20looks,on%20a%20street %20in%20Cologne.

244 *few campaigns of terrorism have succeeded*: Only 6 percent of terrorist groups succeed in achieving their political objectives according to one study. Audrey Kurth Cronin, *Ending Terrorism: Lessons for Defeating al-Qaeda*, Adelphi Paper 394 (Abingdon, Oxon: Routledge for the International Institute for Strategic Studies, 2008), 37.

244 *Zionist terrorism*: Bruce Hoffman, in *Anonymous Soldiers: The Struggle for Israel, 1917–1947* (New York: Alfred A. Knopf, 2015), authoritatively recounts this history.

245 *few other terrorist groups*: Lawrence Wright, *The Terror Years: From al-Qaeda to the Islamic State* (New York: Little, Brown, 2016), 343.

245 *In 2002 there was*: Seth G. Jones, *In the Graveyard of Empires: America's War in Afghanistan* (New York: W. W. Norton, 2009), 263.

245 *burned themselves out*: David C. Rapoport, "The Four Waves of Rebel Terror and September 11," *Anthropoetics* 8, no.1 (Spring/Summer 2002): 14.

246 *size of Portugal*: Ben Wederman and Lauren Said-Moorhouse, "ISIS Has Lost Its Final Stronghold in Syria, the Syrian Democratic Forces Says," CNN, March 23, 2019, https://www.cnn.com/2019/03/23/middleeast/isis-caliphate-end-intl/in dex.html. This paragraph draws upon Peter Bergen, *United States of Jihad: Who Are America's Homegrown Terrorists and How Do We Stop Them?* (New York: Crown, 2016), 251.

246 *more than six weeks*: "Ayman al-Zawahiri Appointed as al-Qaeda Leader," BBC, June 16, 2011, https://www.bbc.com/news/world-middle-east-13788594.

246 *al-Qaeda and ISIS, which formally split*: Liz Sly, "Al-Qaeda Disavows Any Ties with Radical Islamist ISIS Group in Syria, Iraq," *Washington Post*, February 3, 2014, https://www.washingtonpost.com/world/middle_east/al-qaeda-disavows-any -ties-with-radical-islamist-isis-group-in-syria-iraq/2014/02/03/2c9afc3a-8cef -11e3-98ab-fe5228217bd1_story.html.

246 *officially rejected*: Daniel Byman and Jennifer R. Williams, *ISIS vs. Al Qaeda: Jihadism's Global Civil War*, February 24, 2015, Brookings, February 24, 2015.

246 *his rightful heir*: Aaron Zelin, "The War between ISIS and al-Qaeda for Suprem-

acy of the Global Jihadist Movement." The Washington Institute for Near East Policy, June 2014.

247 *Trump often claimed . . . was false:* "Trump 'Wrong' in Claiming US Arabs Cheered 9/11 Attacks," BBC, November 23, 2015, https://www.bbc.com/news /world-us-canada-34902748; Glenn Kessler, "Trump's Outrageous Claim That 'Thousands' of New Jersey Muslims Celebrated the 9/11 Attacks," *Washington Post,* November 22, 2015, https://www.washingtonpost.com/news/fact-checker /wp/2015/11/22/donald-trumps-outrageous-claim-that-thousands-of-new-jer sey-muslims-celebrated-the-911-attacks/.

247 *Trump's presidential campaign also took place:* For a fuller discussion of how Trump used terrorism as an issue to win votes, see Peter Bergen, *Trump and His Generals: The Cost of Chaos* (New York: Penguin, 2019), 19–42.

247 *just over half of Americans:* "Terrorism," Gallup News, accessed April 14, 2021, https://news.gallup.com/poll/4909/terrorism-united-states.aspx.

247 *"total and complete shutdown":* "Trump Urges 'Shutdown' on Muslims Entering US," Associated Press, YouTube, November 16, 2016, https://www.youtube .com/watch?v=Dz2wn3iPDNg.

247 *Polling in early 2016:* Murtaza Hussain, "Majority of Americans Now Support Donald Trump's Proposed Muslim Ban, Poll Shows," *Intercept,* March 30, 2016, https://theintercept.com/2016/03/30/majority-of-americans-now-support -trumps-proposed-muslim-ban-poll-shows/; "Super Tuesday Republican Exit Poll Analysis," ABC News, March 1, 2016, https://abcnews.go.com/Politics/live -super-tuesday-republican-exit-poll-analysis/story?id=37309493.

247 *Other polls showed:* "Top Voting Issues in 2016 Election," Pew Research Center, July 7, 2016, https://www.people-press.org/2016/07/07/4-top-voting-issues-in -2016-election/.

248 *"Have you ever heard of the Baader-Meinhof":* Author's interview with Gina Bennett via FaceTime, February 20, 2021.

SELECTED BIBLIOGRAPHY

DOCUMENTS BY MEMBERS OF AL-QAEDA AND OTHER JIHADISTS

Abd al-Hakim, Umar [Abu Mus'ab al-Suri] "Afghanistan, the Taliban, and the Battle for Islam Today," Combating Terrorism Center, October 1998. AFGP-2002-602383. https://ctc.usma.edu/harmony-program/afghanistan-the-taliban-and-the-battle-for-islam-today-original-language-2/.

Abd al-Rahman, Atiyah. "Atiyah's Letter to Zarqawi." Combating Terrorism Center, December 12, 2005. https://ctc.usma.edu/harmony-program/atiyahs-letter-to-zarqawi-original-language-2/.

Adl, Saif al-'. "A Report from Saif Al-Adl." Combating Terrorism Center, January 17, 1994. Harmony Documents. AFGP-2002-600114. https://ctc.usma.edu/harmony-program/a-report-from-saif-al-adl-original-language-2/.

"Al-Qa'ida Bylaws." Combating Terrorism Center, n.d. Harmony Documents. AFGP-2002-600048. https://www.ctc.usma.edu/harmony-program/al-qaida-bylaws-2/.

Anas al-Subay'i, Abu Abd al-Rahman. "Letter Dtd 13 Oct 2010." Office of the Director of National Intelligence, October 13, 2010. Bin Laden's Bookshelf. https://www.dni.gov/files/documents/ubl/english/Letter%20dtd%2013%20Oct%202010.pdf.

Bin Laden, Hamzah. "Letter from Hamzah to Father Dated July 2009." July 2009. Bin Laden's Bookshelf. https://www.dni.gov/index.php/features/bin-laden-s-bookshelf?start=3.

Bin Laden, Osama. "In Regard to the Money That Is in Sudan—Bin Laden's Will." Office of the Director of National Intelligence, n.d. Bin Laden's Bookshelf. https://www.dni.gov/index.php/features/bin-laden-s-bookshelf?start=2.

———. "Letter from UBL to Atiyatullah Al-Libi 2." Combating Terrorism Center, April 26, 2011. SOCOM-2012-0000010. https://ctc.usma.edu/harmony-program/letter-from-ubl-to-atiyatullah-al-libi-2-original-language-2/.

———. "Letter from UBL to Atiyatullah Al-Libi 3." Combating Terrorism Center,

October 21, 2010. SOCOM-2012-0000015. https://ctc.usma.edu/harmony-pro
gram/letter-from-ubl-to-atiyatullah-al-libi-3-original-language-2/.

———. "Letter from UBL to Atiyatullah Al-Libi 4." Combating Terrorism Center, n.d.
SOCOM-2012-0000019. https://ctc.usma.edu/harmony-program/letter-from-ubl
-to-atiyatullah-al-libi-4-original-language-2/.

———. "Letter from Usama Bin Laden to Mukhtar Abu Al-Zubayr," Combating Terrorism Center, August 7, 2010. https://ctc.usma.edu/harmony-program/letter
-from-usama-bin-laden-to-mukhtar-abu-al-zubayr-original-language-2/.

———. "Letter to Mullah Muhammed Umar from Bin Laden." Combating Terrorism
Center, n.d. AFGP-2002-600321. https://ctc.usma.edu/harmony-program/letter
-to-mullah-muhammed-umar-from-bin-laden-original-language-2/.

———. "Letter to Our Honored Commander of the Faithful." Office of the Director of
National Intelligence, November 5, 2010. Bin Laden's Bookshelf. https://www.dni
.gov/index.php/features/bin-laden-s-bookshelf?start=2.

———. "Letter to Sons Uthman and Muhammad," Safar 1432. Bin Laden's Bookshelf.
https://www.dni.gov/index.php/features/bin-laden-s-bookshelf?start=1.

———. "Letter to Um Abd-Al-Rahman dtd 26 April 2011," April 26, 2011. Bin Laden's
Bookshelf. https://www.dni.gov/index.php/features/bin-laden-s-bookshelf?start
=3. Cultural Commission of the Islamic Emirate. Biography of Mullah Omar.
April 6, 2015.

"Excerpts from the Videotape Transcript." Washington Post, December 14, 2001.
https://www.washingtonpost.com/archive/politics/2001/12/14/excerpts-from
-the-videotape-transcript/16340450-2507-44e9-a0c8-76c91ccaa9b4/.

"An Exclusive Interview with Adam Yahiye Gadahn." *Resurgence* (Al-Qaeda's English-
language magazine), Summer 2015.

Jihad magazine. All Issues. Peshawar, Pakistan. 1984–1993. Author's collection.

"Letter from Adam Gadahn." Combating Terrorism Center, January 2011. SOCOM-
2012-0000004. https://ctc.usma.edu/harmony-program/letter-from-adam-gad
ahn-original-language-2/.

"Letter from Hafiz Sultan." Combating Terrorism Center, March 28, 2007. SOCOM-
2012-0000011. https://ctc.usma.edu/harmony-program/letter-from-hafiz-sultan
-original-language-2/.

"Letter to bin Laden from Atiyah." Government Exhibit 431. *USA v. Abid Naseer*,
United States District Court Eastern District of New York, early April 2011.

"Letter to Nasir al-Wuhayshi." Combating Terrorism Center, n.d. SOCOM-2012-
0000016. https://ctc.usma.edu/harmony-program/letter-to-nasir-al-wuhayshi-ori
ginal-language-2/.

"Letter to the leader of the Pakistani Taliban, Hakimullah Mahsud." Combating Terrorism Center, December 3, 2010. SOCOM-2012-0000007. https://ctc.usma.edu
/harmony-program/letter-to-hakimullah-mahsud-original-language-2/

"Letter to Wife." Office of the Director of National Intelligence, n.d. Bin Laden's Bookshelf. https://www.dni.gov/files/documents/ubl2016/english/Letter%20to%20 wife.pdf.

"Report on the External Operations." Office of the Director of National Intelligence, n.d. Bin Laden's Bookshelf. https://www.dni.gov/index.php/features/bin-laden-s -bookshelf?start=3.

"The September 11th Attacks or the Impossible Becoming Possible," n.d. AQ-SHPD-D-001-285. Conflict Records Center. https://conflictrecords.wordpress.com/col lections/aqam/.

"A Suggestion to Change the Name of Al-Qa'ida." Combating Terrorism Center, n.d. SOCOM-2012-0000009. https://ctc.usma.edu/harmony-program/a-suggestion -to-change-the-name-of-al-qaida-original-language-2/.

"Various Admin Documents and Questions." Combating Terrorism Center, n.d. AFGP-2002-801138. https://ctc.usma.edu/harmony-program/various-admin-doc uments-and-questions-original-language-2/.

"Zarqawi Letter: February 2004 Coalition Provisional Authority English Translation of Terrorist Musab al Zarqawi Letter Obtained by United States Government in Iraq." U.S. Department of State, February 2004. https://2001-2009.state.gov/p/nea /rls/31694.htm.

Zawahiri, Ayman al-. "Zawahiri's Letter to Zarqawi." Combating Terrorism Center, July 9, 2005. https://ctc.usma.edu/harmony-program/zawahiris-letter-to-zarqawi -original-language-2/.

STATEMENTS BY OSAMA BIN LADEN AND LEADERS OF OTHER JIHADIST GROUPS

"10/29/04: Osama Bin Laden Video Message." ABC News, October 29, 2004. https:// abcnews.go.com/Archives/video/oct-29-2004-osama-bin-laden-video-message -11700438.

"The Al-Qa'idah Group Had Nothing to Do with the 11 September Attacks." Khila-fah.com, September 28, 2001. Archived at https://web.archive.org/web/200201110 73623/http://www.khilafah.com/1421/category.php?DocumentID=2392.

Bin Laden, Osama. "Communiqué 5, Important Telegram to Our Brothers in the Armed Forces." Khartoum, Sudan. September 19, 1994,

———. "Communiqué 11." Khartoum, Sudan. December 29, 1994.

———. "Communiqué#17." Khartoum, Sudan. August 3, 1995.

———. "Our Invitation to Give Advice and Reform," Al Qaeda Statements Index, April 12, 1994. https://scholarship.tricolib.brynmawr.edu/bitstream/handle/10066 /15196/OBL19940912.pdf?sequence=4&isAllowed=y.

"Compilation of Usama bin Laden Statements, 1994-January 2004." FBIS report, January 2004. https://fas.org/irp/world/para/ubl-fbis.pdf

"Dangers and Signs of the Indian Nuclear Explosions." Bin Laden statement. May 14, 1998. Author's Collection.

"Full Transcript of Bin Ladin's Speech." Al Jazeera, November 1, 2004. Archived at: https://web.archive.org/web/20081116092323/http://english.aljazeera.net/archive /2004/11/200849163336457223.html.

"My Testimony to History." Pamphlet published by Supporters of Omar Abdel Rahman in the United States. 1996. Author's collection.

"Osama Bin Laden to the Iraqi People," December 30, 2004. Al-Qaeda Statements Index. Global Terrorism Research Project, Haverford College. https://scholarship .tricolib.brynmawr.edu/bitstream/handle/10066/4802/OBL20041227P.pdf?se quence=3&isAllowed=y.

Rahman, Omar Abdel. "The Fatwa of the Prisoner Sheikh Doctor Abdel Rahman." Author's collection.

"Recorded Message from Osama Bin Laden, October 21, 2001." Associated Press, YouTube, July 21, 2015. https://www.youtube.com/watch?v=IHInbQcyg2Y.

"So, congratulations to the Taliban." Bin Laden statement. May 16, 1998. Author's collection.

Tahreek/Osama documents. Author's collection.

"Text: Bin Laden's Statement." Guardian (translation supplied by the Associated Press), October 7, 2001. https://www.theguardian.com/world/2001/oct/07/afghan istan.terrorism15.

"Transcript of Bin Laden's October Interview." CNN, February 5, 2002. https://edi tion.cnn.com/2002/WORLD/asiapcf/south/02/05/binladen.transcript/.

"Transcript: VOA Interview with Taliban Leader." Washington Post, September 23, 2001. https://www.washingtonpost.com/wp-srv/nation/attack/transcripts/omarin terview092301.htm.

Zarqawi, Abu Musab al-. "Zarqawi's Pledge of Allegiance to al-Qaeda: From Mu'asker al-Battar, Issue 21," December 15, 2004. Al-Qaeda Statements Index. Global Terrorism Research Project, Haverford College. https://scholarship.tricolib.brynmawr .edu/bitstream/handle/10066/4757/ZAR20041017P.pdf?sequence=3&isAl lowed=y.

Zawahiri, Ayman al-. "Days with the Imam," October 19, 2014. Al-Qaeda Statements Index. Global Terrorism Research Project, Haverford College. https://scholarship .tricolib.brynmawr.edu/bitstream/handle/10066/17025/ZAW20141019_2.pdf?se quence=1.

———. "Knights Under the Prophet's Banner, extracts." Al Sharq al Awsat. December 2001.

———. "Zawahiri Calls for Revenge for Slain Libyan Officials, Remembers Tora Bora," July 16, 2014. Al-Qaeda Statements Index. Global Terrorism Research

Project, Haverford College. https://scholarship.tricolib.brynmawr.edu/bitstream /handle/10066/17140/ZAW20140716.pdf?sequence=3

———. "Zawahiri Recalls Siege, Escape from Tora Bora, Advises Jihadi Media to Stop Promoting Discord Between Fighters," August 15, 2015. Al Qaeda-Statements Index. Global Terrorism Research Project, Haverford College. https://scholarship .tricolib.brynmawr.edu/bitstream/handle/10066/17131/ZAW20150815.pdf?se quence=4

U.S. GOVERNMENT DOCUMENTS

"9/11 Chronology Part 01 of 02." FBI, November 14, 2003. https://vault.fbi.gov/9-11 %20Commission%20Report/9-11-chronology-part-01-of-02/view.

"9/11 Chronology Part 02 of 02." FBI, November 14, 2003. https://vault.fbi.gov/9-11 %20Commission%20Report/9-11-chronology-part-02-of-02.

"11 September the Plot and the Plotters." Central Intelligence Agency, Directorate of Intelligence, June 1, 2003. https://www.documentcloud.org/documents/368989 -2003-06-01-11-september-the-plot-and-the.html.

"Afghanistan: Demarche to Taliban on New Bin Laden Threat." U.S. Embassy Islamabad. September 14, 1998.

"Afghanistan: Taliban's Mullah Omar's 8/22 Contact with State Department." Cable. U.S. Department of State, August 23, 1998.

"Amerithrax or Anthrax Investigation." FBI.gov. https://www.fbi.gov/history/famous -cases/amerithrax-or-anthrax-investigation.

"Bin Ladin Determined to Strike in US." Central Intelligence Agency Presidential Daily Brief, August 6, 2001. https://nsarchive2.gwu.edu//NSAEBB/NSAEBB116 /pdb8-6-2001.pdf.

Card carried by the Navy Seals during the May 2, 2011, Abbottabad raid. Copy in Author's collection.

"Committee Study of the Central Intelligence Agency's Detention and Interrogation Program." Senate Select Committee on Intelligence, December 13, 2012. https://fas .org/irp/congress/2014_rpt/ssci-rdi.pdf.

"Conduct of Operation Enduring Freedom." United States Senate Committee on Armed Services, 2002. https://www.govinfo.gov/content/pkg/CHRG-107shrg83471/html /CHRG-107shrg83471.htm.

"Declassified Key Judgments of the National Intelligence Estimate 'Trends in Global Terrorism: Implications for the United States' Dated April 2006." Office of the Director of National Intelligence, April 2006. https://www.dni.gov/files/documents /Newsroom/Press%20Releases/2006%20Press%20Releases/Declassified_NIE _Key_Judgments.pdf.

"Draft: DCI Report: The Rise of UBL and Al-Qa'ida and the Intelligence Community

Response." Central Intelligence Agency, March 19, 2004. https://www.document-cloud.org/documents/368992-2004-03-19-dci-report-the-rise-of-ubl-and-al.html.

[Excised]. "'[Title Excised]' 'Planning for the UBL Rendition Is Going Very Well,' to Michael F. Scheuer, From [Excised] Central Intelligence Agency Email," May 5, 1998. https://www.documentcloud.org/documents/368929-1998-05-05-title-excised-planning-for-the-ubl.html.

"[Excised] Terrorism Targeting Study of U S Embassy, Nairobi, Kenya." Central Intelligence Agency, April 5, 1999. https://www.documentcloud.org/documents/368947-1999-04-05-excised-terrorism-targeting-study-of.html.

"Executive Order 12333—United States Intelligence Activities." Federal Register, National Archives, December 4, 1981. https://www.archives.gov/federal-register/codification/executive-order/12333.html#2.11

"FD-302. Interview of John Philip Walker Lindh," December 9–10, 2001. Federal Bureau of Investigation. Author's collection.

"FD-302. Interview with Sulaiman Abu Ghaith." Federal Bureau of Investigation. Author's collection.

"FD-302. Interview with Abu Jandal." Federal Bureau of Investigation. Author's collection.

"FD-302. Interview with Ramzi Yousef." Federal Bureau of Investigation. February 7, 1995. Author's collection.

Hudson, Rex A. "The Sociology and Psychology of Terrorism: Who Becomes a Terrorist and Why?" Federal Research Division: Library of Congress, September 1999. https://fas.org/irp/threat/frd.html.

"International: Bin Ladin Attacks May Be Imminent [Excised]." Central Intelligence Agency Senior Executive Intelligence Brief, June 23, 2001. https://www.documentcloud.org/documents/369166-2001-06-23-international-bin-ladin-attacks-may.html.

"JTF-GTMO Detainee Assessment: Abu Al-Libi." Department of Defense, September 10, 2008. Wikileaks Guantánamo Files. https://wikileaks.org/gitmo/prisoner/10017.html.

"JTF-GTMO Detainee Assessment: Awal Gul." Department of Defense, February 15, 2008. WikiLeaks Guantánamo Files. https://wikileaks.org/gitmo/pdf/af/us9af-000782dp.pdf.

"JTF-GTMO Detainee Assessment: Ayman Saeed Abdulla Batarfi." Department of Defense, April 29, 2008. WikiLeaks Guantánamo Files. https://wikileaks.org/gitmo/prisoner/627.html.

"JTF-GTMO Detainee Assessment: Maad Al-Qahtani." Department of Defense, October 30, 2008. Wikileaks Guantánamo Files. https://wikileaks.org/gitmo/prisoner/63.html.

"JTF-GTMO Detainee Assessment: Salim Hamed." Department of Defense, September 4, 2008. WikiLeaks Guantánamo Files. https://wikileaks.org/gitmo/pdf/ym/us9ym-000149dp.pdf.

"JTF-GTMO Detainee Assessment: Salman Fouad al Rabai." Department of Defense, May 12, 2008. Wikileaks Guantánamo Files. https://wikileaks.org/gitmo/pdf/ku/us9ku-000551dp.pdf.

Kean, Thomas H., and Lee H. Hamilton. "9/11 Commission Report." National Commission on Terrorist Attacks Upon the United States, August 21, 2004. https://govinfo.library.unt.edu/911/report/index.htm.

Keaney, Thomas A., and Eliot A. Cohen. Gulf War Air Power Survey: Summary Report. Washington, DC: U.S. Government Printing Office, 1993.

Kerry, John F. "Tora Bora Revisited: How We Failed to Get bin Laden and Why It Matters Today: A Report to Members of the Committee on Foreign Relations United States Senate." United States Senate Committee on Foreign Relations Majority Staff, November 30, 2009.

"'Millennium Threat,' Briefing for DCI." Central Intelligence Agency, December 17, 1999. https://www.documentcloud.org/documents/368958-1999-12-17-millennium-threat-briefing-for-dci.html.

"Minority Views of Vice Chairman Chambliss Joined by Senators Burr, Risch, Coats, Rubio, and Coburn: Committee Study of the Central Intelligence Agency's Detention and Interrogation Program." Senate Select Committee on Intelligence, December 5, 2014. https://www.feinstein.senate.gov/public/_cache/files/d/b/db587bbf-f52d-47eb-b90c-a60ff3f92484/B184465DC41EB54A90B740167B0BA173.ssci study3.pdf.

"Office of the Inspector General Report on Central Intelligence Agency Accountability Regarding Findings and Conclusions of the Report of the Joint Inquiry into Intelligence Community Activities Before and After the Terrorist Attacks of September 11, 2001." Office of the Inspector General, CIA, June 19, 2005. https://www.cia.gov/readingroom/docs/DOC_0006184107.pdf.

"Opening of the Letter to Senator Leahy." FBI.gov. https://archives.fbi.gov/archives/about-us/history/famous-cases/anthrax-amerithrax/the-leahy-letter.

"Patterns of Global Terrorism: 1997." Department of State Publication 10535. Office of the Secretary of State Office of the Coordinator for Counterterrorism, April 1998. https://fas.org/irp/threat/terror_97/1997index.html.

Scheuer, Michael F. "'Your Note,' Email to [Excised]," Central Intelligence Agency Email, May 17, 1999. https://www.documentcloud.org/documents/368949-1999-05-17-your-note-from-michael-f-scheuer-to.html.

State Department Factsheet on Bin Laden. August 14, 1996. Author's collection.

Storer, Cynthia. "Fatwas or Religious Rulings by Militant Islamic Groups Against the United States." CIA Counterterrorist Center, February 23, 1998.

"Terrorism: Bin Ladin Public Profile May Presage Attack." Central Intelligence Agency Senior Executive Intelligence Brief, May 3, 2001. https://www.document cloud.org/documents/369162-2001-05-03-terrorism-bin-ladin-public-profile .html.

"Terrorism: Planning for Bin Ladin Attacks Continues, Despite Delay [Excised]." Central Intelligence Agency Senior Executive Intelligence Brief, July 2, 2001. https://www.documentcloud.org/documents/369168-2001-07-02-terrorism-plan ning-for-bin-ladin.html.

"Terrorism: Terrorist Groups Said Cooperating on US Hostage Plot." Central Intelligence Agency Senior Executive Intelligence Brief, May 23, 2001. https://www .documentcloud.org/documents/369163-2001-05-23-terrorism-terrorist-groups -said.html.

"United States Special Operations Command History." United States Special Operations Command, 2007. https://fas.org/irp/agency/dod/socom/2007history.pdf.

"Usama bin Ladin: Who's Chasing Whom?" Bureau of Intelligence and Research, U.S. Department of State. July 18, 1996.

"U.S. Department of State Daily Press Briefing #156, 96-09-27." U.S. Department of State, September 27, 1996. http://www.hri.org/news/usa/std/1996/96-09-27.std .html.

U.S. State Department Bureau of Intelligence and Research chronology regarding bin Laden, 1995. Author's collection.

"The Wandering Mujahidin: Armed and Dangerous." United States Department of State Bureau of Intelligence and Research, Weekend Edition, August 21–22, 1993. http://www.nationalsecuritymom.com/3/WanderingMujahidin.pdf.

"(U) What Does the Death of Usama Bin Laden Mean?" NSA SIDtoday, May 17, 2011. Snowden Files. https://theintercept.com/document/2015/05/18/sidtoday-in terview-ubl/.

U.S. COURT DOCUMENTS

Affidavit Filed by Daniel J. Coleman in USA v. Mohamed Rashed Daoud Al-Owhali. United States District Court, Southern District of New York, August 25, 1998. https://fas.org/irp/news/1998/08/98090103_npo.html.

Affidavit in Support of Application for a Search Warrant. Filed by FBI Special Agent David Kane in Support of Search of the Residence of Tariq Hamdi. United States District Court, Eastern District of Virginia, May 13, 2002.

Deposition of Mr. Abdel Bari Abu Atwan. USA v. Khalid al-Fawwaz. United States District Court, Southern District of New York, October 1, 2014.

"Exhibt C1." USA v. Khalid al-Fawwaz. United States District Court, Southern District of New York.

"Indictment." USA v. Usama Bin Laden et al. United States District Court, Southern District of New York, November 5, 1998. https://fas.org/irp/news/1998/11/indict1.pdf.

"Plea." USA v. Ali Mohamed. United States District Court, Southern District of New York, October 20, 2000.

Proceedings of a military commission. USA v. Ali Hamza Ahmad Suliman al Bahlul. May 7, 2008.

"Substitution for the Testimony of Khalid Sheikh Mohammed." USA v. Zacarias Moussaoui. United States District Court, Eastern District of Virginia, undated.

Summation of Patrick J. Fitzgerald. USA v. Usama bin Laden et al. United States District Court, Southern District of New York, May 8, 2001.

Testimony of Ambassador Prudence Bushnell. USA v. Usama bin Laden et al. United States District Court, Southern District of New York, March 1, 2001.

Testimony of Ahmed Ressam. USA v. Mokhtar Haouari. United States District Court, Southern District of New York, July 5, 2001.

Testimony of Essam al-Ridi. USA v. Usama bin Laden et al. United States District Court, Southern District of New York, February 14, 2001

Testimony of FBI Special Agent Daniel Coleman. USA v. Usama bin Laden et al. United States District Court, Southern District of New York, February 21, 2001.

Testimony of FBI Special Agent Steve Gaudin. USA v. Usama bin Laden et al. United States District Court, Southern District of New York, March 7, 2001.

Testimony of Jamal Fadl. USA v. Usama bin Laden et al. United States District Court, Southern District of New York, February 6, 7, 13, and 20, 2001.

White, Mary Jo, and Andrew C. McCarthy. "To: All Counsel of Record Re: US v. Omar Ahmad Ali Abdel Rahman, et Al. (S5) 93 Cr. 181 (MBM)," February 2, 1995. http://www.danielpipes.org/rr/1995-02-02-usgusa049115235.pdf.

STATEMENTS BY U.S. OFFICIALS

AP (YouTube). "Trump Urges 'Shutdown' On Muslims Entering US." November 16, 2016. https://www.youtube.com/watch?v=Dz2wn3iPDNg.

Clinton, Bill. "Address to the Nation on Military Action Against Terrorist Sites in Afghanistan and Sudan." U.S. Government Publishing Office, August 20, 1998. https://www.govinfo.gov/content/pkg/PPP-1998-book2/html/PPP-1998-book2-doc-pg1460-2.htm.

———. "Remarks in Martha's Vineyard, Massachusetts, on Military Action Against Terrorist Sites in Afghanistan and Sudan." U.S. Government Publishing Office, August 20, 1998. https://www.govinfo.gov/content/pkg/PPP-1998-book2/html/PPP-1998-book2-doc-pg1460.htm.

Mueller, Robert S., III. "Speech at the Global Initiative Nuclear Terrorism Conference, Miami, Florida." FBI.gov, June 11, 2007. https://archives.fbi.gov/archives/news/speeches/nuclear-terrorism-prevention-is-our-endgame.

————. "Statement Before the Senate Committee on Homeland Security and Governmental Affairs." FBI.gov, September 13, 2011. https://archives.fbi.gov/archives/news/testimony/ten-years-after-9-11-are-we-safer.

Obama, Barack. "Remarks by the President on Osama Bin Laden." White House Office of the Press Secretary, May 2, 2011. https://obamawhitehouse.archives.gov/the-press-office/2011/05/02/remarks-president-osama-bin-laden.

"A Policy of Evasion and Deception: Transcript of U.S. Secretary of State Colin Powell's Speech to the United Nations on Iraq." Washington Post, February 5, 2003. https://www.washingtonpost.com/wp-srv/nation/transcripts/powelltext_020503.html.

"September 30, 2004 Debate Transcript: The First Bush-Kerry Presidential Debate." Commission on Presidential Debates, September 30, 2004. https://www.debates.org/voter-education/debate-transcripts/september-30-2004-debate-transcript/.

"State of the Union: Text of George W. Bush's Speech." Guardian, September 21, 2001. https://www.theguardian.com/world/2001/sep/21/september11.usa13.

"Transcript for Sept. 14: EXCLUSIVE: Vice President Dick Cheney, in His First Sunday Interview in Six Months, Discusses the War in Iraq." NBC News, September 14, 2003. https://www.nbcnews.com/id/wbna3080244.

"Transcript of Cheney Interview." ABC News, January 6, 2006. https://abcnews.go.com/Primetime/story?id=132168&page=1.

"Vice President and Mrs. Cheney's Remarks and Q&A in Carroll, Ohio." George W. Bush White House Archives, October 19, 2004. https://georgewbush-whitehouse.archives.gov/news/releases/2004/10/text/20041020-2.html.

NON–U.S. GOVERNMENT DOCUMENTS

"Constitution of Joint Investigation Team." Office of the Inspector General of Police Islamabad, Pakistan, January 19, 2012. https://www.cbsnews.com/htdocs/pdf/JIT_Report_033012.pdf.

Iqbal, Justice Javed, et al."Abbottabad Commission Report," Pakistan, 2013. https://www.documentcloud.org/documents/724833-aljazeera-bin-laden-dossier.html.

"Police Report 1969, Falun," Sweden. Copy in Author's collection.

"Letter Dated 19 May 2020 from the Chair of the Security Council Committee Established Pursuant to Resolution 1988 (2011) Addressed to the President of the Security Council." United Nations Security Council, May 27, 2020. https://digitallibrary.un.org/record/3862716?ln=en.

"Security Council Demands That Taliban Turn Over Usama bin Laden to Appropriate Authorities." United Nations Security Council Press Release SC/6739, October 15, 1999. https://www.un.org/press/en/1999/19991015.sc6739.doc.html.

United Nations Security Council. "ABDELMALEK DROUKDEL," April 17, 2018.

https://www.un.org/securitycouncil/sanctions/1267/aq_sanctions_list/summa
ries/individual/abdelmalek-droukdel.

BOOKS

Abbasi, Feroz Ali. Guantánamo Bay Prison Memoirs,2002–2005. Author's collection.

Allen, Jonathan, and Amie Parnes. HRC: State Secrets and the Rebirth of Hillary Clinton. New York: Crown, 2014.

Anas, Abdullah, and Tam Hussein. To the Mountains: My Life in Jihad, from Algeria to
Afghanistan. London: Hurst, 2019.

Azzam, Sheikh Abdullah. Defense of Muslim Lands, The Most Important Personal
Duty. Published in booklet form by Modern Mission Library, 1984

———. The Lofty Mountain. London: Azzam Publications, undated.

Bahri, Nasser al-. Guarding bin Laden: My Life in Al-Qaeda. London: Thin Man Press,
2013.

Bahri, Nasser al-, and Georges Malbrunot. Dans l'ombre de Ben Laden: Révélations de
Son Garde du Corps Repenti. Neuilly-sur-Seine: Michele Lafon, 2010.

Bakos, Nada, and Davin Coburn. The Targeter: My Life in the CIA, Hunting Terrorists
and Challenging the White House. New York: Little, Brown and Company, 2019.

Baweja, Harinder, ed. Most Wanted: Profiles of Terror. New Delhi: Lotus Collection,
Roli Books, 2002.

Bearden, Milt, and James Risen. The Main Enemy: The Inside Story of the CIA's Final
Showdown with the KGB. New York: Random House, 2003.

Benjamin, Daniel, and Steven Simon. The Age of Sacred Terror: Radical Islam's War
Against America. New York: Random House, 2002.

Bennett, Gina M. National Security Mom: Why "Going Soft" Will Make America
Strong. Deadwood, OR: Wyatt-Mackenzie, 2009.

Bergen, Peter. Holy War, Inc.: Inside the Secret World of Osama bin Laden. New York:
Free Press, 2001.

———. The Longest War: The Enduring Conflict Between America and al-Qaeda. New
York: Free Press, 2011.

———. Manhunt: The Ten-Year Search for bin Laden from 9/11 to Abbottabad. New
York: Crown, 2012.

———. The Osama bin Laden I Know: An Oral History of al Qaeda's Leader. New York:
Free Press, 2006.

———. Trump and His Generals: The Cost of Chaos. New York: Penguin, 2019.

———. United States of Jihad: Investigating America's Homegrown Terrorists. New
York: Crown Publishers, 2016.

Bergen, Peter L., and Daniel Rothenberg, eds. Drone Wars: Transforming Conflict,
Law, and Policy. New York: Cambridge University Press, 2015.

Berlin, Isaiah. "Two Concepts of Liberty." In *Four Essays on Liberty*. Oxford: Oxford University Press, 1969.

Berntsen, Gary, and Ralph Pezzullo. *Jawbreaker: The Attack on Bin Laden and Al-Qaeda: A Personal Account by the CIA's Key Field Commander*. New York: Crown, 2005.

Bierbauer, Alec, Mark Cooter, and Michael Marks. *Never Mind, We'll Do It Ourselves: The Inside Story of How a Team of Renegades Broke Rules, Shattered Barriers, and Changed a Drone Warfare Revolution*, New York, Skyhorse Publishing, 2021.

Bin Ladin, Carmen, and Ruth Marshall. *Inside the Kingdom: My Life in Saudi Arabia*. New York: Warner Books, 2004.

Bin Laden, Najwa, Omar bin Laden, and Jean P. Sasson. *Growing Up bin Laden: Osama's Wife and Son Take Us Inside Their Secret World*. New York: St. Martin's Press, 2009.

Bin Laden, Osama. *Messages to the World: The Statements of Osama Bin Laden*. Edited by Bruce Lawrence. London: Verso, 2005.

Blehm, Eric. *The Only Thing Worth Dying For: How Eleven Green Berets Forged a New Afghanistan*. New York: Harper, 2010.

Bowden, Mark. *Black Hawk Down: A Story of Modern War*. New York: Atlantic Monthly Press, 1999.

———. *The Finish: The Killing of Osama bin Laden*. New York: Atlantic Monthly Press, 2012.

Bradsher, Henry S. *Afghan Communism and Soviet Intervention*. Oxford: Oxford University Press, 1999.

Brennan, John O. *Undaunted: My Fight Against America's Enemies, at Home and Abroad*. New York: Celadon, 2020.

Bumiller, Elisabeth. *Condoleezza Rice: An American Life: A Biography*. New York: Random House, 2007.

Burke, Jason. *Al-Qaeda: The True Story of Radical Islam*. London: Tauris, 2004.

———. *The 9/11 Wars*. London: Penguin, 2012.

Bush, George W. *Decision Points*. New York: Crown, 2010.

Carter, J. R. L. *Leading Merchant Families of Saudi Arabia*. London: Scorpion Publications/D. R. Llewellyn Group, 1979.

Cheney, Dick, and Liz Cheney. *In My Time: A Personal and Political Memoir*. New York: Threshold, 2011.

Chesney, Will, and Joe Layden. *No Ordinary Dog: My Partner from the SEAL Teams to the Bin Laden Raid*. New York: St. Martin's Griffin, 2021.

Clarke, Richard A. *Against All Enemies: Inside America's War on Terror*. New York: Free Press, 2004.

Clinton, Bill. *My Life*. New York: Vintage, 2005.

Clinton, Hillary Rodham. *Hard Choices*. New York: Simon & Schuster, 2014.

Coll, Steve. *The Bin Ladens: An Arabian Family in the American Century*. New York: Penguin, 2008.

———. *Directorate S: The C.I.A. and America's Secret Wars in Afghanistan and Pakistan*. New York: Penguin, 2018.

———. *Ghost Wars: The Secret History of the CIA, Afghanistan, and bin Laden, from the Soviet Invasion to September 10, 2001*. New York: Penguin, 2005.

Cook, David. *Understanding Jihad*. Oakland: University of California Press, 2015.

Crile, George. *Charlie Wilson's War: The Extraordinary Story of How the Wildest Man in Congress and a Rogue CIA Agent Changed the History of Our Times*. New York: Grove Atlantic, 2007.

Deraz, Essam. *The Battles of the Lon's Den of the Afghan Mujahideen*. Cairo, 1991.

DeLong, Michael, and Noah Lukeman. *A General Speaks Out: The Truth About the Wars in Afghanistan and Iraq*. St. Paul, MN: Zenith Press, 2007.

DeYoung, Karen. *Soldier: The Life of Colin Powell*. New York: Vintage, 2007.

Draper, Robert. *Dead Certain: The Presidency of George W. Bush*. New York: Free Press, 2007.

———. *To Start a War: How the Bush Administration Took America into Iraq*. New York: Penguin, 2020.

Dupree, Louis. *Afghanistan*. New Delhi: Rama Publishers, 1994.

Eichenwald, Kurt. *500 Days: Secrets and Lies in the Terror Wars*. New York: Touchstone, 2012.

Fandy, Mamoun. *Saudi Arabia and the Politics of Dissent*. New York: St. Martin's Press, 1999.

Feith, Douglas J. *War and Decision: Inside the Pentagon at the Dawn of the War on Terrorism*. New York: Harper, 2008.

Field, Michael. *The Merchants: The Big Business Families of Saudi Arabia and the Gulf States*. Woodstock, NY: Overlook Press, 1985.

Fouda, Yosri, and Nick Fielding. *Masterminds of Terror: The Truth Behind the Most Devastating Terrorist Attack the World Has Ever Seen*. New York: Arcade, 2003.

Franks, Tommy. *American Soldier*. New York: Regan Books, 2004.

Frost, Robin M. *Nuclear Terrorism After 9/11*. London: Routledge, 2017.

Fury, Dalton. *Kill Bin Laden: A Delta Force Commander's Account of the Hunt for the World's Most Wanted Man*. New York: St. Martin's Griffin, 2013.

Gall, Carlotta. *The Wrong Enemy: America in Afghanistan, 2001–2014*. New York: Houghton Mifflin Harcourt, 2014.

Gates, Robert M. *Duty: Memoirs of a Secretary at War*. New York: Alfred A. Knopf, 2014.

Gerges, Fawaz A. *The Far Enemy: Why Jihad Went Global*. Cambridge, U.K.: Cambridge University Press, 2005.

————. *The Rise and Fall of al-Qaeda*. New York: Oxford University Press, 2011.

Graff, Garrett M. *The Threat Matrix: The FBI at War in the Age of Terror*. New York: Little, Brown, 2011.

Graham, Bradley. *By His Own Rules: The Ambitions, Successes, and Ultimate Failures of Donald Rumsfeld*. New York, Public Affairs, 2009.

Grau, Lester W., ed. *The Bear Went Over the Mountain: Soviet Combat Tactics in Afghanistan*. Ft. Leavenworth, KS: Foreign Military Studies Office, 2005.

Grenier, Robert L. *88 Days to Kandahar: A CIA Diary*. New York: Simon & Schuster, 2016.

Hamid, Mustafa, and Leah Farrall. *The Arabs at War in Afghanistan*. London: Hurst, 2015.

Hafez, Mohammed M. *Suicide Bombers in Iraq: The Strategy and Ideology of Martyrdom*. Washington DC: United States Institute of Peace, July 21, 2007.

Hart, David M. *Guardians of the Khaibar Pass: The Social Organisation and History of the Afridis of Pakistan*. Lahore: Vanguard Books, 1985.

Hayden, Michael Vincent. *Playing to the Edge: American Intelligence in the Age of Terror*. New York: Penguin, 2016.

Hegghammer, Thomas. *The Caravan: Abdallah Azzam and the Rise of Global Jihad*. Cambridge, U.K.: Cambridge University Press, 2020.

————. *Jihad in Saudi Arabia: Violence and Pan-Islamism Since 1979*. Cambridge, U.K.: Cambridge University Press, 2010.

Hoffman, Bruce. *Anonymous Soldiers: The Struggle for Israel, 1917–1947*. New York: Alfred A. Knopf, 2015.

Hoffman, Bruce, and Fernando Reinares, eds. *The Evolution of the Global Terrorist Threat: From 9/11 to Osama bin Laden's Death*. Columbia Studies in Terrorism and Irregular Warfare. New York: Columbia University Press, 2016.

Huband, Mark. *Warriors of the Prophet: The Struggle for Islam*. Boulder, CO: Westview Press, 1999.

al-Huzaimi, Nasir. *The Mecca Uprising: An Insider's Account of Salafism and Insurrection in Saudi Arabia*. Edited and translated by David Commins. London: I. B. Tauris, 2021.

Ingrams, Doreen. *A Time in Arabia: Life in Hadhramaut*. London: Eland, 2013.

Jacquard, Roland. *Les Archives Secretes d'Al-Qaida*. Paris: Jean Picollec, 2002.

Jones, Seth G. *In the Graveyard of Empires: America's War in Afghanistan*. New York: W. W. Norton, 2009.

Kepel, Gilles. *Muslim Extremism in Egypt: The Prophet and Pharaoh*. Berkeley: University of California Press, 2003.

Kepel, Giles, and Jean-Pierre Milelli, eds. *Al Qaeda in Its Own Words*. Cambridge, MA: Belknap Press of Harvard University Press, 2008.

Kippenberg, Hans G., and Tilman Seidensticker, eds. *The 9/11 Handbook: Annotated*

Translation and Interpretation of the Attackers' Spiritual Manual. London: Equinox, 2006.

Kitfield, James. *Twilight Warriors: The Soldiers, Spies, and Special Agents Who Are Revolutionizing the American Way of War.* New York: Basic Books, 2016.

Lacey, Jim, ed. *A Terrorist's Call to Global Jihad: Deciphering Abu Musab al-Suri's Islamic Jihad Manifesto.* Annapolis, MD: Naval Institute Press, 2008.

Lahoud, Nelly. *The Jihadis' Path to Self-Destruction.* London: Hurst, 2010.

Levy, Adrian, and Cathy Scott-Clark. *The Exile: The Stunning Inside Story of Osama bin Laden and Al Qaeda in Flight.* New York: Bloomsbury, 2017.

Lewis, Bernard. *The Crisis of Islam: Holy War and Unholy Terror.* New York: Modern Library, 2004.

Manning, Frederic. *The Middle Parts of Fortune.* Melbourne: Text Publishing Co., 2012.

Mattis, Jim, and Bing West. *Call Sign Chaos: Learning to Lead.* New York: Random House, 2019.

McChrystal, Stanley A. *My Share of the Task: A Memoir.* New York: Portfolio/Penguin, 2013.

McClellan, Scott. *What Happened: Inside the Bush White House and Washington's Culture of Deception.* New York: PublicAffairs, 2008.

McRaven, William H. *Sea Stories: My Life in Special Operations.* New York: Grand Central Publishing, 2019.

———. *Spec Ops: Case Studies in Special Operations Warfare: Theory and Practice.* New York: Presidio Press, 1996.

Meleagrou-Hitchens, Alexander. *Incitement: Anwar al-Awlaki's Western Jihad.* Cambridge, MA: Harvard University Press, 2020.

Miller, Flagg. *The Audacious Ascetic: What the Bin Laden Tapes Reveal About al-Qa'ida.* New York: Oxford University Press, 2015.

Miller, John, Michael Stone, and Chris Mitchell. *The Cell: Inside the 9/11 Plot, and Why the FBI and CIA Failed to Stop It.* New York: Hyperion, 2002.

Mir, Hamid. *The Story of Osama bin Laden.* Unpublished manuscript. Author's collection.

Moghadam, Assaf. *The Globalization of Martyrdom: Al Qaeda, Salafi Jihad, and the Diffusion of Suicide Attacks.* Baltimore: Johns Hopkins University Press, 2008.

Mohabbat, Kabir, and Leah McInnis. *Delivering Osama: The Story of America's Secret Envoy.* Berlin: First Draft Publishing, 2020.

Mojdeh, Vahid. *Afghanistan Under Five Years of Taliban Sovereignty*, translated by Sepideh Khalili and Saeed Ganji. Unpublished manuscript, 2003.

Morell, Michael J., and Bill Harlow. *The Great War of Our Time: The CIA's Fight Against Terrorism—From al Qa'ida to ISIS.* New York: Twelve, 2015.

Morgan, Wesley. *The Hardest Place: The American Military Adrift in Afghanistan's Pech Valley.* New York: Random House, 2021.

Muhammad, Basil. *The Arab Supporters in Afghanistan.* Jeddah: House of Learning Printing Press, 1991.

Musharraf, Pervez. *In the Line of Fire: A Memoir.* London: Simon & Schuster, 2008.

Myers, Richard B., and Malcolm McConnell. *Eyes on the Horizon: Serving on the Front Lines of National Security.* New York: Pocket Books, 2014.

Obama, Barack. *A Promised Land.* New York: Crown, 2020.

O'Neill, Robert. *The Operator: Firing the Shots That Killed Osama Bin Laden and My Years as a SEAL Team Warrior.* New York: Scribner, 2017.

The Osama Bin Laden Files: Letters and Documents Discovered by SEAL Team Six during Their Raid on Bin Laden's Compound. New York: Skyhorse Publ., 2012.

Owen, Mark, and Kevin Maurer. *No Easy Day: The Firsthand Account of the Mission That Killed Osama Bin Laden: The Autobiography of a Navy SEAL.* New York: Dutton, 2016.

Panetta, Leon, and Jim Newton. *Worthy Fights: A Memoir of Leadership in War and Peace.* New York: Penguin, 2015.

Partner, Peter. *God of Battles: Holy Wars of Christianity and Islam.* Princeton, NJ: Princeton University Press, 1997.

Qutb, Sayyid. *Milestones.* Sime Books, 1997.

Rashid, Ahmed. *Taliban: Militant Islam, Oil and Fundamentalism in Central Asia.* London: I. B. Taurus, 2000.

Rhodes, Ben. *The World as It Is: A Memoir of the Obama White House.* New York: Random House, 2018.

Rice, Condoleezza. *No Higher Honor: A Memoir of My Years in Washington.* New York: Crown, 2011.

Rice, Susan E. *Tough Love: My Story of the Things Worth Fighting For.* New York: Simon & Schuster, 2019.

Rizzo, John. *Company Man: Thirty Years of Controversy and Crisis in the CIA.* New York: Scribner, 2014.

Rodriguez, Jose A., Jr., and Bill Harlow. *Hard Measures: How Aggressive CIA Actions After 9/11 Saved American Lives.* New York: Threshold, 2013.

Roy, Olivier. *Globalized Islam: The Search for a New Ummah.* The CERI Series in Comparative Politics and International Studies. New York: Columbia University Press, 2004.

Rumsfeld, Donald. *Known and Unknown: A Memoir.* New York: Sentinel, 2011.

Rundell, David H. *Vision or Mirage: Saudi Arabia at the Crossroads.* London: I. B. Tauris, 2021.

Sands, Chris, and Fazelminallah Qazizai. *Night Letters: The Secret History of Gulbuddin Hekmatyar and the Afghan Islamists Who Changed the World.* London: Hurst, 2019.

Scheuer, Michael. *Imperial Hubris: Why the West Is Losing the War on Terror.* Washington, DC: Potomac Books, 2005.

Schmitt, Eric, and Thom Shanker. *Counterstrike: The Untold Story of America's Secret Campaign Against Al Qaeda.* New York: Times Books, 2012.

Schroen, Gary C. *First In: An Insider's Account of How the CIA Spearheaded the War on Terror in Afghanistan.* New York: Presidio Press/Ballantine Books, 2005.

Shane, Scott. *Objective Troy: A Terrorist, a President, and the Rise of the Drone.* New York: Tim Duggan Books, 2015.

Sheehan, Michael A. *Crush the Cell: How to Defeat Terrorism Without Terrorizing Ourselves.* New York: Crown, 2008.

Shelton, Hugh, Ronald Levinson, and Malcolm McConnell. *Without Hesitation: The Odyssey of an American Warrior.* New York: St. Martin's Press, 2010.

Shenon, Philip. *The Commission: The Uncensored History of the 9/11 Investigation.* New York: Twelve, 2008.

Soufan, Ali H. *Anatomy of Terror: From the Death of Bin Laden to the Rise of the Islamic State,* New York, Norton, 2017.

Soufan, Ali H., and Daniel Freedman. *The Black Banners (Declassified): How Torture Derailed the War on Terror After 9/11.* New York: W. W. Norton, 2020.

Spain, James W. *Pathans of the Latter Day.* Karachi: Oxford University Press, 1995.

Stark, Freya. *The Southern Gates of Arabia—A Journey in the Hadhramaut.* London: John Murray, 1946.

Stenersen, Anne. *Al-Qaida in Afghanistan.* Cambridge, U.K.: Cambridge University Press, 2017.

Strick van Linschoten, Alex, and Felix Kuehn. *An Enemy We Created: The Myth of the Taliban–Al Qaeda Merger in Afghanistan.* Oxford: Oxford University Press, 2012.

Tenet, George, and Bill Harlow. *At the Center of the Storm: My Years at the CIA.* New York: HarperCollins, 2007.

Trofimov, Yaroslav. *The Siege of Mecca: The Forgotten Uprising in Islam's Holiest Shrine and the Birth of Al Qaeda.* New York: Anchor Books, 2008.

Urban, Mark. *War in Afghanistan.* London: Palgrave Macmillan, 1988.

Wark, Wesley K., ed. *Twenty-First Century Intelligence,* New York: Routledge, 2008.

Whittle, Richard. *Predator: The Secret Origins of the Drone Revolution.* New York: Henry Holt, 2014.

Wohlstetter, Roberta. *Pearl Harbor: Warning and Decision.* Stanford, CA: Stanford University Press, 1966.

Woodward, Bob. *Bush at War.* New York: Simon & Schuster, 2002.

Wright, Lawrence. *The Looming Tower: Al-Qaeda and the Road to 9/11.* New York: Alfred A. Knopf, 2006.

———. *The Terror Years: From al-Qaeda to the Islamic State.* New York: Little, Brown, 2016.

Yousaf, Mohammad, and Mark Adkin, *Afghanistan—the Bear Trap: The Defeat of a Superpower* Lahore: Jang Publishers,1993.

Zaidan, Ahmad Muaffaq. "Bin Laden Revealed." Unpublished manuscript. Based on Zaidan, *Bin Laden Unmasked* (Arabic). Beirut, 2015.

Zaeef, ʿAbd al-Salām, Alex Strick van Linschoten, and Felix Kuehn. *My Life with the Taliban.* New York: Columbia University Press, 2010.

Zayyat, Montasser al-. *The Road to Al-Qaeda: The Story of Bin Laden's Right-Hand Man.* Critical Studies on Islam. London: Pluto Press, 2004.

Zegart, Amy B. *Spying Blind: The CIA, the FBI, and the Origins of 9/11.* Princeton, NJ: Princeton University Press, 2007.

DOCUMENT SETS AND REPORTS

Aftergood, Steven. "Intelligence Budget Data." Federation of American Scientists. https://fas.org/irp/budget/.

Bell, Kevin. "Usama bin Ladin's 'Father Sheikh': Yunus Khalis and the Return of Al-Qaʾidaʾs Leadership to Afghanistan." Combating Terrorism Center, May 14, 2013, https://ctc.usma.edu/wp-content/uploads/2013/05/CTC_Yunus-Khalis-Report -Final1.pdf.

Bergen, Peter, David Sterman, and Melissa Salyk-Virk. "America's Counterterrorism Wars: The Drone War in Pakistan." New America, August 13, 2020. https:// www.newamerica.org/international-security/reports/americas-counterterrorism -wars/the-drone-war-in-pakistan/.

Bergen, Peter, Albert Ford, David Sterman, and Alyssa Sims. "Terrorism in America After 9/11." New America. https://www.newamerica.org/in-depth/terrorism-in -america/who-are-terrorists/.

Bin Laden's Bookshelf. Office of the Director of National Intelligence. https://www .dni.gov/index.php/features/bin-laden-s-bookshelf?start=1.

Cook, Joana. "'Their Fate Is Tied to Ours' Assessing AQAP Governance and Implications for Security in Yemen." ICSR, October 2019. https://icsr.info/wp-content /uploads/2019/10/ICSR-Report-Their-Fate-is-Tied-to-Ours-Assessing-AQAP -Governance-and-Implications-for-Security-in-Yemen.pdf.

Crawford, Neta C. "Human Cost of the Post-9/11 Wars: Lethality and the Need for Transparency." Costs of War Project, November 2018. https://watson.brown.edu /costsofwar/files/cow/imce/papers/2018/Human%20Costs%2C%20Nov%20 8%202018%20CoW.pdf.

———. "United States Budgetary Costs and Obligations of Post-9/11 Wars Through FY2020: $6.4 Trillion," November 13, 2019. https://watson.brown.edu/costsofwar /files/cow/imce/papers/2019/US%20Budgetary%20Costs%20of%20Wars%20No vember%202019.pdf.

Cronin, Audrey Kurth. *Ending Terrorism: Lessons for Defeating Al-Qaeda.* Adelphi

Paper 394. Abingdon, Oxon: Routledge for the International Institute for Strategic Studies, 2008.

The Early History of al-Qa'ida. RAND, 2007. Unpublished manuscript. Author's collection.

Fenner, Lorry M. and Mark E. Stout with Jessica L. Goldings, eds. *9/11, Ten Years Later: Insights on Al-Qaeda's Past & Future Through Captured Records: Conference Proceedings.* Washington, DC: Conflict Records Research Center, Institute for National Strategic Studies, National Defense University, 2012. https://www.google .com/books/edition/9_11_ Ten_Years_Later/9ryXNXALLvsC?hl=en&gbpv=0.

Gibbs, David N. "Review Essay: Afghanistan: The Soviet Invasion in Retrospect." *International Politics* 37, no. 2 (June 2000), 233–46. https://dgibbs.faculty.arizona .edu/sites/dgibbs.faculty.arizona.edu/files/afghan-ip.pdf.

"Hugh Shelton Oral History: Transcript." UVA Miller Center, May 29, 2007. https:// millercenter.org/the-presidency/presidential-oral-histories/henry-hugh-shelton -oral-history-chairman-joint-chiefs.

"Interview with Michael V. Hayden." University of Virginia Miller Center, November 20, 2012. George W. Bush Oral History Project. http://web1.millercenter.org /poh/transcripts/hayden_michael_2012_1120.pdf.

Jenkins, Brian Michael. "New Age of Terrorism." RAND, 2006. https://www.rand.org /content/dam/rand/pubs/reprints/2006/RAND_RP1215.pdf

Lahoud, Nelly. "Al-Qa'ida's Contested Relationship with Iran." New America, September 7, 2018. https://www.newamerica.org/international-security/reports/al -qaidas-contested-relationship-iran/.

———. "Beware of Imitators: Al-Qa'ida Through the Lens of Its Confidential Secretary." Combating Terrorism Center, June 4, 2012. https://ctc.usma.edu/wp-con tent/uploads/2012/06/CTC-Beware-of-Imitators-June2012.pdf.

"November 2017 Release of Abbottabad Compound Material." Central Intelligence Agency, November 2017. https://www.cia.gov/library/abbottabad-compound/in dex.html.

Pew Research Center. "Chapter 7. Attitudes Toward Extremism Among Muslim Publics." June 17, 2010. https://www.pewresearch.org/global/2010/06/17/chapter-7 -attitudes-toward-extremism-among-muslim-publics/.

Rappaport, David C. "The Four Waves of Rebel Terror and September 11." *Anthropoetics* 8, no. 1 (Spring/Summer 2002).

Statement from Bakr bin Laden. April 1994. Author's collection

NEWSPAPERS, MAGAZINES, JOURNALS, NEWS WEBSITES, BROADCAST NEWS

Arab News, Al Akhbar, Al Sharq al Aswat, Al Quds al Arabi, Associated Press, Baltimore Sun, BuzzFeed, El Correo, Chicago Tribune, Dalarnes Tidningar, Dallas Morning News

Express Tribune, Guardian, Independent, Intercept, Los Angeles Times, Mail on Sunday, Mideast Mirror, Military.com, Military Times, New York Times, Le Nouvel Observateur Ottawa Citizen, Politico, Reuters, Rose al-Yusuf, Sunday Times, Task & Purpose, Telegraph, The News, UPI, USA Today, U.S. News & World Report, Washington Post, Wall Street Journal

MAGAZINES AND JOURNALS

Al Majalah, Esquire, Humanitarian Law & Policy, London Review of Books, Military History Quarterly, Mother Jones, Nation, National Geographic, New Republic, New Yorker, New York Review of Books, Prospect, Time, Refugees Magazine, Washington Monthly, Weekly Standard

BROADCAST NEWS AND RADIO

Al Jazeera, BBC, CBS, CNN, FOX, NBC, NPR, PBS, VOA.

DOCUMENTARIES AND FILMS

Amanpour, Christiane. *In the Footsteps of bin Laden.* CNN, August 23, 2006. Produced by Peter Bergen, Cliff Hackel, and Ken Shiffman. https://www.cnn.com/videos/international/2012/04/26/amanpour-footsteps-cnn-part-1.cnn.

Arnett, Peter, Peter Bergen, and Richard Mackenzie. *Terror Nation? U.S. Creation?* CNN Films, 1994.

Barker, Greg. *Legion of Brothers*, CNN Films, 2017. Produced by John Battsek, Peter Bergen, Tresha Mabile.

———. *The Longest War.* Showtime, 2020. Produced by Peter Bergen, Tresha Mabile.

———. *Manhunt: The Inside Story of the Hunt for Bin Laden.* HBO, January 20, 2013.

Bergen, Peter, Simon Epstein, and Tresha Mabile. "American War Generals." National Geographic, 2014.

Bigelow, Kathryn. *Zero Dark Thirty*, 2012.

Bergen, Peter. *Bin Laden's Hard Drive.* National Geographic Channel, 2020. Produced by Aaron Kunkel/Karga Films.

The Hunt for Bin Laden. History Channel. May 2, 2021.

"Interview: Maha Elsamnah & Zaynab Khadr." PBS *Frontline*, February 22, 2004. https://www.pbs.org/wgbh/pages/frontline/shows/khadr/interviews/mahazaynab.html.

"Interview: U.S. Army General Tommy Franks." PBS *Frontline*, June 12, 2002. https://www.pbs.org/wgbh/pages/frontline/shows/campaign/interviews/franks.html.

Najm, Salah. "Usama Bin Ladin, the Destruction of the Base." Al Jazeera. June 10, 1999.

The Road to 9/11. History Channel. September 4 and 5, 2017. Produced by Left/Right.

INTERVIEWS

Several hundred people were interviewed during the reporting of this book, many of whom chose to be unnamed. The most useful on-the-record interviews for this book were with: Abdullah Abdullah, Christina Akerblad, Hazarat Ali, Abdullah Anas (Boudjema Bounoua), Salman al-Awdah, Abdel Bari Atwan, Hudayfa Azzam, Peter Arnett, Jeremy Bash, Khaled Batarfi, Milt Bearden, Gina Bennett, Noman Benotman, Gary Berntsen, Cofer Black, Tony Blinken, John Brennan, Vincent Cannistraro, Robert Cardillo, James "Hoss" Cartwright, James Clapper, Hillary Clinton, David Cohen, Daniel Coleman, Henry "Hank" Crumpton, Essam Deraz, Charles "Sam" Faddis, Saad al-Fagih, Khalid al-Fawwaz, Michèle Flournoy, Yosri Fouda, Tommy Franks, Brian Fyfield-Shayler, Mary Galligan, Susan Glasser, Robert Grenier, Kemal Halbawy, Michael Hayden, Thomas Hegghammer, Gulbuddin Hekmatyar, Faraj Ismail, Jamal Ismail, Peter Jouvenal, Wael Julaidan, Jamal Khalifa, Mullah Abdul Samad Khaksar, Adam Khan (a pseudonym), Ihsan Mohammad Khan, Ismail Khan, Jamal Khashoggi, Khalid Khawaja, Khalid Khan Kheshgi, Osama bin Laden, Nelly Lahoud, Michael Leiter, Ahmad Shah Massoud, Stanley McChrystal, Denis McDonough, John McLaughlin, William "Bill" McRaven, John Miller, Hamid Mir, Vahid Mojdeh, Haji Deen Mohammed, Philip Mudd, Michael Mullen, Asad Munir, Muhammad Musa, Barack Obama, Leon Panetta, George Piro, Mohammed Asif Qazizanda, Nick Rasmussen, Ben Rhodes, Robert Richer, Nic Robertson, Osama Rushdi, Marc Sageman, Safiwullah, Amarullah Saleh, Michael Scheuer, David Sedney, Mohammed Al-Shafey, Michael Sheehan, Ali Soufan, Cindy Storer, Barbara Sude, Abu Musab al-Suri (Mustafa Setmariam Nasar), Wisal al-Turabi, Michael Vickers, Lawrence Wright, Junaid Younis, Mohammad Yousaf, Rahimullah Yusufzai, Mohammed Zahir, and Ahmad Zaidan.

ACKNOWLEDGMENTS

Thanks to those who agreed to be interviewed for this book. The key on-the-record interviews are listed on page 363.

I'm lucky to have worked with David Sterman for the past eight years at New America. David worked on all phases of the book, performing research, fact checking, footnoting, and making important editorial suggestions. Thanks also to Nadia Oweidat, a highly regarded scholar of Islamism, who helped me interpret the bin Laden family journal and also other documents and videos about the Afghan Arabs. Thanks to Nelly Lahoud, the leading authority on the Abbottabad documents, for several useful discussions about them. Thanks to Melissa Salyk-Virk and Brianna Kablack, who also helped with research for the book, and to Emily Schneider for her review of the final draft. All these smart people work or have worked at New America, my home for the past two decades. I am also lucky to work there with Anne-Marie Slaughter, Awista Ayub, Paul Butler, Kevin Carey, Cecilia Muñoz, Candace Rondeaux, Yulia Panfil, Peter Singer, Sharon Burke, Heather Hurlburt, Shaena Korby, Barry Howard, Cathy Bryan, Dana Ju, Ariam Mohamed, Joanne Zalatoris, Maria Elkin, Alison Yost, Tanya Manning, Jewel Stafford, Angela Spidalette, and Jason Stewart. Sadly, two of the founders of New America died during the past year—Ted Halstead and Sherle Schwenninger. They created an institution that has lasted. Thanks to my fellow editors of the *Coronavirus Daily Brief*: David Sterman, Melissa Salyk-Virk, Narisara Murray, and Emily

Schneider. Thanks also to the former president of New America, Steve Coll, who suggested I start a program at New America focused on national security, which is now in its twelfth year. Steve has also contributed much to our collective understanding of the long war between al-Qaeda and the United States.

Thanks to Michael Crow, the president of Arizona State University (ASU), who hired me as a professor, and to Jim O'Brien, ASU senior vice president and chief of staff. It has been a pleasure to launch under their guidance, and that of Anne-Marie Slaughter, the Center on the Future of War, which is now in its seventh year. Thanks also at ASU to Pardis Mahdavi, Magda Hinojosa, Pat Kenney, Stefanie Lindquist, Jeffrey Kubiak, Thomas Just and H.R. McMaster. And also thanks to our partners in our annual Future Security Forum, Carol Evans of the Army War College, and Ike Wilson of the Joint Special Operation University.

A great deal of thanks is owed to Daniel Rothenberg, my partner in the Future of War/Future Security Forum projects, who is brilliant, hardworking, and thoughtful. Daniel read the manuscript of this book carefully, and his observations improved it. A number of other friends also weighed in. Richard Galant, managing editor at CNN.com and a mensch of the first order, generously read and commented on the manuscript. A number of the stories and themes of this book first emerged in pieces that I wrote for Rich, with whom I have worked closely for the past dozen years. Former federal prosecutor Ken Ballen, *60 Minutes'* Henry Schuster, the director Paul Berczeller, and Fordham University's Karen Greenberg all had very helpful feedback on the book. Thomas Hegghammer, one of the world's leading authorities on jihadism, critiqued the manuscript. Thanks also to the three anonymous reviewers who commented on an outline of the book. Any errors in the book remain mine alone.

In Afghanistan, thanks to Khalid Mafton, Yousuf Yahyapur, Hamid Hamidullah, Gianni Koskinas, Peter Jouvenal, and Hassina Syed. In Pakistan, thanks to Rahimullah Yusufzai, Ismail Khan, Ahmad Zaidan, Jamal Ismail, Commodore (ret.) Zafar Iqbal, Khalid Khan Kheshgi, and Ihsan Khan. For their guidance in Iraq, thanks to Joel Rayburn, Razzaq

Al-Saiedi, and Christine van den Toorn. In Saudi Arabia, thanks to Essam Al-Ghalib, Khaled Batarfi, and Saad Al-Jabri.

Thanks to Motley Rice's Michael Elsner, who made available valuable materials about the Afghan Arabs. Ahmad Zaidan and Hamid Mir kindly gave me their unpublished manuscripts about bin Laden.

I have worked at CNN in one capacity or another for three decades and am grateful to continue to work there today with so many of its excellent anchors, reporters, executives, and producers. In particular: Wolf Blitzer, Amy Entelis, Fareed Zakaria, Brian Todd, Dugald McConnell, Ken Shiffman, Jay Shaylor, Jim Sciutto, Charlie Moore, Anderson Cooper, Kerry Rubin, Susan Chun, Poppy Harlow, Rebecca Kutler, Michael Smerconish, Rick Davis, Pat Wiedenkeller, Yaffa Frederick, Arlene Getz, Jessica Chia, Kirsi Goldynia, Jane Carr, Jhodie-Ann Williams, Fuzz Hogan, Jamie Crawford, Adam Levine, Debbie Berger, Sam Feist, Courtney Sexton, Brianna Keilar, and Jeff Zucker.

At CNN, Pam Hill and the late John Lane were wonderful mentors who indulged my interest in bin Laden. In 1997 I visited Afghanistan with Peter Arnett and Peter Jouvenal to interview al-Qaeda's leader. We had made a previous trip together to Afghanistan after the first World Trade Center terrorist attack in 1993, together with Richard Mackenzie, which was my first introduction to the Afghan Arab phenomenon. In 1983 I made a film in Pakistan with two friends, George Case and Barney Thompson, about the Afghan refugees escaping the Soviet occupation of their country, which launched my longstanding interest in Afghanistan. Thanks to all of you.

Thanks also to the supporters of New America's International Security Program, particularly Tom Freston, and also Bob Niehaus, Aaron Stopak, the George Wasserman Family Foundation, and Ken Ballen. And thanks to David and Katherine Bradley, Kati Marton, and Brian Fishman. Thanks also to the foundations and program officers who have supported our work, especially Marin Strmecki of the Smith Richardson Foundation and Hillary Wiesner at Carnegie.

Thanks to Tim Barrett and Sara Lichterman at the CIA, Ken McGraw at Special Operations Command, and Susan Miller at the National Counterterrorism Center.

Thanks to Greg Barker for the work we have done together making several films about America's long post-9/11 wars. And thanks to Frank Lehmann, Vinnie Malhotra at Showtime, Nancy Abrahamson at HBO, Aaron Kunkel, Banks Tarver, Pete Ross, and Jon Meyersohn of Left/Right, who involved me in their 2017 series for History Channel *The Road to 9/11*. Thanks also to Howard Gordon, Alex Gansa, Russ Smith, John Battsek, Simon Epstein, and Cliff Hackel. Thanks to Matt Jones and Rainey Foster of Leading Authorities and to Clark Forcey, Chris Clifford, and Matthew Parker for your help over the years. Thanks also to Jennie Malloy, Igor Aronov, and Aleksander Ferguson.

Thanks to Bruce Hoffman for involving me both in the scholarly journal *Studies in Conflict and Terrorism* and in RAND's study of the early history of al-Qaeda, and for your work and friendship. Thanks also to Meena and Liaquat Ahamed, Chris and Holly Fussell, Joel Rayburn and Clare Lockhart, Henry and Sandra Schuster, Tom Carver and Katty Kay, Gavin and Odile Wilson, Kate Boo and Sunil Khilnani, Gianni Koskinas and Zena Rabia, Rachel Klayman, Josh Geltzer and Katherine Boone, Jen and Jason Easterly, Chris and Donna Costa, Nick Rasmussen, Rachel Martin and Luke Hartig, Elizabeth Campbell and Nabil Mohamad, Mark Isaksen and Daniel Walth, Adam Kushner and Maria Simon, Scott Moyers, Tina Bennett, Jim Sciutto and Gloria Rivera, Paul Berczeller and Yasmin Hai, Nir Rosen, Thomas and Holly Espy, Neil Barrett and Julia Cohen, Scott Wallace and Meg Walsh, George and Pauline Case, Paddy and Catherine Gibbs, John Micklethwait, Tim and Amanda de Lisle, Shaun and Kiki Waterman, Johnnie Boden, Rupert Smith, Jock Encombe, Robert Noel, Gerry Lampert, Diana Bergen, Carolyn Hammonds, Kirsten Bade, Kari Delaviez, Jennifer Willis, Paula Rosenstock, and Michel Eig.

Thanks to the 9/11 Museum's Alice Greenwald and Clifford Chanin, who asked Mary Galligan, Bruce Hoffman, Mark Stout, and myself to advise them on their exhibit on the hunt for bin Laden. Cliff kindly made available the transcript of the History Channel documentary that was based on the interviews that the museum performed for its superlative exhibit. Thanks also to the James Foley Foundation and to Diane Foley and her family, and to my fellow board members at the Global Special Operations Foundation and to Stu Bradin, Meaghan Keeler-Pettigrew and Keenan Yoho. Thanks to the Homeland Security Group, led by Jane Harman and Michael Chertoff, and its executive director, Rob Walker. I have learned much from these institutions and groups.

At WME, thanks to Eric Simonoff for his excellent advice, and also many thanks to Henry Reisch for his wise counsel and to Bradley Singer for his sage support.

I have known Priscilla Painton for many years, but this was the first book I had the good fortune to work on with her, and she vastly improved it. The book was also significantly sharpened by assistant editor, Hana Park. Working with Priscilla and Hana was a real joy. The rest of the team at Simon & Schuster—Jonathan Evans, Fred Chase, Kimberly Goldstein, Jackie Seow, Ruth Lee-Mui, Larry Hughes, and Elise Ringo—are all consummate professionals.

Thanks to the Mabile, Gould, and Takacs families. Above all, thanks to my wife, Tresha Mabile, who had many valuable ideas about how to shape the book and who traveled to Pakistan with me when she was pregnant with our son as we tried to learn more about bin Laden's final days. Tresha is the most wonderful wife and mother, and it is to her and to our daughter, Grace, and our son, Pierre, that this book is dedicated. Pierre, age nine, took a strong interest in the progress of this book. Many mornings he quizzed me: "What page are you on?" I look forward to telling him: Now it's done. Finally.

INDEX

ABOUT THE AUTHOR

PETER BERGEN has written or edited eight previous books, including three *New York Times* bestsellers and four *Washington Post* best nonfiction books of the year. A vice president at New America, Bergen is a professor at Arizona State University and a national security analyst for CNN. He has testified before congressional committees eighteen times about national security issues and has held teaching positions at Harvard and Johns Hopkins University.

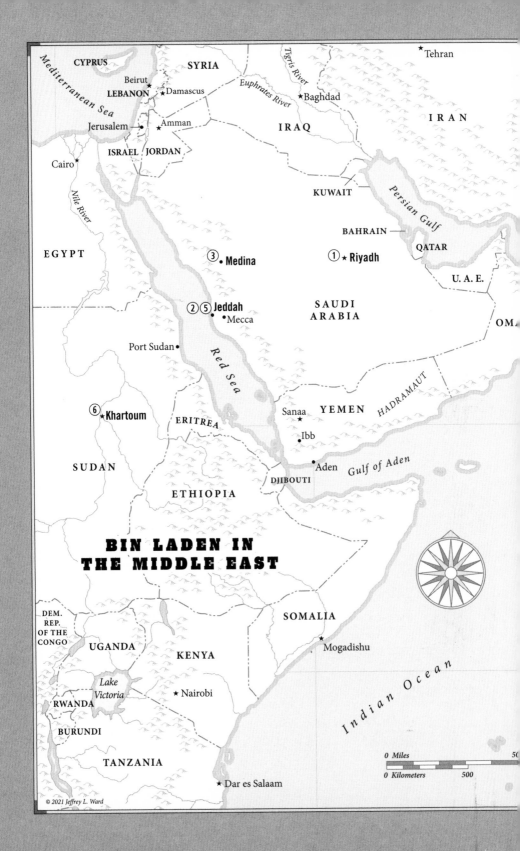

CYPRUS

Mediterranean Sea

SYRIA

★ Tehran

Beirut ★
LEBANON ★ Damascus

Euphrates River

Tigris River

★ Baghdad

IRAN

Jerusalem →

★ Amman

ISRAEL JORDAN

Cairo ★

EGYPT

Nile River

IRAQ

KUWAIT

Persian Gulf

BAHRAIN —

QATAR

U. A. E.

③ • Medina

① ★ Riyadh

②⑤ Jeddah
• Mecca

SAUDI
ARABIA

OM

Port Sudan •

Red Sea

HADRAMAUT

⑥ ★ Khartoum

ERITREA

Sanaa
★

YEMEN

• Ibb

SUDAN

ETHIOPIA

DJIBOUTI

• Aden Gulf of Aden

**BIN LADEN IN
THE MIDDLE EAST**

DEM.
REP.
OF THE
CONGO

UGANDA

SOMALIA

KENYA

★ Mogadishu

Lake
Victoria

RWANDA

★ Nairobi

Indian Ocean

BURUNDI

TANZANIA

★ Dar es Salaam

0 Miles   50

0 Kilometers   500

© 2021 Jeffrey L. Ward